THE
Actors'
YEARBOOK
2005

THE
Actors'
YEARBOOK
2005

The essential resource for anyone wanting to work as an actor

Edited by Simon Dunmore and Lucia Latimer

A & C Black • London

First published 2004
A & C Black Publishers Limited
37 Soho Square, London W1D 3QZ
www.acblack.com

Edited by Simon Dunmore and Lucia Latimer, with additional research by Madeline Clements

ISBN 0–7136–6943–8

A CIP catalogue record for this book is available from the British Library.

Typeset by Pracharak Technologies (P) Ltd, Madras, India
Printed and bound in Great Britain by William Clowes, Beccles

Contents

Introduction

It is well known that an actor's life is not an easy one. Those who aspire to the 'bright lights' face a seemingly bewildering array of courses, audition processes and funding methods. Drama school graduates confront a bedazzling array of agents, casting directors and production companies (in all media) to whom they could send their precious CVs and photographs. Experienced actors try to become philosophical about how secure-seeming 'contacts' they once had have been superseded by a new generation. ('There's a new bunch of schoolboys running the networks each week.' Joan Collins) The art and crafts of acting are difficult enough – the prospect of navigating through 'bald' lists of services and potential employers can overwhelm all but the most determined. Those with time and money can simply blitz every agent (for instance) that they can find, in the hope that some may respond with offers of representation – this will cost several hundred pounds, let alone the time spent stuffing envelopes. And the chances of success, with this kind of unfocused approach, will be extremely limited. Judicious targeting, using the information in this book and your own research (especially on the Internet), can save a considerable amount of money and will give you a greater chance of satisfaction and success.

The aim of this book is also to make some more detailed sense of the ever-diversifying world of professional acting – from training to the wide range of companies offering work in all media, via the 'brokers' (agents and casting directors) of much of that work. In addition, you will find more details of the available services (photographers, showreel companies, and so on) so that you can make detailed comparisons before committing your precious funds. In order to help you cut your way through the 'jungle' of performing arts information, the listings are restricted to those directly relevant to aspiring and work-seeking actors. (For instance, agents who only represent directors, designers, and so forth, are not included.) Careful study of the section(s) appropriate to you at a particular moment could save you time and money through more accurate 'targeting' of your intentions – whether looking for appropriate training, whom to send your CV and photograph to, where to get your showreel made, and so forth.

This book contains details of those organisations and individuals from whom we were able to glean more full information, beyond the basic contact details. Some were prepared to provide helpful information but requested that their telephone numbers, for instance, should not be included. You'll find more organisations listed in *Contacts* (published annually by The Spotlight). Some organisations declined to contribute to this book, apparently fearful of attracting even more actor-submissions. Some simply did not respond. Some information will go out of date – new companies will start up and others will go out of business – and personnel will change; this profession has a highly mobile population. However, the listings will help focus your researches and enable you to 'target' more accurately and efficiently.

The Actors' Yearbook is designed to work in harmony with my *An Actor's Guide to Getting Work* (4th edition, A&C Black, 2004), in which you will find much more detailed advice on how to market yourself and enhance your chances as a professional actor.

Simon Dunmore
February, 2004

Training

Introduction

This section is largely devoted to those who are 18 and older. This is not to dismiss the fact that there is training (of varying kinds) for those under that age. However, the field is so wide that the confines of this book limit listings to the major organisations only.

In spite of the fact that a minority of well-known actors did not formally train, it is very important for today's aspirant to do so. There are an increasing number of people wanting to become actors, so those with 'casting clout' (agents, casting directors and directors) have more and more people to choose from. Doesn't it make more sense to select from those who've undergone the rigours of a respected training process? It is an essential fact that the acting industry works on very tight time-scales and budgets –trained actors will be quicker, more reliable and, usually, more inventive than their untrained counterparts. For instance, an untrained voice that cracks up after a few days of live performance is time-consuming and costly for a management –only the larger productions can afford understudies. An untrained actor, who may look good on camera, will take time to learn how to work on a television set –where time spent keeping technicians waiting is very, very expensive. A fight (in a theatre or on camera) has to be staged so that it (a) looks real, (b) is safe for the participants and (c) can be seen properly by camera and/or audience –actors who've been trained in the essentials of combat will make this staging process much, much quicker. Moving correctly in period costumes, all kinds of formal dance and using microphones properly are just a few of the other time-saving skills that the trained actor can bring to a production. It is only an exceptional few who, nowadays, have the opportunity to 'learn on the job'.

For today's aspiring actor, it is important to train on a professionally recognised course. The established drama schools are the focus of such training. There are acting-related university degree courses which have a reasonable proportion of vocational training (as well as academic work) and there are numerous part-time, short-term and 'foundation' courses which will give you basic insights into the many crafts involved in acting. However, because of the intense competition, a full-time drama school course of at least a year is essential for most people.

For those who have already trained, there are opportunities to learn new skills and refine those already acquired, or simply to keep them in trim when the acting-work is not coming in. The latter is very important as you can be asked to demonstrate your skills at very short notice. Being an actor is a bit like being a fireman –without the regular salary. Also, the more you can legitimately add to the 'Skills' section of your CV, the more you can enhance your chances of acting work.

Training for the Under-18s

It is a fact that many child stars do not succeed as adult actors. There are notable exceptions – Nicholas Lyndhurst, Dennis Waterman and Jenny Agutter, for instance – but they are the exceptions that prove the rule. I also wonder whether a childhood largely devoted to performing is entirely healthy: what about learning about life? And what about learning other essential skills in order to earn one's living when the acting work is not coming in?

Generally speaking, the best thing for the stage-struck child is to send him or her to one of the numerous youth theatre groups and drama workshops that exist in almost every town and city. These are often listed in *Yellow Pages*, and many are members of the National Association of Youth Theatres – see below. Public productions are often the last priority of such groups – especially for the younger ages – but a terrific amount can be learnt by the young from what seem like simple make-believe games. Children in such groups won't learn many of the technical skills necessary to acting, but they will learn a lot of important social skills and the fundamental business of 'interacting' that is so important to an acting ensemble: that it's not just what you can create that matters, it's what you can create with other people. Some youth theatres are allied to agencies who will promote their members for professional work, but it is important to note that employment of the under-16s is very strictly regulated.

National Association for Youth Drama in Ireland (NAYD)

34 Upper Gardiner Street, Dublin 1, Ireland
tel 00353 1878 1301 *fax* 00353 1878 1302
email info@nayd.ie
website www.youthdrama.ie

The National Association for Youth Drama is the umbrella organisation for youth drama and youth theatre in Ireland, providing support for more than 70 youth theatre groups in both Northern and Southern Ireland. Every 4-5 years it organises the National Youth Theatre –an event which brings together young people from all over the country, who work with a youth theatre director and a professional crew to produce a theatre production.

National Youth Theatre shows are produced to a professional standard, and are performed for an audience consisting of members of the general public and representatives from the theatre world. Previous productions have included: *The Young Europeans* (1986), written and directed by Gerry Stembridge; *Our Town* (1984) and *The Crucible* (1987), both directed by the Abbey Theatre's current Artistic Director, Ben Barnes; and *Strawberries in December* (1996), written by Antoine O'Flatharta and directed by Brian Brady. The 2001 National Youth Theatre production entitled *The Old Lady Says 'No!'*, by Denis Johnston, was directed by John White and featured a cast of 35 from 19 youth theatres throughout the country.

The National Youth Theatre has also launched the acting careers of a host of young performers, including Cathy Belton, Jasmine Russell, Anthony Brophy, Noelle Brown, Eunice McMenamin and Tom Murphy.

National Association of Youth Theatres (NAYT)

Arts Centre, Vane Terrace,
Darlington DL3 7AX
tel (01325) 363330 *fax* (01325) 363313
email naytuk@aol.com
website www.nayt.org.uk

Founded in 1982, the National Association of Youth Theatres is the leading member-ship organisation for youth theatre prac-tice in England and Wales. On behalf of its members it works with the Department for Education and Skills (DfES), Arts Council England, Regional Arts Councils and local authorities to achieve greater recognition and improved funding for the sector. Membership is open to any group or indi-vidual using theatre techniques in their work with young people, outside of formal education.

The NAYT provides a range of resources, information and support for its members including training programmes, advice on a wide range of policy and strategy issues, an archive with project reports, surveys and case studies and a monthly *Bulletin* containing the latest news on funding, training, performances and vacancies. With online information and contact details for more than 700 members, the organisation also enables young people to contact youth theatres directly.

National Youth Arts Wales (NYAW)

245 Western Avenue, Cardiff CF5 2YX
tel 029-2026 5060 *fax* 029-2026 5014
email nyaw@nyaw.co.uk
website www.nyaw.co.uk/nytw.html
Artistic Director Greg Cullen

The NYAW represents the National Youth Brass Band of Wales, National Youth Choir of Wales, National Youth Chamber Ensemble of Wales, National Youth Dance Wales, National Youth Orchestra of Wales and National Youth Theatre of Wales.

The National Youth Theatre of Wales was founded in 1976 and has since provided opportunities for hundreds of young people, many of whom are now actively involved with the theatre as professional actors, directors, writers, designers and stage managers. The NYTW is aimed at young people aged 16-21 who are drawn from all over Wales. With guidance from its Artistic Director, the youth theatre pre-pares and rehearses during the summer of each year for a series of high-profile public performances.

In addition, the NYTW spearheads a development programme of workshops and education activities, designed to increase interest and participation in the youth theatre.

The NYTW recently produced the play *Frida and Diego*, a love story with a Welsh-language twist provided by Ian Staples. The play was a multi-media spectacle incorporating the paintings of the Mexican artists Frida Kahlo and Diego Rivera.

National Youth Music Theatre (NYMT)

5 Chancery Lane, Cliffords Inn,
London EC4A 1BU
email nymtenquiries@hotmail.com
website www.nymt.org.uk

Established 27 years ago, the NYMT very nearly closed down in the late summer of

2003 but is now looking forward to steady growth over the course of 2004. It has plans to stage a fundraising Gala Concert and to audition for and mount a major new production for young people. It also hopes to ensure the continuation of its programme of Lab workshops. Consult the website for news of current developments and plans.

National Youth Theatre (NYT)

443-45 Holloway Road, London N7 6LW
tel 020-7281 3863
website www.nyt.org.uk
Membership, Auditions & Courses Stephen Daly

Founded in 1956, the NYT is one of the UK's premier youth arts organisations. It provides young people aged 13-21 with the opportunity for creative participation through theatre arts. Offers courses in Acting, Stage Management, Lighting and Sound, Costume, Scenery and Prop Building at a professional standard which culminate in a season of productions in professional venues in London, across the country and abroad.

Many leading names in the entertainment industry started out with the company, including Sir Ben Kingsley, Sir Derek Jacobi, Dame Helen Mirren, Daniel Craig, Timothy Dalton, Daniel Day-Lewis, Chiwetel Ejiofor, Gina McKee, Timothy Spall, Liza Tarbuck, Alex Kingston and Orlando Bloom.

The NYT auditions roughly 3000 applicants every year at one of 13 audition centres across the UK. Approximately 500 new members are recruited annually from all over the country. Successful applicants are offered a place on one of the courses at either the NYT Headquarters in London or across the UK. Having completed a course, members are entitled to audition for NYT productions. A major production

is mounted in August/September with other tours and seasons occurring throughout the year. Recent productions include: *Watch Over Me, Murder in the Cathedral, Kes* and *Immaculate Conceit.*

Also runs an Outreach programme which aims to include many young people who would not otherwise have the opportunity of becoming involved in drama.

Scottish Youth Theatre

3rd Floor, Forsyth House,
111 Union Street, Glasgow G1 3TA
tel 0141-221 5127 *fax* 0141-221 9123
email info@scottishyouththeatre.org
website www.scottishyouththeatre.org
Artistic Director Mary McCluskey
Key contact Julie Austin

Founded in 1977, Scottish Youth Theatre is Scotland's national theatre for and by young people. Runs weekly drama classes for young people aged 3-25 in addition to a variety of training courses, festivals, educational workshops, youth theatre projects and productions throughout the year. There is no audition process to attend the drama classes but participants in the annual summer festival are asked to prepare a 2-minute speech and a song. In 2003 almost 2000 applications were received and 1000 places offered. Stages at least 5 productions each year which in recent years have included: *Romeo and Juliet, The Prime of Miss Jean Brodie, The Boyfriend* and *Haroun & the Sea of Stories.* Staff are happy to help applicants with any enquiries.

Youth Music Theatre: UK

London Office Unit 10, Bridge Wharf,
156 Caledonian Road, London N1 9UU
tel 0870-240 5057

Northern Ireland Office Ballyvoy Lodge,
56 Ballybracken Road, Doagh, Ballyclare,
County Antrim BT39 0TG
tel 028-9334 0871
website www.youth-music-theatre.org.uk

Established in 2003, Youth Music Theatre:
UK is a new organisation which involves
young people in all aspects of music
theatre. It is open to all young people
aged 11-21 and plans to run projects
in all the countries of the British Isles and
occasionally abroad.

Many of these projects involve young people
creating and devising the work themselves,
supported by professional directors,
choreographers and musical directors. The
company will be providing a full range of
residential workshops during the school
holidays, offering young people the chance
to improve their skills in a number of areas
from audition techniques to martial arts.

All auditions take the form of 'taster' workshops with about 25 young people taking
part at the same time. Working together, the
group learns songs, dances and short scenes;
individuals may be asked to perform a short
extract on their own. Productions will normally be based at a regional theatre and will
rehearse there for a period of 2-3 weeks
before playing for a further 1-2 weeks.

Projects will cost somewhere between £500
and £1000, which will help to cover the
costs of food, accommodation and pas-
toral care. The exact fee for each project
depends on its duration and where it is
taking place.

Drama Schools

Currently there is a core of established drama schools which belong to an organisation called the Conference of Drama Schools (CDS <www.drama.ac.uk>). Most of these run courses that are 'accredited' by the National Council for Drama Training (NCDT <www.ncdt.co.uk>), which was established in the mid-1970s to monitor standards. This organisation assesses courses every few years and decides whether each is up to a sufficient standard – a process called 'accreditation'. The schools themselves are not 'accredited'; only their individual courses. There are schools outside the CDS which have courses with 'accreditation', there are courses in CDS schools that are not 'accredited' – and there are a few well-respected courses that are neither. The reasons for these variations are too complex to explain here. However, if you get a place on a three-year accredited course, you stand a higher than 'evens' chance of getting funding in the same way as those accepted on conventional university courses. It is important to check the current funding arrangements for each course you intend applying for. Don't simply rely on what arrangements were in place last year, as things have a habit of changing.

Many three-year accredited courses have 'degree' status – in spite of the fact that there is little or no written component to the courses, let alone formal, written exams. (Historically, the schools took the 'degree' route to help students get funding on the same basis as those following conventional academic courses.) Degree status actually means very little in the acting profession, and courses with degree status are not necessarily better than those without it. Some schools have been quite vociferous about not wishing to become embroiled in the whole philosophy and bureaucracy that is fundamental to degree education – believing that joining with a university would compromise the purely vocational character of their courses. One such adds: 'Universities are academic institutions and the intelligence required of an academic is different from that required of an actor. Whilst some are blessed with both kinds, many talented and intelligent actors are of indifferent academic ability. We would not wish to exclude them.' Degree status will enable you to go on to a higher degree and enhance your employment prospects outside the profession – but not within it.

Funding for some accredited one- and two-year courses is available, but not with the same frequency as for three-year courses. However, there is advice on finding funds from private sources on both the NCDT and the CDS websites, and some schools have scholarships and/or are good at helping students with this task.

Once you've checked through all the courses listed below, get prospectuses for any that might be viable for you. (Also, if possible seek the opinion of those with recent knowledge of drama schools.) Important considerations include whether you could be eligible for funding (and a maintenance loan), and potential living costs – central London is significantly more expensive to live in than Manchester, for example. (Bear in mind, too, whether a degree qualification at the end of the course is important to you.) Above all, it's important to try to assess which courses you feel would suit you best, and to apply – some require application via UCAS – to as many as you can afford the audition fees and travel costs for. Don't forget to factor in the cost of overnight accommodation, if necessary. The plain truth is that competition for places is so intense (especially for women) that you need to audition for as many places as possible. Every time you do another audition you will learn more about the techniques of auditioning than any book or class can teach you – particularly if it's your first time. It is important to take on board the fact that many people take two or three years of auditioning, and sometimes more, before they get places. If you are determined to become a professional actor, you have to take rejection in your stride – learn from it and keep on trying until you succeed.

Finally, carefully check the application deadlines, funding details and audition specifications of each school you intend applying to – there are some considerable variations.

Note Some places on accredited courses are currently funded through Dance and Drama Awards (DaDAs). These were introduced in the late 1990s and operate like funding for conventional university courses. Some courses quote fees of either £1125 or £1150 – for 2003/4 and 2004/5 respectively. This means that they are publicly funded (like university courses) and this is the maximum portion of the fees that you will have to pay if you are eligible for UK funding.

* Indicates that the school is a member of the Conference of Drama Schools

---

Academy Drama School
189 Whitechapel Road, London E1 1DN
tel 020-7377 8735
email ask@the-academy.info
website www.the-academy.info
Principal Tim Reynolds
Key contact Judith Reynolds

Full-time acting courses
2 scholarships are available for the courses listed below and are offered at specific auditions in April, May and June. Public funding, however, is not available for any of the courses.

- Evening Acting Course (2 years). Applicants must be over the age of 20. Course fee is £3900 p.a. Received approximately 200 applications in 2003 and offered 30 places. *Audition requirements*: 1 modern and 1 classical speech for solo audition. *Audition fee*: £25

- Postgraduate Acting Course (1 year). Applicants must be over the age of 21 and hold a relevant degree. Course fee is £6300. Received approximately 180 applications in 2003 and offered 12 places. *Audition requirements/fee*: as above

- Medallion Acting Course (1 year). Applicants are normally aged 17-20. Course fee is £3000. Received approximately 200 applications in 2003 and offered 30 places. *Audition requirements*: either 1 classical or 1 modern speech. *Audition fee*: £25

The Academy of Live and Recorded Arts (ALRA)*

The Royal Victoria Building, Fitzhugh Grove, Trinity Road, London SW18 3SX
tel 020-8870 6475 *fax* 020-8875 0789
website www.alra.demon.co.uk

Accredited acting courses
- National Diploma in Professional Acting (3 years). Applicants must be aged 18 or over, preferably with A levels. Course fee is £10,340 p.a.; public funding is available for some students. Applications should be made direct to the school by April. The school received 350 applications in 2003 for 40 places. *Audition requirements*: 1 modern speech and 1 Shakespeare for solo audition. *Audition fee*: £30

- National Advanced Certificate in Professional Acting (1 year postgraduate). Applicants must be aged 21 or over, preferably graduates. Course fee is £11,100 with public funding available for some students. Applications should be made direct to the school by April. The school received approximately 270 applications in 2003 for 24 places. *Audition requirements/fee*: as above

The Arden Theatre School

The Arden Centre, Sale Road, Northenden M23 ODD
tel 0161-957 1715 *fax* 0161-957 1715
email rjenkins@ccm.ac.uk

website www.ccm.ac.uk/ast
Head of Acting Wylie Longmore

The Arden Theatre School was established in 1991 by South Manchester Community College (now City College Manchester) in association with the Royal Exchange Theatre Company.

Full-time acting courses
- BA (Hons) Acting Studies (3 or 4 years). Applicants must be aged 18 or over at the start of course and should have a minimum of 2 A levels (Grade C or above) or BTEC National Diploma in Performing Arts or equivalent. Also welcomes applications from students over the age of 21 who may not have standard entrance qualifications but have relevant experience or skills. Applications should be made through UCAS. Auditions are held between December and June

Arts Ed London*

Cone Ripman House, 14 Bath Road, London W4 1LY
tel 020-8987 6655 *fax* 020-8987 6699
email drama@artsed.co.uk
website www.artsed.co.uk
Head of Acting Jane Harrison
Director of the School of Musical Theatre Ian Watt-Smith
Key contact Nicola Ramsbottom

Provider of Dance and Drama Awards. Applications for courses and awards should be made direct to the school.

Accredited acting courses
- BA (Hons) Acting (3 years). Applicants must be aged 18 or over. Course fee is £8493 p.a.; public funding is available for some students. In 2003 the school received 500 applications for 36 places. *Audition requirements*: 1 modern and

1 classical speech for group audition. *Audition fee*: £30

- BA (Hons) Musical Theatre Programme (3 years). Applicants must be aged 18 or over. Course fee is £8991 p.a. for which some public funding is available. In addition, the school has a limited number of bursaries. Applications will be accepted until February but the Academy advises early applications. *Audition requirements*: first round consists of a movement audition and a song from a musical; second round involves an acting audition, a further singing audition, an interview and an Orthopaedic Assessment. Course is accredited by the Council for Dance Education and Training (CDET <www.cdet.org.uk>). *Audition fee*: £30

- MA Acting (1 year postgraduate). Applicants must be aged 21 or over. Course fee is £8997; public funding is available for some students. In 2003 the school received 300 applications for 25 places. *Audition requirements/fee*: as above

Birmingham School of Acting* (formerly Birmingham School of Speech and Drama)

The Link Building, Paradise Place, Birmingham B3 3HJ
tel 0121-262 6800 *fax* 0121-262 6801
email bssd@bssd.ac.uk
website www.bssd.ac.uk
Principal Stephen Simms
Admissions Manager Roger Franke.

Accredited acting courses
- BA (Hons) Acting (3 years). Applicants must be aged 18 or over with 2 A levels (grade E or above) or equivalent. Course fee is £1150 p.a. Applications should be made direct to the school by 31 March. In 2003 the school received 450 applications for 42 places. *Audition*

requirements: 1 modern and 1 other speech for solo audition. Second audition requires 1 modern and 1 classical speech and 1 song. *Audition fee*: £20 for first round, £10 for second

- Graduate Diploma in Acting (1 year). Applicants must be aged 21 or over with a university degree or relevant professional experience. Course fee is £1150. In 2003 the school received 110 applications for 16 places. Applications should be made directly to the school by 31 March. *Audition requirements/fee*: as above

Birmingham Theatre School

The Old Rep Theatre, Station Street, Birmingham B5 4DY
tel 0121-643 3300 *fax* 0121-643 3300
email info@birminghamts.demon.co.uk
website www.thebirminghamtheatreschool.com
Principal Chris Rozanski
Key contact Mandi Ashwood, Sarah Watts

May be able to provide internal students with some financial assistance if progressing from an open-access course to a full-time course.

Full-time acting courses
- HND Performing Arts/Theatre Acting (2 years). Applicants must be aged 18 or over with 12 points at A level or BTEC. 60 applications were received in 2003 and 20 places offered. *Audition requirements*: 1 modern and 1 classical speech for solo audition. *Audition fee*: no charge

- Acting Diploma (1 year). Applicants must be aged 17 or over. Course fee is £6900 for which no public funding is available. More than 35 applications were received in 2003 and 25 places were offered. *Audition requirements/fee*: as above

The Bridge Theatre Training Company

Cecil Sharp House, 2 Regent's Park Road,
London NW1 3AY
tel 020-7424 0860 *fax* 020-7424 9118
email admin@thebridge-ttc.org
website www.thebridge-ttc.org
Joint Artistic Directors Mark Akrill, Judith
Pollard
Company Administrator Rebecca Smedley

The Bridge is a non-profit-making
organisation which provides intensive training for a career in professional acting.
Courses include comprehensive career guidance, and a graduating season of public productions in London theatres with a West End
showcase at the Criterion Theatre in front of
agents, directors and casting directors.

Full-time acting courses
- Professional Acting Course (2 years).
  Applicants must be aged 18 or over.
  Course fee is £3585 p.a. for which some
  public funding is available. 350 applications were received in 2003 and 40
  places were offered. *Audition fee:* £25

- Acting Course (1 year postgraduate).
  Applicants must be aged 21 or over with
  a university degree or significant relevant experience. Course fee is £3585 p.a.
  for which some public funding is available. 150 applications were received in
  2003 and 20 places were offered.
  Audition fee: £25

Bristol Old Vic Theatre School*

2 Downside Road, Clifton, Bristol BS8 2XF
tel 0117-973 3535 *fax* 0117-923 9371
email enquiries@oldvic.ac.uk
website www.oldvic.ac.uk
Principal Christopher Denys

An affiliate of the Conservatoire for Dance
and Drama. All courses are entirely vocational and are validated by the University
of West England.

Accredited acting courses
Course fees for the courses listed below are
set at £1150 p.a. for 2004/5. The official age
for entry is 18-30 but the school frequently
makes exceptions. Applications should be
made direct to the school.

- BA (Hons) Professional Acting (3 years).
  Audition requirements: 1 classical verse
  speech (preferably Shakespeare), 1 modern prose piece –each lasting no longer
  than 2 minutes for solo audition.
  Candidates should also prepare a short
  song. Recalls take the form of a weekend
  school in Bristol. *Audition fee:* £20 for
  first audition and £10 for the recall

- Diploma of Professional Acting (2 years).
  Audition requirements/fee: as above

Other full-time acting courses
- Certificate of Higher Education in
  Professional Acting (1 year). *Audition
  requirements/fee:* as above

Central School of Speech and Drama*

64 Eton Avenue, London NW3 3HY
tel 020-7722 8183 *fax* 020-7722 4132
website www.cssd.ac.uk
email enquiries@cssd.ac.uk
Principal Professor Gary Crossley
Scholarships/Bursaries Diana Wade
Memorial Award and Gary Bond
Memorial Award

Accredited acting courses
- BA (Hons) Acting (3 years). Applicants
  must be aged 18 or over with 2 A levels
  (grade C or above) and 3 GCSEs (grade
  C or above) or equivalent. Applications
  should be made through UCAS by
  January. Course fee is £1125 p.a. for
  which some public funding is available.
  In 2003 the school received 2132 applications for a maximum of 30-35 places.
  Audition fee: £30

Other full-time acting courses

All the 1-year courses listed below are for postgraduates or actors (aged 21 or over) with significant professional experience. Fees for 2004 are set at £4135. No public funding is available for any of these courses.

- MA/PGDip Acting Musical Theatre. In 2003 the school received 89 applications for a maximum of 36 places

- MA/PGDip Classical Acting. In 2003 the school received 113 applications for a maximum of 24 places

- MA Advanced Theatre Practice /PGDip Performing. In 2003 the school received 146 applications for a maximum of 60 places.

- MA/PGDip Actor Movement. This course will run for the first time in 2004

The Cygnet Training Theatre*

New Theatre, Friars Gate, Exeter EX2 4AZ
tel (01392) 277189 *fax* (01392) 277189
email CygnetArts@btinternet.com
website www.drama.ac.uk
Principal Monica Shallis
Key contact Mary G Evans

A member of the Conference of Drama Schools, Cygnet offers a 3-year, full-time training course based in its own studio theatre. Functions as a small touring company, drawing its members from all over the UK and abroad. The small number of applicants selected each year (6-8) are chosen for their flexibility, maturity, awareness and self-discipline. They are expected to work with professional commitment from the first day in this ensemble training. Financial assistance is occasionally available to third-year students.

Full-time acting courses

- Professional Acting Certificate (3 years). Applicants must be aged 18 or over.

Course fee is £6000 p.a. for which no public funding is available. More than 200 applications were received in 2003 and 8 places were offered. *Audition requirements*: 1 modern and 1 classical speech lasting 1-3 minutes each, and 1 unaccompanied song. Applicants are auditioned on their own and in a group. *Audition fee*: £25

Other options include Acting with Music, Acting with Directing, and Acting with Stage Management. People may come to train straight from school, after a university degree, or as a career change. All need stamina, commitment and an ability to put the work of the ensemble before their personal feelings. This training, regardless of the option, requires serious commitment.

Drama Centre*

176 Prince of Wales Road, Chalk Farm, London NW5 3PT
tel 020-7428 2070 *fax* 020-7428 2071
Note Plans to move during 2004 to: Central Saint Martins College of Art and Design, 7 Saffron House, Back Hill, London EC1R 5EN (check the website for current contact details)
email drama@linst.ac.uk
website www.csmlinst.ac.uk/drama
Principal Dr Vladimir Mirodan
Key contact Maggie Wilkinson

Drama Centre London trains students (18+) to become professional actors and directors. Established 40 years ago it is now part of the London Institute and is a member of the Conference of Drama Schools. The school awards 3 UK/EU scholarships each year and 1 international Leverhulme scholarship to second-year students.

Accredited acting courses

- BA (Hons) Acting (3 years). Applicants must be aged 18 or over with 2 A levels.

Course fee is £1125 p.a.; public funding is available for some students. Applications should be made through UCAS. In 2003 the school received 1043 applications for 32 places. *Audition requirements*: 1 modern speech (post-1830) and 1 classical verse speech (Shakespeare or other Renaissance play-wright) for solo audition. Ear test will be required at recalls. *Audition fee*: £30

Other full-time acting courses
- MA in Performance (60 weeks over 2 years). Applicants must be aged 21 or over with a related degree, a diploma in dance or drama or significant professional experience. 16 places are available. *Audition fee*: £30

Drama Studio London (DSL)

1 Grange Road, London W5 5QN
tel 020-8579 3897 *fax* 020-8566 2035
email admin@dramastudiolondon.co.uk
website www.dramastudiolondon.co.uk
Principal Peter Craze
Key contact Amanda Carrara

Drama Studio London (DSL) provides training for mature and postgraduate students in acting and directing. Auditions are held throughout the year. Contact the office for a prospectus, an application form or information about Open Days.

The Peter Howitt Scholarship is awarded every year and normally consists of 2 awards, each for £4000. Auditions for the scholarships are held in July. All successful DSL candidates may apply for the scholarships which are awarded on the basis of need and talent.

Accredited acting courses
- DSL Diploma in Acting (1 year post-graduate). Applicants must be aged 21 or over. Course fee is £10,400 or

£12,450 p.a. Applications should be made direct to the school by June. A maximum of 72 places are offered each year. *Audition requirements*: 1 speech of any genre of a maximum of 2 minutes and 1 group-based workshop session. *Audition fee*: £30

East 15 Acting School*

Hatfields, Rectory Lane,
Loughton IG10 3RY
tel 020-8508 5983 *fax* 020-8508 7521
email east15@essex.ac.uk
website www.east15.ac.uk
Director John Baraldi
Key contact Linda Humphreys

Accredited acting courses
- BA (Hons) Acting (3 years). Applicants must be aged 18 or over with 2 A levels or equivalent. Course fee is £8050 p.a. for which some public funding is available. 40 places were offered in 2003. Deadline for applications is June. *Audition requirements*: 1 modern speech (post-1950), one Shakespeare or Jacobean speech, 1 other speech from a 20th century play and a short song for a group audition. *Audition fee*: £35
- PG/MA Acting (1 year). Applicants must be aged 21 or over with a university degree or a suitable level of experience. Course fee is £8250; public funding is available for some students. 28 places were offered in 2003. Deadline for applications is June. *Audition requirements/ fee*: as above

Other full-time acting courses
- BA in Contemporary Theatre (3 years). Applicants must be aged 18 or over with 2 A levels or equivalent. Course fee is £8050 p.a. for which some public funding is available. 30 places are offered. *Audition requirements/fee*: as above

- PGDip/MA Acting for TV, Film and Radio (1 year). Applicants must be aged 21 or over with a university degree or equivalent. Course fee is £8450. 16 places were offered in 2003. *Audition requirements/fee*: as above
- Foundation in Acting (1 year). Applicants must be aged 18 or over with 2 A levels or equivalent. Course fee is £8050. 48 places were offered in 2003. *Audition requirements/fee*: as above

GSA Conservatoire* (formerly Guildford School of Acting)

Millmead Terrace, Guildford GU2 4YT
tel (01483) 560701 *fax* (01483) 535431
email enquiries@conservatoire.org
website www.conservatoire.org
Head of Acting Peter Barlow

Accredited acting courses
Applications for the courses listed below should by made direct to the school by March.

- BA (Hons) Acting (3 years). Applicants must be aged 18 or over with 2 A levels. Course fee is £8895 p.a. for which some public funding is available. 30 places were offered in 2003. *Audition requirements*: 1 modern and 1 classical speech each lasting 2 minutes for solo audition. *Audition fee*: £30
- Diploma in Acting (1 year postgraduate). Applicants must be aged 21 or over. Course fee is £8995. 15 places were offered in 2003. *Audition requirements/fee*: as above
- BA (Hons) Theatre & Musical Theatre (3 years). Applicants must be aged 18 or over with 2 A levels. Course fee is £9800 p.a. for which some public funding is available. 30 places were offered in 2003. *Audition requirements*: any 2-minute speech and a 2-minute musical

theatre repertoire for solo audition. *Audition fee*: £30
- Diploma in Musical Theatre (1 year postgraduate). Applicants must be aged 21 or over. Course fee is £9800. 15 places were offered in 2003. *Audition requirements/fee*: as above

Guildhall School of Music & Drama*

Silk Street, Barbican, London EC2Y 8DT
tel 020-7628 2571 *fax* 020-7256 9438
email registry@gsmd.ac.uk
website www.gsmd.ac.uk

Founded in 1880, the Guildhall School is acknowledged internationally as a leading conservatoire for both music and drama. The Drama Department and the Technical Theatre Department benefit greatly from collaboration with the other departments. The Main Theatre and the Studio Theatre mount at least 14 productions a year, of which at least 8 are drama productions.

Accredited acting courses
- BA (Hons) Acting (3 years). Applicants must be aged 18 or over with 1 A level pass and 2 AS level passes or equivalent. Applicants over the age of 21 will be assessed on their own merits only. Applications should be made direct to the school as early as possible and by mid-February at the latest. Course fees in 2003/4 were £4055 p.a. *Audition requirements*: 1 Shakespeare or Jacobean speech, 1 modern and 1 other contrasting speech, each lasting no longer than 2 minutes. A short unaccompanied song is also required. Recall auditions include voice, movement and improvisation work (some of this in small groups), more detailed work on audition pieces and a short interview. *Audition fee*: £36. In the final year of training, clear guidance is given on starting in the acting

profession. There are regular talks and visits by regional theatre directors, agents, casting directors, income tax advisers and representatives from Equity

Hertfordshire Theatre School
Queen Street House, 40 Queen Street, Hitchin SG4 9TS
Principals Kirk Foster, John Gardiner
Bursar & key contact Annie Wilkinson

Has been providing training for actors for 14 years. Current total of 50 students. Graduation showcase takes place at a West End theatre.

Full-time acting courses
- Acting and Musical Theatre Course (3 years). Applicants must be aged 18 or over with a good level of education, either at A level or at BTEC. Course fee is £6000 p.a.; no public funding is available, but the school has a charitable trust offering reduced fees to students paying privately. A maximum of 20 places are available. *Audition requirements*: 1 modern, 1 classical and 1 comedy speech and 1 song. *Audition fee*: £25

- Advanced Acting and Musical Theatre (1 year postgraduate). Applicants must be aged 21 or over with a university degree or relevant professional experience. Course fee is £6000 for which no public funding or bursaries are available. A maximum of 6 places are available. *Audition requirements/fee*: as above

Italia Conti Academy of Theatre Arts Ltd.*
Avondale Hall, 72 Landor Road, London SW9 9PH
tel 020-7733 3210 *fax* 020-7737 2728
email acting@lsbu.ac.uk
website www.italiaconti-acting.co.uk

Member of the Conference of Drama Schools, the Academy offers a 3-year BA (Hons) Acting Degree, validated by London South Bank University and accredited by the National Council for Drama Training. This course is a unique approach to actor training. Based loosely on the teachings of Sanford Meisner, whose work now dominates in the United States, it trains actors to be open, responsive and spontaneous.

Accredited acting courses
- BA (Hons) Acting (3 years). Applicants must be aged 18 or over with 5 GCSEs (grade C or above) including English and 2 A levels (grade E or above) or equivalent. Applications can be made via UCAS or direct to the school. Public funding is available towards the cost of tuition fees. *Audition fee*: £30

The Liverpool Institute for Performing Arts (LIPA)
Mount Street, Liverpool L1 9HF
tel 0151-330 3232/3116/3084/3022
fax 0151-330 3131
email admissions@lipa.ac.uk
website www.lipa.ac.uk

LIPA is dedicated to providing the best teaching and learning for people who want to pursue a lasting career in the arts and entertainment economy, and offers a variety of styles of courses aimed at different age groups. It looks for more than acting talent in its students, and applicants should show evidence of versatility and trainable ability in other performance-related skills.

Full-time acting courses
- BA (Hons) Performing Arts –Acting (3 years). Applicants must be aged 18 or over; there is no upper age limit. Educational attainment, relevant experience and interdisciplinary interest and

ability will be taken into account when applying. Applications should be made through UCAS initially. If invited to audition, further information will be required. Course fee is £1125 p.a. with some public funding available

- Postgraduate diploma in Acting (1 year). Applicants are usually aged 21 or over and educated to degree-level standard with some acting experience. Mature students without degree qualifications but with considerable related professional experience are welcome to apply. Course fee is £8250. This is a new, intensive year-long programme enabling students to become flexible, multi-skilled practitioners

London Academy of Music and Dramatic Arts (LAMDA)*

155 Talgarth Road, London W14 9DA
tel 020-8834 0500 *fax* 020-8834 0501
email enquiries@lamda.org.uk
website www.lamda.org.uk
Principal Peter James

The London Academy of Music and Dramatic Art traces its antecedents back to 1861, making it the oldest institution of its kind in the UK. Trains approximately 250 students each year on a number of different acting and stage-management theatre courses. Around 30 students are admitted for the LAMDA 3-year acting course. There are a number of bursaries and scholarships available to students, which are awarded at the Academy's discretion and for which there is a separate application process. Some government Dance and Drama Awards are also available to EU students on the 3-year acting course.

Accredited acting courses
- National Diploma in Acting (3 years). Applicants must be aged 18 or over. Course

fee is £11,550 p.a. Applications should be made direct to the school by May. In 2003 the Academy received 1325 applications for this course and offered 28 places. *Audition requirements:* 1 20th or 21st century speech and 1 Shakespeare or Jacobean speech, each lasting no longer than 3 minutes. Solo audition. *Audition fee:* £30

Other full-time acting courses
- Postgraduate Acting Course (2 years). Course fee is £11,550 p.a.; public funding is available for some students. *Audition requirements/fee:* as above
- Double Semester Classical Acting Course (1 year). Course fee is £11,550; no public funding is available. *Audition requirements/fee:* as above
- Foundation Course (1 year). Course fee is £8250; no public funding is available. *Audition requirements/fee:* as above

London Academy of Performing Arts

St Matthews Church, St Petersburgh Place, London W2 4LA
tel 020-7727 0220 *fax* 020-7727 0330
email admin@lapadrama.com
website www.lapadrama.com
Principal Cecilia Hocking
Key contact Administrator

Conservatory-style drama school founded in 1981 by Cecilia Hocking to provide postgraduate training in classical acting.

Full-time acting courses
- Classical Acting with options in Musical Theatre and Directing (1 year postgraduate). Most students are aged 21 with a university degree. Also takes older students looking for a career change, and other students without a university degree, who have considerable performance experience and personal maturity. Course fee is £7260 for which

no public funding is available. 80 applications were received in 2003 and 20
places were offered. *Audition requirements*: 1 modern and 1 classical speech
for solo audition. A song is required for
the musical option only. *Audition fee*:
£25

London Centre for Theatre Studies

The Impact Centre, 12-18 Hoxton Street,
London N1 6NG
tel 020-7739 5866 *fax* 020-7739 5866
email ldncts@aol.com
website www.thelondoncentrefortheatre
studies.co.uk

Provides vocational training for mature
graduates. Average age of students is
32 and the minimum age for entry is
22. The Actors Company is not a
traditional drama school 'but a company
in training'. The course culminates in a
6-week repertory season at the Jermyn
Street Theatre in the West End. Students
may continue in employment while training 40 hours per week if they wish.

Full-time acting courses
• The Actors Company (4 terms: 46
weeks). Course fee is £9150 for which
some public funding is available. 370
applications were received in 2003 and
45 places were offered. *Audition requirements*: 1 modern and 1 classical speech
for solo audition. *Audition fee*: £27.50

London Drama School

30 Brondesbury Park, London NW6 7DN
tel 020-8830 0074 *fax* 020-8830 4992
email enquiries@startek-uk.com
website www.startek-uk.com
Key contact Sarah Mann

Established 8 years ago. All teachers are
actors, directors, writers or producers currently working in the industry. 2 bursaries

are available to talented students with
financial difficulties; these bursaries cover
half the tuition fees.

Full-time acting courses
• One Year Acting Course. Course fee is
£5950 for which some public funding is
available. More than 60 applications
were received in 2003 and 20 places were
offered. *Audition requirements*: 1 modern
speech (from a play or film) lasting 3-5
minutes for solo audition. An unaccompanied song is optional. Advises applicants to choose a character close to own
age and experience. *Audition fee*: £20

London School of Musical Theatre

83 Borough Road, London SE1 1DN
tel 020-7407 4455 *fax* 020-7407 4455
email info@lsmt.co.uk
website www.lsmt.co.uk
Principal Glenn Lee
Key contact Nikki Rose

Full-time acting courses
• Musical Theatre Diploma Course
(1 year). Age range for entry is 18-35.
Course fee is £10,000 with public funding available for some students. 350
applications were received in 2003 and
40 places were offered. *Audition requirements*: 1 speech of applicant's choice
lasting 2-3 minutes and 2 contrasting
musical theatre songs (i.e. 1 ballad and
1 up-tempo) for solo audition. *Audition
fee*: £20

Manchester Metropolitan University
School of Theatre*

Mabel Tylecote Building, Cavendish Street,
Manchester M15 6BG
tel 0161-247 1305 *fax* 0161-247 6875
email k.daly@mmu.ac.uk
website www.capitoltheatre.co.uk

Principal Niamh Dowling
Key contact Kath Daly

See entry under *University Courses* for further details.

Accredited acting courses

- BA (Hons) Theatre Arts/Acting (3 years). Applicants must be aged 18 or over with 2 A levels or equivalent. Course fee is £1125 p.a. for which some public funding is available. Applications should be made through UCAS by January. 1390 applications were received in 2003 for 28 places. *Audition requirements:* 1 modern, 1 classical and 1 other speech for both group and solo auditions. *Audition fee:* £30

Mountview Theatre School*

Ralph Richardson Memorial Studios,
Clarendon Road, London N22 6XF
tel 020-8881 2201 *fax* 020-8829 0034
email enquiries@mountview.ac.uk
website www.mountview.ac.uk
Principal Paul Clements
Scholarships/Bursaries Sir John Mills
Scholarship, Dame Judi Dench
Scholarship, Margaret Rutherford
Scholarship, Peter Coxhead Scholarship
(all for postgraduate performance courses)

Accredited acting courses

Applications for the courses listed below should be made direct to the school, by March for the BA (Hons) and by July for the postgraduate diploma.

- BA (Hons) Acting (3 years). Applicants must be aged 18 or over, usually with A levels but these are not essential. Course fee is £9084 p.a.; public funding is available for some students. The school received more than 600 applications in 2003 and offered 32 places. *Audition requirements:* 1 modern speech (post-1945) and 1 Shakespeare for both group and solo auditions. *Audition fee:* £30

- BA (Hons) Musical Theatre (3 years). Applicants must be aged 18 or over, usually with A levels but these are not essential. Course fee is £9735 p.a.; public funding is available for some students. The school received more than 600 applications in 2003 for 32 places. *Audition requirements:* 1 modern speech (post-1945), 1 contrasting speech and 2 contrasting songs for both group and solo auditions. *Audition fee:* £30

- PG Dip in Acting (1 year). Applicants must be aged 21 or over, usually with a university degree. Course fee is £11,948. The school received 350 applications in 2003 for 30 places. *Audition requirements/fee:* as above

Oxford School of Drama*

Sansomes Farm Studios, Woodstock,
Oxford OX20 1ER
tel (01993) 812883 *fax* (01993) 811220
email info@oxforddrama.ac.uk
website www.oxforddrama.ac.uk
Principal George Peck
Key contact Jane Whitehead

Provides a significant number of Dance and Drama Awards (DADAs) for its 1-year and 3-year courses. Also offers its own Hardship fund which is distributed each year to students on full-time courses at the school. Students not in receipt of a DADA are prioritised for funding. The Lionel Bart Foundation and the Sir John Gielgud Charitable Trust currently support the school: in addition students have also won the Henry Cotton Memorial Fund Award and the *Evening Standard*/Patricia Rothermere Award.

Accredited acting courses

Applications for the courses listed below should be made direct to the school by

April. The fees for both courses are set at £9180 p.a for 2004/5.

- Diploma in Acting (3 years). Applicants must be aged 18 or over. 18 places were offered in 2003. *Audition requirements*: 1 modern and 1 classical speech, each lasting no longer than 90 seconds for solo audition, and 1 group movement/ improvisation session. *Audition fee*: £30
- One Year Acting Course. Applicants must be aged 21 or over. 18 places were offered in 2003. *Audition requirements/ fee*: as above

Poor School

242 Pentonville Road, London N1 9JY
tel 020-7837 6030 *fax* 020-7837 5330
email acting@thepoorschool.com
website www.thepoorschool.com
Principal Paul Caister

The school was created in 1986 with the aim of providing high-quality acting training that is financially within the reach of all, or almost all. Training lasts 2 years and operates in the evenings and at weekends until the final 2 terms, when daytime work is involved. Since March 1993 the Poor School has owned its own theatre, the Workhouse. This is a flexible studio theatre seating 50-80.

Full-time acting courses
- Two Year Acting Course (6 terms). Most students are in their early 20s but the school offers many places to older and younger people. Course fees are £1350 per term. Accepts 39 students each October. *Audition requirements*: 2 dramatic speeches (1 from Shakespeare) each lasting between 90 seconds and 2 minutes. *Audition fee*: £20

Queen Margaret University College*

Department of Drama, Gateway Theatre,

Elm Row, Edinburgh EH7 4AH
tel 0131-317 3900 *fax* 0131-317 3902
email lbains@qmuc.ac.uk
website www.qmuc.ac.uk
Principal Professor Maggie Kinloch
Key contact Lynn Bains

See entry under *University Courses* for further details.

Accredited acting courses
- BA (Hons) Acting and Performance (3-4 years). Applicants must be aged 18 or over with Scottish Higher CCC, A level at grade E, BTEC or HNC/NC. Applications should be made through UCAS by March. Course fee is £1125 p.a. with public funding available to some students. In 2003 the College received 950 applications for this course and offered 22 places. *Audition requirements*: 1 modern and 1 classic speech for first audition, may also be asked to sing. Recall involves improvisation and movement workshops, sight reading, singing, 2 additional pieces and an interview. *Audition fee*: £30 for first audition and £10 for recall

Initially the core subjects of acting, voice, text and movement are taught separately; as the course progresses, they combine and focus on performance through a wide variety of productions and projects. In the past few years, highly successful collaborations with students on other courses (stage managers, directors, playwrights, etc.) have become a feature of the course. Close collaborations with professional theatre companies provide another dimension to the training.

The REP College

17 St Mary's Avenue, Purley on Thames, Berks RG8 8BJ

Provides acting students with 1 year of practical education, including 14 public performances. Course includes classes on audition techniques and planning. 4-8 scholarships of £1187-2375 are awarded annually.

Full-time acting courses
- Acting Course (1 year). Applicants must be aged 18 or over. Course fee is £9500 with public funding available for some students. 289 applications were received in 2003 and 20 places were offered. *Audition requirements*: group full-day workshop. *Audition fee*: £25

Richmond Drama School
Parkshot Centre, Parkshot, Richmond TW9 2RE
tel 020-8439 8944 *fax* 020-8332 6560
email David.Whitworth@racc.ac.uk
Principal and key contact David Whitworth

Provides an intensive 1-year performance-based training course with many public performances during the year. Students can apply for learning support grants towards fees; these are usually several hundred pounds. Most applicants receive help.

Full-time acting courses
- Richmond Drama School Access Certificate (1 year). Applicants must be aged 18 or over, preferably with A levels. Course fee is £2725 for which no public funding is available. 59 applications were received in 2003 and 20 places were offered. *Audition requirements*: 1 modern and 1 classical speech for solo audition. *Audition fee*: £20

Rose Bruford College*
Lamorbey Park, Burnt Oak Lane, Sidcup DA15 9DF
tel 020-8300 3024 *fax* 020-8308 0542
email enquiries@bruford.ac.uk
website www.bruford.ac.uk
Principal Professor Alastair Pearce

Accredited acting courses
Applicants for the courses listed below must be over the age of 18 with 2 A levels at grade C or above. Course fees in 2003/4 were £1125 p.a. with some public funding available. Applications should be made through UCAS.

- BA (Hons) Acting (3 years). *Audition requirements*: 1 modern speech (post-1960) lasting no longer than 90 seconds, 1 Shakespeare speech from list provided and 1 song from musical theatre repertoire for group audition. *Audition fee*: £25

Other full-time acting courses
- BA (Hons) Actor Musicianship (3 years). *Audition requirements/fee*: as above but with an additional group musicality audition

Royal Academy of Dramatic Art (RADA)*
62-64 Gower Street, London WC1E 6ED
tel 020-7636 7076 *fax* 020-7323 3865
email enquiries@rada.ac.uk
website www.rada.org
Principal Nicholas Barter
Key contact Sally Power

Founded in 1904 by Sir Herbert Beerbohm Tree at His Majesty's Theatre, the Academy moved to its present premises a year later. In 1996 the Academy received a Lottery Grant from the Arts Council and embarked on a £32 million rebuilding programme, opening its new premises in 2000. The final stage of the estate's strategy will be completed at the end of 2004. Some maintenance bursaries are available for students to supplement their own fundraising efforts. Applications should be made direct to the school by March.

Accredited acting courses

- BA (Hons) Acting (3 years). Normal age range for entry is 18-30. Course fee is £1150 p.a. for which some public funding is available. Received 2000 applications in 2003/4 for a maximum of 32 places. *Audition requirements:* 1 Shakespeare or Jacobean speech and 1 contrasting speech, each lasting no longer than 3 minutes for solo audition. Recalls may take the form of second audition, group workshop or individual working session; an unaccompanied song is also required. The auditions are 'lengthy and rigourous' and the process may span several months. *Audition fee:* £30.

The course is for students who wish to earn a living working not only in the more traditional outlets but also in the many alternative areas of theatre, film, television and radio. It is intensive, with a minimum working day of 10.00 a.m. to 6.00 p.m. and individual classes in the evening. When public performances take place the working day can be from 10.00 a.m. to 11.00 p.m.

Royal Scottish Academy of Music and Drama*

100 Renfrew Street, Glasgow G2 3DB
tel 0141-332 4101 *fax* 0141-332 8901
email registry@rsamd.ac.uk
website www.rsamd.ac.uk
Principal John Wallace

Accredited acting courses

Applications for the courses listed below should be made direct to the school by March. Public funding is available for some students.

- BA (Hons) Acting (3 years). Applicants are normally aged 18-21 but this is flexible. Course fee is £1125 p.a. Received 564 applications for 24 places in 2003.

Audition requirements: 1 Shakespeare speech and 1 other for solo audition. *Audition fee:* £35

Other full-time acting courses

- Master of Performance in Musical Theatre (1 year). Course fee is £7500. 12 places will be available. *Audition requirements:* to be confirmed. *Audition fee:* £35

- BA (Hons) Contemporary Theatre Practice (4 years). Applicants must hold 3 highers, 2 advanced highers or 2 A levels. Course fee is £1125 p.a. In 2003 the Academy received 65 applications for 13 places. *Audition requirements:* group workshop and written exercise. *Audition fee:* £35

Royal Welsh College of Music and Drama*

Castle Grounds, Cathays Park,
Cardiff CF10 3ER
tel 029-2039 1327
email drama.admissions@rwcmd.ac.uk
website www.rwcmd.ac.uk
Principal Edmond Fivet
Drama Admissions Officer Lucie Healy

Accredited acting courses

- BA (Hons) Acting (3 years). Applicants should be aged 18 or over. Course fee is £1150 for which some public funding is available. Applications should be made through UCAS. Normally offers 20 places each year

- PG/Dip in Acting (1 year). Applicants should be aged 21 or over. Course fee is £3640, with no public funding available. Applications should be made direct to the College. Normally offers 10 places

The School of the Science of Acting

Dept E, 67-83 Seven Sisters Road,
London N7 6BU
tel 020-7272 0027 *fax* 020-7272 0026

email find@scienceofacting.org.uk
website www.scienceofacting.org.uk
Principal Sam Kogan
Key contact Jack Curzon

Full-time acting courses
No public funding is available for
the courses listed below, but students
may apply for a limited number of scholarships.

- Three Year Acting Course. Applicants
  must be aged 18 or over. Course fee is
  £9990 p.a. Offers 14 places each year.
  Audition requirements: 1 modern,
  1 classical and one other speech and 1
  song for solo audition. *Audition fee*: £25

- One Year Acting Course. Applicants
  must be aged 18 or over. Course fee is
  £9990. Offers 14 places each year.
  Audition requirements/fee: as above

- Two Year Evening Acting Course.
  Applicants must be aged 16 or over. Course
  fee is £4160 p.a. Offers 14 places each year.
  Audition requirements/fee: as above

Webber Douglas Academy of Dramatic Art*

30 Clareville Street, London SW7 5AP
tel 020-7370 4154 *fax* 020-7373 5639
email webberdouglas@btclick.com

website www.webber-douglas-academy.
sageweb.co.uk
Principal R.B. Jago
Academy Secretary Kamaal Hussain

Accredited acting courses
Applications for the courses listed below
should be made direct to the school by
April. Candidates should send an sae to the
value of 75p for an application form and
prospectus.

- Three year Acting Diploma. Applicants
  must be aged 18 or over. Course fee is
  £9588 p.a. with public funding available
  for some students. The Academy received
  1100 applications in 2003 for 28 places.
  Audition requirements: one modern
  speech (post-1850) and one Shakespeare
  speech plus a verse of song to test pitch.
  Solo audition. *Audition fee*: £30

- Two year Acting Diploma. Applicants
  must be aged 18 or over. Course fee is
  £9588 p.a. with public funding available
  for some students. Offers 14 places
  each year. *Audition requirements/fee*: as
  above

- One year Acting Certificate. Applicants
  must be aged 21 or over. Course fee is
  £9996; no public funding is available.
  Offers 14 places each year. *Audition
  requirements/fee*: as above

University Acting-Oriented Courses

On the positive side, on one of these courses you'll have much more free time to 'do your own thing' than your drama school counterpart; on the negative side, they don't provide nearly enough vocational acting training for today's professional. However, one of these courses can be a viable option for those who simply wish to pursue drama as a career, but are not yet convinced that an actor's life is for them. Those who don't get drama school places (or funding) could also consider such a course. If, at the end, you decide that you want to be a professional actor, it is very important to get at least one year's vocational training on a recognised, 'postgraduate' acting course – some of which now offer the chance of also adding 'MA' after your name.

If you are determined to be a professional and choose the university route, it's also worth considering other subjects that might better enhance your earning-power when not in acting-work. Whilst one of these might not enhance your knowledge of dramatic literature, you will embark on your postgraduate acting course uncluttered by the intellectual 'baggage' that can inhibit a complete connection with a vocational acting training. Instinctive impulses are probably more important than intellect in acting – and some people find it difficult to properly readjust the 'brain/gut balance' in the short space of a single year.

The following is a selected sample of university acting-oriented courses; more can be found from UCAS <www.ucas.ac.uk> and the Standing Conference of University Drama Departments <www.art.ntu.ac.uk/scudd>.

University of Birmingham

Department of Drama and Theatre Arts, University of Birmingham, Edgbaston, Birmingham B15 2TT
website www.bham.ac.uk/drama

Courses offered: Drama and Theatre Arts as a Single, Joint or Minor Honours degree. Undergraduate degree programme integrates theoretical and practical approaches to theatre.

University of Bristol

Department of Drama, University of Bristol, Cantocks Close, Woodland Road, Bristol BS8 1UP
tel 0117-928 7833 *fax* 0117-928 7832
website www.bristol.ac.uk/drama

Courses offered: BA (Hons) Drama or Joint Honours with English or a modern language. Plays are studied in the light of their historical background as well as for their own interest as dramatic texts. Opportunities are provided for students to develop practical skills within areas such as acting and directing, design, lighting and stage management through workshop sessions and productions.

Brunel University

Department of Performing Arts, Brunel University, Uxbridge, Middlesex UB8 3PH
tel (01895) 274000 ext. 4486
fax (01895) 816224
email barry.edwards@brunel.ac.uk
website www.brunel.ac.uk/depts/pfa

Courses offered: BA (Hons) in Modern Drama Studies. Course has strong practical emphasis covering the key skill areas of performing, devising, critical analysis, performance analysis, directing and writing for performance.

Chester College, University of Liverpool

Department of Performing Arts, University College Chester, Parkgate Road, Chester, Cheshire CH1 4BJ
tel (01244) 375444 ext. 3138
fax (01244) 392820
email performingarts@chester.ac.uk
website www.chester.ac.uk/performingarts

Courses offered: BA (Hons) Drama and Theatre Studies. Focuses upon the study and practice of performance with practical workshops, performances, lectures, seminars and research.

University of Exeter

Department of Drama, Thornlea, New North Road, Exeter EX4 4LA
tel (01392) 264580 *fax* (01392) 264594
email drama@exeter.ac.uk
website www.ex.ac.uk/drama

Courses offered: BA (Hons) Drama. Composed of a series of modules, all of

which place emphasis on the social nature of theatre. The relationship between theory and practice is key. All drama students get equal opportunities to act, direct and write.

Goldsmiths College, University of London

Drama Department, Goldsmiths College, University of London, New Cross, London SE14 6NW
tel 020-7919 7414 *fax* 020-7919 7413
email drama@gold.ac.uk
website
www.goldsmiths.ac.uk/departments/drama

Courses offered: BA (Hons) Drama and Theatre Arts, Certificate in Performance Skills and Theatre Studies. Explores the theory and practice of performance across a range of media with a strong focus on performance and production work.

University of Huddersfield

School of Music and Humanities, St Peter's Building, St Peter's Street, Huddersfield HD1 1RA
tel (01484) 478455 *fax* (01484) 478428
website www.hud.ac.uk/theatre

Courses offered: BA (Hons) Theatre Studies. A diverse range of modules is on offer, all of which combine studio-based practical work with theoretical study. Joint Honours with Media and Music are also offered.

University of Hull

Drama Department, University of Hull, Hull HU6 7RX
tel (01482) 466210
website www.drama.hull.ac.uk

Courses offered: BA (Hons) Drama. Introduces and develops key practical and theoretical approaches to the study of drama. Allows students to tailor the course to suit their specific academic and practical interests at a later stage.

University of Kent

School of Drama Film and Visual Arts, Rutherford College, University of Kent, Canterbury CT2 7NY
tel (01227) 764000 *fax* (01227) 827850
email isquery@ukc.ac.uk
website www.kent.ac.uk/sdfva/sdfva

Courses offered: MDrama. The BA (Hons) Drama and Theatre Studies has recently become a Masters degree due to its additional 4th year. A range of approaches to performance in practice and theory are studied in the first 3 years, while the 4th year allows students to pursue a specialism in depth. There are also limited opportunities to spend the 3rd year at a European University or in America.

King Alfred's College of Higher Education

School of Community and Performing Arts, King Alfred's, Sparkford Road, Winchester SO22 4NR
tel (01962) 841515 *fax* (01962) 842280
email contact@kingalfred's
website www.wkac.ac.uk/cparts

Courses offered: BA (Hons) Drama Studies, BA (Hons) Performing Arts, and BA (Hons) Drama, Theatre and Television Studies.

The Drama Studies programme is designed to offer an experience of drama in its social, theoretical and practical contexts as well as a critical analysis of the relationships between practice and theory.

Performing Arts is an interdisciplinary programme looking to the role of performance in communities of the future. Work in theatre, dance and music is combined with approaches to live and virtual art,

comedy and innovation in performance technology and design.

Drama, Theatre and Television Studies is split between the study of theatre and documentary. Encourages students to combine the mediums in innovative and creative ways. The emphasis of the drama element is on community/alternative forms of theatre, while the television part of the course focuses on researching and producing documentaries.

University of Lancaster

Department of Theatre Studies, Lancaster University, Lancaster LA1 4YW
tel (01524) 594156 *fax* (01524) 39021
email k.beale@lancaster.ac.uk
website www.lancs.ac.uk/users/theatre

Courses offered: BA (Hons) Theatre Studies. Department has extensive links with professional performance, theatre, drama groups and individual practitioners through their work in the Nuffield Theatre and other projects.

University of Leeds

School of Performance and Cultural Industries, University of Leeds, Bretton Hall Campus, West Bretton, Wakefield, West Yorkshire WF4 4LG
tel 0113-343 9109
email enquiries-pci@leeds.ac.uk
website www.leeds.ac.uk/paci

Courses offered: BA (Hons) Acting. Combines technical work in voice, movement, singing and dancing with performance theory. Allows students to specialise in defined aspects of theatre and to represent their talents in a number of professional contexts.

Liverpool Hope University College

Department of Drama and Theatre Studies, Liverpool Hope, University

College, Hope Park, Liverpool L16 9JD
tel 0151-291 3000
website www.hope.ac.uk

Courses offered: Drama & Theatre Studies
is offered as part of the BA Combined
Honours programme and should be studied with another subject such as Fine Art
or English.

University of Loughborough
Department of English and Drama,
Loughborough University, Loughborough,
Leicestershire LE11 3TU
tel (01509) 222951
email p.higgs@lboro.ac.uk
website www.lboro.ac.uk/departments/ea

Courses offered: BA (Hons) Drama, BA
(Hons) Drama with English. Examines the
history and theory of performance and develops students' practical and technical skills.

University of Manchester
Department of Drama, School of Music
and Drama, University of Manchester,
Oxford Road, Manchester M13 9PL
tel 0161-275 3347 *fax* 0161-275 3349
email drama@man.ac.uk
website www.art.man.ac.uk/DRAMA

Courses offered: BA (Hons) Drama, BA
(Hons) Drama and Screen Studies, BA
(Hons) Drama with English.

Founded in 1961 following a gift from
Granada Television, the Drama department aims to provide an academic study of
theatre and drama based on history, theory
and practical performance.

Manchester Metropolitan University
All Saints Building, All Saints,
Manchester M15 6BH
tel 0161-247 2000 *fax* 0161-247 6390

email enquiries@mmu.ac.uk
website www.mmu.ac.uk/contact/

Courses offered: BA (Hons) Contemporary
Theatre and Performance, BA (Hons)
Theatre Arts (Acting). Contemporary
Theatre and Performance offers a broad
experience of practical work in both
devised and scripted theatre and covers a
variety of performing traditions. The
Acting course develops the range of skills
and abilities required for a career in acting
including voice, movement, acting, textual
analysis and research. The programme is
accredited by the National Council for
Drama Training and students receive full
Equity Cards upon graduation.

See entry under *Drama Schools* for further
information.

University of Middlesex
School of Arts, Middlesex University,
Cat Hill, Barnet, Hertfordshire EN4 8HT
tel 020-8411 5000
website www.mdx.ac.uk/arts/

Courses offered: BA (Hons) Drama and
Theatre Studies, BA (Hons) Drama and
Theatre Arts, BA (Hons) Drama and
Theatre Arts with Performing Arts, BA
(Hons) Drama and Technical Theatre Arts.
A study of modern drama and theatre
allowing extensive practical exploration of
a wide range of material.

University College Northampton
Avenue Campus, St Georges Avenue,
Northampton, Northamptonshire NN2 6JD
tel (01604) 735500
website www.northampton.ac.uk

Courses offered: BA (Hons) Drama.
Students develop skills in improvisation, in
adaptation, in physical and vocal technique
as well as in critical analysis.

University of Nottingham

School of English Studies, University Park, Nottingham NG7 2RD
tel 0115-951 5900 *fax* 0115-951 5924
email english-undergrad@nottingham.ac.uk
website www.nottingham.ac.uk/english

Courses offered: BA (Hons) Drama. The course is committed to a performance-based understanding of drama. Close links with professional theatre are maintained through the school's relationship with the Nottingham Playhouse.

Queen Margaret College, Edinburgh

School of Drama and Creative Industries, Corstorphine Campus, Clerwood Terrace, Edinburgh EH12 8TS
tel 0131-317 3000 *fax* 0131-317 3256
email marketing@qmuc.ac.uk
website www.qmuc.ac.uk/faculties/
schools_drama.htm

Courses offered: BA (Hons) Acting, BA (Hons) Acting Conversion, BA (Hons) Drama and Theatre Arts. The Acting course offers highly intensive and practical training for work in the theatre and related media, while the Conversion course is aimed at diplomates from courses accredited by the National Council for Drama Training (NCDT) wishing to convert their acting diplomas to a degree. Drama and Theatre Arts offers a more theoretical approach.

See entry under *Drama Schools* for further information.

Queen Mary, University of London

School of English and Drama, Queen Mary, University of London, Mile End Road, London E1 4NS
tel 020-7882 3172 *fax* 020-7882 3357
email sedadmissions@qmul.ac.uk
website www.english.qmul.ac.uk/

Courses offered: BA (Hons) Drama. Examines the theory and practice of performance across a range of social and historical contexts.

Roehampton, University of Surrey

Digby Stuart College, Roehampton Lane, London SW15 5PH
tel 020-8392 3213
website www.roehampton.ac.uk/arts

Courses offered: BA/BSc Drama, Theatre & Performance Studies. Focuses on analysing the art of performance through integrated practical and theoretical study. Offers a wide range of emphases but is not designed for those wishing to pursue vocational actor training.

University of Salford

Faculty of Arts, Media and Social Sciences, University of Salford, Salford, Greater Manchester M5 4WT
tel 0161-295 5000 *fax* 0161-295 4704
website www.famss.salford.ac.uk

Courses offered: BA (Hons) Performing Arts, BA (Hons) Media and Performance. Performing Arts focuses on the development of creative performance skills to a professional level. Media and Performance allows students to combine key aspects of performance activity with practical media production and performance.

St Mary's University College, University of Surrey

School of Communication, Culture and Creative Arts, St Mary's College, Waldegrave Road, Twickenham TW1 4SX
tel 020-8240 4008
website www.smuc.ac.uk

Courses offered: BA (Hons) Drama. Building on its programme of practical theatre-making and theoretical investigation, the course will expand in 3 new directions from 2004: Drama and Performance Studies, Physical Theatre, and Drama in the Community.

University of Staffordshire
School of Humanities and Social Sciences, Staffordshire University, College Road, Stoke-on-Trent ST4 2XW
tel (01782) 294415 ext. 4869
email a.dinnivan@staffs.ac.uk
website www.staffs.ac.uk/dta

Courses offered: BA (Hons) Drama and Theatre Arts. Develops knowledge and understanding of performance skills, theory, texts and contexts.

University of Sunderland
School of Arts, Design, Media and Culture, University of Sunderland, Langham Tower, Ryhope Road, Sunderland SR2 7EE
tel 0191-515 2182
email greta.archer@sunderland.ac.uk
website www.sunderland.ac.uk

Courses offered: BA (Hons) Drama. Offers a programme of practical and theoretical work focusing on the development of collaborative work in a contemporary context.

University of Ulster at Coleraine
School of Media and Performing Arts, University of Ulster, Northland Road, Londonderry, Co. Londonderry BT48 7JL
tel 0870-040 0700
website
www.ulst.ac.uk/faculty/humanities/mpa

Courses offered: BA (Hons) Drama. Develops skills and knowledge associated with the various disciplines of drama,

with particular emphasis on collaborative work.

University of Wales, Aberystwyth
Department of Theatre, Film and Television Studies, Parry-Williams Building, University of Wales Aberystwyth, Penglais Campus, Aberystwyth, Ceredigion SY23 3AJ
tel (01970) 622828
fax (01970) 622831
website www.aber.ac.uk/tfts

Courses offered: BA (Hons) Drama, BA (Hons) Drama and Performance Studies, BA (Hons) Drama and Film & Television Studies, BA (Hons) Drama and English. Focuses attention on a variety of different aspects of theatre as an artform and as a social phenomenon.

University of Warwick
School of Theatre Studies, University of Warwick, Coventry CV4 7AL
tel 024-7652 3020
fax 024-7652 4446
email tsraj@warwick.ac.uk
website www.warwick.ac.uk/fac/arts

Courses offered: BA (Hons) Theatre and Performance Studies.

University of the West of England, Bristol
St Matthias Campus, Oldbury Court Road, Fishponds, Bristol BS16 2JP
tel 0117-965 6261
website www.uwe.ac.uk/humanities

Courses offered: BA (Hons) Drama, BA (Hons) Drama and Education, BA (Hons) Drama and English, BA (Hons) Film Studies and Drama. The Drama programme is not intended to provide a vocational training for work in the theatre. Offers a balance between practical, contextual and theoretical approaches to the study of theatre and has close links with the Bristol Old Vic.

University of Wolverhampton

Humanities, Languages and Social Sciences, Wolverhampton City Campus, Wulfruna Street, Wolverhampton WV1 1SB
tel (01902) 321056 *fax* (01902) 323379
website www.asp.wlv.ac.uk

Courses offered: BA (Hons) Drama, HND Performing Arts. The Drama programme covers practical, creative and critical skills, allowing students to develop performance skills and learn from visiting professionals. HND Performing Arts focuses on acting techniques and performance theory. It also offers practical and theoretical knowledge in a wide range of related areas.

University College Worcester

Department of Arts, Humanities and Social Science, University College Worcester, Henwick Grove, Worcester WR2 6AJ
tel (01905) 855000
website www.worc.ac.uk

Courses offered: BA (Hons) Drama and Performance Studies. Explores drama and performance through a variety of contexts and media and develops practical performance skills.

York St John College

York St John College, Lord Mayor's Walk, York YO31 7EX
tel (01904) 624624 *fax* (01904) 612512
email admissions@yorksj.ac.uk
website www.yorksj.ac.uk

Courses offered: BA (Hons) Performance: Theatre. Theory is integrated with practice at all points throughout the degree programme and there are many opportunities to become involved in work placements, independent performance projects and the International Exchange Programme (IEP).

Short-Term and Part-Time Courses

This section lists both 'taster' opportunities for drama school aspirants and further training for professional actors. In *Contacts*, you will also find many individual teachers. If you are thinking of approaching one of these, try to get some advice on his/her current knowledge of the profession and abilities as a teacher before spending your money.

Pre-drama-school courses

Competition for drama school places seems to be growing even more ferocious and many applicants will enhance their chances if they go on a pre-drama-school course. You may for example have done A level Drama, but the actual acting-training on such courses is extremely limited – and, from my observations, is sometimes misleading. (School and college courses are generally geared more towards the exam-passing university entrant – not towards auditioning for drama school.) Whatever your acting background, a 'taster' course (for just a week, for instance) can give you a good idea of what further help/training you need in order to prepare you properly for drama school auditions.

Additional skills

As well as the organisations listed below, there are periodic 'one-off' workshops around the country. These are usually 'trailed', and sometimes advertised, in *The Stage*. Equity occasionally subsidises such enterprises (some, away from the major cities), so it is worth checking with your local Branch/Organiser.

Actors Centres are not just places to sharpen up your existing skills and develop new ones, but also great meeting places for actors to exchange ideas and information.

Academy Drama School
189 Whitechapel Road, London E1 1DN
tel 020-7377 8735
email ask@the-academy.info
website www.the-academy.info
Principal Tim Reynolds
Key contact Judith Reynolds

Courses offered
- Part-time Evening Acting Course (1 year). Course fee is £1350 with 6 hours of classes per week. Entry is by audition
- Saturday Foundation Acting (overall duration of course is flexible). Fee for 4

weeks with 2.5 hours of classes per week is £65. No audition required

- Audition Course (1 week). Course fee is £200 for 26 hours' tuition. Entry is by audition
- Summer Evening Acting Course (2 weeks). Overall fee is £300; no audition required

Actors Centre (London)

1A Tower Street, Covent Garden, London WC2H 9NP
tel 020-7240 3940
email act@actorscentre.co.uk
website www.actorscentre.co.uk

Full membership is open to Equity members, registered graduates from the Conference of Drama Schools in their first year of registration (must hold a student Equity card), and foreign actors holding an Equity letter of exemption. Members are entitled to a wide range of subsidised classes and workshops led by experienced directors and tutors who are active in the industry, plus full use of the centre, café facilities when available and a quarterly schedule. Membership fees are £40 per year or £25 per 6 months. Associate membership is also available for £25 per year; associates are entitled to observe designated workshops but not to participate in them.

Regular classes and workshops include Acting, Tool Box, TV and Film, Auditions, Advice, Labwork, Voice, Shakepeare, Stage Combat, Directing, Musical Theatre and Writing. In addition, members can book individual sessions to work on singing, acting, sight-reading, Alexander Technique, dialect, voice and movement. Contact the centre for a membership form or a current brochure.

Actors Centre North East

2nd Floor, 1 Black Swan Court, Westgate Road, Newcastle upon Tyne NE1 1SG
tel 0191-221 0158 *fax* 0191-221 0158
email actorscentre@yahoo.com
website www.actorscentrene.co.uk

The Actors Centre North East exists to provide support for, and further the interests of, all professional actors and performers living and working in the North East of England. Offers classes in which professional actors and performers can share existing skills and learn new ones, and provides a meeting place for members to exchange ideas and information. Classes and workshops cover all aspects of the performing arts. Equity members, performing arts graduates and performing arts students are eligible for membership. Membership fees are £25 per year or £5 for students.

Courses offered
- Camera Technique for beginners, intermediates and advanced. Offers 6-12 hours of classes for £18-36 with a class size of 12. Courses begin at various points throughout the year
- Audition Technique for beginners, intermediates and advanced. Offers 6-12 hours of classes for £18-36 with a class size of 12. Courses begin at various points throughout the year
- Stage Radio for beginners, intermediates and advanced. Offers 6-12 hours of classes for £18-36 with a class size of 12. Courses begin at various points throughout the year
- IT Training for beginners, intermediates and advanced. Offers 15 hours of free individual tuition available at any time throughout the year

A wide range of courses and classes is available; those listed above are a sample only.

Arts Ed London

Cone Ripman House, 14 Bath Road,
London W4 1LY
tel 020-8987 6655 *fax* 020-8987 6699
email drama@artsed.co.uk
website www.artsed.co.uk
Head of Acting Jane Harrison
Director of the School of Musical Theatre
Ian Watt-Smith
Key contact Nicola Ramsbottom

Courses offered
- Foundation in Performance (1 year part-time). Course fee is £1000-1250 with 7.5 hours of classes per week. Entry is by audition
- Various short courses (10 weeks). Course fee is £150-250 with 2-3 hours of classes per week. Entry is in January, April, July and October. No audition required
- Intensive courses (1-2 weeks at Easter or in the summer). Course fee is £150-350 with 25-30 hours of classes per week. No audition required
- Post Diploma BA (Hons) in Acting

Birmingham School of Acting

The Link Building, Paradise Place,
Birmingham B3 3HJ
tel 0121-262 6800 *fax* 0121-262 6801
email bssd@bssd.ac.uk
website www.bssd.ac.uk
Principal Stephen Simms
Admissions Manager Roger Franke

Courses offered
- Creative Drama (30 weeks part-time). Course fee is £306 with 3 hours of classes per week
- Acting Summer School. Course fee is £510 for 2 weeks in August
- Shakespeare Summer School. Course fee is £299 for 4 days in August

- Musical Theatre Week. Course fee is £350 for 6 days in August
- Musical Theatre Weekend. Course fee is £185 for 2 days in August

Birmingham Theatre School

The Old Rep Theatre, Station Street,
Birmingham B5 4DY
tel 0121-643 3300 *fax* 0121-643 3300
email info@birminghamts.demon.co.uk
website
www.thebirminghamtheatreschool. com
Principal Chris Rozanski
Key contacts Mary Ashwood, Sarah Watts

Courses offered
- Acting for Beginners (11 weeks). Covers the basics of character creation, voice, improvisation and performance discipline for acting beginners. Students participate in all aspects of the creative process from basic exercises to final presentations. Course fee is £69 per term, classes take place in the evening
- Creating Performance (11 weeks). Each term, students will create and perform using a variety of techniques and using both texts and devised work. All aspects of character creation and working with an audience will be explored. Suitable for people with previous experience in acting. Course fee is £69 per term, classes take place in the evening
- Pub Theatre (11 weeks). Provides students with the chance of experiencing exactly what working in a fringe theatre company is all about. Course fee is £69 per term, classes take place in the evening

British Academy of Dramatic Combat

3 Castle View, Helmsley, North Yorkshire
Y062 5AU

email enquiries@badc.co.uk
website www.badc.co.uk

Offers a Performance Certificate in Stage Combat at Foundation, Basic, Basic Level 2, Recommended and Advanced levels. Training is available in the following methods: Broadsword & Shield, Double Handed Broadsword, Quarterstaff, Rapier & Dagger, Rapier & Cloak, Rapier & Buckler, Smallsword, Unarmed Combat. Programmes of workshops are arranged throughout the country, and anyone with suitable venue spaces or wanting to be added to the workshop mailing list should email: Workshops@badc.co.uk

Central School of Speech and Drama

64 Eton Avenue, London NW3 3HY
tel 020-7722 8183
fax 020-7722 4132
website www.cssd.ac.uk
email enquiries@cssd.ac.uk
Principal Professor Gary Crossley

Courses offered

- Saturday Drama Classes (1 term). Course fee is £140, entry is possible throughout the year

- Easter Youth Theatre Workshop (5 days). Course fee is £350

- Introduction to Audition Speeches (3 days). Course fee is £250, entry is in December

- Musical Theatre (2 weeks). Course fee is £820, entry is in June/July

- Summer Shakespeare (2 weeks). Course fee is £820, entry is in June/July

- Actors' Audition Pieces (2 weeks). Course fee is £520, entry is in July

- Youth Theatre (2 weeks). Course fee is £360, entry is in July

- Devising (2 weeks). Course fee is £700, entry is in July/August

- Directed Scenes (2 weeks). Course fee is £700, entry is in August

The City Lit

16 Stukeley Street, London WC2B 5LJ
tel 020-7430 0544 *fax* 020-7405 3347
email v.rochester@citylit.ac.uk
website www.citylit.ac.uk
Head of Drama, Dance & Speech Vivienne Rochester

The college offers an eclectic mix of activities such as acting, movement, voice, mime, circus, stage fighting, magic, comedy, dance, self-presentation, accents, sight-reading and pronunciation which develop vocational, social and personal skills. The John James Bursary is open to Access Course students and there are various other small access grants that might cover travel, books or child-care. Students may ring or come into the office for an interview between 12.30 and 1.30 p.m. (Monday to Saturday) or 5.30 and 6.30 p.m. (Monday to Friday).

Courses offered

- Foundation course (1 year part-time). Applicants must be aged 19 or over. Course fee is £400 or £87 for concessions with 6 hours 40 minutes of tuition per week. Entry is by audition

- Musical Theatre Diploma (1 year part-time). Applicants must be aged 19 or over. Course fee is £535 or £220 for concessions with 6 hours 40 minutes of tuition per week. Entry is by audition

- Cacchetti Ballet School (1 year part-time). Applicants must be aged 19 or over. Course fee is £600 or £306 for concessions with 6 hours 40 minutes of tuition per week. Entry is by interview

- Stage Fighting (1 year part-time). Applicants must be aged 19 or over.

Course fee is £250 or £100 for concessions with 2 hours of tuition per week. Entry is by interview

- A range of acting, voice, movement and self-presentation classes is also available. Courses run for 12 weeks with entry at various points throughout the year

The Desmond Jones School of Mime and Physical Theatre

20 Thornton Avenue, London W4 1QG
tel 020-8747 3537 *fax* 020-8742 3537
email enquiries@desmondjones.co.uk
website www.desmondjones.co.uk
Principal & key contact Desmond Jones

Established in 1979, the school provides professional training in all aspects of mime and physical theatre.

Courses offered
- Foundation Course (3 months). Applicants must be aged 18 or over. Course fee is £930 with half-day classes Monday to Friday. 25 places are available. Entry is by interview, fee is £10

- Advanced Course (3 months). Applicants must be aged 18 or over. Course fee is £930 with half-day classes Monday to Friday. 25 places are available. Entry is by interview, fee is £10

- Masks (2 days). Course fee is £115 with 12 hours of classes per week

- Verbal Improvisation (2 days). Course fee is £115 with 12 hours of classes per week. No audition is required

Drama Studio London (DSL)

1 Grange Road, London W5 5QN
tel 020-8579 3897 *fax* 020-8566 2035
email admin@dramastudiolondon.co.uk
website www.dramastudiolondon.co.uk
Principal Peter Craze
Key contact Amanda Carrara

Courses offered
- Summer Acting Course (4 weeks). Course fee is £950, entry is in August

East 15 Acting School

Hatfields, Rectory Lane, Loughton
IG10 3RY
tel 020-8508 5983 *fax* 020-8508 7521
email east15@essex.ac.uk
website www.east15.ac.uk
Principal John Baraldi
Key contact Linda Humphreys

Courses offered
All courses listed below take place in July:

- Introduction to Acting (1 week), fee is £190

- Approaches to Shakespeare and Jacobean Theatre (2 weeks), fee is £280

- Devised Theatre (3 weeks), fee is £390

- Audition Technique (1 week), fee is £190

- Physical Theatre (1 week), fee is £190

Equity (Wales and South West England Office)

Transport House, 1 Cathedral Road, Cardiff CF11 9SD
tel 029-2039 7971 *fax* 029-2023 0754
email Cardiffequity@altavista.net
website www.equity.org.uk

In the past, Equity has run the Actors Lab in Cheltenham and a series of Theatre Training workshops in Devon and Cornwall for its members. Subjects have included improvisation, movement, working with text, puppetry, fooling, and taking direction; these have been offered at various points throughout the year. Contact the office to find out if and when more workshops are scheduled.

GSA Conservatoire (formerly Guildford School of Acting)

Millmead Terrace, Guildford GU2 4YT
tel (01483) 560701 *fax* (01483) 535431
email enquiries@conservatoire.org
website www.conservatoire.org
Head of Acting Peter Barlow

Courses offered

- Advanced Musical Theatre (1 week).
  Courses take place at Easter and are
  aimed at students over the age of 20 who
  have already achieved a degree of training for the theatre or who are actively
  involved in the field. Classes are held in
  acting, singing and dancing plus a masterclass with a West End performer.
  Course fee is £295

- Singing in the Theatre (1 week). A summer course designed for students over
  the age of 17 who wish to improve their
  singing. Other disciplines relating to the
  voice will also be explored. Entry is in
  July and the fee is £295

- Musical Theatre (2 weeks). Culminating
  in a performance in the Bellairs
  Playhouse, this course is open to
  students aged 17 or over and takes place
  in July/August. Course fee is £495

- Audition Techniques (1 week). Course
  takes place in August and is geared
  towards students aged 17 or over. Course
  fee is £195

Hope Street Ltd.

13a Hope Street, Liverpool L1 9BQ
tel 0151-708 8007 *fax* 0151-709 3242
email peter@hopestreet.org
website www.hope-street.org
Principal Peter Ward
Key contact Alan Richardson

Provides actors with training for physical
theatre and young people's theatre. Places
are also available for trainee directors and
workshop leaders. Courses culminate in
4 public performances directed by professionals. Fees stated below cover the
6-month course period and are applicable
only to non-Merseyside residents.
Merseyside residents may apply for an £80
weekly allowance.

Courses offered

- Physical Theatre (26 weeks full-time).
  Applicants must be aged 18 or over.
  Course fee is £2800. 55 applications were
  received in 2003 and 8 places were offered

- Young People's Theatre (26 weeks full-
  time). Applicants must be aged 18 or
  over. Course fee is £2800. 15 applications
  were received in 2003 and 4 places were
  offered

London Academy of Music & Dramatic Art (LAMDA)

155 Talgarth Road, London W14 9DA
tel 020-8834 0500 *fax* 020-8834 0501
email enquiries@lamda.org.uk
website www.lamda.org.uk
Principal Peter James

Housing is available for short courses in
London; contact the Admissions office for
details.

Courses offered

- Shakespeare Summer Workshop
  (4 weeks). Disciplines include textual
  analysis, history seminars, practical
  voice classes, movement, dance,
  physical theatre, singing (choral and
  solo), scene study, Alexander technique
  and stage combat. Course culminates in
  a non-public open rehearsal and
  includes visits to the Royal Shakespeare
  Company in Stratford-upon-Avon and
  performances at London theatres. Entry
  is by application and references.
  Course takes place from July to August;
  tuition fees for 2004 were set at £1500.

No scholarships are available for this course

- Shakespeare and his Contemporaries Workshop (8 weeks). Featured playwrights include Shakespeare, Marlowe, Jonson and the Jacobeans. Disciplines covered as for 4-week workshops (see above). Includes visits to the Royal Shakespeare Company in Stratford-upon-Avon and performances at London theatres. Entry is by application and references. Course takes place from June to August; tuition fees for 2004 were set at £3000. No scholarships are available for this course

- Stage Combat for Beginners (2 weeks). This course is aimed at anyone wishing to learn about stage combat. No experience is necessary. The course introduces the technical repertoire and develops students' understanding and application of the principles of combat. Includes a visit to the Royal Armouries Museum in Leeds. At the end of the course, it may be possible for certain students to take British Academy of Dramatic Combat Level One Examination. Entry is by application and references. Course takes place in August; tuition fees for 2004 were set at £600

- Advanced Stage Combat (2 weeks). Participants must have at least a Level 2/Intermediate certificate from the BADC or recognised equivalent. Broadens students' technical repertoire and improves their understanding and application of the principles of combat. Includes a visit to the Royal Armouries Museum in Leeds. Entry is by application and references. Course takes place in August; tuition fees for 2004 were set at £600

- Singing for Beginners (2 weeks). This course is aimed at students who are considering an acting training or for actors who wish to gain knowledge of basic techniques and improve confidence in their singing ability. Entry is by application and references. Course takes place in July; tuition fees for 2004 were set at £600

- Advanced Singing for Actors (2 weeks). This course is designed to help actors at all career stages to assemble a portfolio of varied audition songs, tailored to their individual needs. Entry is by application and references. Course takes place in July; tuition fees for 2004 were set at £600

- Physical Theatre Summer School (2 weeks). Comprising work on Le Jeu, Neutral Mask, Musicality of Movement, Clown and the Bouffon, this is an intensive training course suited for the professional or student actor. Entry is by application and references. Course takes place in August; tuition fees for 2004 were set at £600

London Academy of Performing Arts

St Matthews Church, St Petersburgh Place, London W2 4LA
tel 020-7727 0220 *fax* 020-7727 0330
email admin@lapadrama.com
website www.lapadrama.com
Principal Cecilia Hocking
Key contact Administrator

Courses offered

- Classical Acting Course (1 semester full-time). An intensive course for professional performers, directors, drama students and teachers, who want practical work on Shakespearean texts. Classes are timetabled between 9.00 a.m. and 6.00 p.m., 5 days a week. Students must also be available for occasional extra evening and weekend rehearsals, if required. Course fee is £2420. *Audition requirements:* 2 Shakespeare monologues. *Audition fee:* £25

- Summer School Shakespearean Acting (1 month). Course takes place in July and August and is intended for professional performers, drama students (aged 17 and over) and other interested people who wish to explore the English Classical Theatre tradition. Course fee is £850. No audition is required

London Centre for Theatre Studies
The Impact Centre, 12-18 Hoxton Street, London N1 6NG
tel 020-7739 5866 *fax* 020-7739 5866
email ldncts@aol.com
website www.thelondoncentrefortheatre studies.co.uk

Courses offered
Minimum age for entry on the courses listed below is 21 years:

- The Night School (30 weeks). Course fee is £1200 with 6 hours of classes per week
- All Day Acting Class (10 weeks). Course fee is £425 with 6 hours of classes per week
- Evening Acting Class (10 weeks). Course fee is £425 with 6 hours of classes per week
- The Shakespeare Class (10 weeks). Course fee is £300 with 3 hours of classes per week

London Drama School
30 Brondesbury Park, London NW6 7DN
tel 020-8830 0074 *fax* 020-8830 4992
email enquiries@startek-uk.com
website www.startek-uk.com
Key contact Sarah Mann

Courses offered
- Saturday Drama Workshop (10 weeks). Course fee is £450 for 6 hours of classes per week or £250 for 3 hours of classes per week

- Thursday Evening Workshop (10 weeks). Course fee is £180 for 2 hours of classes per week
- Summer Beginners (3 weeks). Course fee is £650. Entry is by audition
- Summer Advanced (6 weeks). Course fee is £1350 or £1800 for both beginners and advanced. Entry is by audition

Morley College Theatre School
61 Westminster Bridge Road, London SE1 7HT
tel 020-7450 1855
email keith-brazil@morleycollege.ac.uk
website www.morleycollege.ac.uk
Key contacts Jane Carr, Keith Brazil

Offers part-time acting classes which lead to London Open College Network accreditation. Classes are led by specialist acting tutors with extensive professional experience. An Access Hardship Fund and concessionary fees are available to some students.

Courses offered
- A range of evening and part-time acting skills courses are available, including: Actors Voice Workshop, The Acting Business, Singing for Actors and Dancers, Absolute Beginners Drama Workshop, Developing Acting Skills, Introduction to Physical Theatre and many different styles of Dance
- Intermediate Foundation Theatre Arts (1 year part-time). Covers Acting Techniques (including voice, improvisation, text work and scenes) and Dance Techniques (Jazz and Contemporary) leading to performances in term 3. Course fee is approximately £1200 with concessions and hardship grants available. Entry is by audition
- Acting Studies (1 year evening school). Develops improvisation, characterisa-

tion, voice and movement skills through a series of workshops and rehearsals. Course fee is approximately £600 with concessions and hardship grants available. Entry is by audition

Mountview Theatre School

Ralph Richardson Memorial Studios, Clarendon Road, London N22 6XF
tel 020-8881 2201 *fax* 020-8829 0034
email enquiries@mountview.ac.uk
website www.mountview.ac.uk
Principal Paul Clements

Courses offered

- Foundation Acting (1 year). Course fee is £1100 with 9 hours of classes per week. Entry is by audition

- Foundation Musical Theatre (1 year). Course fee is £1200 with 9 hours of classes per week. Entry is by audition

- Acting for Screen (2 terms). Course fee is £750 with 3 hours of classes per week. Entry is by audition

- Professional Masterclass, available from 1 day to 1 week during spring and autumn. Fees vary. No audition required

- Summer School Acting (2 weeks). Courses take place in July/August, fee is £600. No audition required

- Summer School Musical Theatre (2 weeks). Courses take place in July/August, fee is £600. No audition required

- Audition Technique (4-6 weeks). Courses take place in spring and autumn, fee is £175. No audition required

Northern Actors Centre

21-31 Oldham Street, Manchester M1 1JG
tel 0161-819 2513 *fax* 0161-819 2513
email info@northernactorscentre.co.uk
website www.northernactorscentre.co.uk

Core provision of ongoing professional development for trained actors. Provides workshops for all Equity members covering every aspect of an actor's toolbox and led by leading industry professionals. Equity members or professional actors with sufficient experience are eligible for membership. Membership fees are £25 per year or £14 for 6 months. Students in their first year following graduation from an NCDT-accredited course are entitled to a reduced membership fee of £5. Email or call the office for a membership form and to receive a current brochure.

Courses offered

- Towards the Text, tutored by George Pensalli. A 2-day workshop in Manchester from 10.30 a.m. to 5.30 p.m. Course fee of £30 with a class size of 12. Aimed at beginners

- So You Want to Be in Voiceovers/Acting for Radio, tutored by Bernard Shaw. Course fee of £15 for 3.5 hours of tuition. Based in Manchester with a class size of 12. Intermediate level

- The Politics of Love and Hate, tutored by Natalie Wilson. 1-day workshop in Leeds. Fee of £18 for 7 hours of tuition in a class of 12. Advanced level

A wide range of courses and classes is available; those listed above are a sample of what was on offer in November 2003.

Oxford School of Drama

Sansomes Farm Studios, Woodstock, Oxford OX20 1ER
tel (01993) 812883 *fax* (01983) 811220
email info@oxforddrama.ac.uk
website www.oxforddrama.ac.uk
Principal George Peck
Key contact Jane Whitehead

Courses offered
- Six-month Foundation course. Aimed at students aged 17 and over, the course covers acting methods and technique, movement, voice, singing, film and television, stage fighting, stage management and history of theatre. Most students on the course are 18-19 years old. Course fee is £4200 with 30.5 hours of classes per week. Entry is by audition

The Questors Theatre Ealing
12 Mattock Lane, London W5 5BQ
tel 020-8567 0011 *fax* 020-8567 8736
email enquiries@questors.org.uk
website www.questors.org.uk
Principal David Emmet
Key contact Administrator

Provides part-time training for actors in the context of a working theatre. Financial support is available from a private trust fund for a limited number of students.

Courses offered
- Acting: Foundation and Performance (2 years). Course fee is £280 with 15 hours of classes per week. Entry is by audition
- Introduction to Acting (1 year). Age range for entry is 17-20. Course fee is £115 with 5 hours of classes per week. Entry is by audition

Richmond Drama School
Parkshot Centre, Parkshot, Richmond TW9 2RE
tel 020-8439 8944 *fax* 020-8332 6560
email David.Whitworth@racc.ac.uk
Principal & key contact David Whitworth

Courses offered
- AS Level Performing Arts (31 weeks). Course fee is £240 with 4.5 hours of classes per week. Entry is by interview

- Physical Theatre (13 weeks). Course fee is £100 with 2 hours of classes per week
- Acting Skills (30 weeks). Course fee is £169 with 2 hours of classes per week
- Shakespeare in Performance; courses take place for 3 weeks in June. Course fee is £91

Rose Bruford College
Lamorbey Park, Burnt Oak Lane, Sidcup DA15 9DF
tel 020-8300 3024 *fax* 020-8308 0542
email enquiries@bruford.ac.uk
website www.bruford.ac.uk
Principal Professor Alastair Pearce

Courses offered
- Acting Summer School (2 weeks). Designed for participants over the age of 18, this programme includes classes, rehearsals and workshops on voice, movement, acting and improvisation

Royal Academy of Dramatic Art (RADA)
62-64 Gower Street, London WC1E 6ED
tel 020-7636 7076 *fax* 020-7323 3865
email enquiries@rada.ac.uk
website www.rada.org
Principal Nicholas Barter

Courses offered
- Acting Shakespeare (8 weeks). Designed for experienced actors, this course offers an opportunity to expand, explore and deepen awareness of Shakespeare's texts. Covers all aspects of vocal technique, with classes to develop the resonance and range of each student's voice. The last 2 weeks of the course are spent in full-time rehearsal for a workshop production culminating in 3 performances in a RADA theatre. Entry is deliberately restricted and places are awarded by competitive audition. Students below the age of 18 are not

normally accepted; most students are in their 20s. Course fee is £4320 which includes breakfast, lunch and refreshments Monday-Friday. Course takes place in June and July. *Audition requirements*: 1 speech from Shakespeare and 1 from a modern play, each lasting no longer than 3 minutes. *Audition fee*: £30

- The RADA Summer School (4 weeks). Based on exploring Shakespeare from an actor's point of view, this course mixes rehearsing scenes and speeches with intensive classes in essential acting skills. Students below the age of 18 are not normally accepted; most students are in their 20s. Course fee is £2460 which includes breakfast, lunch and refreshments Monday-Friday. Course takes place in July and August. No audition required

The School of the Science of Acting

Dept E, 67-83 Seven Sisters Road, London N7 6BU
tel 020-7272 0027 *fax* 020-7272 0026
email find@scienceofacting.org.uk
website www.scienceofacting.org.uk
Principal Sam Kogan
Key contact Jack Curzon

Courses offered
- Intensive Acting Course (33 weeks). Course fee is £1440 with 6 hours of classes per week. No audition required
- Spring Workshop (2 weeks). Course takes place in March and the fee is £500. No audition required
- Summer Workshop (2 weeks). Course takes place in July and the fee is £400. No audition required
- Autumn Workshop (2 weeks). Course takes place in March and the fee is £500. No audition required

Webber Douglas Academy of Dramatic Art

30 Clareville Street, London SW7 5AP
tel 020-7370 4154 *fax* 020-7373 5639
email webberdouglas@btclick.com
website www.webber-douglas-academy. sageweb.co.uk
Principal RB Jago
Academy Secretary Kamaal Hussain

Courses offered
- London Theatre Workshop (4 weeks). Course takes place in July/August with a fee of £1480

Agents and Casting Directors

Introduction

Actors have probably existed since before the invention of writing; actors' agents have only been around since the invention of the telephone, just over a century ago. Prior to this, work-seeking actors had to make themselves known in person to potential employers – for instance, certain hostelries in the Covent Garden area of central London were well-known 'talent-spotting' haunts. Actors would also 'catch a ride' with one of the touring companies in the hope of proving themselves to the manager –and then being put on the payroll. Others would pay managers to let them play small parts in the hope of being noticed. All this meant a lot of hard work and/or expense (let alone the time needed to earn his/her living by other means) for the pre-electronic-age actor. The invention of actors' agents seemed to fill a vital gap.

In the 1970s, a number of actors dissatisfied with the (by then) traditional agent system formed the first co-operative agencies (see also pp. 81-89). This apparently simple idea –with all members taking turns to man the office –took a while to become established. Like many 'simple ideas', the pioneers found that there were more complications involved than they'd initially envisaged, and employers were slow to accept the idea. Thirty years later, the best 'co-ops' have as much professional credibility as their conventional counterparts.

It used to be the case that only the biggest companies used casting directors. The administrative burden inherent in running such a company (let alone directing productions) meant that assistance in the casting process became essential. The 1990s saw a rise in the use of casting directors and in the number of freelancers working on short-term contracts: most of the latter work in a wide variety of fields.

The simple fact is that a significant proportion of properly paid acting work is 'brokered' by casting directors and agents.

Being an Agent

Brian Taylor

The image of an agent –Woody Allen in *Broadway Danny Rose*, on the phone at a desk piled chaotically high in a crowded office, ringing around and touting for business, responding to rumours of possible castings and going out to lunch an awful lot! –still holds fast in many minds. But much has changed: the electronic age has arrived; agents now work in a sophisticated way, making great use of the Internet, faxes, emails, etc.

Brian Taylor –Nina Quick Associates is an established, middle-sized agency with two full-time members of staff and two part-time, and about 80 clients. As such, we are typical of most actors' agencies. Over many years we have established strong, friendly and important contacts with the major television companies –providers of a great deal of work; with theatre producers and directors; with theatre companies in London and theatres around the country; and with casting directors, both commercial and non-commercial, across all aspects of the business. As a result our suggestions have become respected and are taken seriously: we do not suggest actors inappropriately, simply because they are not working. This is essential to the successful running of the business. On a busy day the agency can be kept occupied simply responding to the casting breakdowns that are fed to us from all directions: by phone, email, fax and post. We respond with our suggestions, sending out letters with photographs and CVs; sometimes by fax, with names and Spotlight numbers only; by email, attaching jpeg photos and CVs; and most frequently now, by Spotlight Link. So it's important that actors go into Spotlight, even impoverished students just out of drama school, if they are not to miss out on casting.

When not putting up suggestions, talking to casting directors, giving appointments to clients, listening to their worries and concerns, etc., time has to be found to interview actors looking for representation. Actors writing in, please think carefully about how you address us. 'Dear Sir/Madam' gets nowhere; 'To Whom It May Concern' receives even less consideration! Do not be over-familiar. Be brief and concise. Do not try to be witty and facetious. Always include an sae if you want a reply. Do not 'slag off' your old agent.

Time must also be found to go and see clients in performance. This is always a priority, sometimes involving long journeys, and it's not always possible. Requests are received to go and see other actors, again involving long journeys . . . and all this at the end of a hard day in the office. Actors often forget that.

In touch with the major drama schools, we try to see their student productions, and eventually their showcases, in our search for new and exciting talent. In fact there is a period, starting even before Easter, when if one chose (or was able to) one could be out at a showcase almost every day of the week, such is the proliferation of drama schools today.

So a typical agent's day, in and out of the office, will involve most of the above plus the administrative, book-keeping and accounting work involved in running any busy office. Hopefully this will go some way towards rectifying some actors' image of their agent as a wining, dining, do-nothing layabout. Not true!

Brian Taylor was born in Bolton, Lancashire and educated at Leeds University. He was Head of History at a London comprehensive school before leaving to work as a Producer/Director for ILEA Television, responsible for a variety of programmes including history documentaries, drama series and art programmes. He has taught at LAMDA and set up his own video production company. Brian has also written, produced and directed a number of plays including Then There Was A Star Danced, *a dramatisation of the life of Ellen Terry performed at the Pleasance Theatre, Edinburgh as part of the Festival (and on many occasions since). He changed direction to work as an agent, eventually buying out the business some ten years ago, to become Brian Taylor – Nina Quick Associates.*

Agents

A good agent understands contracts, knows the currents rates in every field of work and – most importantly – has plenty of professional contacts and access to far more casting information than most individuals can ever have. Directors and casting directors rely on the agents whom they know and trust to help with the filtering process of whom to interview. A good agent will work hard at promoting each of his/her clients. In return, it is not unreasonable that they charge commission on every contract they negotiate for you – generally, 10-20% (plus VAT, if appropriate). A good agent will also (a) have only as many clients as they can reasonably handle and (b) ensure that they have a good range of ages and types of actors to cover as many casting opportunities as possible.

When you are seeking representation, it is advisable to contact agents by post in the first instance – unless specifically informed otherwise. It is a good idea to include a separate 10×8in (25×20cm) photograph and it is important that all your enclosures contain your name and the best way to contact you (not a long list of confusing alternatives). Agents receive many requests for representation, and photographs can become separated from their accompanying letters and CVs, so proper labelling is essential.

Use the listings that follow to (a) target your submission as accurately as possible (by writing to a specific, named person, for example), (b) check for any details that could inform the content of your letter and (c) find out whether each would be interested in any extras, like a showreel. Time spent checking details can save money and enhance your chances of being noticed more than the next person.

Unless you have a good collection of professional credits, it is generally best to write to agents when there's an opportunity for them to see you in something.

If you are invited to meet an agent, that is often a good sign. You should approach the occasion in much the same way as you would an interview for a production. The major difference is that you should be prepared to ask (reasonable) questions – rates of commission, for instance.

When seeking representation, it can be a good idea to target only those agencies that you think might suit you. For instance, might you feel lost in a large agency, but feel more comfortable with a smaller one? On the other hand, some larger agencies have huge 'clout' and can be the first 'port of call' for the casting of prestigious productions.

When you've been taken on by an agent, it is important to establish how your working relationship will function. Be clear about any areas of work that you don't want to be suggested for, discuss your availability for auditions and interviews, agree how much promotion you should do for yourself, and so on.

These listings only contain agents who represent adult actors – there are many others who represent children, models, extras and so on.

21st Century Vaux Casting
The Corn Exchange, Fenwick Street,
Liverpool L2 7QS
tel 0151-258 1679 *fax* 0151-231 1067
email 21stcenturyvaux@beeb.net
Key personnel David Williamson

Established in 1991, the agency represents 20 actors. Areas of work include theatre, television, film, commercials, corporate and voice-overs.

Will consider attending performances at venues in Greater London and the North West with at least 1 week's notice. Accepts submissions (with CVs and photographs) from actors previously unknown to the company sent by post or email. Will also accept showreels, voice tapes, and invitations to view individual actors' websites. *Commission*: 7.5%

41 Management
3rd Floor, 74 Rose Street, North Lane,
Edinburgh EH2 3DX
tel 0131-225 3585 *fax* 0131-225 4535
email mhunwick@41man.co.uk
Key personnel Maryam Hanwick

A personal management established in 1999. 1 agent represents actors. Areas of work include theatre, musicals, television, film, commercials and voice-overs. Also represents vocal coaches for theatre, musicals, television and film industries.

Will consider attending performances at venues within Greater London and in Scotland given 4 weeks' notice. Accepts submissions (with CVs and photographs) from actors previously unknown to the company

if sent by post. Will also accept showreels. *Commission*: Theatre 10%; TV and Broadcast Media 12.5%; Commercials 15%

A&J Management
242A The Ridgeway, Botany Bay, Enfield
EN2 8AP
tel 020-8342 0542 *fax* 020-8342 0842
email ajmanagement@bigfoot.com
website www.ajmanagement.co.uk
Managing Director Jackie Mitchell
Key personnel Joanne Michael

Established in 1984. 3 agents represent actors. Areas of work include theatre, musicals, television, film, commercials, corporate and voice-overs.

Will consider attending performances at venues within Greater London with a minimum of 2 weeks' notice. Accepts submissions (with CVs and photographs) from actors previously unknown to the company if sent by post. Invitations to view individual actors' websites are also accepted. *Commission*: 15% plus VAT

June Abbott Associates
The Courtyard, 10 York Way,
London N1 9AA
tel 020-7837 7826 *fax* 020-7833 0870
email jaa@thecourtyard.org.uk
website www.thecourtyard.co.uk
Assistant Agent Lottie Berrill

Established in 1994. 2 agents represent 50 actors. Areas of work include theatre, musicals, television, film, commercials, corporate and voice-overs.

Attendance at performances is dependent on potential client submissions/interviews. Accepts submissions (with CVs and photographs) from actors previously unknown to the company if sent by post. Enclose an sae if a reply is required and for the return of CVs and photographs. Showreels and voice tapes should only be sent on request. Actors should only apply if they have training, and will only be contacted if the agency is interested. Recommends the photographer Peter Simpkin (see entry under *Photographers* for further details). *Commission*: Theatre 10%; Voice-Over and Radio 12%; Film and TV 15%

Acting Associates

71 Hartham Road, London N7 9JJ
tel 020-7607 3562 *fax* 020-7607 3562
email Fiona@actingassociates.co.uk
website www.actingassociates.co.uk
Agent Fiona Farley

Established in 1988. 1 agent represents 45-50 actors.

Will consider attending performances with 1 week's notice. Accepts submissions (with CVs and photographs) from actors previously unknown to the company if sent by post. Recommends the photographer Catherine Shakespeare Lane (see entry under *Photographers* for further details). *Commission*: Theatre 10%; Other 15%

Actors Ireland

Crescent Arts Centre, 2-4 University Rd, Belfast BT7 1NH
tel 028-9024 8861 *fax* 028-9024 8861
email Geraldine@actorsireland.com
website www.actorsireland.com

Established in 2001. 2 agents represent 90 actors. Areas of work include theatre,

musicals, television, film, commercials, corporate and voice-overs.

Will consider attending performances at venues in Northern Ireland. Accepts submissions (with CVs and photographs) from actors previously unknown to the company if sent by post. Will also accept invitations to view individual actors' websites. *Commission*: Theatre 5%; TV 10%

Actual Management

The Studio, 63a Ladbroke Road, London W11 3PD
tel 020-7243 1166 *fax* 0870-874 1149
email agents@actualmanagement.co.uk
website www.actualmanagement.co.uk

Established in 2002. 2 agents represent 50 actors. Areas of work include theatre, television, film and commercials.

Will consider attending performances at venues in Greater London with at least 2 weeks' notice. Accepts submissions (with CVs and photographs) from actors previously unknown to the company sent by post or email. Will also accept showreels, voice tapes, and invitations to view individual actors' websites.

Anita Alraun Representation

5th Floor, 28 Charing Cross Road, London WC2H 0DB
tel 020-7379 6840 *fax* 020-7379 6865
Proprietor/Agent Anita Alraun

1 agent represents a varying number of actors. Areas of work include theatre, musicals, television, film, commercials, corporate and voice-overs. Also represents directors and composers.

Will consider attending performances at venues in Greater London and the North West with 1 week's notice. Accepts submissions (with CVs and photographs) from actors previously unknown to the company if sent by post with sae enclosed for a reply. Also accepts invitations to view individual actors' websites if made in writing. May request showreels and voice tapes following an interview if interested in taking an application further. *Commission*: 7.5-15% depending on job medium

Alvarez Management
86 Muswell Road, London N10 2BE
tel 020-8883 2206 *fax* 020-8444 2646

Established in 1990. 2 agents represent 55 actors. Areas of work include theatre, musicals, television, film, commercials, corporate and voice-overs.

Will consider attending performances at venues within Greater London with 3-4 weeks' notice. Accepts submissions (with CVs, photographs and sae) from actors previously unknown to the company if sent by post. 'When you are on the phone, please introduce yourself.'"Have a really decent photograph taken." *Commission*: Theatre and Radio 10%; Film and TV 12.5%; Commercials 15%

ALW Associates
1 Grafton Chambers, Grafton Place, London NW1 1LN
tel 020-7388 7018 *fax* 020-7813 1398
email alweurope@onetel.net.uk

Established in 1977 as Vernon Conway Ltd. Sole representation of 35 actors. Areas of work include theatre, musicals, television, film and commercials.

Will consider attending performances at venues within Greater London and occasionally elsewhere with 1 week's notice. Accepts submissions (with CVs and pho-

tographs) from actors previously unknown to the company sent by post or email. Also accepts invitations to view individual actors' websites. Showreels and voice tapes should only be sent on request. *Commission*: Theatre and Radio 10-12.5%; Film and TV 12.5%; Commercials 15%

Amber Personal Management Ltd.
189 Wardour Street, London W1F 8ZD
tel 020-7734 7887 *fax* 020-7734 9883
email info@amberltd.co.uk
website www.amberltd.co.uk

Established in 1986. 3 agents represent around 80 actors. Areas of work include theatre, musicals, television, film, commercials, corporate and voice-overs. Also represents directors and presenters (normally as an additional skill of actors already represented by the agency). Management has agents based in London as well as Manchester.

Will consider attending performances at venues within Greater London and elsewhere with 3-4 weeks' notice. Accepts submissions (with CVs, photographs and sae) from actors previously unknown to the company if sent by post. *Commission*: Theatre and Radio 6.5-8.5%; Film, TV and Commercials 15%; Live Presentation 10%

Andrew's Management
203 Links Road, London SW17 9EP
tel 020-8769 7416 or 020-8677 5260
fax 020-8677 8973
email atj@andrewsman.fsnet.co.uk
Sole Proprietor Andrew Thomas James

Established in 1992. 1 agent represents 35-40 actors. Areas of work include theatre, musicals, television, film, commercials and corporate.

Will consider attending performances at venues within Greater London and occasionally elsewhere with 2-3 weeks' notice. Accepts submissions (with CVs and photographs) from actors previously unknown to the company if sent by post. Will also accept follow-up telephone calls, showreels and voice tapes. *Commission*: 10-15%

Susan Angel & Kevin Francis Ltd.

1st Floor, 12 D'Arblay Street,
London W1F 8DU
tel 020-7439 3086 *fax* 020-7437 1712
email angelpair@freeuk.com
Managing Director Susan Angel
Director Kevin Francis

Established in 1976. 2 agents represent 65-70 actors. Areas of work include theatre, musicals, television, film, commercials and corporate.

Will consider attending performances at venues within Greater London and occasionally elsewhere (e.g. Leeds, Bristol, Manchester) with 2 weeks' notice. Accepts brief submissions (with CVs and photographs) from actors previously unknown to the company if sent by post. Emailed applications are not considered due to the volume of mail. *Commission*: 10-12%

APM Associates

PO Box 834, Hemel Hempstead HP3 9ZP
tel (01442) 252907 *fax* (01442) 241099
email apm@apmassociates.net
website www.apmassociates.net
Managing Director Linda French

Established in 1989. 2 agents represent 65-70 actors. Areas of work include theatre, musicals, television, film, commercials, corporate and voice-overs. Also represents actor/writers, presenters and directors.

Will consider attending performances at venues within Greater London with 2 weeks' notice. Accepts submissions (with CVs and photographs) from actors previously unknown to the company if sent by post with sae. Will also accept showreels and voice tapes. Will consider looking at websites only if actor's CV is of interest. *Commission*: Brochure available upon offer of interview

Argyle Associates

St John's Buildings, 43 Clerkenwell Road,
London EC1M 5RS
tel 020-7608 2095 *fax* 020-7608 1642
email argyle.associates@virgin.net
Director Richard Linford
Key personnel Geraldine Pryor

Established in 1995. 2 agents represent 30 actors. Areas of work include theatre, musicals, television, film, commercials and corporate.

Will consider attending performances at venues in Sussex and Surrey (e.g. Eastbourne, Brighton, Guildford, Dorking, Windsor) with 2 weeks' notice. Accepts submissions (with CVs and photographs) from actors previously unknown to the company if sent by post. Invitations to view individual actors' websites are also accepted. 'Be clear about what you think you have to offer the agency –your type and roles. Your photograph should look like you and be a high-grade holiday snap.' *Commission*: Theatre and Radio 10%; TV 12.5%; Commercials, Film, Corporate and CD Rom 15%

Associated International Management

Nederlander House, 7 Great Russell Street,
London WC1B 3NH
tel 020-7637 1700 *fax* 020-7637 8666
email info@a-i-m.net
website www.a-i-m.net
Key personnel Derek Webster, Stephen Gittings, Lisa-Marie Assenheim

An international management established in 1984. 3 agents represent 60 actors. Areas of work include theatre, musicals, television, film, commercials and voice-overs. Also represents directors.

Will consider attending performances at venues within Greater London with 1-2 weeks' notice. Accepts submissions (with CVs and photographs) from actors previously unknown to the company if sent by post. *Commission*: TV 12.5%; Radio and Theatre 10%

BAM Associates

41 Bloomfield Rd, Bristol BS4 3QA
tel 0117-9710 636 *fax* 0117-9710 636
email casting@ebam.tv
website www.ebam.tv

2-3 agents represent 45 actors. Areas of work include theatre, musicals, television, film, commercials, corporate and voice-overs.

Will consider attending performances at venues within Greater London and the South West but requests as much notice as possible. Accepts submissions (with CVs and 10x8in black and white photographs) from actors previously unknown to the company if sent by post. *Commission*: Theatre 10%; Mechanical Media 15%. Rates are halved if the actor generates the work.

Gavin Barker Associates Ltd.

2D Wimpole Street, London W1G 0EB
tel 020-7499 4777 *fax* 020-7499 3777
email gavin@gavinbarkerassociates.co.uk
website www.gavinbarkerassociates.co.uk
Managing Director Gavin Barker
Associate Director Michelle Burke

Established in 1998. 2 agents represent 45 actors. Areas of work include theatre, musicals, television, film, commercials,

corporate and voice-overs. Also represents directors and choreographers.

Will consider attending performances at venues in Greater London given at least 3 weeks' notice. Accepts submissions (with CVs and photographs) from actors previously unknown to the company sent by post or email. Showreels, voice tapes and invitations to view individual actors' websites are also accepted. *Commission*: 10-12.5%

Olivia Bell Ltd.

189 Wardour Street, London W1F 8ZD
tel 020-7439 3270 *fax* 020-7439 3485
email info@olivia-bell.co.uk
Managing Director Xania Segal

Established in 2001. 2 agents represent 90 actors. Areas of work include theatre, musicals, television, film and commercials.

Will consider attending performances at venues within Greater London with a minimum of 1 week's notice. Accepts submissions (with CVs and photographs) from actors previously unknown to the company if sent by post. Invitations to view individual actors' websites and showreels or voice tapes are also accepted. *Commission*: 12.5-20%

Jorg Betts Associates

Gainsborough House, 81 Oxford Street, London W1D 2EU
tel 020-7903 5300 *fax* 020-7903 5301
email jorgbetts@aol.com

Established in 2001. Areas of work include theatre, musicals, television, film, commercials and corporate. Also represents directors and presenters.

Accepts submissions (with CVs and photographs) from actors previously unknown to the company if sent by post.

The Bridge Agency Ltd.
PO Box 261, Loughton IG10 2WS
tel 070-2111 7312 *fax* 070-2164 5220
email the_bridge_agency@yahoo.co.uk
Agent Robert Stokes

Established in 2002. 1 agent represents 10
actors. Areas of work include theatre,
musicals, television, film, commercials,
corporate and voice-overs.

Will consider attending performances
at East 15 Acting School only and with
2 weeks' notice. Accepts showreels and
voice tapes from East 15 graduates.
'Our agency is open to graduates of East
15 Acting School only. We aim to see all
productions at East 15 and to intensify this
cooperation." *Commission*: 8-18%

BROOD
PO Box 21720, London E14 6SU
tel 020-7531 1810 *fax* 020-7531 1810
email broodmanagement@aol.com
Director Brian Parsonage-Kelly

Established in 2003. 1 agent represents 40
actors. Areas of work include theatre,
musicals, television, film, commercials
and corporate. Also represents models.

Accepts submissions (with CVs and
photographs) from actors previously
unknown to the company if sent by post.
Recommends the photographer
Janie Airey (www.janie-airey.com).
Commission: Theatre 10%; Other 15%

Valerie Brook Agency
10 Sandringham Road, Cheadle Hulme,
Cheshire SK8 5NH
tel 0161-486 1631

2 agents represent 75 actors. Areas of work
include theatre, musicals, television, film,
commercials and corporate.

Will consider attending performances at
venues outside Greater London with
2 weeks' notice. Accepts submissions
(with CVs and photographs) from actors
previously unknown to the company if
sent by post. Invitations to view individual
actors' websites are also accepted.
Commission: negotiated with clients individually

Brunskill Management Ltd.
Suite 8A, 169 Queen's Gate,
London SW7 5HE

Agency represents more than 100 actors.
Areas of work include theatre, musicals,
television, film, commercials, corporate
and voice-overs. Also represents producers,
directors and musical directors.

Will consider attending performances at
venues in Greater London and occasionally
elsewhere but requests as much notice as
possible. Accepts submissions (with CVs
and photographs) from actors previously
unknown to the company if sent by post.
Enclose an sae of an appropriate size for
the return of CVs and photographs. Emails
are not encouraged, particularly if they
include large attachments.

Buchanan Associates
Nederlander House, 7 Great Russell Street,
London WC1B 3NH
tel 020-7631 2004 *fax* 020-7631 2034
email info@buchanan-associates.co.uk
website www.buchanan-associates.co.uk

1 agent represents approximately 50 actors.
Areas of work include theatre, musicals,
television, film and commercials.

Will consider attending performances at
venues within Greater London with 2 weeks'
notice. Accepts submissions (with CVs and
photographs) from actors previously

unknown to the company if sent by post. Showreels and voice tapes are also accepted. Recommends the photographer Chris Baker (020-8441 3051). *Commission:* 10% plus VAT

Burnett Granger Associates Ltd.
3 Clifford Street, London W1S 2LF
tel 020-7437 8008 *fax* 020-7287 3239
email associates@burnettgranger.co.uk

2 agents represent 100 actors. Also represents presenters.

Will consider attending performances at venues within Greater London with 3 weeks' notice. Accepts submissions (with CVs, photographs and sae) from actors previously unknown to the company if sent by post. *Commission:* 10-12%

CADS Management
209 Abbey Road, Bearwood,
Birmingham B67 5NG
tel 0121-420 1996 *fax* 0121-434 4909
email info@cadsmanagement.co.uk
website www.cadsmanagement.co.uk
Manager T Smith
Coordinator/Key contact Rosina Chaudry
IT/Administration Ben Steel

Established in 1990. Sole representation of 60-70 actors. Areas of work include theatre, musicals, television, film, commercials, corporate, voice-overs and role-play. Also represents directors and presenters.

Will consider attending performances at venues within Greater London and elsewhere with 3 weeks' notice. Accepts submissions (with CVs and photographs) from actors previously unknown to the company sent by post or email. Showreels and voice tapes are also accepted. Workshops are run in August each year, and contracts are renewed in September. *Commission:* 20%

Campbell Associates
2 Chelsea Cloisters, Sloane Avenue,
Chelsea, London SW3 3DW
tel 020-7584 5586 *fax* 020-7584 8799
email campbellassociates@btopenworld.com
Agents Jackie Williamson, Michelle Holmes, Audrey Campbell

Established in 1996. Agency represents 100 actors, shared between 3 agents. Areas of work include theatre, musicals, television, film, commercials, corporate and voiceovers. Also represents children.

Will consider attending performances at venues within Greater London with 2 weeks' notice. Accepts submissions (with CVs and photographs) from actors previously unknown to the company if sent by post. Showreels and voice tapes are also accepted. *Commission:* Theatre 10%; TV, Film and Commercials 15%

Jessica Carney Associates
Suite 90-92, 87 Regent Street,
London W1B 4EH
tel 020-7434 4143

Established in 1950. 1 agent and her assistants represent 50-60 actors. Areas of work include theatre, musicals, television, film, commercials and corporate. Also represents technicians and directors.

Will consider attending performances at venues within Greater London with 2-3 weeks' notice. Accepts submissions (with CVs and photographs) from actors previously unknown to the company if sent by post. Actors should only write if they are performing in a London show. An sae must be included if a reply is required. Emails with attachments will not be accepted. *Commission:* 10%; Commercials 15%

Casting Couch Productions Ltd.

97 Riffel Road, London NW2 4PG
tel 020-8438 9679 *fax* 020-8208 2373
email moiratownsend@yahoo.co.uk
Key personnel Moira Townsend

Established in 1991. Sole representation of
40 actors. Areas of work include theatre,
musicals, television, film, commercials,
corporate and voice-overs.

Will consider attending performances at
venues within Greater London and
elsewhere with 2-3 weeks' notice.
Accepts submissions (with CVs and photographs) from actors previously
unknown to the company if sent by post.
An sae should be included for the return
of CVs and photographs. Actors will only
be contacted if the agent would like to
meet them. *Commission*: 15% across the
board

See entry under *Casting Directors* for
further details.

The Casting Department

21h Heathmans Road, London SW6 4TJ
tel 020-7384 0388 *fax* 020-7736 2221
email jillscastingpt@aol.com
Key personnel Jill Searle

1 agent represents 200 actors. Areas of
work include television and commercials.

Accepts submissions (with CVs and photographs) from actors previously unknown
to the company if sent by post.

CFA Management

East Trevelmond Farm, Trevelmond,
Liskeard, Cornwall PL14 4LY
tel (01579) 321858 *fax* (01579) 321858
email frances@cfamanagement.fsnet.co.uk
Key personnel Frances Ross

Established in 2000. 1 agent represents 20
actors. Areas of work include theatre, television and film.

Will consider attending performances at
nearby venues in the South West only.
Accepts submissions (with CVs and photographs) from actors previously unknown to
the company if sent by post. Follow-up telephone calls, showreels and voice tapes are
also accepted. 'Please consider whether you
wish to be represented by an agent based in
Cornwall before applying. I would be happy
to discuss this with you.' *Commission*:
Theatre 10%; Film and Television 12.5%

Cinel Gabran Management

Ty Cefn, 14-16 Rectory Road, Canton,
Cardiff, Wales CF5 1QL
tel 029-2066 6600 *fax* 029-2066 6601
email enquiries@cinelgabran.co.uk
website www.cinelgabran.co.uk
Managing Director/Agent David Chance
Agent Sioned James
Company Secretary Mari Gordon-Rice

Established in 1988. 2 agents represent
65 actors. Also represents presenters,
singers who act and actors who write. The
company has a London client list,
although 60% of clients are Wales-based.
It works in both English- and Welsh-
language production.

Will consider attending performances at
venues in Wales and Central London with
2 weeks' notice. Accepts submissions
(with CVs and photographs) from actors
previously unknown to the company if
sent by post. An sae should be included
with CVs and photographs. *Commission*:
Varies according to type of work

Howard Cooke Associates (HCA)

19 Coulson Street, London SW3 3NA

tel 020-7591 0144
Managing Director/Senior Agent Howard Cook
Junior Agent Bronwyn Sanders

2 agents represent 40 actors. Areas of work include theatre, musicals, television, film, commercials and corporate.

Will consider attending performances at venues within Greater London and elsewhere (if within easy travelling distance) with 3 weeks' notice. Hard copy applications (with CVs, photographs and sae) from actors previously unknown to the company are welcome. 'Having trained as an agent at Fraser-Skemp Management, former actor Howard Cooke formed HCA in 1993. The company specialises in a very personal style of representation over a wide range of media and is committed to handling a selective number of clients.' *Commission*: 10-20% depending on type of engagement

Clive Corner Associates

73 Gloucester Road, Hampton, Middlesex TW12 2UQ
tel 020-8287 2726 *fax* 020-8979 4983
email cornerassociates@aol.com
website www.cornerassociates.cwc.net
Key personnel Clive Corner, Duncan Stratton, Bill Upton

Established in 1988. 3 agents represent 75 actors. Areas of work include theatre, musicals, television, film, commercials and corporate.

Will consider attending performances at venues within Greater London with 3 weeks' notice. Rarely prepared to travel elsewhere. Accepts submissions (with CVs and photographs) from actors previously unknown to the company if sent by post. Showreels, voice tapes and invitations to view individual actors' websites are not accepted unless requested following receipt of CV/photograph. *Commission*: Theatre and Radio 10%; TV, Film and Corporate 15%; Commercials 20%

Coulter Management Agency

74 Victoria Crescent Road, Glasgow G12 9JN
Agent Anne Coulter
Assistant S Bartram

2 agents represent 80 actors. Areas of work include theatre, television, film, commercials, corporate and voice-overs.

Will consider attending performances at venues in Scotland with 3 weeks' notice. Accepts submissions (with CVs and photographs) from actors previously unknown to the company if sent by post. Showreels and voice tapes are also accepted. *Commission*: 7.5-15% (sliding scale)

CSM Artistes

St Dunstan's Hall, East Acton Lane, London W3 7EG
tel 020-8743 9982
email csmartists@aol.com
Proprietor Angela Radford
Agent Carole Deamer
Personal Assistant Anthea Francis

Personal management established in 1984. Sole representation of 40-50 actors. Areas of work include theatre, musicals, television, film, commercials and corporate.

Will consider attending performances at venues within Greater London with 3 weeks' notice. Accepts submissions (with CVs and photographs) from actors previously unknown to the company if sent by post. An sae must be included. *Commission*: 15%

Curtis Brown Ltd.

Haymarket House, 28-29 Haymarket,
London SW1Y 4SP
tel 020-7393 4400 *fax* 020-7393 4401
email info@curtisbrown.co.uk
website www.curtisbrown.co.uk
Agents Jacquie Drewe, Maxine Hoffman,
Sarah MacCormick, Sarah Spear, Kate
Staddon

One of Europe's oldest and largest independent literary and media agencies. Established more than 100 years ago, there are now more than 20 agents within the Book, Media, Actors and Presenters Divisions, 5 of whom represent actors. Also represents writers, directors, playwrights and celebrities.

Submissions should be sent by post and addressed to 'Actors Agents'. They should include a covering letter with email address, CV, photograph, showreel on VHS (if actor has one) and sae for the return of the showreel. Tries to respond within 4-6 weeks. Does not meet potential clients before viewing their work. Does not accept email or faxed submissions. *Commission*: 12.5-15%

Lisa D Management Ltd.

Unit 5, Gun Wharf, 241 Old Ford Road,
London E3 5QB

2 agents represent 35-40 actors. Areas of work include theatre, musicals, television, film, commercials and corporate.

Will consider attending performances at venues within Greater London and sometimes elsewhere, given as much notice as possible. Accepts submissions (with CVs and photographs) from actors previously unknown to the company if sent by post. Applicants sending emails should ring first to let the agent know to expect them. Follow-up telephone calls are also accepted.

Caroline Dawson Associates

125 Gloucester Road, London SW7 4TE
tel 020-7373 3323 *fax* 020-7373 1110
email cda@cdalondon.com

3 agents represent 60 actors.

Will consider attending performances at venues within Greater London with 3 weeks' notice. Accepts submissions (with CVs and photographs) from actors previously unknown to the company if sent by post. Showreels, voice tapes and invitations to view individual actors' websites are also accepted. *Commission*: Variable

Felix de Wolfe

Garden Offices, 51 Maida Vale,
London W9 1SD
tel 020-7289 5770 *fax* 020-7289 5731

3 agents represent 100 actors. Areas of work include theatre, musicals, television, film, commercials, corporate and voice-overs. Also represents directors and producers.

Will consider attending performances at venues within Greater London and elsewhere with 10 days' notice. Accepts submissions (with CVs and photographs) from actors previously unknown to the company if sent by post. *Commission*: Variable

Bryan Drew Ltd.

Mezzanine, Quadrant House,
80-82 Regent Street, London W1B 5AU
tel 020-7437 2293 *fax* 020-7437 0561
email bryan@bryandrewltd.com
Managing Director Bryan Drew
Personal Assistant Mina Parmar

Established in 1963. 2 agents represent 40 actors. Areas of work include theatre, musicals, television, film, commercials, corporate and voice-overs. Also represents writers.

Will consider attending performances at venues within Greater London with a minimum of 2 weeks' notice. *Commission*: 12.5-15%

Kenneth Earle Personal Management

214 Brixton Road, London SW9 6AP
tel 020-7274 1219 *fax* 020-7274 9529
email kennethearle@agents-uk.com
website entertainment-kennethearle.co.uk

Established in 2000. 1 agent represents 10-15 actors. Areas of work include theatre, musicals, television, film, commercials, corporate and voice-overs.

Will consider attending performances at venues in Greater London and elsewhere with 1 week's notice. Accepts submissions (with CVs and photographs) from actors previously unknown to the company if sent by post. Follow-up telephone calls and invitations to view individual actors' websites are also accepted. Showreels and voice tapes should only be sent on request. *Commission*: 10-15%

Susi Earnshaw Management

5 Brook Place, Barnet,
Hertfordshire EN5 2DL
tel 020-8441 5010 *fax* 020-8364 9618
email casting@susiearnshaw.co.uk
website www.susiearnshaw.co.uk
Agents Christine Jacquemin, Susi Earnshaw

Established in 1989. 2 agents represent 50 actors. Areas of work include theatre, musicals, television, film, commercials and corporate.

Will consider attending performances at venues within Greater London with 2-3 weeks' notice. Accepts submissions (with CVs and photographs) from actors previously unknown to the company if sent by post. *Commission*: Theatre 10%; TV, Film and Commercials 15%

Annie Elliott Management

Top Floor, 19, Camden Passage,
London N1 8ED
tel 020-7226 4863
email annieelliottmgmt@aol.com
Agent Clare Allen

Established in 2002. 1 agent represents 15 actors. Areas of work include theatre, musicals, television, film, commercials and corporate.

Will consider attending performances at venues within Greater London and occasionally elsewhere, given as much notice as possible. Accepts submissions (with CVs and photographs) from actors previously unknown to the company if sent by post or email. Follow-up telephone calls, showreels, voice tapes and invitations to view individual actors' websites are also accepted. *Commission*: Theatre 5%; Technical 15%

Et-Nik-A Prime Management and Castings Ltd.

3rd Floor, Balfour House, 46-54 Great Titchfield Street, London W1W 7QA
tel 020-7299 3555 *fax* 020-7299 3558
email info@et-nik-a.co.uk
website www.et-nik-a.co.uk
Managing Director Aldo Arcilla

Established in 2000. 3 agents represent 80 actors. Areas of work include theatre, musicals, television, film, commercials, corporate and voice-overs.

Will consider attending performances at venues within Greater London and occasionally elsewhere with 1-2 weeks' notice. Accepts submissions (with CVs and photographs) from actors previously unknown to the company if sent by post. Invitations to view individual actors' websites are also accepted. Showreels and voice tapes should only be sent on request. *Commission*:

Theatre 10%; TV and Films 15%;
Commercials 20%

Evolution Management
Studio 21, The Truman Brewery Building,
91 Brick Lane, London E1 6QB
tel 020-7053 2128 *fax* 020-7375 2752
email info@evolutionmngt.com
website www.evolutionmngt.com
Key personnel Loftus Burton

Established in 1999. 2 agents represent
45 actors. Areas of work include
theatre, musicals, television, film and
commercials. Also represents directors
and presenters.

Will consider attending performances
at venues within Greater London and
sometimes elsewhere with 2 weeks'
notice. Accepts submissions (with CVs
and photographs) from actors previously
unknown to the company sent by post or
email. Showreels and voice tapes are
also accepted. *Commission*: Theatre
negotiable; TV and Films 15%;
Commercials 20%

Fushion
27 Old Gloucester Street,
London WC1N 3XX
tel 08700 111100 *fax* 08700 111020
email enquiries@fushion-uk.com
website www.fushion-uk.com
Key personnel Lee Dennison

Established in 1998. 1 agent represents 35
actors (25 in London; 10 in New York).
Areas of work include theatre, musicals,
television, film, commercials, corporate
and voice-overs. Also represents presenters.

Will consider attending performances at
venues worldwide, given a minimum of 6
weeks' notice. Accepts submissions (with

CVs and photographs) from actors previously unknown to the company sent by
post or email. Showreels, voice tapes and
invitations to view individual actors' websites are also accepted. *Commission*: 15%

Galloways One
15 Lexham Mews, London W8 6JW
tel 020-7376 2288 *fax* 020-7376 2416
email hugh@gallowaysone.com
website www.gallowaysone.com
Directors Hugh Galloway, Jill Moore
Personal Assistant Isabelle Desrochers

Established in 1971. Agency represents
150 actors. Areas of work include television,
commercials, corporate and voice-overs
with the primary focus on commercials.

Will consider attending performances at
venues within Greater London and occasionally elsewhere given as much notice as
possible. Accepts submissions (with CVs
and photographs) from actors previously
unknown to the company if sent by post.
Enclose an appropriately sized sae for the
return of personal details. Invitations to
view individual actors' websites are also
accepted. 'As an agency we prefer to look
up a *Spotlight* entry to see if you are what
we are looking for. If we are interested, we
will call you to request that you send or
email details to us. If we want to take it
further, we will then arrange an interview.'
Commission: TV 10%; Other 18%

Michael Garrett Associates
23 Haymarket, London SW1Y 4DG
tel 020-7839 4888 *fax* 020-7839 4555
email enquiries@michaelgarrett.co.uk
website www.theatricalagent.co.uk

A personal management representing professional actors and actresses. Areas of

work include theatre, musical theatre, television, film, commercials and corporate. Also represents a limited number of theatre designers, choreographers, directors and musical directors.

Accepts submissions from actors previously unknown to the company if sent by post. Does not welcome email submissions or telephone enquiries.

Garricks
5, The Old School House,
The Lanterns, London SW11 3AD
tel 020-7738 1600 *fax* 020-7738 1881
email megan@garricks.net
Key personnel Megan Willis

Established in 1981. Areas of work include theatre, television, film, commercials and corporate. Also represents directors and presenters.

Will consider attending performances at venues within Greater London and elsewhere with 2 weeks' notice. Accepts submissions (with CVs and photographs) from actors previously unknown to the company sent by post or email. Invitations to view individual actors' websites are also accepted. *Commission:* Theatre negotiable; TV and Films 15%; Commercials 20%

Gilbert & Payne
Suite 73-74 Kent House, 87 Regent Street,
London W1B 4EH
tel 020-7734 7505 *fax* 020-7494 3787
email ee@gilbertandpayne.com
Director Elena Gilbert
Key personnel Elaine Payne

Established in 1996. 2 agents represent 50 actors. Areas of work include theatre, musicals, television, film, commercials and corporate, with a particular emphasis

on musical theatre. Also represents choreographers.

Will consider attending performances at venues in Greater London with a minimum of 1 week's notice. Accepts submissions (with CVs and photographs) from actors previously unknown to the company if sent by post. Follow-up telephone calls are also accepted. *Commission:* Theatre 10%

Grantham-Hazeldine
5 Blenheim Street, London W1S 1LD
tel 020-7499 4011 *fax* 020-7495 3370
email grantham-hazeldine@talk21.com
Partners John Grantham, Caroline Hazeldine

Established in 1984. 2 agents represent 75 actors. Areas of work include theatre, musicals, television, film, commercials, corporate and voice-overs. Also represents writers and stunt co-ordinators.

Will consider attending performances at venues in Greater London and elsewhere with 1 month's notice. Accepts submissions (with CVs and photographs) from actors previously unknown to the company if sent by post. Will not accept showreels and voice tapes at the initial stage of contact. *Commission:* Theatre and Radio 10% plus VAT; TV and Film 15% plus VAT

Darren Gray Management
2 Marston Lane, Portsmouth,
Hampshire PO3 5TW
tel 023-9269 9973 *fax* 023-9267 7227
email Darren.gray1@virgin.net
website www.darrengraymanagement.co.uk
Managing Director Darren Gray

Established in 1994. 2 agents represent 60 actors both in England and Australia. Agency mainly represents Australian actors, the majority of whom come from Australian soap operas. Areas of work include theatre, musicals, television, film, commercials, corporate and voice-overs. Also represents directors, producers, writers and presenters.

Will consider attending performances at venues within Greater London and elsewhere at whatever notice possible. Accepts submissions (with CVs and photographs) from actors previously unknown to the company sent by post or email. Showreels, voice tapes and invitations to view individual actors' websites are also accepted. *Commission*: 10%

Joan Gray Personal Management
29 Sudbury Court Island, Sunbury-on-Thames, Middlesex TW16 5PP

1 agent represents a small number of actors. Areas of work include theatre, musicals, television, film, commercials, corporate and voice-overs. Not looking to take on any new actors at the moment. *Commission*: 10%

Sandra Griffin Management Ltd.
6 Ryde Place, Richmond Road, East Twickenham TW1 2EH
tel 020-8881 5676 *fax* 020-8744 1812
email SGmgmt@aol.com
Key personnel Sandra Griffin, Howard Roberts

Established in 1989. 2 agents represent actors. Areas of work include theatre, musicals, television, film, commercials, corporate and voice-overs.

Will consider attending performances at venues in Greater London and occasionally elsewhere with 2 weeks' notice. Accepts submissions (with CVs and photographs) from actors previously unknown to the company if sent by post. Enclosing sae will ensure a reply. *Commission*: Varies according to contract

Hamilton Hodell Ltd.
24 Hanway Street, London W1T 1UH
tel 020-7636 1221 *fax* 020-7636 1226
email info@hamiltonhodell.co.uk
website www.hamiltonhodell.co.uk

3 agents represent 80 actors, working in leading roles in film, television, theatre and radio productions.

Harrispearson Management Ltd.
64-66 Millman Street, London WC1N 3EF
tel 020-7430 9890 *fax* 020-7430 9229
email agent@harrispearson.co.uk
website www.harrispearson.co.uk
Managing Director/Senior Agent Melanie Harris
Senior Agent Paul Pearson

Established in 2001. 2 agents represent up to 50 actors. Areas of work include theatre, musicals, television, film, commercials and corporate.

Will consider attending performances at venues within Greater London given as much notice as possible. Accepts submissions (with CVs and photographs) from actors previously unknown to the company if sent by post. *Commission*: 12.5-15% depending on the type of work

Henry's Agency
53 Westbury, Rochford, Essex SS4 1UL
tel (01702) 541413 *fax* (01702) 541413
email info@henrysagency.co.uk
website www.henrysagency.co.uk

Established in 1995. 1 agent represents 35 actors. Areas of work include theatre, musicals, television, film, commercials and corporate.

Will consider attending performances at venues within Greater London with 2 weeks' notice. Accepts submissions (with

CVs and photographs) from actors previously unknown to the company if sent by post. Emails are accepted if attachments consist of Word documents or small jpeg files. Follow-up telephone calls, showreels and voice tapes are also accepted. Recommends the photographer Ash (ash@ashphotomedia.com). *Commission*: Variable

Edward Hill Management

Teddington Film and Television Studios, Broom Road, Teddington, Middlesex TW11 9NT
tel 020-8614 2678 *fax* 020-8614 2694
email hill@management.freeserve.co.uk

1 agent represents 40 actors. Will accept submissions (with CVs and photographs) from actors previously unknown to the company if sent by post. *Commission*: 10-15%

Dee Hindin Associates

9B Brunswick Mews, Great Cumberland Place, London W1H 7FB
tel 020-7723 3706 *fax* 020-7258 0651

Established in 1991. Represents 15-20 actors. Areas of work include theatre, musicals, television, film, commercials, corporate and voice-overs.

Will consider attending performances at venues in Greater London with approximately 10 days' notice. Recommends the photographer Chris Baker (020-8441 3851). *Commission*: Theatre 12.5-20%

Liz Hobbs Group Ltd.

65 London Road, Newark, Notts NG24 1RZ
tel 0870-070 2702 *fax* 0870-333 7009
email casting@lizhobbsgroup.com

website www.lizhobbsgroup.com
Managing Director Liz Hobbs
Associate Director/Agent Richard Kort

2 agents represent 50-60 actors. Areas of work include theatre, musicals, television, film, commercials, corporate and voice-overs.

Will consider attending performances at venues in Greater London and elsewhere with 1-2 months' notice. Accepts submissions (with CVs and photographs) from actors previously unknown to the company sent by post or email. Will also accept showreels, voice tapes and invitations to view individual actors' websites.
Commission: 10-15% depending on the type of work

Hobson's Actors

62 Chiswick High Road, Chiswick, London W4 1SY
tel 020-8995 3628 *fax* 020-8996 5350
website www.hobsons-international.com
Drama Agent Christina Beyer
Commercial Agent Linda Sacks

Areas of work include theatre, musicals, television, film, commercials and corporate.

Will consider attending performances at venues within Greater London given 2 weeks' notice. Accepts submissions (with CVs and photographs) from actors previously unknown to the company if sent by post. Showreels and voice tapes are also accepted.

ICM

Oxford House, 76 Oxford Street, London W1D 1BS

11 agents represent actors. Areas of work include theatre, musicals, television, film,

commercials, corporate and voice-overs. Also represents directors, writers, technicians and presenters.

Will consider attending performances at venues within Greater London. Accepts submissions (with CVs and photographs) from actors previously unknown to the company if sent by post. 10x8in photographs are preferred. *Commission*: 10%

Icon Actors Management

Tanzaro House, Ardwick Green North, Manchester N12 6FZ
tel 0161-273 3344 *fax* 0161-273 4567
email info@iconactors.net
website www.iconactors.net
Agent Philip Hammond

Established in 2000. 1 agent represents 50 actors. Areas of work include theatre, musicals, television, film, commercials, corporate and voice-overs.

Will consider attending performances at venues in the North West/Yorkshire region given at least 1 week's notice. Accepts submissions (with CVs and photographs) from actors previously unknown to the company if sent by post.

Inter-City Casting

Portland Tower, Portland Street, Manchester M1 3LF
tel 0161-226 0103 *fax* 0161-226 0103
email intercity@bigfoot.com
website iccast.co.uk
Agent Caroline Joynt

Established in 1983. 2 agents represent approximately 60 actors. Areas of work include theatre, musicals, television, film, commercials and corporate.

Will consider attending performances at venues in Manchester and Liverpool. Accepts

submissions (with CVs and photographs) from actors previously unknown to the company if sent by post. Showreels, voice tapes and invitations to view individual actors' websites also accepted. Recommends the photographer Michael Pollard (see entry under *Photographers* for further details). *Commission*: 10-12.5% plus VAT

International Artistes Ltd.

4th Floor, Holborn Hall, 193-197 High Holborn, London WC1V 7BD

4 agents represent approximately 100 actors. Also represents producers, directors, casting directors, presenters, light entertainment artists and comedians. The company has a separate voice-over department. Artists are represented by a total of 11 agents.

Will consider attending performances at venues within Greater London and occasionally elsewhere, given 4 weeks' notice. Accepts submissions (with CVs and photographs) from actors previously unknown to the company if sent by post. Showreels, voice tapes and invitations to view individual actors' websites are also accepted. *Commission*: 10-12.5% plus VAT

International Theatre & Music Ltd.

Shakespeare House, Theatre Street, London SW11 5ND
tel 020-7801 6316 *fax* 020-7801 6317
email inttheatre@aol.com
website www.internationaltheatreandmusic.com
Managing Director Piers Chater-Robinson
Personal Assistant Claire Lloyd
Assistant Emma Bokin

2-3 agents represent 35 actors. Areas of work include musicals, television and commercials.

Will consider attending performances at venues in Greater London and occasionally elsewhere, given as much notice as possible. Accepts submissions (with CVs and photographs) from actors previously unknown to the company if sent by post. Will also accept voice tapes/CDs of singing voices. 'It is likely that all prospective clients will be auditioned, unless their work is established in the industry." *Commission*: Theatre 10%; Film and TV 12.5%

JB Associates

1st Floor, 3 Stevenson Square, Manchester M1 1DN
tel 0161-237 1808 *fax* 0161-237 1809
email info@j-b-a.net
website www.j-b-a.net
Proprietor John Basham

Established in 1996. 2 agents represent 60 actors. Areas of work include theatre, musicals, television, film, commercials, corporate and voice-overs.

Will consider attending performances at venues in the North and occasionally within Greater London given 3-4 weeks' notice. Accepts submissions (with CVs and photographs) from actors previously unknown to the company if sent by post. Will also accept showreels, voice tapes, and invitations to view individual actors' websites. *Commission*: Theatre 10%; TV 15%

Jeffrey & White Management

9-15 Neal Street, London WC2H 9PW
tel 020-7240 7000 *fax* 020-7240 0007
Partners Judith Jeffrey, Jeremy White
Key personnel Laura Elgar

Established in 1986. 3 agents represent 85 actors. Areas of work include theatre, musicals, television, film, commercials and corporate.

Will consider attending performances given as much notice as possible. Accepts submissions (with CVs and photographs) from actors previously unknown to the company if sent by post. *Commission*: Theatre, Film and TV 12.5%; Commercials 15%

JLM Personal Management

259 Acton Lane, London W4 5DG
tel 020-8747 8223 *fax* 020-8747 8286
email jlm@skynow.net
Theatrical Agents Sharon Henry, Janet Malone

Established in 1978. 2 agents represent 40-50 actors. Areas of work include theatre, musicals, television, film, commercials, corporate and voice-overs.

Will consider attending performances at venues within Greater London given 2 weeks' notice. Showreels and voice tapes should only be sent on request. *Commission*: Theatre 10%; TV 15%

KAL Management

95 Gloucester Road, Hampton, Middlesex TW12 2UW
tel 020-8783 0039 *fax* 020-8979 6487
email kaplan222@aol.com
website www.kaplan-kaye.co.uk
Key personnel Kaplan Kaye

Established in 1982. Sole representation of approximately 25 actors. Areas of work include theatre, musicals, television, film, commercials, corporate and voice-overs.

Will consider attending performances at venues within Greater London given as much notice as possible. Accepts submissions (with CVs and photographs) from actors previously unknown to the company if sent by post. Showreels and voice tapes should only be sent on request. *Commission*: Theatre 10%; TV 15%

Langford Associates

17 Westfields Avenue, Barnes,
London SW13 0AT
tel 020-8878 7148
Key personnel Barry Langford

Established in 1987. 1 agent represents 45-50 actors. Areas of work include theatre, musicals, television, film, commercials, corporate and voice-overs.

Will consider attending performances at mainstream venues within Greater London given 3 weeks' notice. Accepts brief submissions (with CVs and photographs) from actors previously unknown to the company if sent by post. Recommends 10×8in photographs which are true representations of an actor's appearance. An sae should be enclosed for the return of personal details. Emails and faxes will not be accepted. 'Limit your CV to relevant information. Make a follow-up call only if you have something relevant to say, for example if you are appearing on the television at short notice. I am always happy to receive postal enquiries and regularly meet with new actors.' *Commission*: 10-15% depending on contract

L'Brooke Personal Management

7 Malt House Place, High Street,
Romford RM1 1AR
tel (01708) 723883 *fax* (01708) 723883
email lbrooke@btopenworld.com
Director Nancy Walker

Established in 2002. 1 agent represents 20 actors. Areas of work include theatre,

musicals, television, film, commercials and corporate.

Will consider attending performances at venues within Greater London and elsewhere given 2 weeks' notice. Accepts submissions (with CVs and photographs) from actors previously unknown to the company sent by post or email. Showreels, voice tapes and invitations to view individual actors' websites are also accepted.

Jane Lehrer Associates

100a Chalk Farm Road,
London NW1 8EH
tel 020-7482 4898 *fax* 020-7482 4899
email janelehrer@aol.com
Sole Proprietor Jane Lehrer
Agent Caz Swinfield

Established in 1986. 2 agents represent 80 actors. Areas of work include theatre, musicals, television, film, commercials, corporate and voice-overs. Also represents presenters.

Will consider attending performances at venues in Greater London with 2-3 weeks' notice. Accepts submissions (with CVs and photographs) from actors previously unknown to the company if sent by post. An sae must always be included with CVs and photographs. Showreels and voice tapes should only be sent on request.

Leigh Management

14 St David's Drive, Edgware HA8 6JH
tel 020-8951 4449 *fax* 020-8951 4449
email leighmanagement@aol.com

Established in 1989. 2 agents represent 75 actors. Areas of work include theatre, musicals, television, film, commercials and corporate. Also represents presenters.

Will consider attending performances at venues within Greater London given a minimum of 1 week's notice. Accepts submissions (with CVs and photographs) from actors previously unknown to the company if sent by post. Follow-up telephone calls and invitations to view individual actors' websites are also accepted. *Commission*: 10-15%

Lime Actors Agency & Management Ltd.
First Floor, Alexandra Buildings,
28 Queen Street, Lincoln Square,
Manchester M2 5LF
tel 0161-835 3550 *fax* 0161-835 2550
email Debbie.pine@limemanagement.co.uk
Director Debbie Pine

Established in 1999. 1 agent represents 40 actors. Areas of work include theatre, musicals, television, film, commercials, corporate and voice-overs. Also represents musical directors.

Will consider attending performances at venues within Greater London and elsewhere, given 4 weeks' notice. Accepts submissions (with CVs and photographs) from actors previously unknown to the company sent by post or email. Follow-up telephone calls, showreels, voice tapes and invitations to view individual actors' websites are also accepted. Recommends the photographer Michael Pollard (see entry under *Photographers* for further details). *Commission*: Theatre 5%; TV 15%

Linkside Agency
21 Poplar Road, Leatherhead KT22 8SF
tel (01372) 802374 or (01372) 378398
fax (01372) 801972

Established in 1986. 2 agents represent 40 actors. Areas of work include theatre, musicals, television, film, commercials, corporate and voice-overs.

Will consider attending performances at venues within Greater London given a minimum of 2 weeks' notice. Accepts submissions (with CVs and photographs) from actors previously unknown to the company if sent by post. An sae should be included for the return of CVs and photographs. Showreels and voice tapes are also accepted.

LSW Promotions
181a Faunce House, Doddington Grove,
London SE17 3TB
tel 020-7793 9755 *fax* 020-7793 9755
email lswpromos@hotmail.com
website www.londonshakespeare.org.uk
Executive Director Bruce Wall
Development Associate James Croft

Established in 1998. 2 agents represent 20 actors. Areas of work include theatre, musicals, television and film.

Will consider attending performances at venues within Greater London and elsewhere, given 2 weeks' notice. Accepts submissions (with CVs and photographs) from actors previously unknown to the company sent by post or email. Invitations to view individual actors' websites are also accepted. *Commission*: 10% donation to charity (LSW Prison Project)

Magnolia Management
136 Hicks Avenue, Greenford,
Middlesex UB6 8HB
tel 020-8578 2899 *fax* 020-8575 0369
email jaffreymag@aol.com
Proprietor Jennifer Jaffrey

Established in 1982. 2 agents represent 55-60 actors. Areas of work include theatre, musicals, television, film, commercials, corporate and voice-overs.

Will consider attending performances at venues within Greater London and occasionally elsewhere, given as much notice as possible. Accepts submissions (with CVs and photographs) from actors previously unknown to the company if sent by post. Photographs should have the actor's name written on the back, and sae(s) enclosed for the return of personal details. Follow-up telephone calls should only be made if the agency has shown an interest in the actor. Showreels, voice tapes and invitations to view individual actors' websites should only be sent on request. *Commission*: 10-15%

Management 2000

23 Alexandra Road, Mold,
Flintshire CH7 1HJ
tel (01352) 771231 *fax* (01352) 771231
email jackey@management-2000.co.uk
website www.management-2000.co.uk

Established in 2000. 1 agent represents 40 actors. Areas of work include theatre, musicals, television, film, commercials, corporate and voice-overs.

Will consider attending performances at venues within Greater London and else-where, given at least 1 week's notice. Accepts submissions (with CVs and pho-tographs) from actors previously unknown to the company if sent by post. Follow-up telephone calls, showreels and voice tapes are also accepted. *Commission*: 10-15%

Andrew Manson Personal Management

288 Munster Road, London SW6 6BQ
tel 020-7386 9158
email post@andrewmanson.com
website www.andrewmanson.com

Established in 1988.

Will consider attending performances at venues within Greater London given as much notice as possible. Industry referrals are preferred. Follow-up telephone calls, showreels, voice tapes and invitations to view individual actors' websites are accepted. Advises actors to visit the Talent Room website (www.talentroom.com).

John Markham Associates

1a Oakwood Avenue, Purley,
Surrey CR8 1AR

Areas of work include theatre, musicals, television, film, commercials, corporate and voice-overs.

Ronnie Marshall Agency

66 Ollerton Road, London N11 2LA
tel 020-8368 4958

Established in 1980. 1 agent represents 25 actors. Areas of work include theatre, musicals, television, film, commercials, corporate and voice-overs.

Will consider attending performances at venues within Greater London with 2 weeks' notice. Accepts business-like submissions (with CVs and photographs) from actors previously unknown to the company if sent by post. Photographs should be a good likeness. Enclose an sae for return of personal details. Follow-up telephone calls and invitations to view individual actors' websites are also accepted. *Commission*: If instigated by client 10%; Otherwise 20%

Scott Marshall Partners

Suite 9, 54 Poland Street,
London W1F 7NJ
tel 020-7432 7240 *fax* 020-7432 7241
email smpm@acottmarshall.co.uk

Agents/Company Directors Manon Palmer, Amanda Evans, Suzy Kenway

Areas of work include theatre, musicals, television, film, commercials, corporate and voice-overs. Also represents directors (theatre and TV), sound designers and composers.

Will consider attending performances at venues within Greater London if given as much notice as possible. Accepts submissions (with CVs and photographs) from actors previously unknown to the company if sent by post. *Commission:* Commercials 15%; Other 10%

Cassie Mayer Ltd.
5 Old Garden House, The Lanterns, Bridge Lane, London SW11 3AD
tel 020-7350 0880 *fax* 020-7350 0890
Agents Cassie Mayer, Jayne Billington, Rachel Dyson, Karen Beesley

Established in 1985. 4 agents represent 50-60 actors. Areas of work include theatre, musicals, television, film, commercials and corporate. Also represents directors, presenters and designers.

Will consider attending performances at Equity venues within Greater London if given 3 weeks' notice. Accepts submissions (with CVs and photographs) from actors previously unknown to the company sent by post or email. All artists' applications will receive an answer. *Commission:* PMA recommended rates

MBA
Concorde House, 18 Margaret Street, Brighton BN2 1TS
tel (01273) 685970 *fax* (01273) 685971
email mba.concorde@virgin.net
website mbagency.fsnet.co.uk

Key personnel Bo Keller, Andrea Todd, Peter Stanford

Established in 1964. Sole representation of 85-90 actors. Areas of work include theatre, musicals, television, film, commercials and corporate.

Will consider attending performances at venues within Greater London and on the South Coast with 1 month's notice. Accepts submissions (with clearly written CVs and photographs) from actors previously unknown to the company if sent by post. Photographs should be of a good quality. Enclose an sae for return of personal details. Showreels, voice tapes and invitations to view individual actors' websites are also accepted. *Commission:* 10-17% depending on the type of work

Bill McLean Personal Management Ltd.
23b Deodar Road, London SW15 2NP
tel 020-8789 8191 *fax* 020-8789 8192

Established in 1972.

Will consider attending performances in Greater London with sufficient notice. Accepts submissions (with CVs and photographs) from actors previously unknown to the company if sent by post. Follow-up telephone calls are also accepted. *Commission:* Theatre 10%; TV 15%

MCS Agency
47 Dean Street, London W1D 5BE
tel 020-7734 9995 *fax* 020-7734 9996
email info@mcs-group.freeserve.co.uk
Agent Keith Bishop

Established in 1994. 2 agents represent actors. Areas of work include theatre, musicals, television, film, commercials and voice-overs. Also represents presenters.

Will consider attending performances at venues within Greater London with 2 weeks' notice. Accepts submissions (with CVs and photographs) from actors previously unknown to the company if sent by post. Showreels, voice tapes and invitations to view individual actors' websites are also accepted. *Commission*: 15-20%

MKA

11 Russell Kerr Close, London W4 3HF
tel 020-8994 1619 *fax* 020-8994 2992
email mka.agency@virgin.net
Key personnel Malcolm Knight

Founded under a different name in 1955, MKA was established under its present name in 1995. 2 agents represent 70 actors. Areas of work include theatre, musicals, television, film, commercials, corporate and voice-overs.

Will consider attending performances at venues within Greater London with 2 weeks' notice. Accepts submissions (with CVs and photographs) from actors previously unknown to the company if sent by post. *Commission*: 10-20% depending on the job

Morgan & Goodman

Mezzanine, Quadrant House, 80-82 Regent Street, London W1B 5RP
tel 020-7437 1383 *fax* 020-7437 5293
email mgl@btinternet.com
Proprietor Lyndall Goodman
Key personnel Tanya Greep, Natalie Elliott

Established in 1981. 2 agents and 1 assistant represent 70-80 actors. Areas of work include theatre, musicals, television, film, commercials, corporate and voice-overs.

Will consider attending performances at venues within Greater London with 2

weeks' notice if an actor is playing a substantial role. Accepts submissions (with CVs and photographs) from experienced actors if sent by post. An sae must always be included for the return of CVs and photographs. Showreels and voice tapes should only be sent on request. *Commission*: 12.5%

The Narrow Road Company

Grampion House, 4th Floor, 144 Deansgate, Manchester M3 3EE
tel 0161-833 1605 *fax* 0161-833 1605
email Manchester@narrowroad.co.uk
Agent Elizabeth Stocking

2 agents represent 40 actors. Areas of work include theatre, musicals, television, film, commercials, corporate and voice-overs.

Will consider attending performances. Accepts submissions (with CVs and photographs) from actors previously unknown to the company if sent by post. Will also accept follow-up telephone calls, showreels, and voice tapes. The agency also has offices in London and Brighton.

Northern Lights Management

Dean Clough Mills, Halifax HX3 5AX
tel (01422) 330101
Agents Maureen Magee, Angie Forrest

Established in 1998. 2 agents represent 40 Northern and Northern-based actors. Areas of work include theatre, musicals, television, film, commercials, corporate and voice-overs.

Will consider attending performances at venues within Greater London and elsewhere, given 2 weeks' notice. Accepts submissions (with CVs and photographs) from actors previously unknown to the company if sent by post. Showreels and voice tapes are also accepted. Enclose an sae for the return of items sent. Telephone calls and emails with attachments are not accepted. Advises actors that the agency is small and rarely takes on new clients.

Norwell Lapley Associates
Lapley Hall, Lapley ST19 9JR
tel (01785) 841991 *fax* (01785) 841992
email norwellapley@freeuk.com
website www.norwellapley.co.uk
Director Chris Davis
Artist Manager Claire Sibley
Personal Assistant Kerry Foley

Sole representation of more than 50 actors. Areas of work include theatre, musicals, television, film, commercials, corporate and voice-overs. Also represents directors, presenters, technicians and musical directors.

Will consider attending performances at venues within Greater London and elsewhere, given as much notice as possible. Accepts submissions (with CVs and photographs) from actors previously unknown to the company sent by post or email. Follow-up telephone calls, showreels, voice tapes and invitations to view individual actors' websites are also accepted. *Commission:* Various rates

Pat Lovett Associates
43 Chandos Place, London WC2N 4HS
tel 020-7379 8111 *fax* 020-7379 9111
email London@pla.uk.com
website www.pla.uk.com
Key personnel Dolina Logan

Scottish office: 5 Union Street, Edinburgh EH1 3LT
tel 0131-478 7878 *fax* 0131 478 7070

Established in 1981. Areas of work include theatre, musicals, television, film, commercials, corporate and voice-overs.

Will consider attending performances at venues in Greater London and Scotland (handled by Scottish office) with 2-3 weeks' notice. Accepts submissions (with CVs and photographs) from actors previously unknown to the company if sent by post. Invitations to view individual actors' websites are also accepted.

Nyland Management Ltd.
20 School Lane, Heaton Chapel, Stockport SK4 5DG

2 agents represent 60 actors. Areas of work include theatre, musicals, television, film, commercials, corporate and voice-overs.

Will consider attending performances at venues within Greater Manchester and the North West given at least 1 week's notice. Accepts submissions (with CVs, photographs and sae) from actors previously unknown to the company if sent by post. *Commission:* 15%

Parr & Bond
The Tom Thumb Theatre, Eastern Esplanade, Cliftonville CT9 2LB
tel (01843) 221791 *fax* (01843) 221791

Established in 1969. Sole representation of 12-20 actors. Areas of work include theatre, musicals, television, film, commercials, corporate and voice-overs.

Will consider attending performances at venues within Greater London and elsewhere, given 2 weeks' notice. Accepts submissions (with CVs and photographs) from actors previously unknown to the company if sent by post.

Commission: Theatre 10%; TV and Film 20%

Pelham Associates

The Media Centre, 9-12 Middle Street, Brighton BN1 1AL
tel (01273) 323010 *fax* (01273) 202492
email petercleall@pelhamassociates.co.uk
website www.pelhamassociates.co.uk
Agent Peter Cleall

Established in 1993. 1 agent represents 50-60 actors. Areas of work include theatre, musicals, television, film, commercials, corporate and voice-overs.

Will consider attending performances at venues within Greater London and elsewhere, given at least 1 month's notice. Accepts submissions (with CVs and photographs) from actors previously unknown to the company if sent by post.
Commission: 8-12.5%

Pemberton Associates Ltd.

Suite 35-26, Barton Arcade, Deansgate, Manchester M3 2BH
tel 0161-832 1661 *fax* 0161-835 3319

Established in 1989. 4 agents represent 100 actors. Areas of work include theatre, musicals, television, film, commercials, corporate and voice-overs.

Will consider attending performances at venues in the North West with 2-3 weeks' notice if looking for new clients. Accepts submissions (with CVs and photographs) from actors previously unknown to the company if sent by post.

Performers Directory

PO Box 29942, London SW6 1FL
tel 020-7610 6699 *fax* 020-7736 6088
email admin@performersdirectory.co.uk
website www.performersdirectory.co.uk
Directors Antonia Stratton, Clive Stevens

Established in 1995. 5 agents represent the actors. Areas of work include theatre, musicals, television, film, commercials and corporate.

Will consider attending performances at venues within Greater London with 7-10 days' notice. Accepts submissions (with CVs and photographs) from actors previously unknown to the company if sent by post. Also accepts follow-up telephone calls, showreels, voice tapes and invitations to view individual actors' websites. 'We do not welcome emails, but feel free to enter your details on our website and call us to let us know they are there. We also encourage companies to post audition or casting information free of charge on the website.' Recommends the photographer <absoluteportfolio@yahoo.co.uk>.
Commission: 10-20%

See also entry under *Casting Directories and Information Services*.

PFD

Drury House, 34-43 Russell Street, London WC2B 5HA
tel 020-7344 1010 *fax* 020-7836 9544
website www.pfd.co.uk
Agents Lucy Brazier, Duncan Hayes, Thea Murphy, Maureen Vincent, Kathryn Fleming, Lindy King, Dallas Smith, Ruth Young
Head of Commercials Department Ruth Cooper

In 1924 A.D. Peters established what has now become 'PFD'. Previously known as Peters, Fraser and Dunlop, it is one of Europe's leading literary and talent agencies in terms of both turnover and breadth of representation. PFD became part of the CSS Stellar group in 2001. The PFD Actors Department represents a diverse portfolio of clients working in leading roles in film, television, theatre and radio productions. 8 agents represent approximately 500 actors. The agency also represents writers, presenters, directors, producers, technicians, composers, editors, sportsmen and women, and make-up artists.

Accepts submissions (with CVs and photographs) from actors previously unknown to the company if sent by post; tries to respond within 8 weeks, although the company cannot guarantee a response. Does not welcome email enquiries or follow-up telephone calls. The Commercials Department works in the areas of voice-overs, corporate and commercial work but only considers existing clients. It does not take on any artists from outside the agency.

Frances Phillips

Millennium Studios, Elstree Way, Borehamwood, Hertfordshire WD6 1SF
tel 020-8236 1366 *fax* 020-8236 1362
email derekphillips@talk21.com

Established in 1983. 2 agents represent more than 40 actors. Areas of work include theatre, musicals, television, film, commercials, corporate and voice-overs.

Will consider attending performances at mainstream theatre venues within Greater London with 4 weeks' notice. The agency does not cover fringe work, however. Accepts submissions (with CVs, photographs and sae) from actors previously unknown to the company if sent by post. Showreels and voice tapes are also accepted. 'Particularly interested in artists with good CVs." *Commission*: 10-15%

PHPM

184 Bradway Road, Sheffield S17 4QX
tel 0114-235 3663
email philippa@phpm.co.uk
Key personnel Philippa Howell

Established in 1996. 1 agent represents 80 actors. Areas of work include theatre, musicals, television, film, commercials, corporate and voice-overs. Also represents directors.

Will consider attending performances at venues outside Greater London given as much notice as possible. Accepts submissions (with CVs and photographs) from actors previously unknown to the company if sent by post. Enclose an sae bearing the correct postage. Showreels and voice tapes are also accepted. Recommends the photographer Andrew Chapman (see entry under *Photographers* for further details). *Commission*: Theatre, Radio and Voice-over 10%; Film, TV and Commercials 15%

Janet Plater Management Ltd.

Floor D, Milburn House, Dean Street, Newcastle upon Tyne NE1 1LF
tel 0191-221 2490 *fax* 0191-221 2491
email magpie@tynebridge.demon.co.uk

Established in 1997. 1 agent represents approximately 50 actors. Areas of work include theatre, musicals, television, film, commercials, corporate and voice-overs. Also represents directors.

Will consider attending performances at venues in North East England with 1-2 weeks' notice. Accepts submissions (with CVs and photographs) from actors previously unknown to the company if sent by post. Showreels and voice tapes should only be sent on request. *Commission*: Maximum of 15%

PPM

73 Leopard Street, Shoreditch,
London EC2A 4QS
tel 020-7739 7552 *fax* 020-7739 7552
Managing Director Polo Piatti

Established in 1996. Agency represents
2 actors and works mainly in musicals.

Will consider attending performances at
venues within Greater London with 3-4
weeks' notice. Accepts submissions (with
CVs and photographs) from actors previously
unknown to the company sent by
post or email. Showreels and voice tapes are
also accepted. 'We will always consider
actors wishing to expand into music work
including pop music." *Commission*: 15-20%

Principal Artistes

4 Paddington Street, London W1U 5QE
tel 020-7224 3414 *fax* 020-7486 4668
email principalartistes@hotmail.com

Established in 1993. 2 agents represent 60
actors. Areas of work include theatre,
musicals, television, film, commercials and
corporate.

Will consider attending performances at
venues in Greater London with at least
1 week's notice. Accepts submissions (with
CVs and photographs) from actors
previously unknown to the company if
sent by post. Always enclose an sae bearing
the correct postage for the return of
photographs and CVs, and if a response is
required. *Commission*: Theatre 10%;
Other 15%

Profile Management

2nd Floor, 213 Chalk Farm Road,
London NW1 8AB
tel 020-7485 0441
Key personnel George Perry

Agency represents 35 actors. Areas of work
include theatre, television, film and commercials.
Also represents physical theatre
artists.

Will consider attending performances (particularly
of physical theatre) at venues within
in Greater London and elsewhere, given 3
weeks' notice. Accepts submissions (with
CVs and photographs) from actors previously
unknown to the company if sent by
post. Showreels and voice tapes are also
accepted. Does not welcome telephone calls.

RDF Management

The Gloucester Building, Kensington
Village, Avonmore Road, London W14 8RF
tel 020-7013 4103 *fax* 020-7013 4101
website www.rdfmanagement.com
Agent/Head of Agency Debi Allen

Established in 2002. 3 agents represent
40-50 actors. Areas of work include theatre,
musicals, television, film, commercials,
corporate and voice-overs. Also represents
writers, directors and presenters.

Will consider attending performances at
venues within Greater London but
requests as much notice as possible.
Accepts submissions (with CVs and
photographs) from actors previously
unknown to the company sent by post or
email. Follow-up telephone calls,
showreels, voice tapes and invitations to
view individual actors' websites are also
accepted. *Commission*: 15%

Rossmore Personal Management

70-76 Bell Street, London NW1 6SP
tel 020-7258 1953 *fax* 020-7258 0124
email agents@rossmoremanagement.com

Established in 1993. 4 agents represent 120
actors. Areas of work include theatre,

musicals, television, film, commercials, corporate and voice-overs.

Will consider attending performances at venues within Greater London. Accepts submissions (with CVs and photographs) from actors previously unknown to the company if sent by post. *Commission*: Theatre and Radio 10%; Film, TV and Commercials 15% plus VAT

Royce Management

34a Sinclair Road, London W14 0NH
tel 020-7602 4992 *fax* 020-7371 4985
email roycemanagement@btconnect.com

Established in 1980. 1 agent represents 100 actors. Areas of work include theatre, musicals, television, film, commercials, corporate and voice-overs.

Will consider attending performances at venues within Greater London with a minimum of 1 week's notice. Accepts submissions (with CVs and photographs) from actors previously unknown to the company if sent by post. Include an sae if a reply is required. *Commission*: Commercials 15%; All other work 10%

Saraband Associates

265 Liverpool Road, London N1 1LX

2 agents represent actors. Areas of work include theatre, musicals, television, film and commercials.

Will occasionally consider attending performances at venues in Greater London, given 1 month's notice. Accepts submissions (with CVs and photographs) from actors previously unknown to the company if sent by post. An sae should be included with CVs and photographs. *Commission*: Varies

SCA Management

77 Oxford Street, London W1D 2ES
tel 020-7659 2027 *fax* 020-7659 2116
email agency@sca-management.co.uk

Established in 1980. 2 agents represent 50 actors. Areas of work include theatre, musicals, television, film, commercials and corporate.

Will consider attending performances within Greater London given sufficient notice. Accepts submissions (with CVs and photographs) from actors previously unknown to the company if sent by post. Showreels and voice tapes are also accepted. *Commission*: 15%

Tim Scott

284 Grays Inn Road, London WC1X 8EB
tel 020-7833 5733 *fax* 020-7278 9175
email timscott@btinternet.com

Established in 1988. Areas of work include theatre, television, film, commercials and corporate.

Accepts submissions (with CVs and photographs) from actors previously unknown to the company if sent by post.

Vincent Shaw Associates

51 Byron Road, London E17 4SN
tel 020-8509 2211 *fax* 020-8521 1588
email info@vincentshaw.com
website www.vincentshaw.com

Sole representation of 100 actors. Areas of work include theatre, musicals, television, film, commercials and corporate.

Will consider attending performances at venues within Greater London with 2 weeks' notice. Accepts submissions (with CVs and photographs) from actors previously unknown to the company if sent by post. *Commission*: 10-15%

Splats Entertainment
5 Denmark Street, London WC2H 8LP
tel 020-7240 8400 *fax* 020-7240 8409
email mike@splats.uk.com

Established in 2002. 1 agent represents 25 actors. Areas of work include theatre, musicals, television, film, commercials, corporate and voice-overs. Also represents directors.

Will consider attending performances at venues within Greater London with 2 weeks' notice. Accepts submissions (with CVs and photographs) from actors previously unknown to the company if sent by post. *Commission*: Theatre 10%; Commercials 15%

Helen Stafford Management
14 Park Avenue, Bush Hill Park, Enfield EN1 2HP
tel 020-8360 6329 *fax* 020-8482 0371
email Helen.Stafford@blueyonder.co.uk
Agent Helen Stafford

Established in 1991. Sole representation of 20 actors. Areas of work include theatre, musicals, television, film, commercials, corporate and voice-overs.

Will consider attending performances at venues within Greater London with 2 weeks' notice. Accepts submissions (with CVs and photographs) from actors previously unknown to the company if sent by post. Showreels and voice tapes should only be sent on request. 'Hard work pays off –don't ever give up!"Recommends the photographer Mark Davis, MAD Photography (200 Gladbeck Way, Enfield Chase, Enfield EN2 7HS; *tel*. 020-8363

4182). *Commission*: Commercials 15%; Everything else 10%

Natasha Stevenson Management Ltd. (NSM)
85 Shorrolds Road, London SW6 7TU
tel 020-7386 5333 *fax* 020-7385 3014
email nsm@netcomuk.co.uk
Director Natasha Stevenson

3 agents represent 85 actors. Areas of work include theatre, musicals, television, film, commercials, corporate and voice-overs.

Will consider attending performances at venues within Greater London with 2 weeks' notice. Accepts submissions (with CVs and photographs) from actors previously unknown to the company if sent by post. *Commission*: Theatre 10%; TV 15%

St James's Management
19 Lodge Close, Stoke D'Abernon, Cobham KT11 2SG
tel (01932) 860666 *fax* (01932) 860444
Managing Director Jacqueline Leggo

Established in 1965. 1 agent represents approximately 50 actors. Areas of work include theatre, musicals, television, film, commercials, corporate and voice-overs.

Actors should approach the company by letter and should enclose an sae.

Brian Taylor – Nina Quick Associates
50 Pembroke Road, London W8 6NX
tel 020-7602 6141 *fax* 020-7602 6301
email briantaylor@nqassoc.freeserve.co.uk
Director Brian Taylor

Established in 1975. 3 agents represent 80 actors. Areas of work include theatre, musicals, television, film, commercials, corporate and voice-overs.

Will consider attending performances at venues within Greater London and occasionally elsewhere, if given as much notice as possible. Accepts submissions (with CVs and photographs) from actors previously unknown to the company if sent by post. *Commission*: 10-15%

TCG Artist Management
4th Floor, 6 Langley Street,
London WC2H 9JA
tel 020-7240 3600 *fax* 020-7240 3606
email info@tcgam.co.uk
website www.spotlightagent.info/tcgam

Established in 1998. 3 agents represent 60 actors. Areas of work include theatre, musicals, television, film, commercials and corporate.

Will consider attending performances at venues within Greater London given as much notice as possible. Accepts submissions (with CVs and photographs) from actors previously unknown to the company if sent by post. Follow-up telephone calls, showreels and voice tapes are also accepted. *Commission*: 10-15% depending on the job

Paul Telford Management
23 Noel Street, London W1F 8GT
tel 020-7434 1100 *fax* 020-7434 1200
email info@telford-mgt.com
Partner Paul Telford

Established 1994. 2 agents represent 75 actors. Areas of work include theatre, musicals, television, film, commercials and corporate.

Will consider attending performances at venues within Central London given at least 2 weeks' notice. Accepts submissions (with CVs and photographs) from actors

previously unknown to the company if sent by post. Showreels and voice tapes are also accepted. Include sae for return of material. *Commission*: Variable

Urban Talent
1st Floor, Alexandra Buildings,
28 Queen Street, Lincoln Square,
Manchester M2 5LF
tel 0161-834 0990 *fax* 0161-834 0014
email liz@nmsmanagement.co.uk
Key personnel Liz Beeley

Agency represents 30-50 actors. Areas of work include theatre, television, film, commercials, corporate and voice-overs. Also represents presenters.

Will consider attending performances at venues in the North West with 2 weeks' notice. Accepts submissions (with CVs and photographs) from actors previously unknown to the company sent by post or email. Also accepts invitations to view individual actors' websites. *Commission*: 15%

Waring & McKenna Ltd.
22 Grafton Street, Mayfair, London W1S 4EX
tel 020-7491 2666 *fax* 020-7409 7932
email dj@waringandmckenna.com
Agents Daphne Waring, John McKenna

Established in 1993. 2 agents represent approximately 80 actors. Areas of work include theatre, musicals, television, film, commercials, corporate and voice-overs.

Will consider attending performances at venues within Greater London and occasionally elsewhere, given at least 1 month's notice. Accepts submissions (with CVs and photographs) from actors previously unknown to the company if sent by post. Follow-up telephone calls are also accepted. Showreels and voice tapes should only be sent on request. *Commission:* Theatre 10%; TV and low-budget Films 12.5%; Commercials and Feature Films over £4 million 15%

Janet Welch Personal Management

11 Sunbury Court Island, Lower Hampton Road, Sunbury-on-Thames TW16 5PP
tel (01932) 766190 *fax* (01932) 766191
email info@janetwelcg.pm.co.uk

Established in 1990. 1 agent represents 60-70 actors. Areas of work include theatre, musicals, television, film, commercials, corporate and voice-overs.

Will consider attending performances at venues within Greater London and sometimes elsewhere, given sufficient notice. Accepts submissions (with CVs and photographs) from actors previously unknown to the company if sent by post.

Newton Wills Management

The Studio, 29 Springvale Avenue, Brentford TW8 9QT
tel (07989) 398381
email newtoncttg@aol.com
Managing Director Newton Wills
International Christopher Socci
Talent Julia Hunt
Office Administrator Helene Barber

Established in 1963. 4 agents represent 70 actors. Areas of work include theatre, musicals, television, film and commercials. Also represents TV presenters, cameramen (film) and location-finders (Europe).

Will consider attending performances at venues within Greater London and elsewhere, but requests as much notice as possible. Accepts submissions (with CVs and photographs) from actors previously unknown to the company sent by post or

email. Showreels and voice tapes are also accepted. 'Find out as soon as possible what an agent does. The relationship between actor and agent should be a partnership – work with your agent to develop your talents and add new ones to your repertoire.' *Commission:* Theatre 10%; Film 15%

Edward Wyman Agency

67 Llanon Road, Llanishen, Cardiff CF14 5AH
tel 029-2075 2351 *fax* 029-2075 2444
email Edward@wymancasting.fsnet.co.uk
website www.wymancasting.fsnet.co.uk
Managing Director Edward Wyman
Casting/Accounts Judith Gay
Casting Audrey Williams

Established in 1969, the agency represents more than 200 actors. Areas of work include television, film, commercials, corporate and voice-overs. Also represents directors, singers, dancers, circus performers, models, look-alikes, extras and promotions people.

Accepts submissions (with CVs and photographs) from actors previously unknown to the company sent by post or email. Initial correspondence should include sae. Follow-up telephone calls and invitations to view individual actors' websites are also accepted. 'The large majority of our work is in the Welsh language and is filmed in the South Wales area, so Welsh actors are particularly welcome.'Recommends the photographer Brian Tarr (6 Bangor Street, Cardiff CF24 3LR). *Commission:* OAPs 12.5%; Others 15%

Yellow Balloon Productions Ltd.

Freshwater House, Outdowns, Effingham KT24 5QR
tel (01483) 281500 or (01483) 281501

fax (01483) 281502
email yellowbal@aol.com
Managing Director Mike Smith
Producer/Head of AR Daryl Smith
Consultant Sally James

A management company established in 1974 covering all aspects of clients' career and long-term development. Represents around 10 actors. Areas of work include television, film, commercials, corporate and voice-overs. Also represents radio and TV presenters and sports stars.

Will consider attending performances at venues in Greater London and elsewhere, given 2-3 weeks' notice. Accepts submissions (with CVs and photographs) from actors previously unknown to the company sent by post or email. Also accepts showreels and voice tapes. Invitations to view individual actors' websites are only accepted if sent via email. Submitted CVs should be as complete as possible and clearly separate professional experience from student productions. Applicants should always state if they have yet to acquire a professional role. *Commission:* 15-20% according to press, accountancy, and PR agreements

Voice-Over Agents

This section lists agencies that specialise in voice-over work. Check the details of how each wishes to be approached and refer to the 'Showreel & Voice-Demos Companies' section for more about getting a voice demo made. Some of the larger conventional agencies have their own voice-over departments – generally, for their existing clients only.

Calypso Voices

25-26 Poland Street, London W1F 8QN
tel 020-7734 6415 *fax* 020-7437 0410
email calyso@calysovoices.com
website www.calypsovoices.com
Manager Jane Savage

2 agents represent 65 clients. Areas of work include musicals, television, film, commercials and audiobooks. Also represents clients working in animation, documentaries and the corporate sector.

Lip Service

60-66 Wardour Street, London W1F 0TA
tel 020-7734 3393 *fax* 020-7734 3373
email booksings@lipservice.co.uk
Key personnel Susan Mactavish

3 agents represent 200 clients. Areas of work include television, film, commercials and audiobooks.

Accepts submissions (with CVs) from individual actors previously unknown to the company sent by email or post. Also accepts voice tapes.

Shining Management Ltd.

82c Shirland Road, London W9 2EQ
tel 020-7286 6092 *fax* 020-7286 6133
email info@shiningvoices.com
website www.shiningvoices.com

Director Claire Daintree
Key personnel Jennifer Taylor

2 agents represent 55 clients. Areas of work include voice-overs for television, film, commercials and audiobooks.

Accepts submissions (with CVs and voice CDs) from individual actors previously unknown to the company if sent by post. Include sae for the return of submissions. Also accepts voice tapes, though CDs are preferred. 'Please do not ring with submission enquiries." *Commission*: 15%

Speak Ltd.

140 Devonshire Road, Chiswick, London W4 2AW
tel 020-8742 1001 *fax* 020-8742 1333
email info@speak.ltd.uk
website www.speak.ltd.uk
Senior Agent Graeme Legg
Managing Director Abigail Wells-Hardy

3 agents represent more than 100 clients. Areas of work include television and commercials.

Accepts submissions (with CVs and voice CDs) from individual actors previously unknown to the company if sent by post. Also accepts voice tapes but requests sae for their return. 'Please view our website for showreel advice." Recommends the voice-tape producer

USP (24 Newman Street, London W1).
Commission: 15%

Speak-Easy Ltd.
1 Dairy Yard, High Street, Market
Harborough, Leicestershire LE16 7NL
Voice-Overs Agent Sarah Pickering
Presenters Agent Kate Moon
Corporate Agent Hilary Knight

3 agents represent 80 clients. Areas of work
include television, commercials and
audiobooks.

Accepts submissions (with CVs and voice
CDs) from individual actors previously
unknown to the company if sent by post.
Enclose sae for reply.

Talking Heads
2-4 Noel Street, London W1F 8GB
tel 020-7292 7575 *fax* 020-7292 7576
email voices@talkingheadsvoices.com
website www.talkingehadsvoices.com
Key personnel John Sachs, Rebecca
Robinson

5 agents represent 100 clients. Areas of
work include musicals, television, film,
commercials and audiobooks.

Accepts submissions (with CVs and voice
CDs) from individual actors previously
unknown to the company if sent by
post. Invitations to view individual
actors' websites are also accepted.
Commission: 15%

Tongue & Groove
3 Stevenson Square, Manchester M1 1DN
tel 0161-228 2469 *fax* 0161-237 1809
email info@tongueandgroove.co.uk
website www.tongueandgroove.co.uk
Producers Beverley Ashworth, John
Barham

3 agents represent 47 clients. Areas of work
include voice-overs for television, commercials and audiobooks.

Accepts submissions (with CVs and voice
CDs) from individual actors previously
unknown to the company if sent by post.
Also accepts voice tapes and invitations to
view individual actors' websites.
Commission: 15%

Voice & Script International
Aradco House, 132 Cleveland Street,
London W1T 6AB
tel 020-7692 7700 *fax* 020-7692 7711
email info@vsi.tv
website www.vsi.tv
Voice-Over Coordinator Jenny Morris
Voice-Over Project Managers Bea
Potashnik, Isobel George
Key contacts Maja Ludford-Thomas,
Anna Jury

5 voice-over agents represent approximately
750-1000 foreign-language voice-over
clients. Areas of work include voice-overs
for television, film and commercials.

Accepts submissions (with CVs) from
individual actors previously unknown to
the company sent by post or email. Also
accepts voice tapes and invitations to view
individual actors' websites. 'We only use
mother-tongue foreign-language speakers.'

Voice Box Agency Ltd.
Laser House, Waterfront Quay, Salford
Quays, Manchester M50 3XW
tel 0161-874 5741
Manager Elinor Stanton

1 agent represents 40 clients. Areas of work
include voice-overs for television, film,
commercials and audiobooks.

Accepts voice tapes from individual actors previously unknown to the company. *Commission:* 15%

Voice Squad

62 Blenheim Gardens, London NW2 4NT
tel 020-8450 4451 *fax* 020-8452 7944
email voices@voicessquad.com
website www.voicesquad.com
Director Neil Conrich

2 agents represent 45 clients. Areas of work include television, film, commercials and audiobooks.

Accepts submissions (with CVs and voice CDs) from individual actors previously unknown to the company if sent by post. Also accepts voice tapes. *Commission:* 15%

Suzy Wootton Voices

75 Shelley Street, Kingsley,
Northampton NN2 7HZ
tel 0870-765 9660 *fax* 0870-765 9668
email suzy@suzywoottonvoices.com
website www.suzywoottonvoices.com

1 agent represents 38 clients. Areas of work include television, film, commercials and audiobooks.

Accepts submissions (with CVs) from individual actors previously unknown to the company sent by post or email. Also accepts follow-up telephone calls, voice tapes, showreels and invitations to view individual actors' websites. *Commission:* 15%

Yakety Yak

8 Bloomsbury Square, London WC1A 2NE
tel 020-7430 2600 *fax* 020-7404 6109
email info@yaketyyak.co.uk
website www.yaketyyak.co.uk
Proprietor Jolie Williams

3 agents represent 55 clients. Areas of work include voice-overs for television, film, commercials and audiobooks.

Accepts submissions (with CVs and voice CDs) from individual actors previously unknown to the company if sent by post. Include sae for the return of submissions. Also accepts voice tapes, though CDs are preferred. 'Please do not ring with submission enquiries.' *Commission:* 15%

The Co-operative Agency

Kim Gillespie

One of the standard questions asked to applicants seeking to join my agency is, 'Why do you want to join a co-operative personal management?' We get various replies depending on age, experience and level of honesty, but tucked away somewhere in most of them is the word 'control'.

Most people working in our industry will at some point testify to feeling a lack of control over the direction and/or purpose of their career. At such moments they may feel they are having little active input into their own professional lives. If they have an agent, they may describe sitting at home waiting for the phone to ring. They may feel frustrated because they have no knowledge of what parts, if any, they are being submitted for; they may even feel part of a large, anonymous and cynically commercial outfit where the promise of getting personal attention is noticeably absent. If they don't have an agent, then the lack of control and focus becomes even more acute since there is no-one –even nominally –working on their behalf.

So, either to get their first agent or to change from an existing conventional one, people come to co-ops for more control – as well as more knowledge of the industry, more contact with other actors, more advice and help from colleagues and more camaraderie. And, of course, more work.

The most common question that people ask *us* at audition is, 'What kind of work comes into the agency?' Most co-ops I know, and certainly my own, will deal with a very wide range of work opportunities. In common with conventional agents and personal managers, co-ops will receive daily casting breakdowns for theatre, TV, film and commercials. Unlike most conventional agents they will also seek corporate training work, role-play, voice-overs, new writing development work and educational workshops. Because most co-ops are small and because they are active and entrepreneurial, they are busy and they try to keep their actors busy too.

I'm biased, but I've never really seen the disadvantages of being in a co-op. There are some, let's be honest; some casting directors still have prejudices and some people find the decision-making process boring. For most, though, this democratic control and participation is the whole point. As for casting directors, the Co-operative Personal Management Association works hard to dispel any myths there might be about co-ops not being completely efficient or not having a commercial attitude. The Association is also seeking to establish high standards of professionalism through its code of conduct and training events.

All co-ops will have different entry requirements, procedures for running the office, and ways of making decisions and forming policy; but they all give members –often after a probationary period –an equal share, and an equal voice and equal responsibility. This is not for everyone, but for many actors –especially those new to the industry –co-ops provide the kind of supportive structure they seek. In turn, this reduces the trials and tribulations of an already pressurised job.

Kim Gillespie is a freelance director and actor. He runs an arts education consultancy and is a teacher, examiner, certified life coach, and role-player/facilitator for corporate training companies. He has been a member of the Central Line co-op for five years and is Secretary of the Co-operative Personal Management Association.

Co-operative Agencies

Before making an approach, it is important to understand what being a member of one of these entails, and to be clear about your reason(s) for wanting to join.

1984 Personal Management Ltd.
Suite 508, Davina House, 137 Goswell Road, London EC1V 7ET

Co-operative management representing 22 actors. Areas of work include theatre, musicals, television, film, commercials, corporate and voice-overs. Members are expected to work 4 days in the office per month unless paying commission.

Will consider attending performances at venues in Greater London with 1 month's notice. Accepts letters (with CVs and photographs) from actors previously unknown to the company following an initial phone-call. Actors should always enquire whether the agency is recruiting before sending CVs. Will also accept showreels and follow-up telephone calls. *Commission*: 12.5%

21st Century Actors Management
E10 Panther House, 38 Mount Pleasant, London WC1X 0AP
tel 020-7278 3438 *fax* 020-7833 1158
email twentyfirstcenturyactors@yahoo.co.uk
Administrator Penny Sands

Co-operative management established in 1992. Represents 21 actors. Areas of work include theatre, musicals, television, film, commercials, corporate and voice-overs. Members are expected to work 3 days in the office per month.

Will consider attending performances at venues in Greater London. Accepts submissions (with CVs and photographs) from actors previously unknown to the company if sent by post. Actors requesting representation should write stating why they wish to join a co-operative and outlining their casting and skills. *Commission*: Theatre 10%; TV, Advertisements and Film 12%

Actors Alliance
Disney Place House, 14 Marshalsea Road, London SE1 1HL
tel 020-7407 6028 *fax* 020-7407 6028
email actors@actorsalliance.fsnet.co.uk

Co-operative management established in 1977. Represents 15-20 actors. Areas of work include theatre, musicals, television, film, commercials, corporate and voice-overs. Members are expected to work 4 days in the office per month.

Will consider attending performances at venues in Greater London with 1 month's notice. Accepts submissions (with CVs and photographs) from actors previously unknown to the company if sent by post. Follow-up telephone calls are also accepted. *Commission*: Variable

Actors Direct Ltd.
Gainsborough House, 109 Portland Street, Manchester M1 6DN

tel 0161-237 1904 *fax* 0161-237 1904
email actorsdirect@aol.com
Administrators Eilis Hetherington,
Jonathan Byrne

Established in 1994. Co-operative management. Sole representative of approximately
25 actors. Areas of work include theatre,
musicals, television, film, commercials,
corporate and voice-overs. Members are
expected to work 2-3 days in the office
each month.

Will consider attending performances at
venues in the North (Manchester, Leeds,
and Liverpool areas) if given 2 weeks'
notice. Accepts submissions (with CVs and
photographs) from actors previously
unknown to the company if sent by post.
Also accepts showreels and voice tapes.
Will consider applications from trained
professional actors with excellent IT and
communication skills and the ability to
perform office duties to a high standard.
'Actors Direct is constantly striving to
maintain a high professional image and to
provide a first-class service to casting
directors." *Commission*: 10% for members

Actors Exchange Management (AXM)

206 Great Guildford Business Square, 30
Great Guildford Street, London SE1 0HS
tel 020-7261 0400 *fax* 020-7261 0408
email info@axmgt.com
website www.axmgt.com

Established in 1983. Co-operative management representing 20 actors. Areas of work
include theatre, musicals, television, film,
commercials, corporate and voice-overs.
Members are expected to work 4 days in
the office per month.

Will consider attending performances at
venues in Greater London, given 1 month's
notice. Accepts submissions (with CVs and
photographs) from actors previously

unknown to the company if sent by post.
Showreels and voice tapes should only be
sent on request following an interview.
Commission: 10%

The Actors File

Spitfire Studios, 63-71 Collier Street,
London N1 9BE
tel 020-7278 0364 *fax* 020-7278 0364
email mail@theactorsfile.co.uk
website www.theactorsfile.co.uk

Established in 1983. Co-operative management representing 20-25 actors. Areas of
work include theatre, musicals, television,
film, commercials, corporate and voice-
overs. Members are expected to work
4 days in the office per month and to
attend business meetings.

Will consider attending performances at
venues in Greater London and occasionally
elsewhere, if given a minimum of 3 weeks'
notice. Accepts submissions (with CVs and
photographs) from actors previously
unknown to the company sent by post or
email. Will also accept showreels, voice
tapes, and invitations to view individual
actors' websites if an interest has already
been expressed in the applicant.
Commission: 12% (negotiable on low
fees)

The Actors Group

21-31 Oldham Street, Manchester M1 1JG

Co-operative management representing
20 actors. Areas of work include theatre,
musicals, television, film, commercials,
corporate and voice-overs. Members are
expected to carry out various office duties.

Will consider attending performances at
venues in the North West with 2-4 weeks'
notice. Accepts submissions (with

CVs and photographs) from actors previously unknown to the company if sent by post. Will also accept follow-up telephone calls, showreels, voice tapes and invitations to view individual actors' websites.

Actors Network Agency

55 Lambeth Walk, London SE11 6DX
tel 020-7735 0999 *fax* 020-7735 8177
email info@ana-actors.co.uk
website www.ana-actors.co.uk
Coordinator and Administrator Sandie Bakker

Established in 1985. Co-operative management representing 20-30 actors. Areas of work include theatre, musicals, television, film, commercials and corporate. Also represents role-play. Members are expected to work 4 days in the office per month.

Will consider attending performances at venues in Greater London and occasionally elsewhere, given as much notice as possible. Accepts submissions (with CVs and photographs) from actors previously unknown to the company if sent by post. Will also accept showreels. "An interest in, and commitment to, this type of agency is essential." *Commission*: 10%; Commercials repeat fees 2%

Actorum Ltd.

3rd Floor, 21 Foley Street,
London W1W 6DR

Co-operative management representing 20 actors. Members are expected to work 4 days in the office per month.

Will consider attending performances at venues in Greater London and elsewhere with 4 weeks' notice. Accepts submissions (with CVs and photographs) from actors

previously unknown to the company if sent by post. Will also accept showreels, voice tapes and invitations to view individual actors' websites. *Commission*: Theatre 10%; TV, Commercials and Film 15%

Arena Personal Management Ltd.

E11 Panther House, 38 Mount Pleasant,
London WC1X 0AP
tel 020-7278 1661 *fax* 020-7278 1661
email arenapmlts@aol.com

Co-operative management representing 20 actors. Areas of work include theatre, musicals, television, film, commercials, corporate and voice-overs. Members are expected to work 1 day in the office per week.

Will consider attending performances at venues in Greater London given 3-4 weeks' notice. Accepts submissions (with CVs and photographs) from actors previously unknown to the company if sent by post. Will also accept follow-up telephone calls, showreels, voice tapes and invitations to view individual actors' websites. *Commission*: Theatre 10%; Commercials 12%

Billboard Personal Management

The Co-op Centre, 11 Mowll Street,
London SW9 6BG
tel 020-7735 9956 *fax* 020-7793 0426
email billboardpm@btconnect.com
website www.billboard.com
Agent Daniel Tasker

Established in 1985. Co-operative management representing 30 actors. Areas of work include theatre, musicals, television, film, commercials, corporate and voice-overs. Members are expected to work 2 days in the office per month.

Will consider attending performances at venues in Greater London given a minimum of 2 weeks' notice. Accepts submissions (with CVs and photographs) from actors previously unknown to the company if they are currently performing. *Commission*: Commercials 16%; Film and TV 13.5%; Other 11%

Cardiff Casting

Chapter Arts Centre, Market Road, Cardiff CF5 1QE
tel 029-2023 3321 *fax* 029-2023 3380
email admin@cardiffcasting.co.uk
website www.cardiffcasting.co.uk
Key personnel Chris Durnal, Bethan Morgan

Established in 1981. Co-operative management representing 17-20 actors. Areas of work include theatre, musicals, television, film, commercials, corporate and voice-overs. Members are expected to work 2-3 days in the office per month.

Will consider attending performances at venues in Greater London, Cardiff, South West England and Wales given 2 weeks' notice. Accepts submissions (with CVs and photographs) from actors previously unknown to the company if sent by post. Will also accept follow-up telephone calls, showreels, voice tapes and invitations to view individual actors' websites. Applicants are asked to state clearly why they have approached a co-operative. *Commission*: Theatre 8%; Mechanical Media 10%

CCM

Panther House, 38 Mount Pleasant, London WC1X 0AP
tel 020-7278 0507 *fax* 020-7813 3103
email casting@ccmactours.com
Key contact Hayley Williams (Secretary), Lee Moore

Established in 1993. Co-operative management representing 19 actors. Areas of work include theatre, musicals, television, film, commercials and corporate. Members are expected to work 3 days in the office per month.

Will consider attending performances at venues in Greater London given 1 month's notice. Accepts submissions (with CVs and photographs) from actors previously unknown to the company sent by post or email. Will also accept invitations to view individual actors' websites. 'Actors must be aware of how co-operatives work and their role within them. Information is available from Equity and Spotlight." *Commission*: Theatre 10%; TV, Advertisements and Film 12%

Central Line

11 East Circus Street, Nottingham NG1 5AF
tel 0115-941 2937 *fax* 0115-950 8087
email mail@the-central-line.co.uk

Established in 1984. Co-operative management representing 15-25 actors. Areas of work include theatre, musicals, television, film, commercials, corporate and voice-overs. Also represents directors. Members are expected to work in the office as and when appropriate.

Will consider attending performances at venues in Greater London and elsewhere. Accepts submissions (with CVs and photographs) from actors previously unknown to the company sent by post or email. Will also accept follow-up telephone calls, showreels, voice tapes and invitations to view individual actors' websites. *Commission*: 10%

Circuit Personal Management Ltd.

Suite 71 SEC, Bedford Street, Stoke-on-Trent ST1 4PZ
tel (01782) 285388 *fax* (01782) 206821
email mail@circuitpm.co.uk

website www.circuitpm.co.uk
Coordinator Simon Knight

Established in 1988. Co-operative management representing 18-20 actors, with 1 full-time coordinator. Areas of work include theatre, musicals, television, film, commercials, corporate and voice-overs. Members are expected to work 1 day in the office every 6 weeks.

Will consider attending performances at venues in Greater London, the West Midlands, North West and West Yorkshire, given 3-4 weeks' notice. Accepts submissions (with CVs and photographs) from actors previously unknown to the company sent by post or email. Will also accept follow-up telephone calls.

City Actors' Management Ltd.
Oval House, 52-54 Kennington Oval, London SE11 5SW
tel 020-7793 9888 *fax* 020-7793 8282
email info@city-actors.freeserve.co.uk
website www.city-actors.freeserve.co.uk

Co-operative management representing 21 actors. Areas of work include theatre, musicals, television, film, commercials and corporate. Members are expected to work 3 days in the office per month.

Will consider attending performances at venues in Greater London with a minimum of 2 weeks' notice. Accepts submissions (with CVs and photographs) from actors previously unknown to the company if sent by post. Will also accept follow-up telephone calls. *Commission*: Theatre 10%; Mechanical Media 12.5%

Denmark Street Management
Packington Bridge Workspace,
Unit 11, 1b Packington Square,

London N1 7UA
tel 020-7354 8555 *fax* 020-7354 8558
email mail@denmarkstreet.net

Established in 1985. Co-operative management representing 15-25 actors. Areas of work include theatre, musicals, television, film, commercials, corporate and voice-overs. Members are expected to work 4 days in the office per month.

Will consider attending performances at venues in Greater London and elsewhere, given 1 month's notice. Accepts submissions (with CVs and photographs) from actors previously unknown to the company if sent by post. Showreels and voice tapes should only be sent on request. Applicants should state why they would like to join a co-operative. Ethnic minority and older actors are particularly welcome. *Commission*: Theatre 10%; TV and Film 12.5%; Commercials 15%

Direct Line
St John's House, 16 St John's Vale, London SE8 4EN
tel 020-8694 1788 *fax* 020-8694 1788
email daphne.franks@dline.org.uk
website www.dline.org.uk

Established in 1984. Co-operative management representing 30 actors. Areas of work include theatre, musicals, television, film, commercials, corporate and voice-overs. Members are expected to work 2 days in the office each month.

Will consider attending performances at venues within Greater London and elsewhere with 1 month's notice. Accepts submissions (with CVs and photographs) from actors previously unknown to the company by post or email. Follow-up telephone calls, showreels, voice tapes and invitations to view individual actors' websites are also accepted. 'Every applicant's enquiry is discussed at a monthly meeting. We do reply to enquiries but would appreciate it if actors enclosed an sae to help reduce our costs." *Commission*: 5-15%

Frontline Management

Colombo Centre, 34-68 Colombo Street, London SE1 8DP
tel 020-7261 9466 *fax* 020-7261 9466
email frontlineactor@freeuk
Key personnel Holly Richardson

Established in 1984. Co-operative management representing 18-22 actors. Areas of work include theatre, musicals, television, film, commercials and corporate. Members are expected to work 3 days in the office per month.

Will consider attending performances at venues in Greater London given 3-7 days' notice. Accepts submissions (with CVs and photographs) from actors previously unknown to the company sent by post or email. Follow-up telephone calls, showreels, voice tapes and invitations to view individual actors' websites are also accepted. *Commission*: 10-12.5% depending on amount of earnings

Heavy Pencil Management

BAC, Lavender Hill, London SW11 5TF
tel 020-7739 9574 *fax* 020-7924 4636
email heavy.pencil@talk21.com

Co-operative management representing 27 actors. Members are expected to work 2 days in the office per month.

Will consider attending performances at venues in Greater London given 1 month's notice. Accepts submissions (with CVs and photographs) from actors previously unknown to the company sent by post or email. Will also accept showreels, voice tapes, and invitations to view individual actors' websites.

IML

Oval House, 52-54 Kennington Oval, London SE11 5SW
tel 020-7587 1080 *fax* 020-7587 1080
email iml.London@btconnect.com
website www.iml.org.uk
Key contact All members

Co-operative management established in 1983. Represents 22 actors. 2 members work in the office each day on a rotational basis. Areas of work include theatre, musicals, television, film and commercials. Members are expected to work 4 days in the office per month.

Will consider attending performances at venues in Greater London given 3 weeks' notice. Accepts submissions (with CVs and photographs) from actors previously unknown to the company if sent by post. Will also accept follow-up telephone calls. Showreels and voice tapes should only be sent on request. *Commission*: 5-15% depending on the job

Inspiration Management

Room 227, The Aberdeen Centre, 22-24 Highbury Grove, London N5 2EA
tel 020-7704 0440 *fax* 020-7704 8497
email
agent@inspirationmanagement.freeserve.co.uk
website
www.inspirationmanagement.co.uk

Established in 1988. Co-operative management representing 20 actors. Areas of work include theatre, musicals, television, film, commercials, corporate and voice-overs. Members are expected to work 2 days in the office per month.

Will consider attending performances at venues in Greater London with 2 weeks' notice. Accepts submissions (with CVs and photographs) from actors previously unknown to the company sent by post or email. Will also accept invitations to view individual actors' websites. *Commission*: 10%

Links Management

34-68 Colombo Street, London SE1 8DP
tel 020-7928 0806 *fax* 020-7928 0806
email links@eidosnet.co.uk
website www.links-management.co.uk
Office Manager Louise North

Established in 1984. Co-operative management representing 25 actors. Areas of work include theatre, musicals, television, film, commercials and voice-overs. Members are expected to work 1 day in the office per week.

Will consider attending performances at venues within Greater London given 2 weeks' notice. Accepts submissions (with CVs and photographs) from actors previously unknown to the company if sent by post. Also accepts follow-up telephone calls, showreels and voice tapes. *Commission*: Theatre 10%; TV and Film 12.5%

North of Watford Actors Agency

Bridge Mill, Hebden Bridge,
West Yorks HX7 8EX
tel (01422) 845361 *fax* (01422) 846503
email northofwatford@btconnect.com
website www.northofwatford.com
New Applications Coordinator Chris Orton

Established in 1992. Co-operative management representing 25-30 actors. Areas of work include theatre, musicals, television, film, commercials, corporate and voice-overs. Members are expected to work 3-4 days in the office per month.

Will consider attending performances at venues in Northern locations (Leeds, Manchester, etc.) but requests as much notice as possible. Accepts submissions (with CVs and photographs) from actors previously unknown to the company if sent by post. Will also accept follow-up telephone calls, showreels, voice tapes and invitations to view individual actors' websites. *Commission*: Varies depending on the work

North One Management

HG08 Aberdeen Studios, Highbury Grove,
London N5 2EA
tel 020-7359 9666 *fax* 020-7359 9449
email actors@northone.co.uk
website www.northone.co.uk

Established in 1987. Co-operative management representing 25 actors. Areas of work include theatre, television, film, commercials and corporate. Members are expected to work 3 days in the office per month.

Will consider attending performances at venues within Greater London given at least 1 week's notice. Accepts submissions (with CVs and black and white 10×8in photographs) from actors previously unknown to the company if sent by post. Will also accept follow-up telephone calls, showreels and voice tapes. Prefers to hear from actors when currently performing. Administration and technical skills are advantageous. Applications from non-European performers are particularly welcome. *Commission*: 10%

Otto Personal Management Ltd.

The Printer's Loft, 111 Arundel Lane,
Sheffield S1 4RF
tel 0114-275 2592 *fax* 0114-275 0550

email ottopm@hotmail.com
website www.ottopm.freeuk.com

Established in 1985. Co-operative management representing 30-35 actors. Areas of work include theatre, musicals, television, film, commercials, corporate and voice-overs. Also represents directors and presenters. Members are expected to work an average of 3 weeks per year in the office.

Will consider attending performances at venues in Yorkshire, the North Midlands, Manchester and the surrounding areas with approximately 1 month's notice. Accepts submissions (with CVs and photographs) from actors previously unknown to the company sent by post or email. Will also accept follow-up telephone calls, showreels, voice tapes and invitations to view individual actors' websites. 'We mainly recruit actors living within a viable distance of Sheffield – Leeds to the North, Mansfield to Manchester.' *Commission*: 12-15% depending on kind of work

Park Management Ltd.

Unit C3, 62 Beechwood Road, London E8 3DY
tel 020-7923 1498 *fax* 020-7923 1422
email park_management@hotmail.com
Coordinator Stephen Leslie

Established in 1977. Co-operative management representing 20 actors. Areas of work include theatre, musicals, television, film, commercials and corporate. Members are expected to work 3-4 days in the office per month.

Will consider attending performances at venues within Greater London with 3 weeks' notice. Accepts submissions (with CVs and photographs) from actors previ-

ously unknown to the company if sent by post. Will also accept showreels, voice tapes and invitations to view individual actors' websites. 'Only write if you are performing in something.' *Commission*: Theatre 11%; TV and Film 13.5%

Performance Actors Agency

137 Goswell Road, London EC1V 7ET
tel 020-7251 5716 *fax* 020-7251 3974
email performance@p-a-a.co.uk
website www.p-a-a.co.uk
Key personnel Lionel Guyett

Established in 1984. Co-operative management representing 25-30 actors. Areas of work include theatre, musicals, television, film, commercials, corporate and voice-overs. Members are expected to work 4 days in the office per month.

Will consider attending performances at venues within Greater London and occasionally elsewhere, given as much notice as possible. Accepts submissions (with CVs and photographs) from actors previously unknown to the company if sent by post and enclosing sae. Will also accept showreels and voice tapes. *Commission*: 10%

Rattlebag Actors Agency Ltd.

Everyman Theatre Annexe, 13-15 Hope Street, Liverpool L1 9BH
tel 0151-708 7273 *fax* 0151-709 0773
email actors@rattlebag.co.uk
website www.rattlebag.co.uk

Established in 1995. Co-operative management representing more than 20 actors. Areas of work include theatre, musicals, television, film, commercials, corporate and voice-overs. Many of the actors have other, additional skills. Members are expected to work an average of 5 days in the office per month.

Will consider attending performances at venues in the North West (Manchester, Liverpool, North Wales) and occasionally within Greater London with 3-4 weeks' notice. Accepts brief, straightforward submissions (with CVs and photographs) from actors previously unknown to the company if sent by post. Photographs should ideally be current black-and-white head-shots. Showreels, voice tapes and invitations to view individual actors' websites are also accepted. 'If invited to an audition or interview it is always best to call in with a response, whether you wish to accept or not." *Commission*: Theatre 10%; Other recorded work 15%

Rosebery Management Ltd.

Diorama Arts Centre, 34 Osnaburgh Street, London NW1 3ND
tel 020-7813 1026 *fax* 020-7692 3065
email roseberymgt@aol.com

Established in 1993. Co-operative management representing 24 actors. Areas of work include theatre, musicals, television, film, commercials, corporate and voice-overs. Members are expected to work 1 day in the office per week.

Will consider attending performances at all venues within Central London with 2 weeks' notice. Accepts submissions (with CVs and photographs) from actors previously unknown to the company sent by post or email. Will also accept invitations to view individual actors' websites. *Commission*: 10%

Stage Centre Management Ltd.

41 North Road, London N7 9DP
tel 020-7607 0872 *fax* 020-7609 0213
email stagecentre@aol.com

Established in 1984. Co-operative management representing 18-26 actors. Areas of

work include theatre, musicals, television, film, commercials and corporate. Members are expected to work 1 day in the office per week.

Will consider attending performances at venues within Greater London and elsewhere, given at least 2 weeks' notice. Accepts submissions (with CVs and photographs) from actors previously unknown to the company sent by post or email. All applicants are advised to call asking for a specific contact name before applying. Will also accept follow-up telephone calls, showreels, voice tapes and invitations to view individual actors' websites. Applicants should not apply if they are unable to provide visible evidence of their work (e.g. performance notice, showcase or showreel). *Commission*: 10%

West Central Management

E4 Panther House, 38 Mount Pleasant, London WC1X 0AP
tel 020-7833 8134 *fax* 020-7833 8134
email mail@westcentralmanagement.co.uk
website www.westcentralmanagement.co.uk

Established in 1984. Co-operative management representing 15-20 actors. Areas of work include theatre, musicals, television, film, commercials and corporate. Members are expected to work 4 days in the office per month.

Will consider attending performances at venues within Greater London with 2 weeks' notice. Accepts submissions (with CVs and photographs) from actors previously unknown to the company sent by post or email. Will also accept invitations to view individual actors' websites. 'We would need to see an applicant's live performance or showreel, but only after an initial meeting/audition." *Commission*: 10%

A Casting Director's Perspective

Richard Evans CDG

The use of casting directors has escalated over the years. Back in the 1950s and '60s a comparative handful ruled the roost, casting major films and television series, often resident as part of the studio or TV station. These days, however, as in every area of the industry, massive expansion has occurred and there are now well over 200 casters in the marketplace. The majority work on a freelance basis –as only the large companies employ people or departments to specifically cast in-house –with some specialising in one area (perhaps television, theatre or commercials), and others, like me, working in all media.

A casting director is employed by a production company to find the best actors for the characters in a given project. Our job is to act as intermediary between our clients (producers, directors and other creatives) and actors and agents; to have a good working and up-to-date knowledge of the talent around, enabling us to compile sensible lists of artists for a particular part; and, above all, to be on the same wavelength as those who have the final say on who gets the job. Contrary to popular belief, this decision is *not* ours, though we do sometimes have influence and are often asked for our opinion.

Many actors see us as a barrier between them and that all-important job. True to some degree, but as I mentioned, the business has expanded phenomenally – *The Spotlight* casting directory has doubled in the last 20 years, while cast sizes have decreased –so we have never had so much choice. I rarely invite actors to audition without having seen their work or having had a trusted recommendation (you wouldn't employ a builder on the basis of a random leaflet dropped through the door!). It's not what you know, it's who you know . . . *and who knows you.* This goes for all of us, including casting directors. We are not handed blockbusters on a plate 52 weeks a year, and mainly get work from those who know us and trust our judgement –a good casting director is worth their weight in gold. We therefore naturally select the best and most suitable actors available, as we are only as good as our last job and the casting industry is fiercely competitive too.

Research what people cast by watching the credits on TV and films and reading theatre programmes, so you can target accordingly. The Casting

Directors' Guild website <www.castingdirectorsguild.co.uk> is another great resource, though not all casters are members. Invite people to see your work, but bear in mind there's a lot to see and time is limited. Always offer complimentary theatre tickets, even if you have to pay for them yourself –they're tax deductible and a very worthwhile career investment. Try to avoid the blanket approach of general 'Here's my CV and photograph' letters and only make contact when you have something to say. Being specific, knowledgeable and realistic when suggesting yourself for roles will maximise your chances of opening doors.

Richard Evans has been a freelance casting director since 1989, and was an actor for ten years prior. He has since cast in all media, and his work includes the Olivier-Award-nominated musical The Rat Pack –Live From Las Vegas *(West End, UK and European tours);* Dancing In The Streets *(UK tour);* Terry Jones' Gargantua *(Grotesque Features); and many commercials and promos. He also regularly devises and leads career development workshops for performers at the Actors' Centres in London and Manchester and at many top drama schools.*

Casting Directors

The title 'Casting Director' can be misleading as these individuals frequently simply 'facilitate' casting; it is usually the director, sometimes the producer, who actually 'directs' the casting decisions. Essentially, they take on a lot of the nitty-gritty work involved in the casting process – suggesting whom the director should consider meeting. The crucial thing to remember is that each one is employed – by someone else – to suggest suitable actors. Some casting directors are employed on a full-time basis; a significant number work freelance and can be as concerned about where their next job is coming from as you are. Therefore, if one gets you to meet a director, it is important that you live up to that casting director's expectations – carefully absorb any brief that he/she gives you. If you suddenly decide to take a radically different approach, he/she will be put into a difficult position with the director.

Fundamental to the job of being a casting director is a wide knowledge of all kinds of actors. Therefore a good one is seeing as many productions as possible. Like squirrels storing nuts for the winter, they keep extensive notes and are continually adding to their collections of actor-profiles. An empathetic, intuitive and imaginative casting director has immeasurable value to both actors and director.

You should approach casting directors in much the same way as you would agents – however, it's even more important that there's something they can see you in. You can keep reasonably up to date with the activities of some casting directors by looking at the website of the Casting Directors Guild (CDG) <www.castingdirectorsguild.co.uk>.

Joanne Adamson Casting
4 Hillthorpe Square, Leeds LS28 8NQ
tel (07787) 311270
email watts07@hotmail.com

Main areas of work are theatre, musicals, television, film and commercials. Casting credits include: *Flesh and Blood* and *Nice Guy Eddie* (BBC), and *Fat Friends II* (Rollem, Tiger Aspect and Ytelevision).

Will consider attending performances at venues in Greater London and elsewhere given 1-2 weeks' notice. Accepts submissions (with CVs and photographs) from actors previously unknown to the casting director if sent by post, but does not welcome email enquiries. Will also accept showreels. 'I am eager to arrange general meetings with actors.'

Pippa Ailion
3 Towton Road, London SE22 9EE

Main areas of work are theatre, musicals, television, film and commercials. Casting credits include: *Tonight's the Night, The Lion King, We Will Rock You, Simply Heavenly, Cole,* and an advertisement for McDonalds' Happy Meals.

Will consider attending performances at venues in Greater London and occasionally elsewhere (such as Chichester or Stratford), given 2-3 weeks' notice. Accepts submissions (with CVs and photographs) from actors previously unknown to the casting director if sent by post. Does not welcome email enquiries.

Sarah Bird CDG

PO Box 326653, London W14 0XA
tel 020-7371 3248 *fax* 020-7602 8601

Casts for film, television, theatre and commercials. Casting credits include: *Second Sight* (BBC), *Monsignor Renard* (Carlton), and *Wilde* (directed by Brian Gilbert).

Lucy Boulting CDG

Riverbank House, 1 Putney Bridge Approach, London SW6 3JD
tel 020-8898 4761 *fax* 020-8614 3109

Casts mainly for film. Casting credits include: *Besieged* (directed by Bernardo Bertolucci), *Shadowlands* (directed by Richard Attenborough), and *Sexy Beast* (directed by Jonathan Glazer).

Siobhan Bracke CDG

Basement Flat, 22a The Barons, St Margaret's RW1 2AP

Main areas of work are theatre, television and film. Casting credits include: *Sex, Chips and Rock n' Roll* (BBC). Casting director for Mark Rylance (Globe theatre), and Neil Bartlett (Lyric theatre, Hammersmith). See entry for

Shakespeare's Globe under *Producing Theatres*, for further information.

Will consider attending performances at venues in Greater London and occasionally elsewhere, given as much notice as possible (preferably 4-5 weeks). Accepts submissions (with CVs and photographs) from actors previously unknown to the casting director if sent by post. Does not welcome email enquiries.

Susie Bruffin CDG

133 Hartswood Road, London W12 9NG
tel 020-8740 9895 *fax* 020-8749 4571

Casts mainly for television and television films. Casting credits include: 16 Catherine Cookson adaptations (drama serials), *Dinner Ladies* (comedy series), and *Complicity* (film).

Candid Casting

2nd Floor, 111-113 Great Titchfield Street, London W1W 6RY
tel 020-7636 6644 *fax* 020-7636 5522
email mail@candidcasting.co.uk
Casting Director Amanda Tabak CDG
Assistant Casting Director Holly McAllister

Main areas of work are television, film and commercials. Casting credits include: *The Low Down* (film) and *Is Harry on the Boat?* (television film).

Will consider attending performances at venues in Greater London given 2 weeks' notice. Accepts submissions (with CVs and photographs) from actors previously unknown to the casting director if sent by post. Does not welcome email enquiries.

John Cannon

Resident Casting Director for the Royal Shakespeare Company. See entry for RSC under *Producing Theatres* for further details.

Cannon Dudley & Associates

43a Belsize Square, London NW3 4HN
tel 020-7433 3393 *fax* 020-7433 3599
email cdacasting@blueyonder.co.uk
Casting Director Carol Dudley CDG, CSA
Casting Associate Helena Palmer

Main areas of work are theatre, television
and film. Casting credits include: *Sunday
Father* (Hampstead theatre), and *Nine
Lives* and *The Card Player* (feature films).

Will consider attending performances at
venues in Greater London given as much
notice as possible. Accepts submissions
(with CVs and photographs) from actors
previously unknown to the casting director
if sent by post. Does not welcome email
enquiries. However, CVs which are not
submitted for specific projects or with
reference to current shows or television
performances cannot be kept for future
reference. Telephone enquiries about
current casting projects or progress of
mailed submissions are not welcomed.

Anji Carroll CDG

109 Ritherdon Road, London SW17 8QH
tel (01270) 250240 *fax* (01270) 250240

Main areas of work are film, television and
commercials. Casting credits include:
London's Burning (LWT), *This Life* (BBC)
and *Out of Depth* (feature film directed by
Simon Marshall).

Casting Ltd.

PO Box 680, Sutton, Surrey SM1 3ZG
tel 020-8715 1036 *fax* 020-8644 9746
email info@janedaviescasting.co.uk
Casting Directors Jane Davies CDG, John
Connor CDG

Casts mainly for television. Casting credits
include: *My Family*, *The Legend of the
Tumworth Two* and *Beauty* (television).

Will consider attending performances of
light drama, particularly of comedies, at
venues in Greater London.

The Casting Angels (London and Paris)

Suite 4, 14 College Road, Bromley BR1 3NS
fax 020-8313 0443
Key personnel Michael *(Big Decisions)*,
Gabriel *(Announcements)*, Raphael, Uriel
(The Daily Grind), Lucifer *(Special
Consultant)*

Main areas of work are television,
musicals, film and commercials with
"casting across the board". Casts for
the UK and other countries within
Europe.

Will consider attending performances at
venues in Greater London and elsewhere,
given as much notice as possible. Accepts
showreels.

The Casting Company

3rd Floor, 112-114 Wardour Street,
London W1F 0TS
Casting Director Louis Hammond

Main areas of work are theatre, television, film
and commercials. Casting credits include:
Mirrormask and *Arsene Lupin* (films).

Will consider attending performances.
Accepts submissions (with CVs and photographs) from actors previously unknown
to the casting director. 'When sending submissions, I suggest a photograph built into
the CV. 10×8in photographs may not be
retained by the casting director."

Casting Couch Productions Ltd.

97 Riffel Road, London NW2 4PG
tel 020-8438 9679 *fax* 020-8208 2373
Casting Director Moira Townsend

Main areas of work are television, film and commercials. Casting credits include: *Who Killed Tutankhamen?* (documentary), and advertisements for DULA and Lunn Poly.

Will consider attending performances at venues in Greater London and elsewhere, given 2-3 weeks' notice. Accepts submissions (with CVs and photographs) from actors previously unknown to the casting director if sent by post. Does not welcome email enquiries. Actors will only receive a response if the casting director is able to attend a performance.

See entry under *Agents* for further details of the company's work.

Casting UK
88-90 Grays Inn Road, London WC1X 8AA
tel 020-7430 1122 *fax* 020-7430 1155
email drew@castinguk.com
Casting Director Andrew Mann

Casts mainly for film and commercials. Casting credits include: commercials for Bacardi, Ericsson and Pepsi, and videos for Placibo.

Will consider attending performances at venues in Greater London given 2 weeks' notice. Accepts submissions (with CVs and photographs) from actors previously unknown to the casting director if sent by post. Does not welcome email enquiries.

Suzy Catliff CDG
PO Box 32658, London W14 0XA

Casts mainly for film, television and theatre. Casting credits include: *Swimming Pool* (film), *Life x 3* (theatre), and *Casualty* (BBC).

Alison Chard CDG
23 Groveside Court, London SW11 3RQ
tel 020-7223 9125 *fax* 020-7223 9125
email
alisonchard@castingdirector.freeserve.co.uk
website www.castingdirectorsguild.co.uk

Main areas of work are theatre, television, film and commercials. Casting credits include: *M.I.T.* and *The Bill* (television) and casting for the Royal Shakespeare Company.

Will consider attending performances at venues in Greater London and occasionally elsewhere, given 1 month's notice. Accepts submissions (with CVs and photographs) from actors previously unknown to the casting director if sent by post. CVs may also be emailed. Showreels and voice tapes are accepted if they are on VHS, accompanied by an sae and of good quality (does not welcome filmed stage pieces). Invitations to view individual actors' websites are unnecessary; ensuring that *Spotlight* entries are up-to-date is more advisable. Advises actors to: "Target performance notices in accordance with the location of the recipient. Guard against unnecessary expense and disappointment by doing your research; find out what they are working on, who they are working with and if they are familiar with your work."

John Connor CDG
See entry for Casting Ltd.

Lin Cordoray
66 Cardross Street, London W6 0DR

Main areas of work are television and commercials.

Will consider attending performances at venues in Greater London. Accepts submissions (with CVs and photographs) from actors previously unknown to the casting director if sent by post. Does not welcome email enquiries.

Irene Cotton CDG
25 Druce Road, London SE21 7DW

Main areas of work are theatre, musicals, television, film and commercials. Casting credits include: *Hutton Report* (for BBC *Panorama*) and *The Bill* (television), *Being Dead* (feature film) and an advertisement for Thorntons Chocolates.

Will consider attending performances at venues in Greater London given as much notice as possible. Accepts invitations to view individual actors' websites. "Always write and ask if a showreel can be sent. I welcome fliers for fringe productions."

Margaret Crawford
92 Castelnau, London SW13 9EU

Casts mainly for television. Casting credits include: *Bad Girls* (Series 2-6), and *Footballers' Wives* (Series 1-3).

Will consider attending performances at venues in Greater London and occasionally elsewhere, given as much notice as possible. Accepts submissions (with CVs and photographs) from actors previously unknown to the casting director if sent by post. Does not welcome email enquiries. Also accepts showreels, voice tapes and invitations to view individual actors' websites.

Crocodile Casting
9 Ashley Close, Hendon,
London NW4 1PH
tel 020-8203 7009 *fax* 020-8203 7711
website www.crocodilecasting.com

Casting Directors Tracie Saban, Claire Toeman

Established in 1996 with the aim of constantly accessing new faces and fresh talent. The company casts mainly for commercials, pop videos and corporate work and sometimes holds general auditions to meet new actors and models.

Jane Davies CDG
See entry for Casting Ltd.

Gary Davy CDG
33 Fitzroy Street, London W1T 6DU
tel 020-7636 0880 *fax* 020-7636 0881

Casts mainly for film, theatre and television. Casting credits include: *In Arabia We'd Be Kings* (play directed by Robert Delamere), *Band of Brothers* (mini-series directed by Tom Hanks), *Revengers Tragedy* (film directed by Alex Cox), *Babyfather Two* (BBC).

Stephanie Dawes
Casting Department, London Weekend Television, Upper Ground, London SE1 9LT
tel 020-7261 3509 *fax* 020-7737 8541

Works mainly for television. Recent credits include: casting for *Crime Monthly* and *Most Wanted* (LWT), and children and extras casting for *Spaced* (LWT/Paramount Comedy Channel for Channel 4) and *Johnny and the Dead* (LWT).

See entry for Granada under *Independent Television* for further details.

Kate Day CDG
Pound Cottage, 27 The Green South, Warborough OX10 7DR

Main areas of work are television, film and commercials.

Will consider attending performances at venues in Greater London and occasionally elsewhere, given as much notice as possible. Accepts submissions (with CVs and photographs) from actors previously unknown to the casting director if sent by post. Does not welcome email enquiries.

Jack Denman Casting

Burgess House, Main Street, Farnsfield, Notts NG22 8EF

Main areas of work are theatre, musicals, television, film and commercials. Casting credits include: *Peak Practice*, *Doctors*, and *Crimewatch* (television), and videos for PC World and Boots.

Will consider attending performances at venues in the Midlands with as much notice as possible. Accepts submissions (with CVs and photographs) from actors previously unknown to the casting director if sent by post. Does not welcome email enquiries.

Malcom Drury CDG

34 Tabor Road, London W6 0BW
tel 020-8748 9232

Casts mainly for television. Casting credits include: *The Bill*, *Heartbeat*, *The Beiderbecke Affair* and Laurence Olivier's *King Lear*.

Carol Dudley CDG, CSA

See entry for Cannon Dudley & Associates.

Julia Duff CDG

73 Wells Street, London W1T 3QG
tel 020-7436 8860 *fax* 020-7436 8859

Casts mainly for film, television and commercials. Casting credits include: *Hamish Macbeth* and *Lorna Doone* (television), and UK casting for *The House of Mirth* (feature film directed by Terence Davies).

Irene East Casting CDG

40 Brookwood Avenue, Barnes, London SW13 0LR

Main areas of work are theatre and film. Casting credits include: *Jealousy* and *Love Bites* (film), *Romeo and Juliet* and *Murder in Paris* (theatre).

Will consider attending performances at venues in Greater London and occasionally elsewhere, given a couple of days' notice. Showreels should only be sent on request.

EJ Casting

Lower Ground Floor, 86 Vassall Road, London SW9 6JA
email info@EJCasting.com
Director Edward James

Casts for theatre, musicals, television, film, commercials and corporate work. Casting credits include: *Into the Woods*, *The Dumb Waiter* and *A Chorus Line* (theatre), a commercial for Cadbury's Fingers, and *Air on a G String* (film).

Will consider attending performances at venues in Greater London and occasionally elsewhere, given a minimum of 8 weeks' notice. Accepts showreels containing work which has been broadcast. Actors should send an sae for the return of their material.

Richard Evans CDG

10 Shirley Road, London W4 1DD
tel 020-8994 6304

email info@evanscasting.co.uk
website www.evanscasting.co.uk
Key personnel Richard Evans CDG

Main areas of work are theatre, musicals, television, film and commercials. Casting credits include: *The Rat Pack – Live From Las Vegas* (theatre).

Will consider attending performances at venues in Greater London and occasionally elsewhere, given sufficient notice. Requests 1-2 weeks before the opening night for theatre productions and 2-3 days prior to transmission for television shows. Accepts follow-up telephone calls after a production has opened or been broadcast. Welcomes submissions (with CVs and photographs) from actors previously unknown to the casting director if sent by post. Does not welcome email enquiries. Showreels should only be sent on request. Advises actors to: 'Be specific, find out about current projects and suggest yourself for particular roles. Always ensure that the part you are playing is worth casting personnel coming to see. Offer complimentary tickets.'

Janie Frazer CDG
LWT, London Television Centre, Upper Ground, London SE1 9LT
tel 020-7261 3848 *fax* 020-7737 8541

Casts mainly for television (drama and comedy, serials and one-offs) and currently resident Casting Director at Granada and LWT. Casting credits include: *Night and Day* (television soap), *Island at War* (drama series), *Aladdin* (television, pantomime) and *Small Potatoes,* Series 2 (situation comedy, Hat Trick Productions for Channel 4).

See entry for Granada under *Independent Television* for further details.

Nina Gold CDG
10 Kempe Road, London NW6 6SJ
tel 020-8960 6099 *fax* 020-8968 6777

Main areas of work are film, television and commercials. Casting credits include: *Love's Labours Lost* (film directed by Kenneth Branagh), *Topsy Turvey* and several other films directed by Mike Leigh, and *Triumph of Love* (directed by Clare Peoploe).

Jill Green CDG
52 Tottenham Street, London W1T 4RN
tel 020-7580 6037 *fax* 020-7580 6048

Casts for theatre (mainly musicals). Casting credits include: *Westside Story* and *Cats* (for UK tours), *Fosse* and *Thoroughly Modern Millie* (in the West End).

Marcia Gresham CDG
3 Langthorne Street,
London SW6 6JT
tel 020-7381 2876 *fax* 020-7381 4496

Main area of work is television. Casting credits include: *The Debt, The Project* and *Innocents* (television).

Will consider attending performances at venues in Greater London given 1 month's notice. Accepts submissions (with CVs and photographs) from actors previously unknown to the casting director if sent by post, but does not welcome email enquiries. Showreels and voice tapes (with sae for return) are also accepted.

David Grindrod CDG
4th Floor, Palace theatre, Shaftesbury Avenue, London W1D 5AY
tel 020-7437 2506 *fax* 020-7437 2507

Casts for theatre and film (mainly musicals). Casting credits include: *Bombay Dreams, Our House, Jesus Christ Superstar, Sunset Boulevard* and *Mamma Mia!* (West End and UK tours) and *Sleeping Beauty* (video/film).

Janet Hall

1 Shore Avenue, Shaw, Oldham OL2 8DA

Casting credits include: AXA commercial and *The Sound of Music* (theatre).

Will consider attending performances at venues in Greater London and in Manchester, Liverpool and Leeds, given 1 week's notice. Accepts submissions (with CVs and photographs) from actors previously unknown to the casting director sent by post or email. Also accepts showreels, voice tapes and invitations to view individual actors' websites.

Louis Hammond

See entry for the Casting Company.

Gemma Hancock CDG

28 Heber Road, London SE22 9LA
tel (01444) 441398 *fax* (01444) 441398

Main areas of work are theatre, television and film. Casting credits include: *Hero to Zero* (BBC television), *Beau Brummell, The Memory of Water* and *The Browning Version* (national theatre tours), and casting for the Royal Shakespeare Company (2003).

Judi Hayfield CDG

Granada Television, Quay Street, Manchester M60 9EA
tel 0161-832 7211 *fax* 0161-827 2853

Resident Casting Director for Granada. See entry under *Independent Television* for further details.

Polly Hootkins CDG

PO Box 25191, London SW1V 2WN
tel 020-7233 8724 *fax* 020-7828 5051
email phootkins@clara.net
website castingdirectorsguild.co.uk
Key personnel Polly Hootkins

Main areas of work are theatre, television and film. Casting credits include: *A New Day in Old Sana'a.*

Will consider attending performances at venues in Greater London and occasionally elsewhere, given as much notice as possible. Accepts submissions (with CVs and photographs) from actors previously unknown to the casting director if sent by post. Does not welcome email enquiries. Showreels, voice tapes and invitations to view individual actors' websites are also accepted.

Dan Hubbard CDG

Hubbard Casting, 2nd Floor, 19 Charlotte Street, London W1T 1RL
tel 020-7636 9991 *fax* 020-7636 7117

Casts mainly for film, television, theatre and commercials. Casting credits include: *Murder Squad* (Granada television), *Paradise Heights* (BBC), *The Murder of Stephen Lawrence* (Granada), *Tomb Raider 1 and 2* (film for Paramount), and *Dracula 2000* (Miramax/Dimensions films).

Sarah Hughes

Stephen Joseph theatre, Westborough, Scarborough YO11 1JW

Resident Casting Director for the Stephen Joseph theatre. See entry under *Producing Theatres* for further details.

Sue Jackson

Resident Casting Director for Yorkshire TV Ltd. See entry under *Independent Television* for further details.

Trevor Jackson CDG

1 Bedford Square, London WC1B 3RA
tel 020-7637 8866 *fax* 020-7436 2683

Casts mainly for musicals produced by Cameron Mackintosh Ltd. Casting credits include: *My Fair Lady, Les Miserables, Miss Saigon, Phantom of the Opera.*

Will consider attending performances at venues in Greater London given as much notice as possible. Accepts submissions (with CVs and photographs) from actors previously unknown to the casting director if sent by post, but does not welcome email enquiries. Showreels, voice tapes and invitations to view individual actors' websites are also accepted.

Jennifer Jaffrey

136 Hicks Avenue, Greenford, Middlesex UB6 8HB
tel 020-8578 2899 *fax* 020-8575 0369
Key personnel Jennifer Jaffrey *(Proprietor)*

Main areas of work are theatre, musicals, television, film and commercials. Casting credits include: *Cross My Heart, Ten Minutes Older* and *Such a Long Journey.*

Will consider attending performances at venues in Greater London given as much notice as possible. Accepts submissions (with CVs and photographs) from actors previously unknown to the casting director

if sent by post, but does not welcome email enquiries. Photographs should have the actor's name written on the back and an sae must be included for the return of material. Showreels should only be sent on request.

Lucy Jenkins CDG

74 High Street, Hampton Wick, Kingston-upon-Thames KT1 4DQ
tel 020-8943 5328 *fax* 020-8977 0466

Casts mainly for film, television, theatre and commercials. Casting credits include: *Babyfather* (BBC), *The Bill* (television), *Top Dog* (short film) and *Emma* (theatre).

Sue Jones CDG

24 Nicoll Road, London NW10 9AB
tel 020-8838 5153 *fax* 020-8838 1130

Main areas of work are film, television, theatre and commercials. Casting credits include: UK casting for *Star Trek – Nemesis* (film for Paramount Pictures), *Nil by Mouth* (directed by Gary Oldman), *The Man in the Iron Mask* (United Artists), *Messiah* and *Coriolanus* (both plays directed by Stephen Berkoff), *A Day in the Death of Jo Egg* (directed by Lisa Forrell), *The Vicar* (BBC television), and *The Politician's Wife* (Channel 4).

Beverley Keogh

40 Princess Street, Manchester M1 6DE
tel 0161-920 9714 *fax* 0161-920 9715
email Beverley@beverlykeogh.tv

Main areas of work are television, film and commercials. Casting credits include: *Fat Friends, Clocking Off* and *Second Coming.*

Accepts submissions (with CVs and photographs) from actors previously unknown to the casting director sent by post or email.

Suzy Korel CDG
20 Blenheim Road, St John's Wood,
London NW8 0LX

Will consider attending performances at
venues in Greater London given as much
notice as possible. Accepts submissions
(with CVs and photographs) from actors
previously unknown to the casting director
if sent by post, but does not welcome email
enquiries. Invitations to view individual
actors' websites are also accepted.

Matthew Lessall
Unit 5, Gun Wharf, 241 Old Ford Road,
London E3 5QB

Relocated to LA and does not therefore welcome any contact from UK-based actors.

Sharon Levinson
30 Stratford Villas, London NW1 9SG

Main areas of work are television, film and
commercials. Casting credits include: *Two
Thousand Acres of Sky* and *A Christmas
Carol* (television).

Will consider attending performances at
venues in Greater London and occasionally
elsewhere, given 2 weeks' notice. Not currently casting.

Karen Lindsay-Stewart CDG
PO Box 2301, London W1A 1PT

Main areas of work are television and film.
Casting credits include: *Sylvia, Harry Potter
and the Chamber of Secrets* and *Cambridge
Spies.*

Will consider attending performances at
venues in Greater London with sufficient
notice. Accepts submissions (with CVs
and photographs) from actors previously
unknown to the casting director if sent
by post, but does not welcome email

enquiries. Do not send sae(s) for
replies.

Maggie Lunn
Resident Casting Director for the Almeida
and Chichester Festival theatres. See
entries for respective theatres under
Producing Theatres.

Kay Magson
Resident Casting Director for West
Yorkshire Playhouse. See entry under
Producing Theatres for further details.

Lisa Makin
Resident Casting Director for the Royal
Court Theatre. See entry under *Producing
Theatres* for further details.

Andrew Mann
See entry for Casting UK.

Joan McCann CDG
26 Hereford Road, London W3 9JW
tel 020-8993 1747
email joanmccann@lineone.net

Main areas of work are television and film.
Casting credits include: *The Low Down*
(film) and *Is Harry on the Boat* (television
film).

Will consider attending performances at
venues in Greater London given a minimum of 2 weeks' notice. Showreels may
be accepted; suggests calling in advance to
check whether it is a good time to send
them. Invitations to view individual
actors' websites are also accepted. Does
not welcome telephone calls for any other
reason than specified above.

Carolyn McLeod

PO Box 26495, London SE10 0WO
tel 0704-400 1720
email carolynmcleodcasting@hotmail.com

Main areas of work are television, film and commercials. Casting credits include: UK child casting on *Entrusted, Beyond Borders* and *Hitler: The Rise of Evil*; additional UK casting on *Exorcist: In the Beginning*.

Will consider attending performances at venues in Greater London and occasionally elsewhere, given 2-3 weeks' notice. Accepts submissions (with CVs and photographs) from actors previously unknown to the casting director sent by post or email. Showreels, voice tapes and invitations to view individual actors' websites are also accepted. Applicants should only submit their details once. Advises actors that: "As most casting directors have little capacity for storing CVs, it may be worth telephoning to check whether they are accepting submissions —though do be warned that some people may not appreciate the phone call. If you already have an agent, ask them to contact us on your behalf."

Chrissie McMurrich

16 Spring Vale Avenue, Brentford, Middlesex TW8 9QH

Main areas of work are theatre and television. Casting credits include: *The Hobbit, A Christmas Carol*, and *The Commander*.

Will consider attending performances at venues in Greater London given 2 weeks' notice. Accepts submissions with performance notices (containing CVs and photographs) from actors previously unknown to the casting director if sent by post. No unsolicited emails are accepted.

Anne McNulty

Resident Casting Director for Donmar Warehouse. See separate entry under *Producing Theatres*.

Sooki McShane CDG

8a Piermont Road, East Dulwich, London SE22 0LN
tel 020-8693 7411 *fax* 020-8693 7411

Works mainly in theatre, film and television. Casting credits include: *Rainbow Room* (Granada television), *My Brother Rob* (feature film), and casting for the Warehouse Theatre Croydon. Currently resident Casting Director for the Nottingham Playhouse. See entry under *Producing Theatres* for further details.

Carl Proctor CDG

158 Bury Place, London WC1A 2JB
tel 020-7681 0034 *fax* 020-7916 2533
website www.carlproctor.com

Casts mainly for film, television, theatre and commercials. Casting credits include: one-off television dramas, *Twelfth Night* (film directed by Trevor Nunn), more than 100 commercials and *Shadow of the Vampire* (film directed by Elias Merhige).

Andy Pryor CDG

7 Garrick Street, London WC2E 9AR
tel 020-7386 8298 *fax* 020-7836 8299

Casts mainly for film, television and commercials. Casting credits include: *Perfect Strangers* and *The Lost Prince* (both directed by Stephen Poliakoff for BBC television), and *Long Time Dead* (film directed by Marcus Adams).

Gennie Radcliffe

Casting Director for *Coronation Street*. See entry for Granada under *Independent Television* for further details.

Simone Reynolds CDG

60 Hebdon Road, London SW17 7NN

Main areas of work are film, television, theatre and commercials. Casting credits include: *Honeymoon Suite* (theatre), *The Vicar of Dibley* and *Quicksand, Turning Points: Emma's Story* (both for BBC television), *Jack and Sarah* (film for Granada) and *Shining Through* (film for Twentieth Century Fox).

Will consider attending performances at venues in Greater London and elsewhere, given as much notice as possible. Accepts submissions (with CVs and photographs) from actors previously unknown to the casting director if sent by post. Does not welcome email enquiries. Advises actors to: 'Keep CVs clear (separate out the part from the director and venue) and keep covering submissions brief.'

Laura Scott CDG

56 Rowena Crescent, London SW11 2PT
tel 020-7978 6336 *fax* 020-7924 1907

Main areas of work are film, television, theatre and commercials. Casting credits include: *Berkley Square* (costume drama for BBC television), *The Railway Children* (Carlton) and *Where There's Smoke* (Talisman films).

Philip Shaw

Suite 476, 2 Old Brompton Road, London SW7 3DQ
tel 020-8715 8943 *fax* 020-8408 1193
email shawcastlond@aol.com

Main areas of work are theatre, television, film and commercials. Casting credits include: *The Last Post* (film), and *The Turn of the Screw* (theatre).

Will consider attending performances at venues in Greater London given a minimum of 2 weeks' notice. Accepts submissions (with CVs and photographs) from actors previously unknown to the casting director if sent by post. Does not welcome email enquiries.

Sandra Singer Associates

21 Cotswold Road, Westcliff-on-Sea, Essex SSO 8AA
tel (01702) 331616 *fax* (01702) 339393
email Sandrasingeruk@aol.com
website www.sandrasinger.com
Key personnel Sandra Singer (M.I.E.A.M.)

Main areas of work are theatre, musicals and film. Casting credits include: regional casting for *The Sound of Music, Les Miserables, The Lion King* and *Chitty Chitty Bang Bang.*

Will consider attending performances at venues in Greater London given 3 months' notice. Performance notices or any other enquiries are not accepted by email. Accepts submissions (with CVs and photographs) from actors previously unknown to the casting director if sent by post. Showreels should only be sent on request. Enclose an sae for the return of material.

Michelle Smith CDG

220 Church Lane, Woodford, Stockport SK7 1PQ
tel (0161) 439 6825 *fax* (0161) 439 0622

Main areas of work are film, television and commercials. Casting credits include: *This*

Little Life (for BBC films), *Phoenix Nights 2* (Channel 4), and *Cold Feet, Series 1-5* (Granada).

Suzanne Smith CDG
33 Fitzroy Street, London W1T 6DU

Main areas of work are film, television, theatre and musicals. Casting credits include: UK casting for *Black Hawk Down* (film directed by Ridley Scott), *Band of Brothers* (for television), and *Life Force* (television).

Wendy Spon CDG
c/o ACT Productions, 20-22 Stukeley Street, London WC2B 5LR
tel 020-7438 9599 *fax* 020-7242 3578

Main areas of work are film, television, theatre and musicals. Casting credits include: *The Graduate* (theatre, directed by Terry Johnson), *Oklahoma* and *Oh What a Lovely War* (both for the National Theatre), and *Shadow Man* (short film).

Gail Stevens Casting CDG
2 Sutton Lane, 54A Clerkenwell Road, London EC1M 5PS

Main areas of work are television, film and commercials. Casting credits include: *Twenty-Eight Days Later*, *Calendar Girls* and *Spooks*.

Sam Stevenson CDG
103 Whitecross Street, London EC1Y 8JD
tel 020-7256 5727 *fax* 020-7920 0852

Main areas of work are television, theatre and film. Casting credits include: UK casting for *The Life Aquatic* (directed by Wes

Anderson), *Happy Days* (for theatre, directed by Sir Peter Hall), and *Eastenders*, *Holby City* and *Doctors* (for BBC television). Employed as the Casting Coordinator for the Royal Shakespeare Company for two seasons.

Amanda Tabak CDG
See entry for Candid Casting.

Moira Townsend
See entry for Casting Couch Productions Ltd.

Jill Trevellick CDG
123 Rathcoole Gardens, London N8 9PH
tel 020-8340 2734 *fax* 020-8348 7400

Main areas of work are film, television, theatre and commercials. Casting credits include: *The Canterbury Tales* (series of 6 films for BBC television), *Sons and Lovers* (television film for Company television/ITV), *Me Without You* (feature film for Dakota), and *One Last Chance* (feature film for Hero films).

Sarah Trevis CDG
c/o Twickenham Studios, St Margaret's, Twickenham TW1 2AW
tel 020-8607 8888 *fax* 020-8607 8766

Main areas of work are television and film. Recent casting credits include: work for Granada television, the BBC and Twentieth Century Fox.

Will consider attending performances given 2 weeks' notice. Accepts submissions (with CVs and photographs) from actors previously unknown to the casting director if sent by post. Does not welcome email enquiries.

Vital Productions

PO Box 26441, London SE10 9GZ
tel 020-8316 4497 *fax* 020-8316 4497
email mail@vital-productions.co.uk
Key personnel Melissa Waudby

Main areas of work are theatre and television. Casting credits include: *BBC Crimewatch* and *The Great Dome Robbery* (television).

Will consider attending performances at venues in Greater London and elsewhere, given 1 month's notice. Accepts submissions (with CVs and photographs) from actors previously unknown to the casting director if sent by post. Does not welcome email enquiries. "Because of time pressure, we tend to use *Spotlight* and specific agents or individual suggestions rather than CVs and photographs submitted to us."

Anne Vosser CDG

PO Box 203, Aldershot GU12 4YB
tel (01252) 404715
fax (01252) 404716
email vossercasting@ntlworld.com

Main areas of work are theatre and musicals. Casting credits include: *Romeo and Juliet* and *Taboo* (both in the West End), *Fame* and *Saturday Night Fever* (West End and Tour).

June West

Resident Casting Director at Granada. See entry under *Independent Television* for further details.

Matt Western

4th Floor, 193 Wardour Street,
London W1V 3FA

Main areas of work are film, television, theatre and commercials. Casting credits include: *The Other Boleyn Girl* (film for

BBC television), *The Night Detective* (series for Zenith/BBC) and *Essential Poems* (for Talkback Productions).

Toby Whale CDG

80 Shakespeare Road, London W3 6SN
tel 020-8993 2821
fax 020-8993 8096
website www.whalecasting.com

Main areas of work are film, television and theatre. Casting credits include: *East is East* (Assassin Films/FilmFour), *Spoonface Steinberg* (BBC film), *Wire in the Blood* (Series 1 & 2 –Coastal/ITV) and more than 40 theatre productions for the Royal Court Theatre, Out of Joint, the Almeida Theatre, English Touring Theatre and Sheffield Crucible amongst others.

Currently Head of Casting at the National Theatre; see entry under *Producing Theatres* for further information.

Tara Woodward

Top Flat, 93 Gloucester Avenue,
Primrose Hill, London NW1 8LB
tel 020-7586 3487 *fax* 020-7681 8574

Main areas of work are film, television, theatre and commercials. Casting credits include: *The Early Days*, *Post* and *Hello Friend* (all for Shine/Film Four Lab), *Chasing Heaven* (for Venice Film Festival), *The Browning Version* and *Romeo and Juliet* (theatre), and commercials for Parmalat Aqua and Royal Danish Post. Has worked as Casting Assistant to Nina Gold on films including *All Or Nothing* (directed by Mike Leigh), and *Love's Labours Lost* (directed by Kenneth Branagh).

Francesca Woolgar CDG

See entry for Pearce Woolgar Casting below.

Pearce Woolgar Casting

Mayfair House, 14-18 Heddon Street,
London W1B 4DA
tel 020-8667 0527 *fax* 020-8667 0527
email info@pearcewoolgar.com
website www.pearcewoolgar.com
Casting Director Francesca Woolgar CDG

Casts mainly for commercials. Casting
credits include: commercials for Knorr,
Volkswagon and Visa.

Will consider attending performances at
venues in Greater London given sufficient
notice. Accepts submissions (with CVs and
photographs) from actors previously
unknown to the casting director if sent by
post, but does not welcome email
enquiries.

Jeremy Zimmermann Casting

Clareville House, 26-7 Oxendon Street,
London SW1Y 4EL

Main areas of work are television and film.

Will consider attending performances at
venues in Greater London and elsewhere.
Accepts submissions (with CVs and photographs) from actors previously unknown to
the casting director if sent by post. Does not
welcome email enquiries. Invitations to view
individual actors' websites are also accepted.

Theatre

Introduction

Theatres and theatre companies/managements abound in all kinds of different forms, and paid opportunities for live performance are not restricted to putting on productions. The days of the permanent 'repertory' company are almost gone, but there is a much wider diversity of work available. The larger companies/managements often use casting directors (see pp. 92-106), who should usually be your first port of call with your letter, CV and photograph. However, it can be worth exploiting any personal contacts that you may have.

For reasons of space, this section does not include the numerous theatres (often subsidised by a local authority) and arts centres which largely present touring and (sometimes) amateur productions. However, a number of these do mount their own professional pantomimes and it can be useful to look through the 'Theatres – Provincial/Touring' section of *Contacts* to check which. Many have websites. Another way of finding out is to check through the reviews in *The Stage* every Christmas. Pantomimes in such theatres will often be directed by the resident and usually cannot afford the services of a casting director.

For all approaches, it is important to send your submissions to the person named –unless you have a personal contact.

Producing Theatres

Included in this section are the national and regional building-based companies that mount their own productions – sometimes in co-operation with others, and sometimes sending out tours. The majority are subsidised by the national and regional Arts Councils (and use Equity's regional theatre contract), but a few are not (and use Equity's commercial theatre contract), and a few have their own contractual arrangements. Almost all have websites which can be very useful for keeping track of their activities. A little extra insight – beyond that listed on the following pages – into a theatre might just tip the balance in your favour.

In real terms, rates of pay are better than they were a decade and more ago, but they are still only 'adequate' – especially if you are incurring the extra costs of living away from home. However, rehearsing and performing a production in such a theatre can be an exhilarating experience. A well-run theatre has a wonderful 'family' atmosphere and in the close-knit working environment you can often make friendships which sustain for many years afterwards – and contacts who might be useful in years to come. It is well worth checking each theatre's 'casting procedures' very carefully as there are significant variations between them. It is also worth familiarising yourself with their programmes of productions via *The Stage* and/or their websites.

Almeida Theatre

Almeida Street, London N1 1TA
tel 020-7288 4900 *fax* 020-7288 4901
email info@almeida.co.uk
website www.almeida.co.uk
Artistic Director Michael Attenborough
Associate Director Howard Davies
Casting Director Maggie Lunn
Executive Director Neil Constable
General Manager Ros Brooke-Taylor

Production details
The Almeida is committed to staging British and international drama presented to the highest possible standards and productions which reveal the plays in a new light. Embraces international classics, foreign classics in newly commissioned versions, and new plays –in addition to an annual Opera season of specially commissioned operas, music theatre pieces and concerts of contemporary music. Stages approximately 6 productions each year. Recent productions include: Ibsen's *The Lady from the Sea*, *The Mercy Seat* by Neil La Bute, and Edward Albee's *The Goat, Or Who is Sylvia?*

Casting procedures
Actors may write at any time requesting inclusion. Welcomes submissions (with CVs and photographs) sent by post or email. Also accepts showreels and invitations to view individual actors' websites.

Birmingham Repertory Theatre

Centenary Square, Broad Street,
Birmingham B1 2EP
tel 0121-245 2000

website www.birmingham-rep.co.uk
Artistic Director Jonathan Church
Literary Manager Ben Payne
Executive Director Stuart Rogers
Head of Education Steve Ball

Production details
Stages 15 productions in the main house each year and 6 in the studio. Also runs Outreach, Community and Education programmes.

Casting procedures
Sometimes uses freelance casting directors. Welcomes submissions (with CVs and photographs) sent by post or email, preferably in relation to specific productions. Also accepts invitations to view individual actors' websites. Particularly interested to hear from performers in the West Midlands region.

Birmingham Stage Company (BSC)

Suite 228, 162 Regent Street,
London W1B 5TG
tel 020-7437 3391 *fax* 020-7437 3395
email info@birminghamstage.net
website www.birminghamstage.net
Actor-Manager Neal Foster
Producing Assistant Louise Eltringham
Education Eileen Mills
Administrator Philip Compton

Production details
Founded in 1992, the BSC stages 3 shows each year, 1 of which tours nationally. Produces a range of plays with particular emphasis on new writing, and is now recognised for its children's shows which visit 60 venues around the UK. Recent productions include: *Collision at the Old Red Lion* and *George's Marvellous Medicine*.

Casting procedures
Uses freelance casting directors and sometimes holds general auditions. Casting breakdowns are available through postal application (with sae), *PCR* and *Castweb* (see entry under *Casting Directories and*

Information Services). Actors should write requesting inclusion in response to postings in *PCR*. Welcomes submissions (with CVs and photographs) sent by post or email. Also accepts showreels, voice tapes and invitations to view individual actors' websites. 'Do as much research as you can before submitting."

Bristol Old Vic

King Street, Bristol BS1 4ED
tel 0117-949 3993 *fax* 0117-949 3993
email davidandsimon@bristol-old-vic.co.uk
website www.bristol-old-vic.co.uk
Artistic Directors David Farr, Simon Reade
Assistant to the Artistic Directors Kate Yedigaroff
Director of Education and Youth Theatre Heather Williams

Production details
Classical theatre company producing its own repertoire throughout the year. Stages 8 shows in the main house each year and 4 in the studio. Also runs Education programmes. Recent productions include: *Cinderella, True West, The Comedy of Errors* and *The Caretaker.*

Casting procedures
Uses freelance casting directors. Actors may send letters (with CVs and photographs) which will be forwarded to the casting director. Does not welcome email submissions, showreels or requests for meetings. Actors are welcome to call Kate Yedigaroff to find out about the forthcoming season towards the end of the previous one; where possible they will be told which casting directors are being used. A file of local actors is held in the theatre.

Byre Theatre

Abbey Street, St Andrews KY16 9LA
tel (01334) 476288 *fax* (01334) 475370

email enquiries@byretheatre.com
website www.byretheatre.com
Artistic Director Ken Alexander
Associate Directors Rita Henderson,
Steven Little
Managing Director Tom Gardner

Production details
Founded in 1933, it moved into a new
state-of-the-art theatre in 2001. Presenting
a mixed programme of in-house and guest
productions, the theatre stages 6-8 shows
each year in its main auditorium and studio theatres. Also runs TIE, Outreach and
Community programmes. Recent productions include: *Tally's Blood, Educating Rita*
and *Much Ado About Nothing.*

Casting procedures
Holds general auditions. Actors may write
at any time requesting inclusion. Casting
breakdowns are obtainable via postal
application (with sae). Welcomes submissions (with CVs and photographs) sent by
post or email. Also accepts invitations to
view individual actors' websites.

Chichester Festival Theatre
Oaklands Park, Chichester PO19 6AP
Artistic Directors Ruth MacKenzie, Steven
Pimlott, Martin Duncan
Casting Director Maggie Lunn
Executive Director Maggie Saxon

Production details
Consists of the main house set in park-
land, the Minerva Studio and a multi-
purpose auditorium. In-house plays and
musicals are produced in the main house
during the festival season (April-
September) and family shows at
Christmas. The Minerva Studio places
emphasis on new and experimental work
during the festival and also stages an in-
house Christmas production. 4 productions are staged both in the main house

and the Minerva Studio each year. Also
runs TIE, Outreach and Community programmes (contact Alison Roden). Recent
productions include: *The Merchant of
Venice, Pinocchio, The Seagull* and Gilbert
& Sullivan's *The Gondoliers.*

Casting procedures
Occasionally holds general auditions.
Actors should write in December or
January requesting inclusion. Welcomes
submissions (with CVs and photographs)
sent by post or email.

Citizens' Theatre
Gorbals, Glasgow G5 9DS
tel 0141-429 5561 *fax* 0141-429 7374
website www.citz.co.uk
Artistic Director Jeremy Raison
Company Manager Lynn Pullen

Production details
Producing theatre with annual guest
seasons in March/April and host to the
Scottish Youth Theatre Summer Festival.
Stages 3-4 shows in the main auditorium
and 3-4 in the studio theatre each year.
Also runs Education and Outreach
programmes (contact Lynn Pullen).

Casting procedures
Does not use freelance casting directors.
Sometimes holds general auditions. Actors
should write in April requesting inclusion.
Welcomes letters (with CVs and pho-
tographs) but not email submissions.

Clwyd Theatr Cmyru
Mold, Flintshire CH7 1YA
tel (01352) 756331 *fax* (01352) 701558
email mail@clwyd-theatr-cymru.co.uk
website www.clwyd-theatr.cymru.co.uk
Artistic Director Terry Hands
Associate Director Tim Baker
Casting Director Gary Howe (freelancing)

Production details
A major drama-producing company in
Wales. Although most work is presented in
English, some pieces are performed in
Welsh. Stages 5-6 shows in the main house
and 5-6 in the studio each year, with some
mid/large-scale productions touring Wales
and England. Also runs TIE programmes.
Recent productions include: *Rosencrantz,
O What a Lovely War, Song of the Earth*
(trilogy based on Welsh classic novels) and
The Rabbit (new writing from Wales).

Casting procedures
Uses freelance casting directors and does
not welcome enquiries from actors.

Coliseum Theatre
Fairbottom Street, Oldham OL1 3SW
tel 0161-624 1731 *fax* 0161-624 5318
email mail@coliseum.org.uk
website www.coliseum.org.uk
Artistic Director Kevin Shaw
Administrator Joanne Moss

Production details
A traditional repertory theatre producing
8-10 shows each year, with additional
incoming tours and one-off special events.
Also runs TIE, Outreach and Community
programmes (contact Justine Potter
Williams). Recent productions include:
*From a Jack to a King, Brighton
Beach Memoirs* and *I'll be back before
Midnight.*

Casting procedures
Does not use freelance casting directors.
Sometimes holds general auditions; actors
should write in January requesting inclusion. Casting breakdowns are available
through postal application (with sae).
Welcomes letters (with CVs and photographs) but not email submissions. Also
accepts invitations to view individual
actors' websites.

Crucible Theatre
55 Norfolk Street, Sheffield S1 1DA
tel 0114-249 5999 *fax* 0114-249 6003
email info@sheffieldtheatres.co.uk
website www.sheffieldtheatres.co.uk
Associate Directors Michael Grandage,
Anna Mackmin
Chief Executive Grahame Morris
Director of Education Karen Simpson

Production details
Comprises 2 theatres: the Crucible Theatre
(thrust stage, 960 capacity) and the Studio
Theatre (approximately 200 capacity).
Stages 5-6 shows each year in the main
house and 3-4 in the studio. Also runs TIE
programmes. Recent productions include:
The Firework-Master's Daughter by Philip
Pullman, *A Midsummer Night's Dream* and
various new plays.

Casting procedures
Uses freelance casting directors. Casting
breakdowns available twice yearly (June
and October) by postal application (with
sae) to theatre. Welcomes letters (with CVs
and photographs) but suggests that realistically, this may not be the most productive
use of actors' resources. If writing: 'Take
the trouble to find out who to write to!"

Derby Playhouse
Theatre Walk, Eagle Centre, Derby DE1
2NF
tel (01332) 363271 *fax* (01332) 547200
Co-Artistic Leaders Karen Hebden,
Stephen Edwards
Associate Director Uzma Hameed
Casting Director Samantha Relph

Production details
Stages 8 shows in the main house each year.
Also runs Outreach and Community
programmes (contact Kim Miller). Recent
productions include: *My Dad's Corner Shop,
Oh What a Lovely War* and *Blithe Spirit.*

Casting procedures
Welcomes letters (with CVs and photographs) but not email submissions. Actors should write (enclosing sae) in March and September. Showreels and invitations to view individual actors' websites are also accepted.

Donmar Warehouse

41 Earlham Street, London WC2H 9LX
tel 020-7240 4882
website www.donmarwarehouse.com
Artistic Director Michael Grandage
Executive Producer Nick Frankfort
General Manager Tobias Round
Development Director Naomi Russell
Casting Director Anne McNulty

Production details
Independent producing house located in Covent Garden. The building originally served as a vat room and hop warehouse for the local brewery. In 1961 it was purchased by Donald Albery and converted into a rehearsal studio for the London Festival Ballet, which he formed with ballerina Margot Fonteyn. It takes its name from them. In the 1990s the Donmar was redesigned. The current theatre space retains the characteristics of the former warehouse while incorporating a new thrust stage. Recent productions include: *Caligula*, *Proof* and *Pacific Overtures*.

The Dukes

Moor Lane, Lancaster LA1 1QE
tel (01524) 598505 *fax* (01524) 598579
website www.dukes-lancaster.org
Artistic Director Ian Hastings
Theatre Secretary and PA to Artistic Director Jacqui Wilson

Production details
A producing theatre with an independent cinema. Stages 5 shows each year in the main house (313 seats) and 1 in the studio (178 seats) with a focus on contemporary drama and outdoor site-specific productions. Also runs a Youth Arts programme (contact Helen Clugston). Recent productions include: *What the Butler Saw*, *Mojo*, *Dancing at Lughnasa* and *Arabian Nights* (outdoor production).

Casting procedures
Does not use freelance casting directors. Casting breakdowns are obtainable through the website, postal application (with sae), Equity Job Information Service and *PCR*. Welcomes letters (with CVs and photographs) but not email submissions. Showreels and invitations to view individual actors' websites are also accepted.

Dundee Repertory Theatre

Tay Square, Dundee DD1 1PB
tel (01382) 227684 *fax* (01382) 228609
website www.dundeerep.co.uk
Artistic Director Dominic Hill
Chief Executive James Brining

Production details
Producing theatre housing Dundee Repertory Ensemble, Scotland's only permanent acting company. Stages 6 shows each year in the main house. Also runs TIE, Outreach and Community programmes (contact James Brining/Dominic Hill). Recent productions include: *Peter Pan* and *Twelfth Night*.

Casting procedures
Does not use freelance casting directors. Welcomes letters (with CVs and photographs) but not email submissions. Actors should write in the spring.

Gate Theatre

Above Prince Albert Pub, 11 Pembridge Road, London W11 3HQ

tel 020-7229 0906 *fax* 020-7221 6055
email gate@gatetheatre.freeserve.co.uk
website www.gatetheatre.co.uk
Artistic Director Erica Whyman
Literary Associate Penny Black
Producer Tali Pelman

Production details

Presents new writing and undiscovered
classics from around the world in original
and visually imaginative productions.
Stages 7-9 shows each year in the main
house. Also runs a Community programme (contact Erica Whyman). Recent
productions include: *Electra* by Jean
Giraudoux, *The Riot Act* by Tom Paulin,
and *Angels of the Universe* by Icelandic
Take-Away Theatre.

Casting procedures

Does not use freelance casting directors.
Welcomes letters (with CVs and photographs) but not email submissions.
'Individual directors tend to cast from
their own lists —contact with the director
is the best way to ensure that your
application is considered.'

Greenwich Theatre

Crooms Hill, Greenwich, London SE10 8ES
Executive Director Hilary Strong
Associate Director Kenneth Richardson

Production details

Currently mainly receiving touring
productions but occasionally produces
shows in-house. Stages 2 productions each
year in the main house. Recent
productions include: *The External*
(with Prunella Scales and Timothy West),
Sadly Solo Joe and *Golden Boy* (musicals).

Casting procedures

Uses freelance casting directors. 'We don't
respond to unsolicited applications but do
run a professional artists' network and are

interested to hear from performers based
in Greenwich.'

Haymarket Theatre

Wote Street, Basingstoke RG21 7NW
tel (01256) 323073
email Barbara@haymarket.org.uk
website www.haymarket.org.uk
Artistic Director to be announced
PA to Artistic Director Barbara Lilley
Executive Director Zöe Curnow

Production details

Has been producing repertory theatre
since the 1970s using a rolling ensemble
cast. Stages 7 shows each year in the main
house, from light comedy to musicals and
with an emphasis on its international
repertoire. Also runs TIE, Outreach and
Community programmes (contact Alice
Bartlett). Recent productions include:
Daughter-in-Law, April in Paris, Tartuffe
and *Good Golly Miss Molly.*

Casting procedures

Does not use freelance casting directors.
Sometimes holds general auditions; actors
should write in May requesting inclusion.
Welcomes submissions (with CVs and
photographs) sent by post or email. 'We
currently run an ensemble for the autumn
season, then cast individually for the spring.'

Key Theatre

Embankment Road, Peterborough,
Cambridgeshire PE1 1EF
tel (01733) 552437 *fax* (01733) 567025
email michaelcross@thekeytheatre.co.uk
website www.peterboroughkeytheatre.co.uk
Artistic Director Michael Cross
Youth Theatre Officer Paul Collings

Production details

Mainly a receiving house with occasional
in-house productions including an annual

pantomime and TIE company. Stages 4
shows each year in the main house and
1 in the studio. Recent productions
include: *Macbeth, Tom and Mollie's
Jungle Adventure, West End Nights* and
Pinnochio.

Casting procedures
Does not use freelance casting directors.
Sometimes holds general auditions.
Unsolicited communications are
not advised. Casting breakdowns are
sometimes available through the website,
postal application (with sae), Equity Job
Information Service, *PCR* and advertisements in *The Stage.* 'If you are at the
theatre on tour, make a point of visiting
the resident casting officer just to introduce yourself and, if possible, invite them
to the show."

Library Theatre Company
St Peter's Square, Manchester M2 5PD
tel 0161-234 1913 *fax* 0161-228 6481
email ltc@libraries manchester.gov.uk
website www.librarytheatre.com
Artistic Director Chris Honer
Associate Director Roger Haines

Production details
Regional producer of contemporary
drama. Also produces 1 play for families
and children at Christmas. Produces 5-6
shows each year in the main house. Also
runs an Education programme (contact
Liz Postlethwaite). Recent productions
include: *Top Girls, Translations, Schweyk in
the Second World War, Tom's Midnight
Garden, Who's Afraid of Virginia Woolf* and
The Memory of Water.

Casting procedures
Does use freelance casting directors.
Welcomes letters (with CVs and
photographs) but not email submissions.
Actors should write in March or

April. 'Read the plays in our programme
and submit yourself for a specific part
about 12 weeks before the first
performance."

Live Theatre
27 Broad Chare, Quayside, Newcastle upon
Tyne NE1 3DQ
tel 0191-261 2694 *fax* 0191-232 2224
email info@live.org.uk
website www.live.org.uk
Artistic Director Max Roberts
Associate Directors Jeremy Herrin, Paul
James

Production details
New writing theatre established in
1973. Produces 3-4 shows each year in
the main house and 1-2 in the studio
theatre. Also runs TIE, Outreach and
Community programmes (contact Paul
James).

Casting procedures
Does not use freelance casting directors.
Welcomes submissions (with CVs and
photographs) sent by post or email. Actors
may write at any time. Showreels and invitations to view individual actors' websites
are also accepted.

Lyric Theatre
55 Ridgeway Street, Belfast BT9 5FB
email claire@lyrictheatre.co.uk
website www.lyrictheatre.co.uk
Artistic Director Paula McFetridge
General Manager Mike Blair
Education Officer Una Nic Eoin
Production Assistant Clare Gault

Production details
Northern Ireland's only full-time
producer of professional theatre.
Presents a distinctive, challenging and
entertaining programme of new writing

as well as contemporary and classic plays by Irish, European and American writers. Stages 7 shows each year in the main house. Also runs an Education programme. Recent productions include: *The Star Catcher, New Year's Eve Can Kill You, Ghosts* and *Observe the Sons of Ulster Marching.*

Casting procedures
Does not use freelance casting directors. Welcomes submissions (with CVs and photographs) sent by post or email. Actors should write in July. Advises actors to check the website for its future programme.

Lyric Theatre Hammersmith
Lyric Theatre Hammersmith, King Street, London W6 0QL
tel (020) 8741 0824 *fax* (020) 8741 5965
email enquiries@lyric.co.uk
website www.lyric.co.uk
Artistic Director Neil Bartlett

Production details
Produces and co-produces original theatre for a wide audience. Currently working to redevelop the theatre, creating 2 new spaces —a purpose-built rehearsal studio and education/training room. The theatre runs an extensive Education programme and focuses on working with disadvantaged communities and young people in the local area. For further information contact the Education Administrator, Herta Queirazza. Recent productions include: *Oliver Twist* (adapted and directed by Neil Bartlett), and *Good & True/Be Proud of Me* (presented by Stan's Café).

Casting details
Recent productions have been cast by Siobhan Bracke. See separate entry under *Casting Directors.*

Manor Pavilion Theatre
Manor Road, Sidmouth, Devon EX10 8RP
tel 020-7636 4343 *fax* 020-7636 2323
email cvtheatre@aol.com
Artistic Director Charles Vance
Associate Director Imogen Vance

Production details
Summer repertory theatre with a 3-month season (July-September). Now in its 18th year of operation of weekly repertory theatre. Stages 12 shows each year in the main house.

Casting procedures
Welcomes letters (with CVs and photographs) but not email submissions. Actors should write in February sending application to Head Office, Hampden House, 2 Weymouth Street W1W 5BT.

Mercury Theatre
Balkerne Gate, Colchester, Essex CO1 1PT
tel (01206) 577006 *fax* (01206) 769607
email info@mercurytheatre.co.uk
website www.mercurytheatre.co.uk
Chief Executive Dee Evans
Associate Directors Janice Dunn, Adrian Stokes, David Hunt, Nix Rosewarne, Michael Vale

Production details
A regional repertory theatre which opened in 1972, producing 3 ensemble shows each season. Stages 6 shows each year in the main house and 1-2 in the studio. Also runs a Community programme (contact Adrian Stokes). Recent productions include: *Romeo and Juliet, The Europeans, The Three Sisters, The White Devil* and *All My Sons.*

Casting procedures
Each show is cast by the director from within the ensemble. 'Prefer for actors to build up a relationship with the artistic team rather than approach by letter or email."

New Vic Theatre
Etruria Road, Newcastle-under-Lyme ST5 OJG
tel (01782) 717954 *fax* (01782) 712885
email admin@newvictheatre.org.uk
Artistic Director Gwenda Hughes
General Manager Nick Jones

Production details
Purpose-built theatre-in-the-round with a full programme of in-house drama, concerts and occasional touring productions. Stages 10 shows each year in the main house. Also very active with Outreach and Education programmes (contact Sue Moffat and Jill Rezzano respectively). Recent productions include: *Sweeney Todd, My Night with Reg, The Duchess of Malfi, Kes* and *The Marriage of Figaro*.

Casting procedures
Does not use freelance casting directors. Casting breakdowns are obtainable by postal application (with sae). Welcomes letters (with CVs and photographs) but not email submissions. Submissions should be specific and referenced to a particular role. Also accepts invitations to view individual actors' websites.

Nottingham Playhouse
Wellington Circus, Nottingham NG1 5AF
Artistic Director Giles Croft
Associate Director Richard Baron
Casting Director Sooki McShane
Director of Roundabout and Education Andrew Breakwell

Production details
Nottingham Theatre Trust was founded in 1946 and moved to its current location in 1963. Stages 8 shows each year in the main house and 5 Roundabout productions. Also runs TIE, Outreach and Community programmes. Recent productions include: *Rat Pack Confidential, Ethel and Ernest* and *Polygraph* (main house); *Walking the Tightrope* and *Mohammed* (Roundabout).

Casting procedures
Does not use freelance casting directors. Casting breakdowns are available from the casting director, Sooki McShane. Welcomes letters (with CVs and photographs) but not email submissions. Showreels and invitations to view individual actors' websites are also accepted.

Nuffield Theatre
University Road, Southampton SO17 1TR
tel 023-8031 5500 *fax* 023-8031 5511
email info@nuffieldtheatre.co.uk
website nuffieldtheatre.co.uk
Artistic Director Patrick Sandford
Associate Director Russ Tunney
Administrative Director Kate Anderson

Production details
A regional theatre performing a range of classic plays and new writing. Stages 5-7 shows each year in the main house, and 3-4 in the studio. Also runs TIE, Outreach and Community programmes. Recent productions include: *Hamlet, When We Are Rich* (new writing commission), *Not Now Bernard* (touring Primary schools) and *Mr Benn*.

Casting procedures
Uses freelance casting directors. Holds local auditions for actors in the Southampton area. Actors may write at any time requesting inclusion. Casting breakdowns are sometimes available through *PCR* or Equity Job Information Service.

Octagon Theatre
Howell Croft South, Bolton BL1 1SB
tel (01204) 529407 *fax* (01204) 556502
email info@octagonbolton.co.uk
website www.octagonbolton.co.uk
Artistic Director Mark Babych

Executive Director John Blackmore
Head of Production Lesley Chenery

Production details
Stages 8-9 shows each year in the main house and 18 in the studio. Also runs TIE, Outreach and Community programmes (contact Activ8 Department). Recent productions include: *Score* (TIE tour), *Boston Marriage*, *Carmen*, *Cooking with Elvis* and *The Weir*.

Casting procedures
Does not use freelance casting directors. Actors may write requesting inclusion in the company at any time and should enclose an sae. Accepts invitations to view individual actors' websites.

Open Air Theatre
Inner Circle, Regent's Park,
London NW1 4NR
Artistic Director Ian Talbot
Casting Directors Ian Talbot, Jane Salberg
Office Manager Shona McCarthy

Production details
Stages 4 shows each year in the main house and 1 in the studio theatre. Recent productions include: *A Midsummer Night's Dream*, *Two Gentlemen of Verona* and *High Society*.

Casting procedures
Uses freelance casting directors. Sometimes holds general auditions. Actors should write in January or February requesting inclusion. Welcomes submissions (with CVs and photographs) sent by post or email. Also accepts showreels and invitations to view individual actors' websites.

Orange Tree Theatre
1 Clarence Street, Richmond TW9 2SA
tel 020-8940 0141 *fax* 020-8332 0369
email admin@orange-tree.demon.co.uk
website www.orangetreetheatre.co.uk
Artistic Director Sam Walters

Production details
'The Orange Tree Theatre is wholly concerned with the performance of quality live theatre and reaching as wide an audience as possible with its work. Over the 30 years of its existence it has established a reputation for being the leader in its field and is the only permanent theatre-in-the-round in London.' Presents a mixture of new writing, classic plays, comedies and musicals. Education and Community work forms a major area of activity. Stages 7 shows each year.

Casting procedures
Does not use freelance casting directors. Casting breakdowns are obtainable by postal application (with sae). Welcomes letters (with CVs and photographs) but not email submissions. Also accepts invitations to view individual actors' websites.

Perth Theatre
185 High Street, Perth PH1 5UW
tel (01738) 472700 *fax* (01738) 624576
email info@perththeatre.co.uk
website www.perththeatre.co.uk
Artistic Director to be confirmed
Secretary Elaine White
Education Officer Jennifer McGregor

Production details
Scotland's longest-established theatre company with a mixed programme of in-house and guest productions throughout the year, including drama, musical theatre and pantomime. Produces 6-7 shows each year. Also runs Outreach and Community programmes. Recent productions include: *Kidnapped*, *Mother Goose*, *Faith Healer* and *Educating Rita*.

Casting procedures
Does not use freelance casting directors. Welcomes submissions (with CVs and photographs) sent by post or email. Actors should write in the spring. Also accepts

invitations to view individual actors' websites.

Pitlochry Festival Theatre

Port-Na-Craig, Pitlochry PH16 5DR
tel (01796) 484600 *fax* (01796) 484616
email admin@pitlochry.org.uk
website www.pitlochry.org.uk
Artistic Director John Durnin
Chief Executive Nikki Axford
Community and Education Director
Colette McLaughlin

Production details

Founded in 1951, Pitlochry Festival
Theatre is a producing and presenting theatre located in the Perthshire Highlands.
Comprises main house (capacity 544), an
extensive production facility, and the
Scottish Plant Collectors Garden, containing a number of open-air performance
spaces. Between April and October each
year a 20-strong acting ensemble presents
a season of 6 major productions performed in day-change repertoire. Visiting
theatre, music, dance, opera and other
activities are presented during the winter
months. Also runs TIE and Community
programmes. Recent productions include:
*The Matchmaker, Double Indemnity, The
Steamie, Stepping Out, Man and Superman*
and *The Haunted Man.*

Casting procedures

Does not use freelance casting directors.
Recruits new members of the acting
ensemble each autumn and winter with a
detailed casting breakdown published
each October. Auditions are then held in
London and Edinburgh in November,
December and January. Casting breakdowns are obtainable by postal application (with sae) from September.
Submissions at any other time will not be
considered.

Queen's Theatre

Billet Lane, Hornchurch, Essex RM11 1QT
Artistic Director Bob Carlton
Associate Director Matt Devitt
Education Manager Samantha Lane
Administrator Henrietta Duckworth

Production details

Has been a producing theatre since it was
first established in 1953. Currently works
with actor musicians in a permanent
repertory company model. Stages 9 shows
each year in the main house. Also runs
TIE, Outreach and Community programmes. Recent productions include: *A
Midsummer Night's Dream, Jane Eyre* and
Return of the Forbidden Planet.

Casting procedures

Does not use freelance casting directors.
Holds general auditions; actors should
write in April or May requesting inclusion.
Welcomes letters (with CVs and photographs) from actor musicians only.

Royal Court Theatre

Sloane Square, London SW1W 8AS
tel 020-7565 5050 *fax* 020-7565 5001
email info@royalcourttheatre.com
website www.royalcourttheatre.com
Artistic Director Ian Rickson
Associate Director Marianne Elliott
Casting Directors Lisa Makin, Amy Ball

Production details

Since 1956 the English Stage Company
at the Royal Court has focused on
developing, funding and producing new
writing. Productions frequently transfer
to the West End and Broadway. Stages 6
productions each year in the Jerwood
Theatre downstairs and 8 upstairs. Also
presents programmes of rehearsed
readings (contact Lisa Makin). Recent productions include: *Hitchcock Blonde* by
Terry Johnson, *A Number* by Caryl

Churchill and *Terrorism* by Presnyakov Brothers.

Casting procedures
Welcomes submissions (with CVs and photographs) by post or email. Also accepts showreels and invitations to view individual actors' websites.

Royal Exchange Theatre
St Ann's Square, Manchester M2 7DH
tel 0161-833 9833
website www. royalexchange.co.uk
Artistic Directors Greg Hersov, Braham Murray
Casting Directors Jerry Knight-Smith, Camilla Evans
Education Director Amanda Dalton

Production details
Manchester's leading producing theatre company, comprising a main theatre and studio space. Presents 7-8 productions, on average, in the main theatre and 5-6 in the studio each year. Also runs Education and Community programmes involving schools, young people, community groups and theatre enthusiasts of all ages. Work is based around the theatre's repertoire and its unique building. Where possible the department leads sessions in the theatre and frequently works with other departments around the building to give participants an insight into how theatre, and particularly the Royal Exchange, works. Recent productions include: *Great Expectations, Major Barbara, The Importance of Being Earnest* and *Six Degrees of Separation.*

Casting procedures
Has a casting department of 2 who coordinate casting for each show. Actors are contracted for individual plays rather than for a season of work. Occasionally holds general auditions, but this depends

on the director. Releases advance production information to around 200 agents on their website, and to the Actors Centres for their noticeboards. Detailed casting breakdowns are only available for some shows.

Will consider attending performances at venues in the North West and London with sufficient notice. Accepts submissions (with CVs and photographs), but actors should bear in mind that the department expects to receive more than 2000 CVs and photos each season and more in the summer months following graduation at the drama schools. All submissions are considered while a season is being cast (a period of 4-6 months) but they are not kept on file indefinitely.

Also operates a 'cover' system which has been agreed with Equity. Employs 1 actor and 1 actress on each production who read-in for some, or all, of the male and female roles should they be indisposed. These actors are contracted on Equity minimum payment to be at the theatre throughout each show for this purpose, and must therefore be based in Manchester.

Royal National Theatre
South Bank, London SE1 9PX
tel 020-7452 3335 *fax* 020-7452 3340
email info@nationaltheatre.org.uk
website www.nt-online.org
Artistic Director Nicolas Hytner
Head of Casting Toby Whale CDG
Assistant Casting Director Gabrielle Dawes

Production details
A National Theatre was first proposed in 1848. In 1951 a foundation stone was laid by the Royal Festival Hall, and in 1962 Sir Laurence Olivier was appointed the National's first director, based at London's Old Vic Theatre. Finally, in 1976, the new NT officially opened with a production of *Hamlet.* Today, the National stages a range

of classics, musicals, new plays and entertainment 'for all the family". It comprises 3 theatres: the Olivier (open-stage, capacity 1120 people), the Lyttleton (proscenium arch, capacity 890) and the Cottesloe (studio theatre on 3 levels with flexible staging, capacity 300). Recent productions include: *Democracy, The Permanent Way, Jerry Springer – The Opera, Jumpers* and *Anything Goes.*

Casting details

The National Theatre's casting team works with approximately 10 directors a year casting NT shows. Actors known to the theatre may be approached directly, but casting is predominantly carried out thorough agents. The NT will first approach agents to check actors' availability, then audition a shortlist. New talent is actively sought out and the casting team sees several performances a week within London and (less frequently) outside. It also attends drama schools' showcases and will sometimes approach other casting directors known to the NT.

Royal Shakespeare Company (Casting Department)

1 Earlham Street, London WC2H 9LL
tel 020-7845 0500 *fax* 020-7845 0505
email casting.coordinator@rsc.org.uk
website www.rsc.org.uk
Artistic Director Michael Boyd
Casting Director John Cannon
Casting Coordinator Hannah Miller

Production details

One of the best-known theatre companies in the world, the RSC has been operating under its present name since 1961, a year after Peter Hall was appointed director. The repertoire was widened at this time to include modern writing and classics other than Shakespeare. Over the next 30 years the company continued to expand under the artistic directorships of Peter Hall, Trevor Nunn, Terry Hands and Adrian Noble. Michael Boyd succeeded Adrian Noble as artistic director in 2003. The RSC is formed around an ensemble of actors and core of associate actors who are committed to a 'distinctive and unmissable approach to theatre". Stages approximately 15 productions each year. Recent productions include: *Midnight's Children, Alice in Wonderland, Julius Caesar, The Merry Wives of Windsor* and *Brand.*

Casting procedures

Welcomes letters (with CVs and photographs) but not email submissions.

Salisbury Playhouse

Malthouse Lane, Salisbury SP2 7RA
Artistic Director Joanna Read
Casting Coordinator John Manning

Production details

Stages 9 productions each year in the main house and 3 in the studio. Also runs an Outreach programme (contact Gill Foreman).

Casting procedures

Casting breakdowns are available by postal application (with sae). Welcomes submissions (with CVs and photographs) by post or email. Actors should write in August or January. Also accepts invitations to view individual actors' websites.

Shakespeare's Globe

21 New Globe Walk, Bankside, London SE1 9DT
tel 020-7902 1400 *fax* 020-7902 1401
email info@shakespearesglobe.com
website www.shakespeares-globe.org
Artistic Director Mark Rylance
Casting Director Siobhan Bracke
Theatre Administrator Rowan Walker-Brown

Production details

A reconstruction of Shakespeare's Globe, the theatre has a repertoire which includes the work of Shakespeare, his contemporaries and new writing. The season runs from May to October with 3-5 productions staged each year. Also runs Outreach and Community programmes (contact Deborah Callan in the Education Department). Recent productions include: *Richard II, Richard III, The Taming of the Shrew,* Marlowe's *Edward II* and *Dido, Queen of Carthage.*

Casting procedures

Welcomes letters (with CVs and photographs) but not email submissions. Actors should write to Siobhan Bracke (not Mark Rylance) in January.

Sherman Theatre

Senghennydd Road, Cardiff CF24 4YE
tel 029-2064 6901 *fax* 029-2064 6902
website www.shermantheatre.demon.co.uk
Artistic Director Phil Clark
Associate Director Stephen Fisher

Production details

Stages 2 shows each year.

Casting procedures

Does not use freelance casting directors. Sometimes holds general auditions. Welcomes letters (with CVs and photographs) but not email submissions. Also accepts invitations to view individual actors' websites.

Soho Theatre

21 Dean Street, London W1D 3NE
Artistic Director Abigail Morris
Associate Director Jonathan Lloyd
(Freelance) Casting Director Ginny Schiller
Administrative Producer Mark Godfrey

Production details

The Soho Theatre is a new writing venue, staging 8 productions each year. Also runs Outreach and Community programmes (contact Jonathan Lloyd), and presents some guest productions and rehearsed readings. Recent productions include: *Mr Nobody, Protection, A Reckoning* and *Dirty Butterfly.*

Casting procedures

Uses freelance casting directors. Welcomes submissions (with CVs and photographs) by post or email. Actors may write at any time.

Southwold & Aldeburgh Summer Theatre

14 York House, Upper Montagu Street, London W1H 1FR
tel 020-7724 5432 *fax* 020-7724 3210
Artistic Director Jill Freud
Associate Director Anthony Falkingham
Company Coordinator Carol Carey

Production details

Summer theatre with an extensive programme. Stages 15 productions each year in the main house and 14 in the studio. Recent productions include: *Stepping Out, Neville's Island, Blithe Spirit, Dry Rot* and 6 guest children's shows.

Casting procedures

Does not use freelance casting directors. Holds general auditions; actors should write in November requesting inclusion. Casting breakdowns are available by phone. Welcomes letters (with CVs and photographs) but not email submissions, and advises that they cannot see everyone who writes to them.

Stephen Joseph Theatre

Westborough, Scarborough YO11 1JW
tel (01273) 370540 *fax* (01273) 360506
email sarah.hughes@sjt.uk.com

website www.sjt.uk.com
Artistic Director Alan Ayckbourn
Associate Director Laurie Sansom
Casting Director Sarah Hughes
Administrator Stephen Wood

Production details
Stages 6-7 productions each year with
lunchtime shows, late nights, rural and
national touring. Most work is new writing.
Recent productions include: *Making Waves,
Bedtime Stories* and *Sugar Daddies.*

Casting procedures
Does not use freelance casting directors.
Sometimes holds general auditions; actors
may write at any time requesting inclusion.
Welcomes submissions (with CVs and
photographs) by post or email. Also
accepts showreels and invitations to view
individual actors' websites.

Theatre by the Lake
Lakeside Keswick, Cumbria CA12 5DJ
Artistic Director Ian Forrest
Associate Director Stefan Escreet
Artistic Administrator Katherine Anderson
Youth Director Ian Douglas

Production details
Produces a summer season of 6 plays, an
Easter production and a Christmas
production each year. Also promotes a
touring programme of visiting professional
work across all artforms. Stages 5 shows
each year in the main theatre and 3 in the
studio. Also runs an Outreach programme.
Recent productions include: *The Tenant of
Wildfell Hall, Wallflowering, Kiss of the
Spiderwoman* and *Not a Game for Boys.*

Casting procedures
Does not use freelance casting directors.
Casting breakdowns are obtainable by
postal application (with sae). Does not
welcome submissions from actors.

Theatre Royal Stratford East
Gerry Raffles Square, London E15 1BN
tel 020-8534 7374 *fax* 020-8534 8381
email theatreroyal@stratfordeast.com
website www.stratfordeast.com
Artistic Director Philip Hedley
Deputy Artistic Director Kerry Michael
Resident Director Dawn Reid
Head of Education Caroline Barth

Production details
Committed to work which portrays the
experiences of different social and ethnic
communities, the theatre is constantly
striving to present shows which resonate
with its diverse local audiences. Stages 8
shows each year. Also runs TIE, Outreach
and Community programmes. Recent productions include: *Urban Afro Saxons,
People Next Door, Funny Black Women on
the Edge* and *Da Boyz.*

Casting procedures
Casting breakdowns are advertised on
their website. Welcomes submissions (with
CVs and photographs) sent by post or
email. Advises actors to research the theatre's work before writing and to think
carefully about their own suitability.
Invitations to view individual actors' websites also accepted.

Theatre Royal Windsor
Thames Street, Windsor SL4 1PS
tel (01753) 863444 *fax* (01753) 831673
website www.theatreroyalwindsor.co.uk
Artistic Director Mark Piper

Production details
A long-standing, non-subsidised
producing theatre. Shows run for
2-3 weeks. Stages 15 productions each
year with some going on to tour. Recent
productions include: *The Constant
Wife, The Boy Friend* and *The Chalk
Garden.*

Casting procedures
Does not use freelance casting directors.
Welcomes letters (with CVs and photographs) but not email submissions.

Torch Theatre

St Peter's Road, Milford Haven SA73 2BU
tel (01646) 694192 *fax* (01646) 698919
email info@torchtheatre.co.uk
website www.torchtheatre.co.uk
Artistic Director Peter Doran
PA to Artistic Director Lynn Muir
Casting Director Christine O'Reilly

Production details
Stages 4-5 productions each year. Recent
productions include: *Macbeth, One Flew
Over the Cuckoo's Nest* and *Blue
Remembered Hills.*

Casting procedures
Sometimes holds general auditions; actors
should write in June requesting inclusion.
Casting breakdowns are available by postal
application (with sae) and Equity Job
Information Service. Welcomes submissions (with CVs and photographs) sent by
post or email. Showreels and invitations to
view individual actors' websites are also
accepted. Advises actors to join their mailing list so they know what is being planned
6 months in advance.

Traverse Theatre

Cambridge Street, Edinburgh EH1 2ED
tel 0131-228 3223 *fax* 0131-229 8443
email neil@traverse.co.uk
website www.traverse.co.uk
Artistic Director Philip Howard
Associate Director Roxanna Silbert
Casting Director/Literary Assistant Neil Coull

Production details
Scotland's only theatre committed to new
writing. Presents a mixed programme of
in-house and guest productions. Stages 4
shows each year in the main house and 2
in the studio. Also runs Outreach and
Script Development programmes (contact
Neil Coull). Recent productions include:
People Next Door by Henry Adam, *Dark
Earth* by David Harrower, *Iron* by Rona
Munro and *Outlying Island* by David
Greig.

Casting procedures
Does not use freelance casting directors.
Welcomes letters (with CVs and
photographs) but not email submissions.
Actors should write in January, June or
September. Particularly interested to hear
from Scottish actors. Invitations to view
individual actors' websites are also
accepted.

Warehouse Theatre

Dingwall Road, Croydon CR20 2NF
Artistic Director Ted Craig
Administrative Director Evita Bier
Education Coordinator Rose-Marie Vernon

Production details
Runs TIE and Community programmes.
Recent productions include: *Knock Dow
Ginger, Miss Julie* and *Dick Barton V.*

Casting procedures
Uses freelance casting directors. Welcomes
submissions (with CVs and photographs)
sent by post or email. Actors may write at
any time.

Watermill Theatre

Bagnor, Nr Newbury RG20 8AE
tel (01635) 45834 *fax* (01635) 523726
website www.watermill.org.uk
Artistic Director Jill Fraser
Associate Directors John Doyle, Edward
Hall, Euan Smith
Outreach Director Ade Morris

Production details
A producing theatre where actors live on
site. Stages 6 shows each year with runs of
6-8 weeks, and 2 Outreach tours. Recent
productions have included: Shakespeare,
Music Theatre, New Writing and Classics.

Casting procedures
Does not use freelance casting directors.
Casting breakdowns are available by postal
application (with sae) but actors should
call first. Welcomes letters (with CVs and
photographs) with reference to specific
castings only.

West Yorkshire Playhouse

Playhouse Square, Quarry Hill,
Leeds LS2 7UP
tel 0113-213 7800 *fax* 0113-213 7250
website www.wyp.org.uk
Artistic Director Ian Brown
Producer Paul Crewes
Casting Director Kay Magson (for all cast-
ing related matters)

Production details
Founded in 1990, the West Yorkshire
Playhouse has 2 auditoria, the Quarry (750
seats) and the Courtyard (350 seats).
Works include new writing, classics,
Shakespeare and musicals as well as guest
productions from incoming touring com-
panies. Also runs TIE, Outreach and
Community programmes (contact Gail
McIntyre). Their schools company tours 3
times a year. Stages 15-17 productions each
year across both theatre spaces. Recent
productions include: *Hamlet, Singin' in the
Rain, The Wind in the Willows* and *Off
Camera.*

Casting procedures
Sometimes holds general auditions; actors
should write in September or March
requesting inclusion. Casting breakdowns
are available by postal application

(with sae). Welcomes letters (with
CVs and photographs) but not email
submissions.

York Theatre Royal

St Leonard's Place, York YO1 7HD
tel (01904) 658162 *fax* (01904) 611534
website www.yorktheatreroyal.co.uk
Artistic Director Damian Cruden
Chief Executive Ludo Keston

Production details
One of the oldest theatres in the country,
it seats 867 in the main theatre and 106
in the studio. Productions include
classics, new writing and the famous
York pantomime every Christmas. Also
hosts touring companies, premieres and
has a resident young people's company
(Pilot Theatre). Stages 7-8 shows each
year in the main theatre and 6-7 in
the studio. Also runs Outreach and
Community programmes (contact Gill
Adamson). Recent productions include:
Old Mother Goose, Noel Coward's *Private
Lives, Single Spies* by Alan Bennett, and
Bryony Lavery's *Behind the Scenes at the
Museum.*

Casting procedures
Does not use freelance casting directors.
Does not welcome submissions from
actors.

Young Vic

66 The Cut, London SE1 8LZ
tel 020-7922 8400 *fax* 020-7922 8401
email info@youngvic.org
website www.youngvic.org
Artistic Director David Lan
Associate Artistic Director Sue Emmas

Production details
Stages 9 productions each year in the
main house and 2 in the studio. Also

runs TIE, Outreach and Community
programmes (contact Sue Emmas). Recent
productions include: *Skellig* by David
Almond (directed by Trevor Nunn),
Hobson's Choice adapted by Tankia Gupta
(directed by Richard Jones), and *Simply*

Heavenly by Langston Hughes (directed by
Josette Bushell-Mingo).

Casting procedures
Uses freelance casting directors. Does not
welcome submissions from actors.

Independent Managements / Theatre Producers

This section mostly lists commercial organisations that mount West End and touring productions to larger-scale venues – some of which originate in the subsidised sector. Most such productions will be led by well-known actors, but they will usually need supporting actors who can also understudy those leads. (In the West End the under-studies get a chance to do their own performance of the production – a useful oppor-tunity to 'showcase' for agents and casting directors.) Sometimes, such a production will tour to try it out before (hopefully) coming into the West End; at others, a manage-ment will tour to 'milk' further profits from a West End success.

On tour, apart from 'Acting-ASMs' (assistant stage managers who also understudy), you shouldn't be asked to do any of the graft of get-ins and get-outs – unlike on smaller-scale touring. However, if you are also understudying, you will be expected to do an understudy rehearsal every week until the last stages of the tour. This rehearsal will probably be taken by the company manager (rarely, the director) and the whole ambience will feel very unsympathetic to good acting. Despite this, it is very important to be as fully prepared as possible for the chance that the 'name' you are understudying will be unavoidably delayed one night. Touring is fraught with potential delays, and a reputation for being able to 'deliver the goods' at very short notice will enhance future employment prospects. The downside of playing small parts and understudying is that you can become stuck doing this – a good agent will be able to advise in this area.

Touring is not for everyone: long periods away from home, wide variations in the quality of digs (often costing more in holiday resorts during the 'season'), and the fact that you could miss opportunities to be seen for other work are some of the potential disadvantages. On the plus side, contracts for large-scale tours are usually at least three months with at least a week in each venue, and you should have time to see some of the most beautiful sights in the UK (if not Europe and further afield) – 'Being paid to sight-see,' as a friend put it.

Although not as expensive as major films, such productions do cost a lot of money to mount and productions have been known to collapse suddenly without any warning. When accepting work in this area it is important to have a proper Equity contract.

Ambassador Theatre Group (ATG)

Duke of York's Theatre, 104 St Martin's Lane, London WC2N 4BG
Head of Production Meryl Faiers
Production Associate – Casting Neil Rutherford

Production details

ATG is the second-largest theatre owner and operator in the UK, with 22 venues (11 in the West End and 11 regional). It has produced around 22 productions in theatres and community venues across the UK, Japan, Italy and New York. Anywhere between 3 and 30 actors work on each production. Recent productions include: *Ragtime, See you Next Tuesday, Les Liaisons Dangereuses* and *Absolutely Perhaps!* playing to most major UK national venues and ATG venues in the West End.

Casting procedures

Uses freelance casting directors. Welcomes letters (with CVs and photographs) but not email submissions. Actors may write at any time, but prefers contact to be made via an agent and preferably during pre-production. Advises actors against sending expensive photos 'on spec', especially if unaccompanied by a letter.

Nick Brooke Ltd.

The Penthouse, 7 Leicester Place, London WC2H 7RJ
tel 020-7851 0393 *fax* 020-7734 7185
email info@nickbrooke.com
Directors Nick Brooke, Philip Noel

Production details

Founded in 2002 as an independent theatre production company, Nick Brooke Ltd. stages 2 productions each year, averaging an annual total of about 280 performances. Tours to approximately 30 theatres throughout England and Wales annually. In general 6-10 actors work on each production. Recent productions include: *Corpse* and *The Shell Seekers.*

Casting procedures

Occasionally employs freelance casting directors. Also holds general auditions; actors should write in January and in the early summer to request inclusion. Casting breakdowns are publicly available via the website and postal application. Welcomes submissions (with CVs and photographs) from actors previously unknown to the company if sent by post, but does not welcome email enquiries. Also accepts invitations to view individual actors' websites.

Ray Cooney Plays

Everglades, 29 Salmons Road, Chessington KT9 2JE
Director Ray Cooney
General Manager Alan Osman

Production details

Occasionally directs, but no longer produces, plays.

Casting procedures

Sometimes holds general auditions. Welcomes letters (with CVs and photographs) from actors previously unknown to the company, but not email submissions.

CV Productions Ltd.

Hampden House, 2 Weymouth Street, London W1W 5BT
tel 020-7636 4343 *fax* 020-7636 2323
email cvtheatre@aol.com
Director Charles Vance

Production details

Regional touring theatre company.

Casting procedures

Does not use freelance casting directors. Sometimes holds general auditions.

Casting breakdowns are not publicly available. Welcomes submissions (with CVs and photographs) sent by post or email. Invitations to view individual actors' websites are also accepted.

Andrew Fell Ltd.

4 Ching Court, 49-51 Monmouth Street, London WC2H 9EY
tel 020-7240 2420 *fax* 020-7240 2499
email nq@andrewfell.co.uk
Directors Andrew Fell, Sally Hoskins

Production details
Theatre production company and general management. Recent productions include: *Romeo and Juliet, The Lieutenant of Innishmore* and *Taboo*.

Casting procedures
Uses freelance casting directors.

Vanessa Ford Productions Ltd.

Upper House Farm, Upper House Lane, Shamley Green GU5 0SX
tel (01483) 278203 *fax* (01483) 271509
email Vanessa@vfpltd.fsnet.co.uk
website www.vfpltd.com
Managing Director Vanessa Ford
Director Glyn Robbins

Production details
Founded in 1979. Tours to approximately 30 theatres throughout the UK each year. On average, 14 actors work on each production. Recent productions include: *The Hobbit, A Christmas Carol* and *Shirley Valentine*.

Casting procedures
Occasionally uses freelance casting directors, and sometimes holds general auditions. Casting breakdowns are available on the website and through *The Spotlight*. Welcomes submissions (with CVs and

photographs) by post and email. Invitations to view individual actors' websites are also accepted.

Robert Fox Ltd.

6 Beauchamp Place, London SW3 1NG
tel 020-7584 6855 *fax* 020-7225 1638
email info@robertfoxltd.com
website www.robertfoxltd.com
Director Robert Fox

Production details
Founded in 1980. Theatre and film production company specialising in large-scale theatre productions and musicals as well as feature films. Performances are staged in the West End and on Broadway. Recent theatre productions include: *The Breath of Life, The Boy from Oz* and *Gypsy*. Also recently produced the feature films *The Hours* and *Iris*.

Casting procedures
Employs casting directors for specific projects and does not welcome unsolicited submissions from actors. Casting breakdowns are available on the website and details of casting directors are sometimes posted here as well.

David Graham Entertainments Ltd.

72 New Bond Street, London W15 1RR
tel 020-8977 6909 *fax* 020-8977 8707
email info@david graham.co.uk
website www.davidgraham.co.uk
Director David Graham

Production details
Theatre producer and concert promoter. Stages around 8 productions in 70-80 theatres and concert halls on an annual basis, totalling approximately 200 performances per year. Countries covered include Britain, Holland, Germany, Canada and Ireland. In general, 12

performers work on each production. Recent productions include: *The Real Monty, The Wonderful West End* and *Hold Tight, It's 60s Night.*

Casting procedures
Does not use freelance casting directors or hold general auditions. Casting breakdowns are available via the website, *PCR* and advertisements in *The Stage.*

Paul Holman Associates Ltd.
20 Deane Avenue, South Ruislip, Middlesex HA4 6SR
tel 020-8845 9408 *fax* 020-8582 2557
email paulholmanassociates@blueyonder. co.uk
website www.paulholmanassociates.co.uk
Director Paul Holman
Associate Producers Adrian Jeckells, John Ogle

Production details
Founded approximately 15 years ago. Produces pantomimes, summer shows and one-night attractions. Stages 10 productions annually at 10 or more theatre venues. On average, at least 10 actors work on each production. Recent productions include: *Peter Pan* and a *Summer Spectacular.*

Casting procedures
Casting breakdowns are released to agents and are available on *Castweb* (see entry under *Casting Information Services*). Welcomes submissions (with CVs and photographs) sent by post and email. Showreels and invitations to view individual actors' websites are also accepted.

Thelma Holt Ltd.
Waldorf Chambers, 11 Aldwych, London WC2B 4DG
tel 020-7379 0438 *fax* 020-7836 9832
email Thelma@dircon.co.uk
website www.thelmaholt.co.uk
Managing Director Thelma Holt
Executive Director Malcolm Taylor

Production details
Founded in 1990. Theatre producer of classic plays in the West End, on tour and internationally (particularly Japan). Stages 4-5 productions annually and gives 250 performances. Tours 6 theatres across the UK each year. On average, 18 actors work on each production. Recent productions include: *Hamlet, The Taming of the Shrew, All's Well that Ends Well, Othello* and *Pericles.*

Casting procedures
Uses freelance casting directors. Does not hold general auditions. Advises that the company does not encourage unsolicited approaches with letters or photographs, as they will be ignored if not in production. When casting, requirements are made well known via casting directors.

Bruce James Productions Ltd.
68 St George's Park Avenue, Westcliff-on-Sea, Essex SSO 9UD
tel (01702) 335970 *fax* (01702) 304620
email info@brucejamesproductions.co.uk
website www.brucejames.co.uk
Director Bruce James

Production details
Founded in 1995. Produces drama, comedies, thrillers, musicals and children's shows all over the country, both in touring and in repertory at various theatres across the UK. Stages 10-20 productions annually and gives 300 performances in 12 venues during the course of the year. On average 4-20 actors work on each production. Recent productions include: *Funny Money, Murder with Love,* and *Little Shop of Horrors.*

Casting procedures
Holds general auditions. Actors should write in spring and autumn to request inclusion. Casting breakdowns are publicly available via the website and *Castweb* (see entry under *Casting Information Services*). Welcomes letters (with CVs and photographs) sent by post but not by email. Also accepts invitations to view individual actors' websites. Advises that due to the large volume of applications received, individual replies are not always possible.

Andy Jordan Productions Ltd.

5 Underwood Cottages, The Coombe, Streatley-on-Thames, Berkshire RG8 9RA
tel (01491) 871411 *fax* (01491) 871411
email andyjordan@aol.com
Director Andy Jordan

Production details
Founded in 2000. Commerical production company, largely producing new plays of all genres. Stages 2-4 productions annually and gives 50-100 performances per year. Performs annually in 4-10 theatres across the UK, including Northern Ireland and Eire. Also tours overseas. On average, 3-7 actors work on each production. Recent productions include: *Last Song of the Nightingale* and *Kings of the Road.*

Casting procedures
Uses freelance casting directors. Actors may write at any time requesting inclusion. Casting breakdowns are publicly available via Spotlight link. Welcomes submissions (with CVs and photographs) sent by post and email.

Richard Jordan Productions Ltd.

Mews Studios, 16 Vernon Yard,
London W11 2DX
tel 020-7243 9001 *fax* 020-7213 9667

email Richard.Jordan@virgin.net
Director Richard Jordan

Production details
Founded in 1998. Produces theatre in the West End, throughout the UK and internationally. Main area of work is new writing and revivals of plays; occasionally produces musicals. Company also works as general managers and consultants for a wide range of producers and theatres in the UK and abroad. Stages 5-10 productions annually and gives 300 performances during the course of the year. Recent productions include: *The Twits, Single Spies* and *The Lady in the Van.*

Casting procedures
Uses freelance casting directors. Sometimes holds general auditions. Casting breakdowns are sometimes publicly available in *PCR*. Welcomes letters (with CVs and photographs) but not email submissions. Applications are particularly welcome if actors are currently in a production that the company can go and see. Advises that applicants should have an awareness of the type of work produced by the company before sending CVs.

Cameron Mackintosh Ltd.

1 Bedford Square, London WC1B 3RB
tel 020-7637 *fax* 020-7436 2683
Chairman Cameron Mackintosh
Managing Director Nicholas Allot
Casting Director/Associate Producer Trevor Jackson

Production details
Stages musical theatre productions worldwide. Recent productions include: *Les Miserables, Miss Saigon* and *The Phantom of the Opera.*

Casting procedures
In-house casting. Does not hold general auditions. Welcomes letters (with CVs and

photographs) but not email submissions. Also accepts showreels and invitations to view individual actors' websites.

Christopher Malcom Ltd.
1 Calton Road, Bath BA2 4PP
tel (01225) 445459 *fax* (01225) 427778
email cmalcom@btconnect.com
Director Christopher Malcolm
Other key personnel Judith Lloyd

Production details
Founded in 1980, the company works in both licensing and production. Theatre producer for the West End, UK touring and European touring. Manager of *Rocky Horror Co. Ltd.* and first-class rights holders in *The Rocky Horror Show* worldwide. Stages 2-3 productions annually with 200-300 performances during the course of the year. Tours on average 30-40 UK venues, and 100-150 European venues annually. 13-25 actors are involved in each production. Recent productions include: *The Rocky Horror Show* and *Footloose.*

Casting procedures
Uses freelance casting director, Debbie O'Brien. Sometimes holds general auditions. Actors should write to the casting director only, requesting inclusion. Advises actors to use their agents as a means of contact with the casting director. Unsolicited letters and photographs are not considered.

Johnny Mans Productions Ltd.
PO Box 196, Hoddesdon,
Herts EN10 7WG
tel (01992) 470907 *fax* (01992) 470516
Managing Director Johnny Mans
Company Secretary Philip Crowe

Production details
Founded in 1989. Activities include producing one-night stands, celebrity concerts

and touring shows, casting for TV and pantomime, artist management and personal management of Sir Norman Wisdom OBE. Stages about 38 productions annually, totalling 350 performances during the course of the year. Tours to 300 different arts centres and theatres across the UK and Ireland each year. Recent productions include: *Norman Wisdom and Friends, Max Bygraves and the Beverley Sisters,* and *Thoughts of Chairman Alf.*

Casting procedures
Sometimes holds general auditions. Actors requesting inclusion should write at New Year and in mid-summer. Welcomes letters (with CVs and photographs) but not email submissions. Showreels should only be sent on request.

Guy Masterson Productions
The Bull Theatre, 68 High Street,
Barnet EN5 5SJ
Director Guy Masterson

Production details
10-year-old producers of small to mid-scale work. Stages 4-6 productions annually and gives 400 performances during the course of the year. Tours on average to 350 different national and international venues, including arts centres, theatres, and outdoor, educational and community venues. Recent productions include: *Twelve Angry Men, Animal Farm* and *Under Milk Wood.*

Casting procedures
Sometimes holds general auditions. Only works with actors seen on a previous occasion, and then only by invitation.

Norwell Lapley Associates
Lapley Hall, Lapley, Staffs ST19 9JR
tel (01785) 841991

fax (01785) 841992
email norwelllapley@freeserve.com
website www.norewelllapley.co.uk
Director Chris Davis
Artiste Manager Claire Sibley
Personal Assistant Kerry Foley

Production details
Produces theatre in the West End and touring productions. Stages 4-5 productions annually and gives 40-50 performances during the course of the year at theatres nationwide. Recent productions include: *Zipp.*

Casting procedures
Uses freelance casting directors and does not deal directly with actors.

See entry under *Agents* for further details about the company's work.

David Pugh Ltd.

Canaletto Yard, 41-45 Beak Street, London W1F 9SB
tel 020-7434 9757 *fax* 020-7287 8856
Director David Pugh

Production details
Theatre production company staging 2-3 productions annually and touring to theatres throughout the UK. Recent productions include: *Art, The Play What I Wrote* and *Blues Brothers.*

Casting procedures
Uses freelance casting directors. Sometimes holds general auditions. Actors should address requests for inclusion to Sarah Bird CDG (see entry under *Casting Directors*) who is responsible for all casting.

Michael Redington

10 Maunsel Street, London SW1P 2QL
tel 020-7834 5119
Director Michael Redington

Production details
Founded in 1979. Produces new and original plays. Stages 1 theatre production annually. Recent productions include: *Japes.*

Casting procedures
Uses freelance casting directors. Sometimes holds general auditions.

Rho Delta Ltd.

52 Tottenham Street, London W1T 4RN
tel 020-7436 1392 *fax* 020-7436 1395
email info@ripleyduggan.com
Director Greg Ripley-Duggan

Production details
Founded in 1991. Produces West End and Touring Commercial Theatre. Stages 1 production annually which tours to 6 theatres. Recent productions include: *Life x 3* and *The Memory of Water.*

Casting procedures
Uses freelance casting directors and does not deal directly with actors.

Adam Spiegel Productions

2nd Floor, 20-22 Stukely Street, London WC2B 5LR
tel 020-7438 4565 *fax* 020-7438 9577
email bridget@adamspiegel.com
Director Adam Spiegel
Managing Director Bob Eady
General Manager Amanda Riley

Production details
Founded in 1996, the company is responsible for staging *Fame* in London's West End, which is re-cast every year. Each show is performed 416 times annually and tours to 48 different theatres across Great Britain. Occasionally co-produces Scandinavian tours. In general 20-30 actors are involved in each production. Recent productions

include: *Fame, The Mysteries* and *Saturday Night Fever*.

Casting procedures

Uses freelance casting directors. Sometimes holds general auditions as well. Actors may write at any time requesting inclusion. Casting breakdowns are available via *PCR* and advertisements in *The Stage*. Welcomes letters (with CVs and photographs) but not email submissions. Showreels and invitations to view individual actors' websites are also accepted.

Barrie Stacey UK Productions Ltd.

Flat 8, 132 Charing Cross Road,
London WC2H OLA
tel 020-7836 6220/4128 *fax* 020-7836 2949
email hopkinstacey@aol.com
Director Barrie Stacey
Stage Director Tony Joseph

Production details

Founded in 1966. Specialises in children's musicals and songbook concerts. Stages 24 productions annually and gives 100 performances during the course of the year. Tours to 8 different theatres in Southern England, including the London area. In general 8 actors are involved in each production. Recent productions include: *West End to Broadway* and *Movie Memories*.

Casting procedures

All casting is done in-house. Holds general auditions. Casting breakdowns are available on request. Welcomes letters (with CVs and photographs) but not email submissions. Advice for actors: 'Don't be grand when just starting.'

Stage Further Productions Ltd.

Westgate, Stansted Road,
Eastbourne BN22 8LG
tel (01323) 739478 *fax* (01323) 736127

email info@stagefurther.co.uk
Director Garth Harrison
Producer David Nott
Artistic Director Keith Myers

Production details

Founded in 1985. Produces plays and pantomimes for its repertory seasons and national tours. Also provides entertainment and shows to the cruise industry. Stages 10 productions annually and performs in around 18 different venues, including arts centres and theatres nationwide and cruise vessels. In general 6 actors are involved in each production. Recent productions include: *Anybody for Murder* and *Dead of Night*.

Casting procedures

Holds general auditions. Casting breakdowns are available via *PCR, The Stage* and from agents. Welcomes letters (with CVs and photographs) but not email submissions. Invitations to view individual actors' websites are also accepted.

Stanhope Productions Ltd.

The Penthouse, Charles House, 7 Leicester Place, London WC2H 7RJ
tel 020-7734 0710 *fax* 020-7734 7185
email office@stanhopeprod.com
Director Kim Poster
Production Coordinator Chrissie Dugan

Production details

Founded in 2001. Theatrical producing company. Stages 4-5 productions annually and gives 576 performances during the course of the year. Tours to 2-4 different theatres, primarily in the West End and London area. In general 18 actors are involved in each production. Recent productions include: *A Woman of No Importance* and *Brand*.

Casting procedures

Uses freelance casting directors. Holds general auditions. Casting breakdowns are available via Equity Job Information Service.

Kevin Wood Productions
5 Archery Square, Walmer, Deal CT14 7JA
Director Kevin Wood

Production details
Founded in 1980. Produces tours, pantomimes and plays. Stages 4-6 productions with 400 performances each year. Tours to 16 different UK theatres annually. In general 12 actors are involved in each production. Recent productions include: *Godspell.*

Casting procedures
Uses freelance casting directors. Sometimes holds general auditions. Actors should write requesting inclusion in response to advertisements. Casting breakdowns are available on *Castweb* (see entry under *Casting Directories and Information Services*). "Unsolicited letters without an sae are not replied to."

Middle & Smaller-Scale Companies

This section covers a huge range of companies: from the very prestigious, often subsidised (like Out of Joint) who usually only perform in theatres with around 500 seats (or more) to the very small, who frequently have little or no public subsidy and perform wherever they can find a paying audience. The bigger companies operate much like the commercial 'big boys' in the previous section – except they tend to have longer rehearsal periods. The smaller companies rarely use casting directors, tend to do only one or two performances in each venue and often pay below Equity rates – and it's probable that you'll have to help with get-ins and get-outs. It's very hard work and you have to rise to the peak of performance every time in spite of travelling in cramped vans, sharing unsatisfactory digs and rarely, if ever, being seen by anyone who could advance your career. However, some very prestigious companies have grown from such very small beginnings – and a number of now highly respected directors, playwrights and actors have started this way. It is important to assess the potential quality of the product (as well as the pay, and terms and conditions) before accepting such a job.

As such companies tend to come and go with great rapidity, the listings only contain companies that have been in existence for three years or more.

Actors of Dionysus

44-46 Old Steine, Brighton BN1 1NH
tel (01273) 320396/514 *fax* (01273) 220025
email info@actorsofdionysus.com
website www.actorsofdionysus.com
Artistic Directors Tamsin Shasha, David Stuttard
General Manager Alison Fewings

Production details
National and international touring company founded in 1993. A member of the ITC, it receives funding from Arts Council England and specialises in performing new adaptations of Ancient Greek drama through a fusion of poetry, music and movement. Has a strong educational focus and runs international summer schools. Stages 2-3 productions each year with an average annual total of 120-150 performances. Venues include arts centres, theatres (including Greek and Turkish theatres), and educational venues across the UK, EIRE and Turkey. Also performs on cruise ships. In general 4-6 actors work on each production. Recent productions include: *Oedipus* (touring autumn 2003, premiere at The Crucible, Sheffield and residencies at Bath Theatre Royal and London's Cockpit Theatre) and *Agamemnon* (Bath TR, Bridewell Theatre and national tour).

Casting procedures

Does not use freelance casting directors. Holds general auditions; actors should write to request inclusion in August and December. Casting breakdowns are available through the website and *PCR*. Does not welcome general submissions from actors but will accept invitations to view individual actors' websites.

Badapple Theatre Company

7 St Mary's, York YO30 7DD
tel (01904) 623565 *fax* 0870-135 8302
email office@badapple.freeserve.co.uk
website www.badapple.freeserve.co.uk
Director Kate Bramley

Production details

Founded in 1998, the company specialises in small-scale tours of new biography drama. Stages 1-2 productions each year with an average annual total of 60 performances. Venues include arts centres and theatres across Scotland, Wales and England. In general 3-4 actors work on each production. Recent productions include: *Still Marilyn* playing to 35 arts centres in spring 2003.

Casting procedures

Does not use freelance casting directors. Casting breakdowns are available through Equity Job Information Service, *PCR* and advertisements in *The Stage*. Actors should write (with CVs and photographs) in response to casting breakdowns only. Does not welcome email submissions. Invitations to view individual actors' websites are accepted.

Big Telly Theatre Company

Town Hall, The Crescent, Portstewart, Londonderry BT55 7AB
tel 028-7083 6473 *fax* 028-7083 2588
email info@big-telly.com

website www.big-telly.com
Director ZoëSeaton

Production details

Established in 1987, Big Telly works across different artforms to produce strongly visual pieces of work. Using dance, music, circus, magic and film the company aims to create pieces with a unique sense of spectacle. Funded by the Arts Council of Northern Ireland, Big Telly also runs Education and Community projects and has toured across both Northern and Southern Ireland, Scotland, England and India. Stages 1-2 productions each year with an average annual total of 50 performances. Venues include arts centres, theatres, educational and community venues. Anywhere between 1 and 8 actors work on each production. Recent productions include: *The Playboy of the Western World* (spring 2003), *McCool XXL*, a new musical (spring 2002) and *Fish*, a new theatre/illusion piece (autumn 2000).

Casting procedures

Does not use freelance casting directors. Casting breakdowns are available through the website and Equity Job Information Service, and are also released to agents. Welcomes submissions (with CVs and photographs) from actors previously unknown to the company sent by post or email. Invitations to view individual actors' websites are also accepted.

Borderline Theatre Co.

North Harbour Street, Ayr KA8 8AA
tel (01292) 281010 *fax* (01292) 263825
email enquiries@bordertheatre.co.uk
website www.bordertheatre.co.uk
Producer Edward Jackson

Production details

Founded in 1974, the company stages 2-3 productions each year with an average annual total of 60-90 performances. Each tour normally runs for 31 performances across 13 different venues. Venues include arts centres and theatres across Scotland. In general 4 actors work on each production. Recent productions include: *Tally's Blood, Women on the Verge of HRT* and *Angel's Share.*

Casting procedures
Does not use freelance casting directors. Currently releases casting breakdowns to agents but may publish them on their website in future. Welcomes submissions (with CVs and photographs) from actors previously unknown to the company sent by post or email. Also accepts showreels.

Cavalcade Theatre Company
57 Pelham Road, London SW19 1NW
tel 020-8540 3513 *fax* 020-8540 2243
Directors Graham Ashe, Kim Joyce, Carol Crowther
Touring Manager Colin Agate

Production details
Founded in 1972. Stages an average of 5 productions each year, averaging an annual total of about 200 performances. Tours approximately 20 venues per year, including arts centres, theatres, and outdoor, educational and community venues throughout the UK and Ireland. Also performs at conferences and exhibitions and covers publicity and PR events. In general 8 actors work on each production. Recent productions include: *Alice in Wonderland, The Adventures of Brer Rabbit,* pantomimes, musicals and some small-scale plays.

Casting procedures
Does not use freelance casting directors. Sometimes holds general auditions; actors may write at any time to request inclusion. Casting breakdowns are only available in

PCR, The Stage and through agents. Welcomes submissions (with CVs and photographs) from actors previously unknown to the company if sent by post, but does not welcome email enquiries. Also accepts invitations to view individual actors' websites.

Channel Theatre Company
36 Park Place, Margate CT9 1LE
tel (01843) 280077 *fax* (01843) 280088
email info@channel-theatre.co.uk
website www.channel-theatre.co.uk
Director Philip Dart
Outreach Director Claudia Leaf
Administrator Eddie de Souza

Production details
Founded in 1980, the company works in Theatre in Education, Health in Education and produces commissioned pieces on various scales. Stages 5-7 productions each year, averaging an annual total of about 225 performances. Tours to approximately 200 arts centres, theatres, education and community venues in the South East and South West of England annually. In general 3-4 actors work on each production. Recent productions include 3 drug education programmes and a domestic violence project for young people aged 5-14. The company's touring and outreach arm, Chalkfoot Theatre Arts, was founded in 2003. Funded by the Arts Council of England, it is committed to touring non-theatre venues and specialises in rural theatre. 2-3 productions are staged each year, totalling 75 performances at 60 venues. 3-5 actors are involved in each production; recent productions include: an adaptation of *The Phoenix and the Carpet* by E Nesbit.

Casting procedures
Neither Channel Theatre Company nor Chalkfoot Theatre Arts employ freelance

casting directors or hold general auditions. Casting breakdowns are available by postal application with sae. Will only accept invitations to view individual actors' websites when casting.

Close for Comfort Theatre Company

34 Boleyn Walk, Leatherhead, Surrey KT22 7HU
tel (01372) 378613
email close4comf@aol.com
website www.hometown.aol.com/close4comf
Director Janet Gill
Co-Director Glenn Johnson

Production details

Founded in 2001. "Takes theatre to living rooms across the country."Stages 3-4 productions each year, averaging an annual total of 30-40 performances in the same number of private homes in the South East, South West and the Midlands. 2 actors work on each production. Recent productions include: *Dossier: Ronald Ackerman in a house in Bristol.*

Casting procedures

Does not use freelance casting directors or hold general auditions.

Comyns Carr and Tyger's Heart

18 St Ann's Terrace, London NW8 6PJ
tel 020-7586 5252 *fax* 020-7722 1945
email tygersheart@comynscarr.fsnet.co.uk
website www.comynscarr.co.uk
Artistic Director Melissa Holston
Associate Producer Victoria Walker

Production details

Originally founded in 1995, Comyns Carr now includes a new division, Tyger's Hart, founded in 2003. Stages 1-4 productions each year, averaging an annual total of 40-70 performances. Tours 2-22 venues per year, including arts centres, theatres, and outdoor, educational and community venues throughout London and the South East. In general 5-8 actors work on each production. Recent productions include: *Fair Maid of the West* and *The Way of the World.*

Casting procedures

Uses freelance casting directors. Actors should only write to request inclusion when auditions have been announced. Casting breakdowns are available through Equity Job Information Service and *PCR.* Welcomes letters (with CVs and photographs) from actors previously unknown to the company, but not email submissions. Also accepts invitations to view individual actors' websites.

Creation Theatre Company

9 Standingford House, Cave Street, Oxford OX4 1BA
tel (01865) 250636 *fax* (01865) 242234
email enquiry@creationtheatre.co.uk
website www.creationtheatre.co.uk
Director David Parrish

Production details

Produces site-specific Shakespeare. Stages 2-3 productions annually and gives approximately 150 performances per year in outdoor venues and factories in Oxford. 8 actors work on each production. Recent productions include: *Twelfth Night, The Tempest* and *Macbeth.*

Casting procedures

Does not use freelance casting directors or hold general auditions. Casting breakdowns are available by postal application (with sae) and via *PCR* and *Castfax.* Welcomes letters (with CVs and photographs) from actors previously unknown to the company, but not email submissions. Actors should write in October or March.

Dead Earnest Theatre

57 Burton Street, Sheffield S6 2HH
tel 0114-233 4579 *fax* 0114-233 4579
email info@deadearnest.co.uk
website www.deadearnest.co.uk
Director Ashley Barnes
Drama Project Leader Rachel Scott
Administrator Louise Ingham

Production details

Founded in 1993, the company creates
theatre pieces of varying length and for
various audiences. Original
productions tour regionally and
nationally with shorter performances
being created for training or community
empowerment. Characteristically, live
music is used in these productions which
focus on social issues. 1 touring show and
4 shorter forum pieces are staged per
year, with an average annual total of 12
touring and 20 forum productions.
Touring productions perform to arts
centres and theatres, while forum pieces
are staged in educational and community
venues. Tours mainly to Yorkshire and
the North West and less frequently to the
East Midlands and South West. In
general 3-5 actors work on each
production. Recent productions include:
Stalingrad.

Casting procedures

Uses freelance casting directors.
Sometimes holds general auditions.
Welcomes postal or email submissions
(with CVs and photographs) from actors
previously unknown to the company.
Applicants should live locally or aim to
have a local base since company resources
do not extend to assistance with accommodation. Also accepts invitations to
view individual actors' websites. The
company often employs new actors for its
short forum pieces. Those with musical
skills are particularly favoured.

Eastern Angles Theatre Company

Sir John Mills Theatre, Gatacre Road,
Ipswich IP1 2LQ
tel (01473) 218202 *fax* (01473) 384999
email info@easternangles.co.uk
website www.easternangles.co.uk
Director Ivan Cutting
General Manager Jill Streatfield

Production details

Founded in 1982, the company tours theatre productions around East Anglia. New
writing and a flavour of the region colour
all its original work. It stages 4-5 pieces
each year with an average annual total of
200 performances at 80 different venues.
These include arts centres and theatres,
educational and community venues, and
site-specific locations. Tours mainly to East
England but also to the South, South West,
Wales and the Midlands. In general 6
actors work on each production. Recent
productions include: *David Copperfield,
The Last Laugh, Bone Harvest* and *East
Anglian Psychosis.*

Casting procedures

Does not use freelance casting directors or
hold general auditions. Casting breakdowns
are not currently publicly available but may,
in future, be posted on the website.
Welcomes letters (with CVs and
photographs but not saes) but not email
submissions. Advises applicants to consult
the website to get an idea of the sort of
work the company produces. Applicants
should only write once and should specify in
their letter if they are local or native to the
region.

English Touring Theatre

25 Short Street, London SE1 8LJ
tel 020-7450 1990 *fax* 020-7450 1991
email admin@englishtouringtheatre.co.uk
website www.englishtouringtheatre.co.uk

Director Stephen Unwin
Executive Director Tim Highman
Marketing and Press Manager Drew Cowerd

Production details
Founded in 1993. "An artistically led national touring company that aims to achieve the highest artistic standards in acting, directing, lighting and music." Stages 3 productions annually and gives approximately 120 performances per year in arts centres and theatres throughout England and Scotland. 4-15 actors are involved in each production. Recent productions include: *Romeo and Juliet.*

Casting procedures
Uses freelance casting directors. Welcomes submissions (with CVs and photographs) sent by post or email.

Forbidden Theatre Company

Diorama Arts Centre, 34 Osnaburgh Street, London NW1 3ND
tel 020-7813 1025
email info@forbidden.org.uk
website www.forbidden.org.uk
Directors Georgia Bance, Pilar Orti

Production details
Physical and visual theatre company. Produces small-scale productions of adaptations of classics and devised work. Stages 1 production annually and gives approximately 40 performances per year. Tours 2 venues on average and performs in arts centres and theatre venues in London and Scotland. In general, 4-6 actors work on each production. Recent productions include: *Spell, Alice in Wonderland, Antigone* and *Freestyle Performances.*

Casting procedures
Does not use freelance casting directors. Sometimes holds general auditions. Actors can write at any time requesting inclusion. Welcomes letters (with CVs and photographs) but not email submissions. Advises that the company will only reply to actors if inviting them to audition. CVs are kept on file.

Forced Entertainment

The Workstation, 46 Shoreham Street, Sheffield S1 4SP
tel 0114-279 8977 *fax* 0114-221 2170
email fe@forcedentertainment.co.uk
website www.forced.co.uk
Artistic Director Tim Etchells
General Manager Matt Burman
Administration/Education Eileen Evans

Production details
Forced Entertainment is a group of artists who have been working together since 1984, producing new works in theatre and performance as well as projects in digital media, video and installation. The theatre projects frequently explore and experiment with the 'rules' of theatre and the expectations of the audiences. Tours across the UK and mainland Europe to mid-scale theatres, arts centres, studios and site-specific projects. A member of the ITC, it is regularly funded by the Arts Council England and Sheffield City Council. In general a company of 6 actors works on each production. Aside from the permanent ensemble, the company involves artists from other disciplines, introducing fresh skills and ideas to support and develop their work. Recent productions include: *Bloody Mess, Erasure, Imaginary Evidence* and *So Small.*

Forkbeard Fantasy

PO Box 1241, Bristol BS99 2TG

Production details
Founded in 1974; an artist-led, multi-media film and performance company.

Stages 1-2 productions and performs about 50 times per year. Tours to 10 venues both nationally and internationally on an annual basis. As this is an artist-led company, actors are only occasionally involved in productions. Performed recently at the Blackpool Puppet Festival, Warwick Arts Centre and The Lowry, Slaford.

Casting procedures
Never holds general auditions. Advises actors that the company usually performs with artists who are already in the core team.

Foursight Theatre
Newhampton Arts Centre, Dunkley Street, Wolverhampton WV1 4AN
tel (01902) 714257 *fax* (01902) 428413
email foursight.theatre@boltblue.net
website www.foursight.theatre.boltblue.net
Artistic Director Naomi Cooke
Special Projects Coordinator Frances Land
Administrator Emma Beale

Production details
National touring theatre company. Emphasises the need for "total theatre" combining word, movement and music. Specialises in biographical plays about women in history and runs a strong education programme. Stages 1 production annually in addition to its regional and education work. Performs at about 17 different venues during its national tour, including arts centres, theatres and educational venues. Around 8 actors work on each production. Recent productions include: *The Snow Queen* and *Medea*.

Casting procedures
Casting breakdowns are not publicly available. Actors are advised to keep an eye on the website for information posted prior to productions. Welcomes submissions (with CVs and photographs)

by post and email. Invitations to view individual actors' websites are also accepted.

Frantic Theatre Company
32 Wood Lane, Falmouth TR11 4RF
tel (01326) 312985 *fax* (01326) 312985
email info@frantictheatre.com
website www.frantictheatre.com

Production details
Founded in 1990. Stages 2 productions annually with around 1500 performances in 1500 venues throughout the UK and Ireland every year. Venues include arts centres, village halls, theatres, outdoor venues, educational and community venues, private homes and hospitals. On average 4 actors work on each production. Recent productions include: *Can I Do You Now, Sir?* and *Don't Dilly Dally*.

Casting procedures
Holds general auditions. Actors should write in May and November to request inclusion. Casting breakdowns are available by postal application (with sae), Equity Job Information Service, *PCR* and advertisements in *The Stage*. Welcomes submissions (with CVs and photographs) by post or email. Showreels and invitations to view individual actors' websites are also accepted. Actors are advised not to telephone, and to send their details only when they have researched the company's very specific work and can explain their suitability.

Galleon Theatre Company Ltd.
Greenwich Playhouse, Greenwich BR Station Forecourt, 189 Greenwich High Road, London SE10 8JA
tel 020-8858 9256
email boxoffice@galleontheatre.co.uk

website www.galleontheatre.co.uk
Artistic Director Alice de Souza
Theatre Director Bruce Jamieson

Production details
Founded in 1990. Stages 5-8 productions
annually and gives 192 performances at its
own venue, Greenwich Playhouse. Has
toured throughout Britain in previous
years. On average 15 actors work on each
production. Recent productions include:
Absent Friends by Alan Ayckbourn.

Casting procedures
Uses in-house casting director. Holds
general auditions. Actors should write to
request inclusion when the company is
casting for a specific project. Casting
breakdowns are available via the website
and through *PCR* and advertisements *The
Stage*. Welcomes letters (with CVs and
photographs) but not email submissions.
Showreels and invitations to view
individual actors' websites are also
accepted.

Graeae Theatre Company

LVS Resource Centre, 356 Holloway Road,
London N7 6PA
tel 020-7700 2455 *fax* 020-7609 7324
email info@grae.org
website www.grae.org
Artistic Director Jenny Sealey
Associate Director Jamie Beddard
Executive Producer Roger Nelson

Production details
Founded in 1980. Produces theatre made
by disabled people (actors, directors and
other theatre practitioners) with physical
and sensory impairments. Stages 3 productions annually and gives 70 performances
at 50 venues each year. Venues include arts
centres and theatres in England, Scotland,
Wales and Ireland. 3-6 actors are involved
in each production. Recent productions

include: *Peeling* and *Mother Courage and
her Children*.

Casting procedures
Sometimes holds general auditions.
Welcomes postal or email submissions
(with CVs and photographs) from actors
with physical and sensory impairments.
Also accepts showreels and invitations to
view individual actors' websites.

Grassmarket Project

18 Forth Street, Edinburgh EH1 3LH
tel (01355) 583581
email Jeremy@gmptheatre.demon.co.uk
website www.grassmarketproject.org
Artistic Director Jeremy Weller

Production details
Founded in 1989. Independent Theatre
Company producing new work in theatres
across Europe, USA and the UK. Stages 2
productions annually and gives 30-40
performances every year. On average,
5-6 actors work on each production.
Recent productions include: *De Andre
(The Others)*.

Casting procedures
Productions are cast by freelance casting
directors or the company's artistic director.
Sometimes holds general auditions.
Employs a mixture of trained and
untrained actors. Welcomes letters (with
CVs and photographs) but not email submissions. Showreels and invitations to
view individual actors' websites are also
accepted.

Grid Iron Theatre Company

85 East Claremont Street,
Edinburgh EH7 4HU
Director Ben Harrison
Producer Judith Doherty
General Manager Claire Robb

Production details
Founded in 1995. Produces new writing and site-specific theatre. Stages 1-3 productions annually and gives 20-50 performances every year. Performs in theatres, outdoor and site-specific venues in Scotland, England and Northern and Southern Ireland. 2-8 actors work on each production. Recent productions include: *Variety, Decky does a Bronco*, and *Those Eyes, That Mouth*.

Casting procedures
Sometimes holds general auditions. Actors may write requesting inclusion at any time throughout the year. Welcomes submissions (with CVs and photographs) sent by post and email. Showreels and invitations to view individual actors' websites are also accepted.

Handstand Productions
13 Hope Street, Liverpool L1 9BH
tel 0151-708 7441 *fax* 0151-709 3515
email info@handstand-uk.com
website www.handstand-uk.com
Director Han Duijvendak
Producer Nicholas Stanley
Co-Producer Lucy Dossor

Production details
Founded in 1993. Works across a broad range of artforms from live theatre to film and television projects. Theatre work has a strong actor-musician and international bias. Stages 1 production every 2 years with up to 140 performances each year at 1-15 venues. Venues include arts centres, theatres, and community venues in the UK, Netherlands and Greece. On average 5-15 actors work on each production. Recent productions include: *Sweet Charity* and *The Sofa*.

Casting procedures
Never holds general auditions. Casting breakdowns are available via the website, Equity Job Information Service, *PCR* and

agents. Requests that actors do not submit anything to the company unless a specific casting requirement has been made available on the website and via the usual industry channels.

Highly Sprung Performance Company
49 Abercorn Road, Chapelfields, Coventry CV5 8EE
tel 020-7667 0141
email mail@sprunghq.fsnet.co.uk
website www.highlysprungperformance.co.uk
Artistic Director Sarah Hunt
Company Director Mark Worth

Production details
Founded in 1999. Aims to create original and innovative performances exploring the relationship between dance, text and physical theatre. Also runs community and educational activities alongside productions. Stages 1 production annually with 25 performances every year. Tours 10-15 venues annually. These include arts centres, theatres, outdoor and educational venues in the West Midlands, London, Manchester and Edinburgh. On average 2-8 actors work on each production. Recent productions include: *Pretend I'm Not Here* and *More Than Kisses*.

Casting procedures
Holds general auditions. Actors should send CVs and photographs by post or email. These will be kept on file for future auditions. Casting breakdowns are available on the website, by postal application and via Equity Job information Service and advertisements in *The Stage*. Showreels and invitations to view individual actors' websites are also accepted.

Hoipolloi Theatre
Cambridge Drama Centre, Mill Road, Cambridge CB1 2HR

Director Shôn Dale-Jones
Associate Director Stephanie Müller
Production Manager Richard Couldrey

Production details
Founded in 1994. Stages 1-2 productions annually and gives 100 performances every year at 60-70 venues. These include arts centres and theatres in national and international locations. On average 4-5 actors work on each production. Recent productions include: *The Man Next Door.*

Casting procedures
Sometimes holds general auditions. Actors may write at any time requesting inclusion. Welcomes letters (with CVs and photographs) but not email submissions. Invitations to view individual actors' websites are also accepted. Advises actors approaching the company to have some knowledge of its work.

Indigo Entertainments

Tynymynydd, Bryneglwys, Corwen, Denbighshire LL21 9NP
tel (01978) 790211 *fax* (01978) 790626
email info@indigoentertainments.com
website www.indigoentertainments.com
Director Emma Hands

Production details
Founded in 2000. Takes existing small-scale theatre productions, usually with a literary theme, and tours them around the UK and internationally. Stages 5-10 productions annually and gives 50 performances in 50 venues every year. These include arts centres, theatres, outdoor and educational venues, community venues and hotels all over the UK and in the Middle East and Far East. On average 1-3 actors work on each production. Recent productions include: *The Tale of Beatrix Potter*, *Dear Liar*, *Turn of the Screw* and *Testament of Youth.*

Casting procedures
Does not welcome unsolicited CVs. Will accept showreels if they demonstrate productions of interest and are not just an actor's general showreel. Advises that the shows presented are usually intelligent, light, witty commercial pieces rather than experimental work.

Kabosh

The Old Museum Arts Centre, 7 College Square North, Belfast BT1 6AR
tel 028-9024 3343 *fax* 028-9023 1130
email kabosh@dircon.co.uk
website www.kabosh.net (under construction)
Director Karl Wallace
General Manager Sinead Coll
Company Manager Azlicena Avila

Production details
Founded in 1994. Produces innovative physical and visual theatre both local, national and international touring and site-specific work. Stages 2-4 productions annually and gives 56 performances during the course of the year. Tours about 20 venues annually, including arts centres and theatres, and site-specific locations. In general 2-6 actors are involved in each production. Countries covered include Northern Ireland, Republic of Ireland, England (including London), Scotland, Wales and North America. Recent productions include: *Rhinoceros* and *Todd.*

Casting procedures
Sometimes holds general auditions. Actors may write at any time requesting inclusion. Welcomes applications (with CVs and photographs) sent by post and email. Also accepts invitations to view individual actors' websites. Any actor known to the company is welcome to send a CV and headshot (which will be kept on file), and to notify the director of performances

where their work may be seen. The director will endeavour to see new actors, but auditions are by invitation only. Any unseen actor who has sent a CV will be notified of open auditions should they arise.

Kaos Theatre

39-41 North Road, Islington,
London N7 9DP
tel 020-7700 3885 *fax* 020-7700 3885
email admin@kaostheatre.com
website www.kaostheatre.com
Director Xavier Leret

Production details
Founded in 1994. Working ensemble of actors, musicians, designers and artists working with text-based theatre. Stages both new writing and contemporary adaptations of existing work (classic and modern). Receives funding from the Arts Council England. Stages 1-2 productions annually and gives 80 performances during the course of the year. The company tours on average to 30 different venues across the UK (excluding the Highlands and Islands) each year. Recent productions include: *Titus Andronicus* and *The Kaos Importance of Being Earnest.*

Casting procedures
In-house casting. Does not hold general auditions. Casting breakdowns are publicly available via the website, postal application (with sae), Equity Job Information Service, *PCR* and advertisements in *The Stage.* Sometimes welcomes letters (with CVs and photographs) but not email submissions. Accepts invitations to view individual actors' websites. Advises that the company mainly works with a regular ensemble of performers and only occasionally meets or auditions newcomers. Members of the

ensemble come from a diverse training background (rarely straight from drama school). Does not welcome over-persistent enquiries. The company will make the contact if interested in an applicant.

Kneehigh Theatre

14 Walsingham Place, Truro,
Cornwall TR1 2RP
Director B Mitchell
Associates Emma Rice, Mark Shepherd

Production details
Stages 3 productions annually and gives 130 performances during the course of the year. On average tours 15 venues annually. Performs in arts centres, theatres, outdoor and 'out of the ordinary"indoor venues across the UK and internationally. Recent productions include: *Red Shoes, Cry Woolf* and *Tristan and Yseult.*

Casting procedures
Sometimes holds general auditions. Casting breakdowns are publicly available in *PCR* (on occasion). Advises that the company works with a pool of performers, but is interested in meeting new actors, either by personal recommendation or by seeing their work.

Lip Service

The Comedy Suite, 116 Longford Road,
Manchester M21 9NP
tel 0161-881 0061 *fax* 0161-881 0061
email info@lip-service.net
website www.lip-service.net
Joint Artistic Directors Sue Ryding,
Maggie Fox

Production details
Founded in 1985. National touring company specialising in comedy and funded by the Arts Council England. The company's artistic directors write and perform the

majority of the work, which is co-produced with other theatres. Stages 1 production annually and gives 60 performances during the course of the year. 3 actors (including the artistic directors) are normally involved in each production. Tours have covered the North West, Manchester, Yorkshire, Scotland and East Anglia. Recent productions include: *The Importance of Being Earnest, Withering Looks* and *Hector's House.*

Casting procedures
Uses casting directors of co-producing venue. Does not hold general auditions. Actors should write requesting inclusion when extra performers are needed for a new production. Casting breakdowns are available direct from the co-producing theatre; details of these are available via the website. Welcomes invitations from actors to view their work, and information from actors familiar with company's work.

Mad Dogs and Englishmen
The Old Post Office, Green Lane, Quidenham NR16 2AP
tel (01953) 888499 *fax* (01953) 888499
email info@mad-dogs.org.uk
website www.mad-dogs.org.uk
Director Ann Courtney
Administration Jacqui Merryweather

Production details
Founded in 1995. Theatre company based in Norfolk. Its policy is to provide well-balanced, entertaining and educational drama. Main areas of work are new writing, adaptations and classical work. Stages 2 productions annually with 70 performances during the course of the year, plus 30 workshops for schools. Tours to rural venues (churches, public houses) as well as arts centres, theatres, outdoor venues, educational venues, and community venues. Tours have covered East Anglia and venues

across the UK. On average 4-9 actors are involved in each production. Recent productions include: *Henry V* and *Outrageous Nonsense.*

Casting procedures
Sometimes holds general auditions. Audition criteria are published in *PCR* at the appropriate times of the year. Welcomes letters (with CVs and photographs) but not email submissions.

Magnetic North Theatre Productions
18 Brandon Terrace, Edinburgh EH3 5DZ
tel 0131-556 3299 *fax* 0131-556 3299
email mail@magneticnorth.org.uk
website www.magneticnorth.org.uk
Director Nicholas Bone

Production details
Founded in 1999. Commissions and produces new plays. 2 full productions and 1 film have been produced so far. Stages 1 production annually and gives 12 performances during the course of the year. Tours on average to 8 different venues in Scotland annually. About 5 actors are involved in each production. Recent productions include: *Word for Word* and *The Dream Train.*

Casting procedures
Sometimes holds general auditions. Actors should write to request inclusion when productions are announced on the website. Casting breakdowns are publicly available through the website, postal application (with sae) and *PCR*. Welcomes submissions (with CVs and photographs) sent by post or email. Also accepts invitations to view individual actors' websites. Advises that the company has a low turnover of productions and a small staff and finds it difficult to respond to general enquiries about available work.

Meeting Ground Theatre Co.
4 Shirley Road, Nottingham NG3 5DA
tel 0115-962 3009
website www.meetingground.org.uk
Director Tanya Myers

Production details
2003/4 was a year for research and
development; the company is currently
re-organising and preparing for 2004/5.

Casting procedures
Actors are advised not to contact the
company during the re-organisation
period.

Midland Actors Theatre
25 Merrishaw Road, Northfield,
Birmingham B31 3SL
tel 0121-608 7144 *fax* 0121-608 7144
email news@midlandactorstheatre.co.uk
website www.midlandactorstheatre.co.uk
Director David Allen
Secretary Judith Aston

Production details
Founded in 1999. Produces classics and
new work inspired by stories and legends
from different cultures. Stages 3 productions annually and gives 90 performances
during the course of the year. Tours on
average to 75 different theatres, schools,
and other venues in the West Midlands,
East Midlands, North West and Scotland
each year. Around 4-5 actors are involved
in each production. Recent productions
include: *Macbeth* and *Prospero's Island.*

Casting procedures
Sometimes holds general auditions. Actors
should write requesting inclusion when
auditions are advertised. Casting
breakdowns are publicly available via
Equity Job Information Service and *PCR.*
Welcomes letters (with CVs and
photographs) but does not welcome email

enquiries. Advises that the company is
primarily interested in actors who are
Midlands-based.

Mu-Lan Theatre Company
The Albany, Douglas Way,
London SE8 4AG
tel 020-8694 0557 *fax* 020-8694 0618
email mailbox@mu-lan.org
website www.mu-lan.org
Director Paul Courtenay

Production details
Founded in 1988. Stages 1 production
annually and gives 30 performances during
the course of the year. Tours have covered
the North West, South and South West
England. About 8 actors are involved in
each production. Recent productions
include: *Sun is Shining, Romeo and Juliet*
and *Takeaway.*

Casting procedures
Uses freelance casting directors. Does not
hold general auditions. Casting breakdowns are publicly available via *PCR.*
Welcomes submissions (with CVs and
photographs) sent by post or email. Also
accepts invitations to view individual
actors' websites.

NITRO
6 Brewery Road, London N7 9NH
tel 020-7609 1331 *fax* 020-7609 1221
email info@nitro.co.uk
Artistic Director Felix Cross
General Manager Philip Bray
Administrator Sophia Davidson

Production details
Founded in 1978 and formerly known as
Black Theatre Co-operative Ltd. National
touring theatre company that generates and
produces contemporary black musical theatre. First established to provide training

for black writers, directors and artists. Aims to explore ways of using black music as a means of attracting new audiences to theatre. Stages 1-2 productions annually and gives 1-2 performances during the course of the year. Recent productions include: *Nitrobeat* and *A Nitro at the Opera*.

Casting procedures

Sometimes uses agents when casting. Also holds general auditions; actors should write at the start of the year to request inclusion. Welcomes submissions (with CVs and photographs) sent by post or email. Accepts invitations to view individual actors' websites. Advises that the company keeps an up-to-date catalogue of black actors and would particularly welcome CVs from actors of different ethnic backgrounds.

NTC Touring Theatre Company

Alnwick Playhouse, Alnwick,
Northumberland NE66 1PQ
tel (01665) 602586 *fax* (01665) 605837
email admin@ntc-touringtheatre.co.uk
website www.ntc-touringtheatre.co.uk
Director Gillian Hambleton
General Manager Anna Flood
Tour Administrator Hilary Burns

Production details

Founded in 1978 as Northumberland Theatre Company. Small-scale touring theatre company performing at village halls, small theatres and community venues in predominantly rural areas. Main areas of work are new writing and ensemble physical theatre pieces. Stages 3-4 productions annually and gives more than 120 performances during the course of the year. Tours on average to 120 different venues nationally. 5 actors are usually involved in each production. Recent productions include: *Quay Moments* and *Tartuffe*.

Casting procedures

Sometimes holds general auditions. Actors should write in January or February requesting inclusion. Casting breakdowns are available on request via postal application (with sae). Welcomes submissions (with CVs and photographs) sent by post or email. Also accepts invitations to view individual actors' performances and will always reply to individual actors. Particularly interested in locally based actors or actors with local origins, and will keep details on file for future reference unless requested to do otherwise.

Out of Joint

7 Thane Works, Thane Villas,
London N7 7PH
tel 020-7609 0207 *fax* 020-7609 0203
email ojo@outofjoint.co.uk
website www.outofjoint.co.uk
Director Max Stafford-Clark
Administrator and Education Manager
Natasha Ockrent

Production details

Stages 2 productions annually with approximately 230 performances during the course of the year. Tours both nationally and internationally playing to around 12-15 arts centres and theatres each year. Recent productions include: *Duck* and *The Permanent Way*.

Casting procedures

Welcomes letters (with CVs and photographs) but not email submissions. Also accepts performances notices from individual actors.

Ovation Productions

1 Prince of Wales Passage,
London NW1 3EF
tel 020-7387 2342

website www.ovationtheatres.com
Director John Plews
Casting Director Katie Plews

Production details
Founded in 1985. Owns and operates
Upstairs at the Gatehouse, a fringe theatre
in North London (see entry under *Fringe
Theatres*). Recent productions include:
*Little Shop of Horrors, Jeffrey Bernard is
Unwell* and *Rough Crossing.*

Casting details
Casting breakdowns are publicly available
via *PCR* and advertisements in *The Stage.*
Welcomes letters (with CVs and photographs) but not email submissions. 'We
are always looking for actor/musicians.
Always check to see whether there is a casting coming up."

The Oxford Shakespeare Company
3 Gunter Grove, London SW10 0UN
tel 020-7351 5417
email oxfordshakespeare@btopenworld.com
website www.oxfordshakespeare
  company.co.uk
(currently being updated)
Directors Kevin Hosier, Charlotte
Windmill
London Producer Nick Green

Production details
Founded in 2001. Took over from Bold
and Saucy (established in 1992), staging
Shakespeare plays in Wadham College
Gardens, Oxford. Also has a residency at
North Garden, Lincoln's Inn, London.
Stages 3 productions with 90-100 performances during the course of the year. 9-
10 actors are involved in each production. Tours have reached Oxford, London
and Basingstoke. Recent productions
include: *As You Like It* and *The Winter's
Tale.*

Casting procedures
Actors requesting inclusion should write
in March or April. Casting breakdowns
are released to agents and are
available via *PCR.* Welcomes letters (with
CVs and photographs) but not email
submissions. Actors applying should be
able to demonstrate experience of
Shakespeare and the rigours of open-air
performing.

Paines Plough
4th Floor, 43 Aldwych,
London WC2B 4DN
tel 020-7240 4533 *fax* 020-7240 4534
email office@painesplough.com
website www.painesplough.com
Artistic Director Vicky Featherstone
Associate Director John Tiffany
Projects Manager Susannah Matthews
Administrative Assistant Helen Poole

Production details
Founded in 1974, the company is
dedicated to producing new writing. Stages
3-4 productions annually and gives 100
performances during the course of the
year. Tours to 25 different arts centres and
theatres in London, the South Coast,
Yorkshire, Scotland, and the North annually.
Recent productions include: *The Drowned
World* and *The Straits.*

Casting procedures
Sometimes holds general auditions.
Advises that the company cannot accept
unsolicited CVs or photographs as it has
no facility to store such information.

Parasol Theatre
Garden House, 4 Sunnyside,
London SW19 4SL
tel 020-8946 9478 *fax* 020-8946 0228
email parasoltheatre@waitrose.com

website www.parasoltheatre.co.uk
Director Richard Gill
Head of Design Elizabeth Waghorn

Production details
Founded in 1967. Performs largely to children and family audiences in middle-scale regional theatres, mixing classical acting with visual spectacle. Stages 2 new productions annually. Gives 80-100 performances during the course of the year in 5-6 different arts centres and theatres across England, Scotland, Ireland and Wales. Recent productions include: *The Snow Queen, The Gingerbread House* and *The New Adventures of Pinocchio.*

Casting procedures
Holds general auditions. Actors should write in mid-summer requesting inclusion. Welcomes letters (with CVs and photographs) but not email submissions.

Pentabus
Bromfield, Ludlow, Shropshire SY8 2JU
tel (01584) 856564 *fax* (01584) 856254
email john@pentabus.co.uk
website www.pentabus.co.uk
Development Director John Moreton
Artistic Director Theresa Heskins

Production details
Founded in 1974, Pentabus is a national touring company focused on the development and production of new writing. Stages 1-2 productions annually and gives 20-60 performances during the course of the year. In general 5 actors are involved in each production. Tours annually to about 10 different arts centres, theatres and outdoor venues. Recent productions include: *Smashed Eggs* and *Silent Engine.*

Casting procedures
Occasionally uses freelance casting directors. Casting breakdowns are available via Equity Job Information Service, *PCR* and the website. Welcomes letters (with CVs and photographs) but not email submissions. The company advises that it involves actors in writing development workshops as well as in productions.

Purple Fish Productions
197 Goldhawk Road, London W12 8EP
tel (07976) 809693
email info@purplefishproductions.co.uk
website www.purplefishproductions.co.uk
Directors Michelle Seton, Luan de Burgh

Production details
Founded in 2001. Aims to produce both established work and exciting devised pieces for adults and children. Michelle Seton and Luan de Burgh both trained in London and at Le Coq in Paris. Stages 3 productions with 75 performances during the course of the year. Tours to 20 different arts centres, theatres, educational and community venues annually. Tours have covered Greater London, Ireland and Canada. In general 2 actors are involved in each production. Recent productions include: *Told by a Dodo* and *The Two of Us.*

Casting procedures
Casting breakdowns are available via *PCR* and the website. Welcomes letters (with CVs and photographs) but not email submissions. Actors should write only when the company advertises. Invitations to view individual actors' websites are also accepted.

Pursued by a Bear
6 Glenluce Road, London SE3 7SB
Director Stuart Mullins

Production details
Theatre company touring new writing across the UK. Stages 2 productions annually and gives 60 performances during the course of the year. Tours to around 10 different arts centres, theatres, educational and community venues each year. Tours have covered the Easst, North East, South East, South West and London. In general 2 actors are involved in each production. Recent productions include: *Double Helix, You Don't Kiss* and *All Fall Away*.

Casting procedures
Welcomes submissions (with CVs and photographs) sent by post or email.

The Red Room
Cabin Q, Clarendon Buildings, Ronalds Road, London N5 1XJ
email info@theredroom.org.uk
website www.thearedroom.org.uk
Director Lisa Goldman
General Manager Michael White

Production details
Founded in 1995. Produces new work which 'frees the imagination against the status quo.' Develops new plays from concept to production. Engages in cultural activism, and established Actors Against the War in 2001. Stages 1-2 productions annually and gives 25-50 performances during the course of the year. Tours to 12 different theatres in international and national locations. In general fewer than 5 actors are involved in each production. Recent productions include: *Animal, The Bogus Woman* and *Going Public*.

Casting procedures
Accepts letters (with CVs and photographs), but does not welcome any other form of enquiry such as telephone calls or email. 'We are too small and busy to respond.'

Rejects Revenge Theatre Company
The Annexe, 15 Hope Street,
Liverpool L1 9BH
tel 0151-708 8480 *fax* 0151-708 8480
email rejects.revenge@virgin.net
website www.rejectsrevenge.com
Director Ann Farrar
Administrator Adrian Watts

Production details
Founded in 1990. Tours physical comedy to small and mid-scale venues in the UK and abroad. Stages 1-3 productions annually with 60-90 performances during the course of the year. Tours to 50-70 different arts centres, theatres, educational and community venues across the UK each year. In general 3-4 actors are involved in each production. Recent productions include: *Peasouper* and *Bicycle Bridge*.

Casting procedures
Uses freelance casting directors. Sometimes holds general auditions. Casting breakdowns are available via Equity Job Information Service and the website. Welcomes letters (with CVs and photographs) but not email submissions. Invitations to view individual actors' websites are also accepted.

Richmond Productions
47 Moor Mead Road, St Margaret's,
Twickenham TW1 1JS
Director Alister Cameron

Production details
Founded in 1995. International touring company producing small cast comedies. Stages 2 productions annually. Tours to arts centres, theatres, outdoor, educational and community venues and hotels in the Middle East and Eastern Europe.

Casting procedures
Advises that the company only uses actors already known to them.

Suzanna Rosenthal Ltd.

PO Box 40001, London N6 4YA
tel 020-8340 4421 *fax* 020-8340 4421
email admin@suzannarosenthal.com
website www.suzannarosenthal.com

Production details
Founded in 2001 the company produces Off-West End shows. Stages 3-5 productions annually with 100 performances over the year in theatres and outdoor venues across London. In general 5-15 actors are involved in each production. Recent productions include: *Henry VIII* and *The Resistible Rise of Arturo Ui.*

Casting procedures
Uses freelance casting directors. Sometimes holds general auditions. Actors should only write requesting inclusion in response to advertisements. Casting breakdowns are available via the website, *PCR* and advertisements in *The Stage.*

Sgript Cymru

Chapter, Market Road, Canton, Cardiff CF5 1QE
tel 029-2023 6650
email sgriptcymru@sgriptcymru.com
website www.sgriptcymru.com
Director Simon Harris
Administrative Director Mai Jones

Production details
Founded in 2000 and funded by the Arts Council of Wales, Sgript Cymru is a strategic new writing theatre company. Stages 4 productions annually and gives 100 performances during the course of the year. Tours to 25 different arts centres, theatres, and community venues in Wales, Scotland, London and the North West. In general 5 actors are involved in each production. Recent productions include: *Indian Country* and *Past Away.*

Casting procedures
Uses freelance casting directors. Welcomes letters (with CVs and photographs) but not email submissions.

Shared Experience

The Soho Laundry, 9 Dufour's Place, London W1F 7SJ
tel 020-7434 9248 *fax* 020-7287 8763
email admin@sharedexperience.org.uk
website www.sharedexperience.org.uk
Joint Artistic Directors Nancy Meckler, Polly Teale
Administrative Producer Jen Harris

Production details
An award-winning theatre company founded during the 1970s, Shared Experience stages 2-3 productions annually and tours to 12 different arts centres and theatres in the UK and abroad. In general 6-10 actors are involved in each production. Recent productions include: *After Mrs Rochester, Madame Bovary: Breakfast with Emma* and *A Passage to India.*

Casting procedures
Uses freelance casting directors. Advises that actors should contact Liz Holmes to enquire about the current casting director. 'Please do not send unsolicited mail."

Sheringham Summer Theatre

75 Byron Avenue, Colchester CO3 4HQ
tel (01206) 768765
Artistic Director Seymour Matthews

Production details
Founded in the early 1980s and formerly
known as Frinton Summer Theatre, the
company has now moved on to Sheringham
Summer Theatre. Hires out the Little Theatre
and presents a 12-week repertory theatre season (comprising 8 productions) from July to
September. Recent productions include: *Star
Spangled Girl, Make me a Widow, Run for
your Wife* and *Bedside Manners.*

Casting procedures
Holds general auditions. Actors should
write between January and April to request
inclusion. Casting breakdowns are only
occasionally made available via Equity Job
Information Service. Welcomes letters
(with CVs and photographs) but not email
submissions. 'In general, we don't issue
casting breakdowns because we nearly
always use actors known to us. However,
we do look out for extremely versatile
actors."

Sphinx Theatre Company
25 Short Street, London SE1 8LJ
Director Sue Parrish
General Manager Susannah Kraft-Levene

Production details
Former women's theatre group established
approximately 30 years ago. Specialises in
writing and directing by women. Stages
1-2 productions annually and gives 50 performances during the course of the year.
Tours to 8-10 different arts centres, theatres and educational venues nationwide.
In general 6 actors are involved in each
production. Recent productions include:
As You Like It and *Wedding Story.*

Casting procedures
Sometimes holds general auditions. Actors
may write at any time requesting inclusion.
Casting breakdowns are available via postal
application and *PCR*. Welcomes letters

(with CVs and photographs) but not email
submissions.

Talawa Theatre Co. Ltd.
3rd Floor, 23-25 Great Sutton Street,
London EC1V ODN
tel 020-7251 6644 *fax* 020-7251 5969
email nq@talawa.com
website www.talawa.com
Director Paulette Randall
General Manager Kate Sarley

Production details
Founded in 1986. Aims to use black ritual,
political experience and culture to further
inform, enrich and enlighten modern
British theatre. Stages 2-3 productions
annually and gives 40 performances during
the course of the year. Tours to 2-3 different
theatres, educational and community
venues in the West Midlands and Jamaica
annually. In general 4 or more actors are
involved in each production. Recent productions include: *Itsy Bitsy Spider* and *The
Key Game.*

Casting procedures
Welcomes submissions (with CVs and
photographs) sent by post or email.
Invitations to view individual actors' websites are also accepted.

Tamasha Theatre Company
Unit E, 11 Ronalds Road, London N5 1XJ
tel 020-7609 2411 *fax* 020-7609 2772
email Claire@tamasha.org.uk
website www.tamasha.org.uk
Directors Kristine Landon-Smith, Sudha
Bhuchar
General Manager Bryan Savery

Production details
Founded in 1989. Produces 'untold stories"
in mainstream theatre venues. Stages 1-2
productions annually and gives 50

performances during the course of the year. Tours annually to about 6 small and mid-scale theatre venues in London, Yorkshire, Newcastle, the Midlands, the South West and Cornwall. In general 2-15 actors are involved in each production. Recent productions include: *Ryman and the Sheikh, Ghost Dancing* and *Fourteen Songs.*

Casting procedures

Actors requesting inclusion should write in the run-up to productions –suggests 3 months in advance. Casting breakdowns are available by postal application (with sae). Welcomes submissions (with CVs and photographs) sent by post or email.

Tenth Planet Productions

75 Woodland Gardens, London N10 3UD
tel 020-8442 2659 *fax* 020-8883 1708
email admin@tenthplanetproductions.com
website www.tenthplanetproductions.com
Artistic Director Alexander Holt
Literary Manager Mark Underwood
Associate Directors Susan Harriet, Alex Scrivener

Production details

Founded in 1998. Stages 4-6 productions annually and gives 100-120 performances during the course of the year. Tours to 2-10 different theatres in the UK and United Arab Emirates. Also performs dinner theatre in the Emirates and in site-specific locations such as the Rose Theatre in London. In general 4-8 actors are involved in each production. Recent productions include: *Rough Crossing, Tamburlaine* and *Can't Pay, Won't Pay.*

Casting procedures

Holds general auditions. Actors should write in response to advertisements only. Casting breakdowns are available via *PCR, Castnet* and *Castweb* (see entry under *Casting Directories and Information Services*). Showreels and invitations to view individual actors' websites are also accepted. Advises that the company principally casts NCDT-trained actors or established actors with demonstrable experience. As it is unable to retain submissions on file, actors should only write in when casting is advertised, or telephone first.

Theatre Absolute

57-61 Corporation Street,
Coventry CV1 1GQ
tel 024-7625 7380
email info@theatreabsolute.co.uk
website www.theatreabsolute.co.uk
Artistic Director Chris O'Connell
Producer Julia Negus

Production details

Founded in 1998. Develops, produces and tours new plays. Its development arm, The Writing House, works with writers, actors and directors on new scripts. Stages 1 production annually and gives 30-40 performances during the course of the year. Tours to around 20 arts centres and theatres in the North West, West Midlands, East Midlands, London and the South East. In general 6 actors are involved in each production. Recent productions include: *Car, Raw* and *Kid.*

Casting procedures

Actors should consult the website for details of the next project and for casting breakdowns and information. In addition to its annual production, the company works with actors in writing workshops throughout the year. Welcomes letters (with CVs and up-to-date photographs) but not email submissions. Advises actors not to send blanket letters and CVs. 'Find out about our work first –we always see actors who have seen our work if they're suitable for the role offered.'Also happy to give advice to new/emerging actors.

Theatre de Complicite

14 Anglers Lane, Kentish Town, London
NW5 3DE
tel 020-7485 7700 *fax* 020-7485 7701
email email@complicite.org
website www.complicite.org
Artistic Director Simon McBurney
Administrative Producer Judith Dimant
Administrator Anita Ashwick
Education and Marketing Natasha
Freedman

Production details

Award-winning theatre company founded
in 1983. Constantly evolving its ensemble
of performers and collaborators. Work
ranges from entirely devised pieces to theatrical adaptations and revivals of classic
texts. Stages 2 productions annually and
gives 50-100 performances during the
course of the year. Tours to 10-20 different
theatres and major arts centres across the
UK, throughout Europe and worldwide. In
general 4-7 actors are involved in each production. Recent productions include: *The
Elephant Vanishes* and *Mnemonic.*

Casting procedures

Occasionally uses freelance casting directors. Welcomes letters (with CVs and photographs) sent by post rather than email.
'We are always more inclined to meet with
actors previously unknown to us if they
are familiar with our work (i.e. if they have
seen a Complicite show or participated in
an Open Workshop). Complicite's
Education Department programmes 2
Open Workshop seasons for actors each
year. Contact us to join the Open
Workshop mailing list.'

Théâtre Sans Frontières

Queens Hall Arts Centre, Beaumont Street,
Hexham NE46 3LS
tel (01434) 652484 *fax* (01434) 607206

email admin@tsfront.co.uk
website theatresansfrontieres.co.uk
Directors Sarah Kemp, John Cobb
General Manager Helen Green

Production details

Founded in 1991. Set up by former students of Philippe Gaulier and Monika
Pagneux. Specialises in physical theatre
and stages texts in different languages for
adults and children using international
performers. Stages 2-3 productions
annually and gives 60-100 performances
during the course of the year. Tours to 30
different venues annually, including arts
centres and theatres in all regions of the
UK. Also tours to schools. In general 3-6
actors are involved in each production.
Recent productions include: *Le Petit
Chaperon Rouge* and *Le Tour de France.*

Casting procedures

Sometimes holds general auditions. Actors
may write at any time requesting inclusion.
Casting breakdowns are available on
request. Welcomes submissions (with CVs
and photographs) sent by post or email.
Invitations to view individual actors' websites are also accepted. 'We are usually
looking for actors who have languages
other than English (especially French,
Spanish or German), and who have a clear
physical theatre training (i.e. Le Coq,
Gaulier, Pagneux or Complicite).'

Theatre Set-up

12 Fairlawn Close, Southgate,
London N14 4JX
website www.ts-u.co.uk
Charitable Director Wendy Macphee

Production details

Founded in 1976. Presents Shakespeare
productions in historic and beautiful sites.
Stages 1 production annually with 55 performances over the course of the year.

Tours to 40 different outdoor venues annually in the UK, Norway, the Netherlands and Belgium. In general 8 actors are involved in each production. Recent productions include: *Two Gentlemen of Verona.*

Casting procedures

Sometimes holds general auditions. Actors should write in February requesting inclusion. Welcomes letters (with CVs and photographs) but not email submissions. Advises actors that 'the tour is rigorous and not for the faint-hearted'.

Theatre-Rites

The Warehouse, 12 Ravensbury Terrace, London SW18 4RL
tel 020-8946 2236 *fax* 020-8946 0965
email info@theatre-rites.co.uk
website www.theatre-rites.co.uk
Director Sue Buckmaster
General Manager Natalie Highwood

Production details

Founded in 1995, the company creates touring productions and site-specific installations for children and family audiences. Company work is devised, visual and features puppetry, commissioned soundscapes and music. Stages 1 touring show and 1 site-specific piece each year with a total of 12 performances. Tours to 4 different venues annually, including arts centres, theatres and outdoor venues in national and international locations. In general 4 actors are involved in each production. Recent productions include: *Finders Keepers, Catch Your Breath* and *Shopworks.*

Casting procedures

Sometimes holds general auditions. Welcomes letters (with CVs and photographs) but not email submissions. 'Multi-disciplined performers are always very welcome.'

Tinderbox Theatre Company

Imperial Buildings, 22 High Street, Belfast BT1 2BE
tel 028-9043 9313 *fax* 028-9032 9420
email info@tinderbox.org.uk
website www.tinderbox.org.uk
Artistic Director Michael Duke
General Manager Eamon Quinn

Production details

Founded in 1988. Produces, develops and stages new work which interrogates life in Northern Ireland. Stages 2-3 productions and tours to 12 different venues annually, including arts centres, theatres and site-specific locations in Ireland, England and Scotland. In general 6 actors are involved in each production. Recent productions include: *Caught Red Handed* and *The Chairs.*

Casting procedures

Sometimes holds general auditions. Welcomes letters (with CVs and photographs) but not email submissions. Invitations to view individual actors' websites are also accepted.

Told by an Idiot

c/o BAC, Lavender Hill, London SW11 5TF
tel 020-7978 4200 *fax* 020-7978 5200
email ggranger@dial.pipex.com
website www.toldby.dircon.co.uk
Directors Hayley Carmichael, Paul Hunter, John Wright
General Manager Ghislaine Granger
Associate Producer Nick Sweeting

Production details

Founded in 1992, the company tours to arts centres and theatres throughout England.

Casting procedures

Sometimes holds general auditions. Actors may write at any time throughout the year requesting inclusion. The company will make contact if and when a relevant project arises. Casting breakdowns are available on request from the box office. Welcomes submissions (with CVs and photographs) sent by post or email. Invitations to view individual actors' websites are also accepted.

TOSG Gaelic Theatre Company

Sabhal Mor Ostaig, Sleat,
Isle of Skye IV44 8RQ
tel (01471) 888542 *fax* (01471) 888542
email tosg@tosg.org
website www.smo.uhi.ac.uk/tosg
Artistic Director Simon Mackenzie
General Manager Janet Ward

Production details

Founded in 1996. Professional Gaelic Theatre Company producing theatre for both adults and children. Also runs a new writing scheme. All productions are performed in Gaelic. Stages 2 productions annually and gives 50 performances per year. Tours to 30 different venues annually, including arts centres, theatres, educational and community venues in Scotland. In general 5 actors are involved in each production.

Casting procedures

Sometimes holds general auditions. Actors can write in May requesting inclusion. Welcomes letters (with CVs and photographs) but not email submissions. Invitations to view individual actors' websites are also accepted. 'Non-Gaelic speakers need not apply.'

Trestle Theatre Company

Trestle Arts Base, Russet Drive,
St Albans AL4 0JQ
tel (01727) 850950 *fax* (01727) 855558
email admin@trestle.org.uk
website www.trestle.org.uk
Director Toby Wilsher
General Manager Valerie Evans

Production details

Founded in 1981. Small to mid-scale theatre company touring new, devised or commissioned work. Principal medium is the full mask, but also uses text, puppets and live music. Stages 2-3 productions annually and gives more than 100 performances. Tours to 50 different venues each year, including arts centres and theatres in Britain, Europe and other international locations. In general 5 actors are involved in each production. Recent productions include: *Tonight We Fly, Island* and *Inventions of the Stoneheads.*

Casting procedures

Sometimes holds general auditions. Actors may write at any time requesting inclusion. Casting breakdowns are available from the website, *PCR* and advertisements in *The Stage.* Welcomes letters (with CVs and photographs) but not email submissions. 'Don't apply unless you have relevant mask training and experience.'

UK Arts International

2nd Floor, 6 Shaw Street, Worcester
WR1 3QQ

Production details

Stages 1 production annually which tours to approximately 70 different venues, including arts centres, theatres, education and community venues across the UK.

Casting procedures

Does not hold general auditions and does not welcome submissions from actors previously unknown to the company.

Unlimited Theatre

Studio 11, Aire Street Workshops,
30-34 Aire Street, Leeds LS1 4HT
tel 0113-234 5400
email unlimited@unlimited.org.uk
website www.unlimited.org.uk
Director Jon Spooner
Development Manager Liz Margree

Production details

Founded in 1997. Creates work intended
to "explore how personal experience can
illuminate political debate, and which puts
marginalised voices centre-stage." Stages 1-2
productions annually, and gives 50-100
performances. Tours to 10-20 different
venues each year including arts centres and
theatres throughout the UK (including
Glasgow, Edinburgh and Belfast) and overseas. In general 4-6 actors are involved in
each production. Recent productions
include: *Safety* and *Neutrino*.

Casting procedures

Sometimes holds general auditions.
Welcomes letters (with CVs and photographs) but not email submissions.
Invitations to view individual actors' websites are also accepted. 'We are a small to
middle-scale organisation and only occasionally employ freelance actors. We are
always interested in hearing from potential
new collaborators."

Volcano Theatre Company

Swansea Institute, Townhill Road,
Swansea SA2 0UT
tel (01792) 281280
email volcano.tc@virgin.net
website www.volcanotheatre.co.uk
Directors Paul Davies, Fern Smith
General Manager Katie Keeler

Production details

Founded in 1987. Small-scale national and
international touring company based in
Wales. Specialises in physical theatre, new
writing, devised and collaborative work
and adaptations/deconstructions of classics. Stages 2-4 productions and gives
50 performances each year. Tours to 35 different venues annually. Venues have
included arts centres and theatres in Wales,
England, Ireland, Scotland, Europe,
Central Asia, South America, Canada and
Sri Lanka. In general 2-5 actors are
involved in each production. Recent
productions include: *The Imaginary
Woman* and *Talk Sex Show.*

Casting procedures

Casting breakdowns are available by postal
application (with sae). Welcomes letters
(with CVs and photographs) but not email
submissions. Invitations to view individual
actors' websites are also accepted. The
company also runs workshops that can
sometimes lead to casting invitations.

Keith Whitall

10 Woodlands Avenue, West Byfleet,
Surrey KT14 6AT
tel (01932) 343655
Director Keith Whitall

Production details

Founded in 2000. Produces revues, small-
scale musicals and occasionally plays and
one-person shows. Stages 2-3 productions
annually and gives 20 or more performances in theatres in Brighton and the
South East. So far has only toured to 1 arts
centre. In general 9-10 actors are involved
in each production. Recent productions
include: *Broadway Calling.*

Casting procedures

Sometimes holds general auditions. Actors
may write at any time requesting inclusion. Casting breakdowns are usually
made available to casting directors or
actors seen in a production. Welcomes

letters (with CVs and photographs) but not email submissions. The company's director, Keith Whitall, is also a freelance casting director. 'In my reviews I usually use 3-4 experienced artistes plus new young artistes in whom I am especially interested."Musical theatre experience is preferable.

The Wrestling School

42 Durlston Road, London E5 8RR
tel 020-8442 4229
website www.thewrestlingschool.co.uk
Director Howard Barker

Production details
Founded in 1988. 'Develops ways of presenting complex ideas in the theatre through the work of Howard Barker." Stages 1 production annually and gives 35 performances. Tours to 6 different venues each year including arts centres and theatres. In general 5-7 actors are involved in each production.

Casting procedures
Sometimes holds auditions. Welcomes letters when casting (with CVs and photographs) but not email submissions. Actors should telephone in late July to find out if the company is casting.

English-Language European Theatre Companies

This small section seems to be populated by companies set up by enthusiasts who have kept on going with very little subsidy – and sometimes with none at all. Although living away from home and isolated from auditions, it can be fun working for such companies. It is important to note that the work often involves educational projects and/or touring.

ACT Company

51 rue Hoche, 92240 Malakoff, France
tel 0033 146 562318 *fax* 0033 146 562318
email andrew.wilson@wanadoo.fr
website www.actheatre.com
Artistic Director Andrew Wilson
Administrator Anne Wilson

Founded in 1981. An English-language theatre company focusing on research and development to create high-quality productions. Aims to make theatrical experiences in English accessible to a non-native-speaking public. Runs Theatre in Education projects, performing English theatre for young French native speakers. Recent productions include: *Robinson Crusoe, Sir Gawain and the Green Knight* and *The Secret Diary of Adrian Mole*.

Amandla Theatre Company

179 rue de Vaugirad, 75015 Paris, France
tel 0033 630 898881
Artistic Director Caroline Benamza
Administrator Jean-Marie Degove

A bilingual touring theatre company.

Dear Conjunction Theatre Company

6 rue Arthur Rozier, 75019 Paris, France
tel 0033 142 416965
email dearconjunction@wanadoo.fr
Artistic Directors Barbara Bray, Leslie Clack, Patricia Kessler

Company composed of professional actors, directors and writers who are resident in Paris. Presents plays and poetry readings at various venues. Past productions include: *Rough for Theatre I, That Time* and *Footfalls* by Samuel Beckett. Welcomes actors previously unknown to the company. Contact Leslie Clack for more information.

English Pocket Theatre

Internationales Theater Frankfurt, Hanauer Landstrasse 7-9, G-60314 Frankfurt am Main, Germany
tel 0049 69 4990980

Theatre company which performs at the International Theatre in Frankfurt. Regularly presents musicals, readings and Celtic music.

The English Speaking Theatre Oslo (TESTO)

Jacob Aalls Gate 30, 0364 Oslo, Norway
tel 0047 22 466248
email testo-no@online.no
website home.tiscali.no/testo.no

Artistic Director Simon Lay
Director Kristin Zachariassen

Founded in 1996 by actors Simon Lay and Kristin Zachariassen. Main focus of work is Theatre in Education. Produces theatre adaptations targeted at Norwegian students but also appealing to the general Norwegian public. Recent productions include: *How High is Up?, Too Much for Punch and Judy, Pygmalion* and *The Woman in Black.*

The English Theatre Company Ltd.

Nybrogatan 35, 114 39 Stockholm, Sweden
tel 0046 8 6624133 *fax* 0046 8 6601159
email etc.ltd@telia.com
website www.englishtheatre.se
Artistic Director Christer Berg
Director Derek Killeen

Founded in 1981. Stages 2 productions annually. Recent productions include: *Shirley Valentine* and *A Christmas Carol.* Uses freelance casting directors. Holds general auditions; actors requesting inclusion should write between August and September. Casting breakdowns are not publicly available. Welcomes postal enquiries from actors previously unknown to the company.

The English Theatre of Copenhagen

The London Toast Theatre, Kochsvej 18, 1812 Fred C., Copenhagen
tel 0045 3322 8686
email mail@londontoast.dk
website www.londontoast.dk
Artistic Director Vivienne McKee
Administrator Soren Hall

Founded in 1982. The largest English-speaking theatre company in Northern Europe. Presents theatre productions and provides corporate entertainment, stand-up comedy and Murder Mystery shows in Scandinavia and abroad. The company's voice-over bureau, 'Speaker's Corner', provides English and American voices for films and commercials. Recent productions include: *Dracula – a pain in the neck!* and *The Importance of Being Earnest.*

English Theatre Frankfurt

Kaiserstrasse 34, D-60329 Frankfurt, Germany
tel 0049 6924 231610
fax 0049 6924 231614
email mail@english-theatre.org
website www.english-theatre.org
Artistic Adviser Clive Paget
Managing Director Daniel Nicholas

Founded in 1979. Presents contemporary plays, musicals and classics. 5 productions performed in the main house each year, totalling 260 performances. Uses London-based freelance casting directors. Does not hold general auditions. Actors should write requesting inclusion in the company in April. Casting breakdowns are not publicly available.

The English Theatre of Hamburg

Lerchenfeld 14, 22041 Hamburg, Germany
tel 0049 40 2277089 *fax* 0049 40 2295040
email ETHamburg@onlinehome.de
website www.englishtheatre.de
Contact Robert Rumpf, Clifford Dean

Founded in 1976 by 2 Americans, Robert Rumpf and Clifford Dean, who originally trained and worked professionally in the USA. They share general management responsibilities, plan the artistic programme and direct productions. Since 1981 the theatre has occupied its present premises at Mundsburg in 22018 Hamburg. Performs 8 times per week from September to June. A typical season at The

English Theatre includes a classic American or British drama, a comedy and a thriller. Recent productions include: *Over the River and Through the Woods, I Ought to be in Pictures, Educating Rita* and *When the Reaper Calls.* Also runs Education programmes.

Light Nights – The Summer Theatre

The Travelling Theatre Baldursgata 37, IS-101 Reykjavik, Iceland
tel 00354 5519181 *fax* 00354 5515015
Artistic Director Kristine G Magnus

Merlin International Theatre

1052 Budapest, Gerloczy Utca 4, Hungary
tel 0036 1 3179338 *fax* 0036 1 2660904
email angol@merlinszinhaz.hu
website www.szinhaz.hu/merlin/english
Director Laszlo Magacs
Associate Director Emma Vidovsky

Founded in 1991; Hungary's first and currently its only international theatre. Recent productions include: *The Importance of Being Earnest, Don't Drink the Water, Stones in His Pockets* and *Twelfth Night.* Resident companies at the Merlin Theatre are the Atlantis Company, Junion Group and Madhouse.

Onatti Theatre Company

9 Field Close, Warwick, Warwickshire CV34 4QD
tel 01926 495220 *fax* 0870 1643629
email info@onatti.co.uk
website www.onatti.co.uk
Artistic Director Andrew Bardwell
Company Manager Seanna Hardaker-Jones

Presents foreign-language productions for schools, touring productions, theatre in museums, and theatre function

entertainments. Contact Alan Hamlet, Educational Advisor <tie@onatti.co.uk> for details of Theatre in Education programmes. Recent productions include: *The Way of the World, Premier Amour, Greensleeves* and *The Child King.*

Theatre From Oxford (Touring Europe and Beyond)

69-71 Oxford Street, Woodstock, Oxford OX20 1TJ
Contact Robert Southam

Only accepts written correspondence.

Vienna's English Theatre

UK address: VM Theatre Productions Ltd., 16 The Street, Ash, Canterbury CT3 2HJ
tel (01304) 813330 *fax* (01304) 813330
Theatre address: Josefsgasse 12, A-1080 Vienna, Austria
tel 0043 1402 12600 *fax* 0043 1402 126042
email office@englishtheatre.at
website www.englishtheatre.at

Founded in 1963. The oldest English-language theatre in continental Europe. Originally intended as a summer theatre for English-speaking tourists, it has now developed a year-round programme. Productions scheduled for 2004 include: *The Second City, The Syringa Tree, The Kat and the Kings* and *There Goes the Bride.*

White Horse Theatre

Bœrdenstrasse 17, 59494 Soest-Müllingsen, Germany
tel 0049 2921 339339
fax 0049 2921 339336
email theatre@whitehouse.de
website www.whitehouse.de
Artistic Director Peter Griffith
Casting Director Michael Dray

Founded in 1978. Tours schools in Germany with occasional visits to neighbouring countries. Contracts are for 10-11 months. 6 companies of 4 actors each perform 3 plays. Recent productions include: *The Glass Menagerie*, *Oliver Twist*, and numerous plays for 10-13 year olds and for 14-16 year olds. Does not use freelance casting directors. Holds general auditions; actors should write in April requesting inclusion. Casting breakdowns are available through the website, postal application (with sae), Equity Job Information Service, *PCR* and advertisements in *The Stage*. Welcomes postal and email enquiries from actors previously unknown to the company. Invitations to view individual actors' websites are also accepted.

Fringe Theatres

Essentially, the idea of 'fringe theatre' began at the Edinburgh Festival more than half a century ago. It really started taking off (especially in London) in the late 1960s as an arena for 'alternative' and 'experimental' theatre. The 1990s saw a huge expansion in the number of venues being used, and a downturn in the exploration of theatre forms: the 'fringe' became more commercial and much more competitive – and not just in London and Edinburgh. Today, the terms 'alternative' and 'experimental' are far less frequently used, and the Fringe is now largely seen as a way for actors, directors and writers to showcase their work.

Casting for Fringe productions is usually advertised by one or more of the casting information services, and agents and casting directors do scout for new talent in them. However, it's highly unlikely that you will make any money from participating in such a production, and agents and casting directors get blitzed with so many invitations that the chances of getting one of them to see you are quite low. The only reasons for being in a Fringe production are (a) you might be 'seen', (b) you fundamentally believe in the production's potential and (c) it could help keep your acting-juices flowing – you might find classes less time-consuming and possibly more beneficial.

Although it is generally regarded as 'professional' work, there is a tendency in Fringe productions for professional standards (and facilities) to be somewhat lacking – and that is sometimes an understatement. Poor technical back-up, indifferent front-of-house arrangements and general unreliability are too often the case, almost inevitably damaging the quality of the final product.

The listings that follow are restricted to the more 'established' venues, with performance spaces for hire. Some Fringe theatres only programme-in work known to them.

Note If you are thinking of mounting a Fringe production and/or starting your own theatre company, start researching and planning well in advance. It is well worth consulting the Independent Theatre Council (ITC) <www.itc-arts.org>.

Umbrella organisations

Fringe Theatre Network (FTN)

Unit 5a, Imex Business Centre, Ingate
Place, London SW8 3NS
tel 020-7627 4920 *fax* 020-7978 2631
email Frank.Fisher@fringetheatre.org.uk
website www.fringetheatre.org.uk
Coordinator Frank Fisher

The FTN provides services, support and a
network of contacts for venues, producing
companies and individuals working on the
London Fringe with the aim of increasing
the level of professionalism in Fringe theatre. Acting as an umbrella organisation,
the FTN puts forward the interests of
Fringe theatre in its dealings with statutory
authorities, funding bodies, policy-makers
and other arts organisations.

Edinburgh Festival Fringe

The Fringe Office, 180 High Street,
Edinburgh EH1 1QS
tel 0131-226 0026 *fax* 0131-226 0016
email admin@edfringe.com
website www.edfringe.com

The Fringe Society was formed in 1959 to
co-ordinate publicity and ticket sales and
offer a comprehensive information service
to both performers and audiences. It compiles information about venues, press and
suppliers and produces a series of publications designed to answer frequently asked
questions. Its brochure contains details for
183 Fringe venues in Edinburgh. The office
is open all year round and the staff are
available to help by phone, email or personal appointment.

London Fringe venues

Barons Court Theatre

The Curtain's Up, 28A Comeragh Rd, West
Kensington, London Wl4 9RH
tel 020-7602 0235 *fax* 020-7603 8935
email baronstheatre@fsmail.net

A 60-seat theatre in the basement of The
Curtain's Up public house. Usually offers
3-week runs and is booked 4-5 months in
advance.

The Bridewell Theatre

Bride Lane, Fleet Street, London EC4Y 8EQ
tel 020-7353 0259 *fax* 020-7583 5289
email bridewell@freeuk.com
General Manager Simon James Collier

Flexible seating arrangements with a maximum house of 175. Theatre can be booked
up to 7 months in advance, but ring to
check or send a written proposal to Simon
James Collier.

Camden People's Theatre

58-60 Hampstead Road, London NW1 2PY
email cpt@dircon.co.uk
website www.cpt.dircon.co.uk
tel 020-7916 5878 *fax* 020-7813 3889

A 60-seat theatre available for single nights
as well as full runs.

Canal Café Theatre

The Bridge House, Delamere Terrace, Little
Venice, London W2 6ND
tel 020-7289 6056 *fax* 020-7266 1717
email newsrevue@mail.com
website www.newsrevue.com

A 60-seat cafétheatre situated above the
Bridge House pub next to the canal in
Little Venice. Welcomes comedy.

Chelsea Centre Theatre

World's End Place, King's Road,
London SWI0 0DR
tel 020-7352 1967 *fax* 020-7352 2024

A 110-seat theatre which can be booked-up 6 months in advance. Particularly welcomes new writing.

Cockpit Theatre

Gateforth Street, London NW8 8EH
email dave.wybrow@awc.ac.uk
tel 020-7258 2920 *fax* 020-7258 2921

Theatre seats 180 (60 seats on 3 sides) and should be booked 6 months in advance. Welcomes classics, foreign-language theatre and other niche market work.

The Courtyard Theatre

10 York Way, King's Cross, London N1 9AA
tel 020-7833 0870
email info@thecourtyard.org.uk
website www.thecourtyard.org.uk

Flexible seating arrangements for up to 70 with separate rehearsal rooms, foyer and gallery. Normally offers 4-week runs, can be booked up to a year in advance.

Diorama Studio Theatre

34 Osnaburgh Street, London NW1 3ND
tel 020-7916 5467 *fax* 020-7916 5282

Seats up to 50, companies are advised to book as far in advance as possible.

Etcetera Theatre Club

Oxford Arms, 265 Camden High Street, London NW1 7BU
tel 020-7482 4857 *fax* 020-7482 0378
email etceteratheatre@hotmail.com

A black-box studio space with 42 raked seats, the theatre particularly welcomes new writing. Will also consider innovative adaptations of classics. Presents an early and a late show each evening.

Finborough Theatre

Finborough Arms, 118 Finborough Road, London SW10 9ED
tel 020-7244 7439 *fax* 020-7835 1853
email admin@finboroughtheatre.co.uk
website www.finboroughtheatre.co.uk

A member of the ITC, the theatre was nominated for the 2003 Empty Space Peter Brook Award for up-and-coming studio theatre hire. Email the theatre for a copy of their Rental Information Pack.

The Grace Theatre

The Latchmere, 503 Battersea Park Road, London SW11 3BW
Programming Office: c/o 68 Kensington Church Street, London W8 4BY
tel 020-7229 8530 *fax* 020-7229 8140
email mail@latchmeretheatre.com
website www.latchmeretheatre.com

Theatre and comedy venue promoting new writing and new comedians. Situated above a public house, it also has a gallery attached.

Greenwich Playhouse

Greenwich BR Station Forecourt, 189 Greenwich High Road, London SE10 8JA
tel 020-8858 9256 *fax* 020-8969 2910
email Alice@galleontheatre.co.uk
Artistic Director Alice de Sousa

Theatre seats 83 and boasts state-of-the art facilities. Available for hire for short-seasons at very affordable weekly rates. Visiting productions benefit free of charge from the advice and support of the resident Artistic Director –also see entry under Galleon Theatre Company Ltd.

Hackney Empire Studio Theatre

(Above Samuel Pepys Public House) 289 Mare Street, London E8 1EJ
tel 020-8986 0171

Theatre seats up to 250 and will be available for hire again towards the end of 2004.

Hen & Chickens Theatre

Above Hen & Chickens Theatre Bar, 109 St Paul's Road, Islington, London Nl 2NA
tel 020-7704 2001

A 60-seat theatre welcoming new writing. Directly opposite station. Offers 3-4 week runs with Monday nights available separately.

Jacksons Lane Theatre

269A Archway Road, London N6 5AA
tel 020-8340 5226
email mail@jacksonslane.org.uk
website www.jacksonslane.org.uk

Rooms are available for hire on a daily or hourly basis for private parties, rehearsals and performances. The Lavender Room seats up to 40; the Primrose Room seats up to 40; a multi-purpose space seats up to 80; the Youth Space seats up to 25; and the Main Theatre seats 125-163.

King's Head Theatre

115 Upper Street, Islington, London N1 1QN
tel 020-7226 8561
website www.kingsheadtheatre.org

Famous for helping to launch the careers of many new writers, directors and actors including Stephen Berkoff, Anthony Sher and Victoria Wood, the theatre is situated above a public house with flexible seating for up to 105.

The Landor Theatre

70 Landor Road, London SW9 9PH
tel 020-7737 7276 *fax* 020-8480 8536
email info@landortheatre.co.uk
website www.landortheatre.co.uk

A 60-seat theatre situated above a public house.

New End Theatre

27 New End, Hampstead, London NW3 1JD
tel 020-7472 5800 *fax* 020-7472 5808
email mail@newendtheatre.co.uk
website www.newendtheatre.co.uk

Theatre seats 84 and has a strong tradition of presenting new plays and musicals, as well as reviving works from the classical canon. Recent productions include: Sondheim's *Assassins*, *A Dangerous Woman* (starring Fenella Fielding), and *Weill & Lenya* (directed by Ken Russell).

Old Red Lion

418 St John Street, Islington, London EC1V 4NJ
tel 020-7833 3053 *fax* 020-7833 3053
website www.oldredliontheatre.co.uk
Artistic Director Melanie Tait

Founded in 1979, the Old Red Lion Theatre is a 60-seater Fringe theatre primarily dedicated to new writing. Companies wishing to hire the venue should post a script, some company information and a production proposal to the Artistic Director. Normally programmes 3 months ahead.

Oval House Theatre

52-54 Kennington Oval, London SE11 5SW
tel 020-7582 0080
email Karena.Johnson@OvalHouse.com
website www.ovalhouse.com
Programmer Karena Johnson

Comprises 2 spaces; the upstairs theatre seats 50 and the downstairs theatre seats 100. Presents a diverse programme of work.

Pleasance Theatre London

Carpenters Mews, North Road,
London N7 9EF
tel 020-7619 6868 *fax* 020-7700 7366
email info@pleasance.co.uk
website www.pleasance.co.uk/LONDON

The Pleasance now has 2 spaces: the Main Theatre, seating just under 300; and the Pleasance Stage Space, a new venue created to nurture the best in new theatre writing and emerging comedy talent, seating 54.

Riverside Studios

Crisp Road, London W6 9RL
tel 020-8237 1000
website www.riversidestudios.co.uk

Riverside has a varied programme of both domestic and international performance, theatre, dance and other events. Considers work, either hires or co-productions, within the context of the building's artistic policy.

Studio Two is a medium-sized black-box space with a comprehensive motorised grid, suited to all types of production. Flexible configurations seating up to 400. Selected recent shows include: Graeae Theatre's *Mother Courage and Her Children* and Complicite's *Mnemonic*. Studio Three is a small black-box studio, opening off the foyer; raked theatre-style seating available –156 seats installed as standard. Studio Four is a high-quality general-purpose room on the second floor, particularly suited to rehearsals, auditions, workshops and small-scale filming. No permanent seating; capacity up to 100 (not currently accessible by wheelchair). Other spaces available for hire include many smaller office spaces, a cinema auditorium and a television studio.

Rosemary Branch Theatre

2 Shepperton Road, London N1 3DT
email cecilia@rosemarybranch.co.uk
tel 020-7704 6665

Theatre with 50 seats and a separate rehearsal space. Can be booked 3-4 months in advance.

Soho Theatre

21 Dean Street, London W1V 6NE
tel 020-7287 5060 *fax* 020-7287 5061
email hires@sohotheatre.com
website www.sohotheatre.com

A venue for new writing, the theatre has a range of rooms and spaces to hire.

Southwark Playhouse

5 Playhouse Court, 62 Southwark Bridge Rd, London SE1 0AS
tel 020-7652 2224 *fax* 020-7261 1271
email admin@southwarkplayhouse.co.uk
website www.southwarkplayhouse.co.uk

Formed in 1993, this studio theatre has been nominated 3 times for the Empty Space Peter Brook Award. Alongside their own productions, the theatre presents and supports the work of talented young companies with a mixed programme of classic and new plays. Maximum seating capacity is 90. In general the theatre is booked-up 3-4 months in advance but this can vary. Proposals should be sent by post or email to the Playhouse with a 1-page synopsis of the production and all the relevant details.

Tabard Theatre
2 Both Road, Turnham Green,
London W4 1LW
tel 020-8995 6035

Situated above the Tabard pub, close to
Turnham Green tube. Offers 3-4 week
runs which are programmed 3-4 months
ahead.

Theatro Technis
26 Crowndale Road, London NW1 1TT
tel 020-7387 6617 *fax* 020-7388 7971
email info@theatrotechnis.com
website www.theatrotechnis.co.uk

Theatro Technis' ideas and policies are
realised for anyone who is interested in the
development of individuals and communities. The theatre maintains a balance
between both classic and contemporary
work and serves to embrace a variety of
diverse artforms ranging from theatre and
dance to art, photography, music and film.

Union Theatre
204 Union Street, Southwark,
London SE1 0LX
tel 020-7261 9876 *fax* 020-7261 9876
email sasha@uniontheatre.freeserve.co.uk
website www.uniontheatre.freeserve.co.uk

Primarily a new writing venue, the theatre
aims to present a diverse programme featuring the best new talent. Guest performances
are supplemented by regular in-house productions. Normally offers 3-week runs.

Upstairs at the Gatehouse
The Gatehouse Pub, North Road,
London N6 4BD
tel 020-8340 3477
email events@ovationproductions.com
website www.upstairsatthegatehouse.com

Seats 132 (140 in cabaret style). A rehearsal
room is also available. See entry for
Ovation Productions under *Middle &
Smaller-Scale Companies.*

White Bear Theatre
138 Kennington Park Road,
London SE11 4DJ
tel 020-7793 9193

A L-shaped studio space with seating for
up to 50. Generally prefers new writing but
occasionally accepts revivals.

Wimbledon Studio Theatre
(In Wimbledon Theatre) 103 The
Broadway, London SW19 1QG
tel 020-8543 4549 *fax* 020-8543 6637
email live@wimbledontheatre.demon.co.uk

A recently refurbished theatre with seating
for up to 80. Normally offers 3-4 week runs
which are programmed 6 months ahead.

Edinburgh Fringe venues

Many of these venues are only available to
hire during the Edinburgh Festival Fringe
in August. For a full list of venues, contact
the Fringe Society (see above).

Assembly Rooms
Assembly Festival Theatre, The Assembly
Rooms, 2/2 50 George Street,
Edinburgh EH2 2LE
tel 0131-624 2442 *fax* 0131-624 7131
email info@assemblyrooms.com
website www.assemblyrooms.com

The Assembly Rooms have presented more
than 1000 productions featuring most of the
major names in British comedy, as well as a
huge array of theatre, dance and music

events which have been seen by more than 1.5 million people over the last 20 years of the Edinburgh Festival Fringe. The daily programme runs from 11.00 a.m. to 3.30 a.m. with exhibitions, a café, 2 public bars, a club bar and late-night supper club. Aims to programme a balance of theatre, comedy and new work.

Augustine's

Augustine United Church, 41 George IV Bridge, Edinburgh EH1 1EL
tel 0131-220 1677

During the rest of the year this venue is known as Augustine United Church. It is adapted during the Festival to house 2 performance spaces (the upper venue seates 110; the lower venue seats approximately 105). Programmes theatre, musicals, dance and children's theatre from the UK and elsewhere.

Bedlam Theatre

11b Bristo Place, Edinburgh EH1 1EZ
tel 0131-225 9873
email bedlam.theatre@ed.ac.uk
website www.bedlamtheatre.co.uk

A 90-seat black-box theatre in central Edinburgh housed in a neo-gothic church. The theatre is available for hire when not in use by the Edinburgh University Theatre Company.

C Venues

Administration Office: C Venues Limited, 5 Alexandra Mansions, Chichele Road, London NW2 3AS
email info@cvenues.com
website www.cvenues.com

Contains 4 venues: C, C too, CO$_2$ and C cubed. Presents drama, physical theatre,

comedy, music, musicals, mime, opera, children's shows and visual arts with an emphasis on new and dynamic work. C's 4 theatre spaces include a 203-seat thrust space, 2 end-on black-box studios seating 95 and 144, and a permanent 160-seat proscenium arch auditorium in the basement. There is also a platform stage in the bar and extensive exhibition space on each foyer level.

Gilded Balloon

233 Cowgate, Edinburgh EH1 2LG
tel 0131-226 6550 *fax* 0131-226 6554

Has a very strong comedy programme; also presents live music.

Greyfriars (Studios 1 and 2)

Greyfriars Kirk House, 86 Candlemaker Row, Edinburgh EH1 2QA

Studio 1 (upstairs, seats 60) and Studio 2 (seats around 40) are intimate spaces suited to 1-3 handers, storytelling or poetry. Applications should be made by February for hire during the Festival Fringe.

Hill Street Theatre

Hill Street Theatre, Universal Arts, Gateway Theatre, Elm Row, Edinburgh EH7 4AH
tel 0131-478 0195 *fax* 0131-478 0185
email hillstreet@universal-arts.com

Presents a programme of well-known works alongside new writing, musicals, dance, mime and physical theatre. Theatrical production includes comic writing but not stand-up comedy. The main theatre seats 120 while the studio theatre is a more intimate space, seating a maximum of 73. Suited to 1-handers, the studio can accommodate up to 8 performers comfortably.

The Netherbow

43-45 High Street, Edinburgh EH1 1SR
tel 0131-556 9579

Intimate 75-seat theatre presenting drama, poetry, storytelling and puppetry events. Offers a strong programme of family shows.

The Pleasance

The Pleasance Courtyard: 60 The Pleasance, Edinburgh EH8 9TJ
The Pleasance Dome: 1 Bristo Square, Edinburgh EH8 9AL
The Pleasance Administration Office: Carpenters Mews, North Road, London N7 9EF
tel 020-7619 6868
website www.pleasance.co.uk/edin

The Pleasance presents more than 160 shows across its 16 venues during the 4 weeks of the Festival Fringe. With 191,612 visitors in 2003, it remains one of the most popular venues of the Fringe offering a mix of comedy, theatre, dance and music.

Traverse Theatre

10 Cambridge Street, Edinburgh EH1 2ED
email mike@traverse.co.uk
website www.traverse.co.uk
Administrative Director Mike Griffiths

Centre for new playwriting. All-year-round venue in underground purpose-built theatre with 2 auditoria. Has staged premieres of plays by Rona Munro and David Grieg, and productions by Paines Plough. Also presents late-night comedy.

The Underbelly

Off Cowgate, Edinburgh
Permanent Office: 25 Greenside Place, Edinburgh EH1 3AA
tel 0131-622 6566 *fax* 0131-622 6576
email ed@smirnoffunderbelly.co.uk

website www.theunderbelly.co.uk
Venue Manager Ed Bartlam

Comprises 6 spaces over 4 floors with 3 bars. Venues cater for audiences of 60-200 with different seating configurations available. Programmes new writing, theatre, dance and comedy.

Other Fringe locations

Komedia

44-47 Gardner Street, Brighton BN1 1UN
tel (01273) 647101 *fax* (01273) 647102
email info@komedia.co.uk
website www.komedia.co.uk

95-seat theatre with upstairs café/cabaret bar. Has been host to early career performances from names such as Graham Norton, Mel & Sue, League of Gentlemen and The Right Size.

Sevenoaks Stag Theatre

London Road, Sevenoaks, Kent TN13 1ZZ
tel (01732) 451548
email julian.woolford@stagtheatre.co.uk

The theatre can seat up to 453 and has provision for wheelchair users. Companies should book the space up to 6 months in advance. Programmes a wide range of theatre and dance events.

Watermans Arts Centre

40 High Street, Brentford, Middlesex TW8 0DS
tel 020-8847 5651 *fax* 020-8569 8592
email enquiries@watermans.org.uk
website www.watermans.org.uk

Newly refurbished venue comprising 239-seat theatre, cinema space, new studio space, gallery, café and bar. Programmes across a range of artforms.

Children's, Young People's & Theatre in Education Companies

Paul Harman

Work in this very large sector of employment for actors in the UK varies greatly in the style of theatre created and presented, and in the wages and conditions offered by employers. Those taking work in the field should always be clear about the aims and status of the employer.

Most producing theatres offer plays for young audiences as part of a season, and Christmas shows and pantomimes are mounted by a very large number of receiving theatres and commercial touring companies. Some 200 independent touring companies regularly present original theatre productions, usually in schools, reaching a total audience of at least five million annually. Smaller touring companies may operate for profit, or as profit-share partnerships. Companies in membership of ITC (Independent Theatre Council) offer pay and conditions agreed with the performers' trade union, Equity.

Reality check

No official agency collects reliable statistics or regulates the quality of what is offered. Your work may never be publicly reviewed and it can be hard and demanding. Casts are often small, and living conditions on the road are sometimes difficult. The work may involve a lot of driving (if you are over 25 and insurable) as well as humping sets in and out of vans. The rewards for good-quality work conscientiously presented are in the warmth of welcome from audiences and bookers alike, and a directness and openness of audience response which is often less evident at more formal, adult-oriented theatre events. In schools you perform in daylight, very close to children –so it helps if you like them. They can see every blemish on you, and you can see every reaction on a hundred faces.

In addition to physical stamina, an ability to play many parts convincingly, skill at playing an instrument, and the ability to hit a peak of performance two or more times in a day, six days a week, other skills and aptitudes may be called upon. A play may be preceded or followed by workshop activity with young people, from 'hot-seating' in character to involving children in a performance. An understanding of drama education techniques is therefore an advantage, and experience of Youth Theatre useful.

What shows?

For good economic and marketing reasons, most theatre for children presented in larger houses is based on well-known stories by established authors, or on characters from TV shows. Companies may receive financial support from official agencies to present plays on health and social issues. Plays related to the National Curriculum, such as science topics, are in great demand from schools.

Theatre in Education (TIE) is a term commonly used to mean many kinds of theatre in schools. In the strict sense, TIE implies an extended theatre event, combining performance and participatory elements and designed to engage pupils in exploring their own knowledge, feelings and attitudes. This is quite a different process from explaining how magnets work or presenting an account of an historical event. Very few companies nowadays can afford the time and staffing needed to support real TIE, but there are many opportunities to create and present challenging educational plays on a wide variety of subjects.

Independent touring companies receiving public subsidy from Arts Councils in England, Wales, Scotland and Northern Ireland generally aim to present original, commissioned drama. A small group of writers are specialists in this field, addressing personal and social topics, from fear of the dark or the break-up of families, to genetics and migration. This group of companies – whose aims are primarily artistic, rather than just to entertain or deliver educational messages – find like-minded companies in 70 countries through ASSITEJ (International Association of Theatre for Children and Young People). Overseas tours and international collaborations are increasing.

Above all, don't look upon this field as an easy step towards something else. Your first experiences may well be tough, but an apprenticeship served with a supportive company will open a field of work you can return to with growing enjoyment and professional satisfaction.

Paul Harman has worked as an actor and director in professional theatre since 1963. He joined Belgrade Theatre in Education team in 1966, headed Education work at Liverpool Everyman from 1970, and founded Merseyside Young People's Theatre Company in 1978. Since 1994 he has been Artistic Director of CTC Theatre, Darlington. He is the current Chair of ASSITEJ UK.

6.15 Theatre Company
22 Brookfield Mansions, Highgate,
London N6 6AS
tel 020-8342 8239 *fax* 020-8340 5696
email six15@dircon.co.uk
website www.six15.co.uk
Artistic Director James Tillitt
Associate Director Nicola Cussons

Production details
Founded in 1984. Tours to schools, trade
exhibitions and conference venues across
the UK. Singing ability, proficiency with a
musical instrument and a driving licence
are required. Actors may be expected to
lead workshops. Recent productions
include: *Wise Up!*, an interactive drug education project for the Mentor Foundation,
and *CR7*, a musical presentation on cancer
prevention for Cancer Research UK.

Casting procedures
Does not hold general auditions but casting breakdowns are available through their
website, Equity Job Information Service
and *PCR*.

Applause Productions
31 Wimborne Road West, Wimborne,
Dorset BH21 2DG
tel (01202) 887439 *fax* (01202) 849493
email admin@derekgrant.co.uk
website www.derekgrant.co.uk
Artistic Director Derek Grant
Administrative Director Michael Jones

Production details
Founded in 1989. 'We present traditional
children's/family shows and pantomimes.
A strong storyline features in every show
along with colourful costumes and scenery,
bright musical numbers and lots of joining
in!"Normally tours 2 projects each year
with an average annual total of 200 performances and 200 different venues. Venues
include arts centres and theatres across the
UK including Northern Ireland, Channel
Islands and the Isle of Man. In general 5
actors go on tour and play to audiences
aged 3-93. Singing ability, dance/physical
theatre skills and a driving licence are
required. Recent productions include:
Goldilocks and the Three Bears, Pinocchio
and *Humpty Dumpty in Nursery Rhyme
Land.*

Casting procedures
Sometimes holds general auditions; actors
can write at any time requesting inclusion.
Accepts submissions (with CVs and photographs) from actors previously unknown
to the company sent by post or email. Will
also accept showreels and invitations to
view individual actors' websites.

Big Wheel Theatre in Education
The Institute, PO Box 18221, London
EC1R 4WJ
tel 020-7689 8670 *fax* 020-7689 8670
email info@bigwheel.org.uk
website www.bigwheel.org.uk
Artistic Directors Roland Allen, Jeni
Williams

Production details
Has developed interactive theatre to use for
education and training in the UK and
abroad since 1984. Normally tours 10 projects each year with an average annual total
of 400 performances and 200 different
venues. Venues include schools and conference centres across the UK, Europe, Japan,
Kenya and South Africa. In general 2 actors
go on tour and play to audiences aged 7
upwards. Actors are required to hold a driving licence and to lead workshops.
Experience in teaching or training is also
useful. Recent productions include:
Introduction to Shakespeare, a game-show-
based interactive workshop; *Breakfast with
Big Wheel*, a show to teach English in
European schools; and a variety of

workshops for the NHS about communication, partnerships and peripatetic working.

Casting procedures
Sometimes holds general auditions; actors may write at any time requesting inclusion. 'It's quite specialist work. Best to have a good look at the website and only send us your stuff if you think it really is your cup of tea."

Bournemouth Theatre in Education
BCCA, 93 Haviland Road,
Bournemouth BH7 6HJ
tel (01202) 395759 *fax* (01202) 399597
email tie@bournemouth.gov.uk
Artistic Directors Tony Horitz, Sharon Muiruri
Administrator Shaz Watkins

Production details
Founded in 1967. 'Theatre in Education service within a lifelong learning framework.'Works in schools presenting theatrical performances and facilitating drama. Also actively involved in the field of social inclusion. Normally tours 10-15 projects each year to schools, arts centres, outdoor venues, community venues, prisons and hospitals in the South of England. In general 3-4 actors go on tour and play to audiences of all ages. Actors are required to have good workshop skills and the ability to relate well to people. Recent productions include: *My Name is Savitri*, an anti-racism play for Year 4 children; *Angel*, with a disabled actors theatre company; and *Sleeping Beauty*, with Tops (actors with learning difficulties).

Casting procedures
Sometimes holds general auditions; actors may write at any time requesting inclusion. Accepts submissions (with CVs and photographs) from actors previously unknown to the company sent by post or email. Will also accept showreels and invitations to view individual actors' websites. 'We do use professional actors on a fairly regular basis but prefer to use those living in or around the Bournemouth area."

Box Clever Theatre Company
12 G1 The Leathermarket, Weston Street,
London SE1 3ER
tel 020-7357 0550 *fax* 020-7357 8188
email admin@boxclevertheatre.co.uk
website www.boxclevertheatre.com
Artistic Director Michael Wicherek
Administrator Claire Knights

Production details
Founded in 1996, the company produces contemporary theatre for young people – new plays, adaptations of Shakespeare plays, issue-based and educational work. 6 productions are staged per year with an average annual total of approximately 500 performances in 400 different venues. Venues include arts centres, theatres, and educational and community venues nationwide. About 3 actors are involved in each production. Recent productions include: *The Buzz* (for Secondary schools), *Car Story* (Primary schools) and *Boxed Macbeth* (for schools and arts/community centres).

Casting procedures
Does not use freelance casting directors or hold general auditions. Casting breakdowns are available via Equity Job Information Service and *PCR*. Welcomes submissions (with CVs and photographs) from actors previously unknown to the company if sent by post and if in response to casting breakdowns only. Advises actors that the company receives a huge response to advertisements placed in *PCR* and through Equity and is therefore unable to return photographs or respond in writing to applicants not invited to audition.

C&T

University College Worcester, Henwick Grove, Worcester WR2 6AJ
tel (01905) 855436
email info@candt.org
website www.candt.org
Artistic Director Paul Sutton

Production details

Founded in 1988. A theatre company incorporating performance, learning and digital media. Works in schools, colleges and universities in the UK and across Europe. Normally tours 2-3 projects each year with an average annual total of 50-100 performances and 50-100 different venues. In general 2-3 actors go on tour and play to audiences aged 5-65. Dance/physical theatre skills, proficiency with computers and digital media and a driving licence are required. Actors are also expected to lead workshops. Recent productions include: *Living Newspaper.com*, a docu-drama project online for schools.

Casting procedures

Sometimes holds general auditions; actors should write in September requesting inclusion. Accepts submissions (with CVs and photographs) from actors previously unknown to the company sent by post or email. Will also accept showreels and invitations to view individual actors' websites.

Cwmni Theatr Arad Goch

Stryd Y Baddon, Aberystwyth, Ceredigion SY23 2NN
tel (01970) 617998 *fax* (01970) 611223
email post@arodgoch.org
Artistic Director Jeremy Turner
Administrative Manager Nia Wyn Williams

Production details

Founded in 1989. Main focus of work is Theatre in Education. Normally tours 6 projects each year with an average annual total of 150 performances and more than 100 different venues. Venues include schools, theatres and community venues across Wales and occasionally abroad. In general 3-6 actors go on tour and play to audiences aged 4 upwards. Singing ability, proficiency with a musical instrument, fluency in Welsh and a driving licence are required. Actors may also be expected to lead workshops. Recent productions include: *Twm a Mati Tat*, for 7-11 year olds and *Letus*, commissioned for the National Eisteddfod 2003.

Casting procedures

Sometimes holds general auditions; actors requesting inclusion should write before the start of the academic year. Accepts submissions (with CVs and photographs) from actors previously unknown to the company sent by post or email. Will also accept showreels and invitations to view individual actors' websites.

Daylight Theatre

66 Middle Street, Stroud, Gloucestershire GL5 1EA
tel (01453) 763808
Artistic Director Hugh Young
Key personnel Roger Burfield

Production details

Founded in 1977. Tours educational theatre into schools. Topics have included drugs, HIV/AIDS, Shakespeare, history and mythology, and have been linked to the National Curriculum. Normally tours 7 projects each year with an average annual total of 200 performances and 150 different venues. Venues include schools (mainly Primary but some Secondary), arts centres and theatres across the UK, Germany and Luxembourg. In general 2-3 actors go on tour and play to audiences aged 4-18. Actors are required to hold a driving licence and may also be expected to lead workshops. Recent productions include: *Can You Take It* –drugs, alcohol and tobacco education for 9-11 year olds; *A Midsummer Night's Dream* and *Macbeth* for Key Stage 2 level; and *Ghostcliff Grange*, a World War II drama also for Key Stage 2.

Casting procedures
Actors requesting inclusion can write at any time. 'Don't give up, keep trying!'

Gazebo Theatre in Education Company
Multi-Purpose Centre, Victoria Road, Darlaston WS10 8AP
tel 0121-526 6877 *fax* 0121-526 6877
email gazebotie@tiscali.co.uk
website www.gazeboti.com
General Manager Jacqueline Green
Artistic Project Leaders Pamela Cole-Hudson, Michael O'Hara

Production details
Founded in 1979. Normally tours 3-5 projects each year plus workshops, with an average annual total of 300 performances and 250 different venues. Venues include schools and community venues in the West Midlands and South Shropshire. In general 5 actors go on tour and play to audiences aged 4-25. Musical ability and movement skills are sometimes required, as is a driving licence. Actors may also be expected to lead workshops. Recent productions include: *The Search for the Dragon's Tongue* (Key Stage 1), *Macbeth* (Key Stage 3) and *Fighting Back* (Key Stage 3).

Casting procedures
Holds general auditions; actors requesting inclusion should write in May (for performance in July) or November/December (for January).

Casting breakdowns are sometimes available by postal application (with sae) or through Equity Job Information Service. Accepts submissions (with CVs and photographs) from actors previously unknown to the company if sent by post. Does not welcome unsolicited emails. Will also accept invitations to view individual actors' websites.

Gwent Theatre
The Drama Centre, Pen-y-Pound, Abergavenny NP7 5UD
tel (01873) 853167 *fax* (01873) 853910
email gwenttie@aol.com
website www.gwenttie.co.uk
Artistic Director Gary Meredith
Administrator Julia Davies

Production details
Founded in 1976. Tours at least 4 projects each year with an average annual total of 180 performances. Venues include schools, theatres, outdoor venues and community venues in Gwent and across Wales. In general 3-5 actors go on tour and play to audiences aged 6 upwards. Singing ability, proficiency with a musical instrument, dance/physical theatre skills and a driving licence are required. Actors may also be expected to lead workshops. Recent productions include: *The Tinderbox* by Charles Way for family audiences, *The Crooked House, The Merchant of Venice* and *The Canterbury Tales* (all for schools).

Casting procedures
Sometimes holds general auditions and actors can write at any time requesting inclusion. Accepts submissions (with CVs and photographs) from actors previously unknown to the company if sent by post. Does not welcome unsolicited emails. Will also accept invitations to view individual actors' websites.

Half Moon Young People's Theatre

43 Whitehorse Road, London E1 0ND
tel 020-7265 8138 *fax* 020-7709 8914
email admin@halfmoon.org.uk
website www.halfmoon.org.uk
Artistic Director Chris Elwell
Administrative Producer Tracy Brunt

Production details
Founded in 1977. 'Young people's theatre touring in London and nationally with a reputation for high-quality work. Also a receiving venue for young people's work.' Normally tours 2 projects with an average annual total of 170 performances and 45 different venues. Venues include schools, arts centres, theatres and community venues. In general 2-3 actors go on tour and play to audiences aged under 17. Singing ability and physical theatre skills are required and actors may also be expected to lead workshops.

Casting procedures
Casting breakdowns are available through the website, postal application (with sae) and Equity Job Information Service. Sometimes holds general auditions; actors can write at any time requesting inclusion. Accepts submissions (with CVs and photographs) from actors previously unknown to the company sent by post or email. Will also accept invitations to view individual actors' websites.

Hopscotch Theatre Company

2nd Floor, 7 Water Row,
Glasgow G51 3UW
tel 0141-440 2025 *fax* 0141-440 2025
email info@hopscotchtheatre.com
website www.hopscotchtheatre.com
Artistic Director Grant Smeaton
General Manager Susan McGregor

Production details
Founded in 1988. A Theatre in Education company touring 4 productions each year to Primary schools with an average annual total of 520 performances. Venues include schools, arts centres, theatres and community venues across Scotland. In general 4 actors go on tour and play to audiences aged 5-12 years. Singing ability, proficiency with a musical instrument and a driving licence are required. Recent productions include: *The Romans in Scotland, Mary Queen of Scots* and *Tam O' Shanter.*

Casting procedures
Holds general auditions; actors requesting inclusion should write in May or June. Accepts submissions (with CVs and photographs) from actors previously unknown to the company sent by post or email. Will also accept showreels.

Jack Drum Arts

West New Houses, Baldersdale, Barnard Castle, County Durham DL12 9UU
Artistic Director Julie Ward
Administrator Jill Cole

Production details
Founded in 1986. 'Delivers a strong programme of participatory arts for all sectors of the community.' Normally tours 3 projects each year with an average annual total of 60 performances and 60 different venues. Venues include schools, arts centres, theatres, outdoor venues and community venues across the UK and abroad with a focus on rural touring. In general 3-4 actors go on tour and play to audiences of pre-school age and upwards. Singing ability, proficiency with a musical instrument and a driving licence are required for some shows. Actors may also be expected to lead workshops. Recent productions include: *Arch Enemies*, a new writing piece touring

to a variety of venues; *Bambino*, touring to outdoor festivals; and *Jackie and the Beanstalk*, a 3-hander on a smaller scale.

Casting procedures

Accepts submissions (with CVs and photographs) from actors in the North East area only. 'We like to know who is around in the North East, especially if based in County Durham. Can help access local networks and professional development.'

Krazy Kat Theatre Company

173 Hartington Road, Brighton BN2 3PA
tel (01273) 692552 *fax* (01273) 692552
email kkat@kkat.demon.co.uk
website www.krazykattheatre.co.uk
Artistic Director Kinny Gardner
Administrative Director Alastair Macmillan

Production details

A children's theatre company founded in 1972. Normally tours 4-6 projects each year with an average annual total of 150 performances and 75 venues. Venues include schools, arts centres, theatres, outdoor venues and community venues in Essex, Sussex, Kent, London and Scotland. In general 2 actors go on tour and play to audiences aged 3-7. Singing ability, physical theatre skills, sign language and a driving licence are required. Actors may also be expected to lead workshops. Recent productions include: *Hoy Sancho, Three Pigs* and *Red Riding Hood.*

Casting procedures

Sometimes holds general auditions; actors can write at any time requesting inclusion. Accepts submissions (with CVs and photographs) from actors previously unknown to the company if sent by post. Does not welcome unsolicited emails. Will also accept invitations to view individual actors' websites.

M6 Theatre Company

Hamer County Primary School, Albert Royds Street, Rochdale OL16 2SU
tel (01706) 355898 *fax* (01706) 711700
email info@m6theatre.co.uk
website www.m6theatre.co.uk
Producer Dorothy Wood
General Manager Jane Milne

Production details

Theatre in Education company founded in 1977. Normally tours 3 projects each year with an average annual total of 150 performances and 9 different venues. Venues include schools, arts centres, theatres and community venues mainly in the North West, Birmingham and London. In general 3-4 actors go on tour and play to audiences aged 3-18. Actors may also be expected to lead workshops. Recent productions include: *Peacemaker* by David Holman, *Breathing Space* and *Forever* by Mary Cooper, a monologue programme and an early years programme.

Casting procedures

Sometimes holds general auditions; actors can write at any time requesting inclusion. Accepts submissions (with CVs and photographs) from actors previously unknown to the company sent by post or email. Will also accept invitations to view individual actors' websites.

Monster Productions

Buddle Arts Centre, 258b Station Road, Wallsend NE28 8RH
Artistic Directors Chris Speyer, Ievan Einion
Youth Theatre Director Laura Lindon
Administrator Doreen Ford

Production details

Set up in 2000 to continue the work for children under 7 begun by the directors at

Northern Stage. Creates new music theatre for young children and runs a youth
theatre programme for North Tyneside.
Normally tours 2 projects each year with
an average annual total of 150
performances and 30 different venues.
Venues include schools, arts centres, theatres and community venues across the
UK, Wales and Ireland. In general 3-5
actors go on tour and play mainly to
audiences under 7 years old. Actors may
also be expected to lead workshops.
Recent productions include: *The Terrible
Grump* and *Trouble Under Foot* (both for
under-7s), and *Street of Strangers* for
young people and adults.

Casting procedures

Sometimes holds general auditions; actors
should write requesting inclusion when
advertised in *PCR*. Accepts submissions
(with CVs and photographs) from actors
previously unknown to the company if sent
by post. Does not welcome unsolicited
emails. Will also accept invitations to view
individual actors' websites. 'Due to our
scale of work we only employ a small
number of actors each year. We favour
multiracial casts to reflect our audiences.
Musical and movement skills are a great
advantage."

Oily Cart Company

Smallwood School Annexe, Smallwood
Road, London SW17 OTW
tel 020-8672 6329 *fax* 020-8672 0792
email oilies@oilycart.org.uk
website www.oilycart.org.uk
Artistic Director Tim Webb
General Manager Rebecca Farrar
Administrator Kevin Walsh

Production details

'Oily Cart makes gentle, interactive theatre
for carers and babies as young as 6 months

old, and elaborate multi-sensory pieces tran-
scending the most complex sensory and
intellectual impairments."Tours to schools,
arts centres, theatres and special needs
schools across the UK. In general 4 actors go
on tour and play to infant audiences.
Singing ability, proficiency with a musical
instrument, dance/physical theatre skills,
puppeteering ability and a driving licence
are required. Recent productions include:
Moving Pictures, an interactive, highly personal piece for children and young people
with profound and multiple learning dis-
abilities, and *Jumpin' Beans*, a show for children aged between 6 months and 6 years.

Casting procedures

Casting breakdowns are available through
Equity Job Information Service and advertisements in *The Stage*.

Passe-Partout

13 Stanford Avenue, Brighton BN1 6AD
tel (01273) 557595 *fax* (01273) 701694
email office@passe-partout.demon.co.uk
Artistic Director Michele Young
Manager Richard Crane

Production details

Founded in 1986. "Theatre for social
change –assisting people to have a voice
about an issue which concerns them."
Normally tours 3 projects each year with
an average annual total of 20 performances
and 20 different venues. Venues include
schools, outdoor venues, community
venues and office spaces in the UK and
abroad. In general 4 actors go on tour and
play to audiences of all ages. Any additional skills that actors may have will be put to
use. Actors may be expected to lead workshops. Recent productions include:
Bullying in Prisons (UK), *Fashion*
(Belgium), *Terrorism* (Lithuania/Denmark)
and *Youth Pregnancy* (Jamaica).

Casting procedures
'We cast from the group of people who have proposed an issue they want to take forward. We sometimes build in one or two people from outside that group who have interest and energy."

Pied Piper Theatre Company in association with the Yvonne Arnaud Theatre
1 Lilian Place, Coxcombe Lane, Chiddingfold GU8 4QA
tel (01428) 684022 *fax* (01428) 684022
email twpiedpiper@aol.com
website www.yvonne-arnaud.co.uk
Artistic Director Tina Williams

Production details
Founded in 1984 and joined with Yvonne Arnaud in 1994. Has had 3 national tours funded by Arts Council England. Normally tours 2 projects each year with an average annual total of 140 performances. In general 4-8 actors tour to schools across the UK playing to audiences aged 4-19. Work is taken to arts centres and theatres every other year. Singing ability, proficiency with a musical instrument, dance/physical theatre skills and a driving licence are required. Recent productions include: a national tour of Anne Fine's *The Diary of a Killer Cat* for family audiences, and a school tour of *Town Mouse and Country Mouse*.

Casting procedures
Holds general auditions; actors requesting inclusion should write during the summer. Casting breakdowns are available through Equity Job Information Service. 'Actors must be happy to tour. Most music is live. Must have a passion for children/young people's theatre."

Playtime Theatre Company
18 Bennell's Avenue, Whitstable, Kent CT5 2HP
tel (01227) 266272 *fax* (01227) 266648
email Playtime@dircon.co.uk
website www.playtime.dircon.co.uk
Artistic Director Nicholas Champion
Administrator Sara Kettlewell

Production details
Established in 1983 with the aim of bringing imaginative and innovative professional theatre to children and young people. Has grown to become 'one of the leading children's theatre companies in the South East", and tours both nationally and internationally. Normally tours 2-4 projects each year with an average annual total of 200 performances and 190 venues. Venues include schools, arts centres, theatres, community venues and festivals. Tours have covered the South East, Yorkshire and Humberside and various countries in Europe. In general 2-4 actors go on tour and play to targeted audiences of 5-7, 4-11, 7-11 and 9-13. Actors are expected to offer 1-2 additional skills. Singing ability, proficiency with a musical instrument, physical theatre, puppetry and mime skills and a driving licence are all useful. Actors may also be expected to lead workshops. Recent productions include: *A Tale O' Two*, an adaptation of *The Canterbury Tales*; *Secrets*, a fairy-tale; and *The Happy Prince*, a co-production with a Hungarian theatre company.

Casting procedures
Holds general auditions; actors should write in August requesting inclusion. Casting breakdowns are available through the website, postal application (with sae), Equity Job Information Service, *PCR*, *The Stage* and *Castcall* (see entry under *Casting Information Services*). Welcomes submissions (with CVs and photographs) from actors previously unknown to the company sent by post or email. Also accepts showreels and invitations to view individual actors' websites (if actor is

shown performing). Advises actors to: 'Be truthful. Tell us about the things that make you stand out. Tell us briefly why you want to work in children's theatre and why you like touring. Seriously consider the implications of living away from your base for months on end!"

Pop-Up Theatre

27a Brewery Road, London N7 9PU
tel 020-7609 3339 *fax* 020-7609 2284
email admin@pop-up.net
website www.pop-up.net
Artistic Director Michael Dalton
Associate Director Jane Wolfson
Administrator John Johnston

Production details

Founded in 1982. Produces and tours theatre for young people to an annual audience of more than 25,000 across theatres, arts centres, schools and nurseries both in the UK and overseas. Normally tours 3 projects each year with an average annual total of 150 performances and 75 different venues. Venues include schools, arts centres, theatres and community venues across the UK. In general 2-4 actors go on tour and play to audiences aged under 11. Comedy/clowning and puppetry skills are required from actors. Recent productions include: *The Snow Children* by Michael Dalton and *Wild Girl, Wild Boy* by David Almond.

Casting procedures

Accepts submissions (with CVs and photographs) from actors previously unknown to the company sent by post or email. Will also accept invitations to view individual actors' websites.

Q20 Theatre

19 Wellington Crescent, Shipley,
W. Yorks BD18 3PH

Artistic Director John Lambert
Administrators David Smith, Gillie Kerrod

Production details

Normally tours 10 projects each year with an average annual total of 350 performances. Venues include outdoor venues, corporate workspaces and shopping centres in the North East, Yorkshire and Cambridge. In general 2 actors go on tour and play to audiences of all ages. Singing ability and dance/physical theatre skills are required. Recent productions include: *Pirate Pranks* at Wakefield Shopping Centre and *Metro Gnomes* at Metrocentre.

Casting procedures

Sometimes holds general auditions; actors should write in May or October requesting inclusion. Accepts submissions (with CVs and photographs) from actors previously unknown to the company only if sent by post. Does not welcome unsolicited emails. Will also accept invitations to view individual actors' websites.

Quicksilver Theatre

The Glasshouse, 4 Enfield Road,
London N1 5AZ
tel 020-7241 2942 *fax* 020-7254 3119
email talktous@quicksilvertheatre.org
website www.quicksilvertheatre.org
Artistic Directors Guy Holland,
Carey English
Administrative Director Helen Gethin

Production details

Founded in 1977. Normally tours 3 projects each year with an average annual total of 180 performances. Venues include schools and small to mid-scale arts centres and theatres across the UK. Up to 5 actors go on tour and play to audiences of all ages. Singing ability, proficiency with a musical instrument, dance skills and a driving licence are an advantage. Actors may also be expected to lead workshops. Recent productions include: *Idle Pop* (for 7 years upwards) *Sea of Science* (for 7-11 years) and *Upstairs in the Sky* (for 3-5 years).

Casting procedures
Casting breakdowns are available though the website, postal application (with sae), *PCR* and advertisements in *The Stage*. Accepts submissions (with CVs and photographs) from actors previously unknown to the company sent by post or email. Will also accept showreels and invitations to view individual actors' websites.

Replay Productions

Old Museum Arts Centre, 7 College Square North, Belfast BT1 6AR
tel 028-9032 2773 *fax* 028-9032 2724
email replay@dircon.co.uk
website www.replayproductions.org
Artistic Director Richard Croxford
Administrator Ali Fitzgibbon

Production details
'Founded in 1988, Replay aims to produce high-quality theatre and related activities that entertain, educate and stimulate children and young people." Normally tours 3 projects each year with an average annual total of 100 performances. Venues include schools, arts centres, theatres and community venues in Northern Ireland and occasionally the Republic of Ireland. In general 4 actors go on tour and play to audiences aged 3-18. Recent productions include: *Striking Distance* by Raymond Scannell (for 14 years upwards) and *Little Lou Tells a Story* by Sarah Fitzgibbon (for 3-6 years).

Casting procedures
Sometimes holds general auditions; actors should write during June or July requesting inclusion. Casting breakdowns are

available through the news section of the website. Accepts submissions (with CVs and photographs) from actors previously unknown to the company sent by post or email. Will also accept invitations to view individual actors' websites.

Scat Theatre Company

The Old School House, Bedhampton Arts Centre, Bedhampton Road, Havant PO9 3ET
tel 023-9236 6829 *fax* 023-9236 3241
Artistic Directors Paul Hayes, Geraldine Owen

Production details
Founded in 1982. A children's theatre company producing original shows and workshops for schools. Normally tours 3 projects each year (not including workshops) with an average annual total of 180 performances. Although most work is geared towards schools, the company also tours to arts centres, theatres and community venues in Hampshire and local counties. In general 3 actors go on tour between December and February and play to audiences aged 3-11. Actors holding a driving licence will be at an advantage. Recent productions include: *Drumlins and Dragons* and *The King of Cabbage Castle*.

Casting procedures
Holds general auditions; actors should write between July and September to request inclusion. Accepts submissions (with CVs and photographs) from actors previously unknown to the company only if sent by post. Does not welcome unsolicited emails. Usually employs actors with professional experience of performing to children aged 3-11. As they have no technician, actors are also responsible for get-ins. Not an Equity or ITC-registered company.

Shakespeare 4 Kidz
42 Station Road East, Oxted,
Surrey RH8 OPG
tel (01883) 723444 *fax* (01883) 730384
email office@shakespeare4kidz.com
website www.shakespeare4kidz.com
Producer and Director Julian Chenery
Producer Carolyn Chenery
Company Manager Paul Reynolds

Production details
Founded in 1997. 'Recognised as the
national Shakespeare company for children
and young people, it has pioneered its
Music Theatre & Shakespeare and Creative
Shakespeare Education Programme both in
the UK and abroad.'Normally tours 2 projects each year with an average annual total
of 230 performances across 60 different
theatres. In general 13 actors go on tour and
play to audiences aged 8 upwards. Singing
ability and dance/physical theatre skills are
required; marketing skills are also advantageous. Recent productions included:
Shakespeare 4 Kidz Macbeth and
Shakespeare 4 Kidz Twelfth Night.

Casting procedures
Holds general auditions; actors should
write in March requesting inclusion.
Casting breakdowns are available through
their website, *PCR* and *The Stage*. Accepts
submissions (with CVs and photographs)
from actors previously unknown to the
company sent by post or email. Will also
accept showreels and invitations to view
individual actors' websites.

Sixth Sense
The Burkhardt Hall, Swindon College,
Regent Circus, Swindon SN1 1PT
tel (01793) 614864 *fax* (01793) 616715
email sstc@dircon.co.uk
website
www.sixthsensetheatrecompany.co.uk

Artistic Director Benedict Eccles
Administrator Victoria Wicks

Production details
Founded in 1986. Tours to schools and
small-scale venues in the South and South
West. Receives funding from Swindon
Borough Council and Arts Council
England, South West and has an 'excellent
reputation in the region'. Normally tours
3 projects each year with an average annual total of 150 performances across 90
venues. Venues include schools, arts centres and community venues. In general 3
actors go on tour and play to audiences
aged 5-18. Singing ability, proficiency with
a musical instrument, dance skills and a
driving licence may be required. Actors
are usually expected to lead workshops.
Recent productions include: *Aesop's Fables*
(for 5-11 years) and *The Secret Garden*
(for 11-18 years).

Casting procedures
Sometimes holds general auditions; actors
should write in September requesting
inclusion. Accepts submissions (with
CVs and photographs) from actors previously unknown to the company sent by
post or email. Will also accept invitations
to view individual actors' websites.
Issues ITC/Equity contracts for 5-10
week tours. 'Happy to receive actors'
details but can't always respond. Please
don't chase us; if we're interested we'll
contact you."

Theatr Iolo
The Old School Building, Cefn Road,
Cardiff CF14 3HS
tel 029-2061 3782 *fax* 029-2052 2225
email admin@theatriolo.com
website www.theatriolo.com
Artistic Director Kevin Lewis
Administrative Director Wendy York

Production details

'Formed in 1987, Theatr Iolo aims to produce and programme the best of live theatre, making it widely accessible to children and young people in Cardiff and the Vale of Glamorgan to stir the imagination, inspire the heart and challenge the mind. Theatr Iolo works alongside teachers and advisers to enhance teaching and learning across the curriculum.' Normally tours 5 projects each year with an average annual total of 150 performances across 120 venues. Venues include schools, arts centres and theatres in Wales and occasionally England. In general 4 actors go on tour and play to audiences aged 3-18. Singing ability, proficiency with a musical instrument, dance/physical theatre skills and a driving licence are frequently required. Actors may also be expected to lead workshops. Recent productions include: *Grimm's Tales* (for 7-10 years) and *Are We There Yet* (for 3-5 years).

Casting procedures

Sometimes holds general auditions; actors should write in July requesting inclusion. Casting breakdowns are available through Equity Job Information Service. Accepts submissions (with CVs and photographs) from actors previously unknown to the company it sent by post. Emails are also welcome, as long as the file is not too big.

Theatr Na N'Og

Unit 3, Millands Road Industrial Estate, Neath SA11 1NJ
tel (01639) 641771 *fax* (01639) 647941
email cwmni@theatr-nanog.co.uk
website www.theatr-nanog.co.uk
Artistic Director Geinor Jones
Administrator Janet Huxtable

Production details

'Formerly Theatre West & Glamorgan, the company has been producing high-quality original theatre for young people for more than 20 years. We provide a first-class Theatre in Education service to schools in three county boroughs, and tour to general audiences in venues across the UK.' Normally tours 3 projects each year with an average annual total of 200 performances. In general 3 actors go on tour. Singing ability is required and actors may also be expected to lead workshops.

Casting procedures

Holds general auditions; actors may write at any time requesting inclusion. Casting breakdowns are available through their website. Accepts submissions (with CVs and photographs) from actors previously unknown to the company sent by post or email. Will also accept invitations to view individual actors' websites. 'Please learn to spell the names of the company's personnel properly!'

Theatr Powys

The Drama Centre, Tremont Road, Llandrinod Wells LD1 5EB
tel (01597) 824444 *fax* (01597) 824381
email theatre.powys@powys.gov.uk
website www.theatrepowys.co.uk
Artistic Director Ian Yeoman
Acting General Manager Nikki Leopold

Production details

Founded in 1976. Has an average annual total of 250 performances across 150 different venues. Venues include schools, arts centres, theatres and community venues across Wales. In general 4 actors go on tour and play to audiences aged 4 upwards. Singing ability, proficiency with a musical instrument, dance/physical theatre skills and a driving licence are required. Actors are also expected to lead workshops. Recent productions include: *Margiona's Dance* and *Towers of Ilium*.

Casting procedures

Holds general auditions; actors may write at any time requesting inclusion. Casting breakdowns are available through postal application (with sae), Equity Job Information Service, *PCR* and advertisements in *The Stage*. Accepts submissions (with CVs and photographs) from actors previously unknown to the company sent by post or email. Will also accept invitations to view individual actors' websites.

Theatre Centre

Units 7&8 Toynbee Workshops, 3 Gunthorpe Street, London E1 7RQ
tel 020-7377 0379 *fax* 020-7377 1376
email admin@theatre-centre.co.uk
website www.theatre-centre.co.uk
Artistic Director Rosamunde Hutt
Administrator Thomas Kell

Production details

Founded in 1953. A new writing company commissioning, developing and producing new plays which are toured nationally and internationally to schools, arts centres and theatres. Normally tours 3 projects each year with an average annual total of 180 performances across 100 different venues. In general 3-4 actors go on tour and play to targeted groups aged between 4-18. Singing ability, proficiency with a musical instrument and dance/physical theatre skills may be required. An affinity with new writing and touring audiences is an advantage. Recent productions include: *Devotion* by Leo Butler and *Glow* by Manjinder Virk.

Casting procedures

Casting breakdowns are available through their website, postal application (with sae), Equity Job Information Service, *PCR* and advertisements in *The Stage*. Accepts submissions (with CVs and photographs) from actors previously

unknown to the company sent by post or email; actors should write around New Year or Easter. 'We keep all unsolicited CVs on file and do consult them when casting –therefore do send refreshed CVs! Get to know us and our work, there are regular free open day/showcase performances to which people on the mailing list are always invited.'

Theatre Company Blah Blah Blah!

East Leeds Family Learning Centre, Brooklands View, Leeds LS14 6SA
tel 0113-224 3171 *fax* 0113-224 3685
email admin@blahs.co.uk
website www.blahs.co.uk
Artistic Director Anthony Haddon
General Manager Kate Rose

Production details

A Leeds-based Theatre in Education company founded in 1985; also produces theatre for young people with integrated workshops. Normally tours 2-3 projects each year with an average annual total of 100 performances across 60 different venues. Venues include schools, arts centres, community venues and youth centres in Yorkshire. In general 3-4 actors go on tour and play to audiences aged 5 upwards. Singing ability, proficiency with a musical instrument, dance/physical theatre skills and a driving licence are all potentially useful. Experience of TIE work is also helpful as actors are generally expected to lead workshops. Recent productions include: *Big Sister, Little Brother,* a primary school series of workshops; and *Silas Marner,* toured to schools and community venues with related workshops.

Casting procedures

Sometimes holds general auditions; actors may write at any time requesting inclusion, as CVs are kept on file. Accepts submissions (with CVs and photographs) from actors previously unknown to the company only if sent by post. Does not welcome unsolicited emails. Will also accept invitations to view individual actors' websites. 'We are particularly interested in hearing from people with both acting and facilitation skills.'

Theatre Exchange Ltd.

The Village, Caterham, Surrey CR3 5ZU
Artistic Director Katy Potter
Education Director Stephen Cordwent

Production details

An educational theatre company focusing on the creative exchange between young people, artists and those who work with young people. Works on up to 21 projects each year with an average annual total of 650 performances across 400 different venues. Venues include schools, arts centres, theatres and community venues across the South East of England. In general 6 actors go on tour and play to audiences aged 4-13. Interest in and some experience of working with young people is necessary and a driving licence is also useful. Actors are also expected to lead workshops. Recent productions include: *Monsters, Myths & Legends, Luverly Jubilee* and *The Greeks.*

Casting procedures

Holds general auditions; actors requesting inclusion should write between May and July. Casting breakdowns are available through their website, postal application (with sae), Equity Job Information Service and advertisements in *The Stage.* Accepts submissions (with CVs and photographs) from actors previously unknown to the company sent by post or email. Will also accept invitations to view individual actors' websites. 'Please send a letter detailing why you are interested in working with young people, along with your CV.'

Travelling Light Theatre Company

13 West Street, Old Market,
Bristol BS2 ODF
tel 0117-377 3166 *fax* 0117-377 3167
email info@travlight.co.uk
website www.travlight.co.uk
Producer Jude Merrill
General Manager Cath Creig

Production details

'Since 1984 the company has produced innovative and inspiring work for young audiences. Uses live music, visual and physical performance in its work.' Normally tours 2 projects each year with an average annual total of 200 performances across 25 different venues. Venues include schools, arts centres, theatres, community venues and festivals across England, Northern Ireland, Scotland, Wales, North America and the Republic of Ireland. In general 2-3 actors go on tour and play to audiences aged 3-18. Singing ability, proficiency with a musical instrument and physical theatre skills are required. Actors may also be expected to lead workshops. Recent productions include: *Cloudland* (for 3-6 years) and *The Stones* (for 12 years upwards).

Casting procedures

Casting breakdowns are available through Equity Job Information Service, *PCR* and *Castweb* (see entry under *Casting Directories and Information Services*). Accepts submissions (with CVs and photographs) from actors previously unknown to the company only if sent by post. Does not welcome unsolicited emails. Will also accept invitations to view individual actors' websites.

Unicorn Theatre for Children

St Mark's Studios,
Chillingworth Road, London N7 8QJ
tel 020-7700 0207
fax 020-7700 3870
email admin@unicorntheatre.com
website www.unicorntheatre.com
Artistic Director Tony Graham
Associate Director Rebecca Gatward
Education Director Alison Barry

Production details
Founded in 1947. "The UK's premier professional theatre company, in the process
of building the first purpose-designed theatre for children in the UK."Opens in 2005
near London Bridge. Performed 5 projects
in 2002/3 with a total of 200 performances;
9 projects are planned for 2005/6 with a
total of 460 performances. Has produced
site-specific works across England and in
Cardiff, Glasgow and Edinburgh. In general 7-8 actors are involved in each production and play to audiences aged 4-11.
Singing ability, proficiency with a musical
instrument and dance/physical theatre
skills are required. Recent productions
include: *Diary of an Action Man*, a co-production with Graeae Theatre Company for
London and touring; *Granny and the
Gorilla*, for Regents Park Open Air Season
2003; and *Finders Keepers*, a site-specific
project with Theatre Rites Company.

Casting procedures
Sometimes holds general auditions;
actors may write at any time requesting
inclusion. Accepts CVs and
photographs from actors previously
unknown to the company only if sent by
email. Advises actors to send an
interesting covering note detailing why
they are interested in working with
Unicorn in particular.

Whirlwind Theatre Productions

54 High Road, Halton, Lancaster LA2 6PS
tel (01524) 812851
email enquiries@whirlwindtheatre.org.uk
website www.whirlwindtheatre.org.uk
Artistic Director Myette Godwyn
Associate Artistic Director Alistair Ganley

Production details
Formed in 2000 to produce a community
play at the Museum of Cannock Chase in
association with Illyria Theatre Company.
New touring productions are being
devised and a programme is being put
together in partnership with community
associations in the Lancaster/Morecambe
area. Normally tours 2-3 projects each year
with an average annual total of 75 performances across 35 different venues. Venues
include schools, arts centres, theatres, outdoor venues and community venues across
England. In general 5-8 actors go on tour
and play to audiences aged 5 upwards.
Singing ability, proficiency with a musical
instrument, dance/physical theatre skills
and a driving licence are required. Actors
are also expected to lead workshops.
Recent productions include: *Miners'
Memories*, for the Museum of Cannock
Chase, and *Goldilocks & the Three Bears* for
a South England tour.

Casting procedures
Holds general auditions; actors requesting
inclusion should write between August and
December. Casting breakdowns are available through *PCR* and advertisements in
The Stage. Accepts letters (with CVs and
photographs) from actors previously
unknown to the company sent by post or
email. "Actors must be experienced in
working with young children and be will-
ing to be CRB (Criminal Records Bureau)
checked before working.

Must also be prepared to assist in fit-ups, etc. on tour."

Zip Theatre

Newhampton Arts Centre, Dunkley Street,
Wolverhampton WV1 4AN
tel (01902) 572250 *fax* (01902) 572251
email admin@ziptheatre.co.uk
website www.ziptheatre.co.uk
Artistic Director Jon Lingard-Lane
Administrator Alyson Lanning

Production details

Founded in 1980. Normally tours 6 projects each year with an average annual total of 300 performances. Venues include schools, arts centres, theatres, outdoor venues and community venues mainly in the West Midlands area. In general 7 actors go on tour and play to audiences aged 5 upwards. Singing ability and dance skills are required. Actors are also expected to lead workshops. Recent productions include: *Behind a Smile,* Theatre in Education pieces based on sexual exploitation and *Wind Dragons,* an outdoor summer show.

Casting procedures

Sometimes holds general auditions; actors may write at any time requesting inclusion any time. Accepts submissions (with CVs and photographs) from actors previously unknown to the company only if sent by post. Does not welcome unsolicited emails.

Festivals

These are populated by all kinds of companies listed in previous sections. Some are hired-in by a festival's organisers; others 'hire' space in order to participate – the latter predominate at the most famous festival of all, in Edinburgh. Participation in a festival can be enormous fun and a great opportunity to meet other actors and see other productions. However, the chances of such a production transferring, let alone making money, are limited.

Umbrella organisations

British Arts Festivals Association (BAFA)
3rd Floor, The Library, 77 Whitechapel High Street, London E1 7QX
tel 020-7247 4667 *fax* 020-7247 5010
email info@artsfestivals.co.uk
website www.artsfestivals.co.uk

Provides information and a professional network for the festivals movement in the UK, working to promote the profile and status of arts festivals. As well as the arts festivals website, which catalogues festivals in the UK and provides links to festivals in Europe, BAFA also publishes a free Calendar and Directory of the 105 festival members in print, and produces an advance festivals press pack each January. Members have the opportunity to attend BAFA conferences, training courses and focus meetings. Membership is open to all arts festivals in the UK and associate membership to other arts organisations. Does not promote individual artists, companies or tours.

British Federation of Festivals for Music, Drama and Speech
Festivals House, 198 Park Lane, Macclesfield, Cheshire SK11 6UD
tel 0870-7744 290 *fax* 0870-7744 292
email jt@festivals.demon.co.uk
website www.festivals.demon.co.uk

Provides information and a network for amateur and competitive festivals in the UK. The Federation includes more than 300 festivals.

The European Festivals Association
General Secretariat, Château de Coppet, Case Postale 26, CH-1296 COPPET, Switzerland
tel 0041-22-776 86 73
fax 0041-22-776 42 75
email info@euro-festival.net
website www.euro-festival.net/Efichome

Represents more than 93 high-quality festivals in 31 European countries and 4 non-European countries. The website offers a general overview of these festivals, together with a detailed list of thousands of events and performances in its annual calendar.

UK arts festivals

Arundel Festival
tel (01903) 883474
email arundelfestival@btopenworld.com
website www.arundelfestival.co.uk

For 10 days each August, the market town of Arundel is host to a multi-arts festival which began more than 25 years ago. Street theatre and a festival Fringe are regular features, as are concerts, exhibitions, fireworks and jazz. The festival culminates in an open-air production of a Shakespeare play in the ground of Arundel Castle. Each production is led by a cast of experienced professional actors and extended with members of the local community who work with the professionals throughout the 6-week rehearsal period.

Barbican International Theatre Event (BITE)

Barbican Centre, Silk Street, London EC2Y 8DS
tel 020-7638 4141
email theatre@barbican.org.uk
website www.barbican.org.uk/bite/
Theatre Administrators Toni Racklin, Griselda Yorke, Angie Smith

Since its first programme in 1998, BITE has sought to create a venue in London dedicated to presenting some of the most significant and innovative artists around the world. The Spring 2004 season featured music, theatre and dance pieces from 12 different countries. Events included *Jimmy* from Infrarouge Théâtre, written, directed and performed by Marie Brassard, and *Continental Divide*, 2 new plays from award-winning writer David Edgar and directed by Tony Taccone (a Berkeley Repertory Theatre and Oregon Shakespeare Festival production).

Bath Shakespeare Festival

Theatre Royal, Sawclose, Bath BA1 1ET
tel (01225) 448844
website www.bathshakespeare.org.uk

Presenting premieres, international productions and new commissions, the 6th Bath Shakespeare Festival took place from 1-13 March 2004. Opening with a new family production of *A Midsummer Night's Dream*, the programme also included Bremer Shakespeare Company's multinational production of *Much Ado About Nothing*, Forkbeard Fantasy's new play about Shakespeare on film, and *Al-Hamlet Summit*, an exploration of contemporary Arab politics through Shakespeare's tragedies.

Belfast Festival at Queens

25 College Gardens, Belfast BT9 6BS
tel 028-9027 2600
email a.mcGrath@qub.ac.uk
website www.belfastfestival.co.uk

Founded in 1963, the Belfast Festival is an annual 3-week international arts festival held in October and November each year. The largest festival of its kind in Ireland, it covers all artforms including theatre, dance, classical music, literature, jazz, comedy, visual arts, folk music and popular music, attracting more than 50,000 visitors. Theatre performances in 2003 included Bill Kenwright's production of *A Picture of Dorian Gray* and the National Theatre's production of *Vincent in Brixton*. Artists wishing to participate in the festival should submit a written proposal to the address listed above.

Birmingham ArtsFest

tel 0121-685 2605
email mail@artsfest.org.uk
website www.artsfest.org.uk

ArtsFest is one of the UK's largest free arts festivals and is held in venues across Birmingham for 2 days in September. It programmes a range of free performances including theatre, jazz, opera and dance events. Street theatre also features heavily, with musicians, jugglers, visual artists and stand-up comedians all presenting their work outside.

ArtsFest 2003 played host to names from all kinds of artforms, such as the City of Birmingham Symphony Orchestra, the Royal Shakespeare Company, Mercury Music Prize nominee Soweto Kinch, Musical Youth featuring Pato Banton, Dhol Foundation, Birmingham Royal Ballet and Spanish street theatre company Sarruga.

Bradford International Festival Ltd.

Business Innovation Centre, Angel Way, Listerhills, Bradford BD7 1BX
tel (01274) 722272 *fax* (01274) 736600
email info@bethere2003.com

The Bradford Festival has been established for 14 years and continues to grow each summer. For 2 weeks in July the festival celebrates a creative fusion of cultures from across the District and West Yorkshire. The main events are the Mela, which is the largest event of its kind in Europe, the Lord Mayor's Carnival Procession and the Street Theatre Festival. Last year's programme included Improbable Theatre's production of *Sticky* and performances from Polish company Teatr Osmigo Dnia.

Brighton Festival

email info@brighton-festival.org.uk
website www.brighton-festival.org.uk

Founded in 1967. For 3 weeks in May, more than 300 separate arts events take place in venues across Brighton and Hove. Artists from a number of different countries are represented in theatre, dance, music, opera, books, events and outdoor spectaculars.

Running alongside Brighton Festival, Brighton Festival Fringe (previously called 'the Open') has been in existence for 37 years and is the biggest in England showcasing a variety of artforms and activities. In 2003 the Fringe featured 203 artists in open houses, 105 exhibitions, 67 theatre events, 54 classical and opera recitals, 48 city tours, 45 music concerts, 21 events for children, 25 comedy events, 15 nightlife events and 15 literature events. Theatre events scheduled for 2004 include the premiere of Peter Brook's *The Death of Krishna*, performed by the French Company Thêâtre de Bouffes du Nord.

Cambridge Hotbed Festival

Junction CDC, Clifton Road, Cambridge CB1 7GX
tel (01223) 578000
email cat@junction.co.uk
website www.hotbedfest.co.uk

Following the success of the original Hotbed 2002, Menagerie Theatre Company (www.menagerie.uk.com) and Junction CDC (www.junction.co.uk) have joined forces to present Hotbed 2004, the second Cambridge New Writing Theatre Festival. From 1-18 July, venues around Cambridge –including CB2, Cambridge Drama Centre and Cambridge Arts Theatre's Playroom –will host a variety of new plays by a selection of regional and national writers including Claire Macdonald, Fraser Grace and Steve Waters. Productions range from 15-minute lunchtime shorts to full evening performances, with a selection of workshops, talks, masterclasses and seminars also included in the programme.

The festival presents opportunities for both writers and actors to get involved. Any writer may submit a complete play for 2 actors lasting 15-20 minutes.

Successful writers will see their production professionally developed and performed at various central Cambridge venues throughout the 3-week festival. A repertory company based around the members of Menagerie Theatre Company will be supporting the festival, and actors are welcome to audition for the company a few months in advance. For further information about the next Hotbed and how to get involved, contact Cat Moore by phone, email or post.

Canterbury Festival

Christ Church Gate, The Precincts, Canterbury, Kent CT1 2EE
tel (01227) 452853
email info@canterburyfestival.co.uk
website www.canterburyfestival.co.uk

Founded in 1929, the dates for Canterbury Festival 2004 are 9-24 October. The festival will feature music, dance, drama, opera, film, community events, talks, walks and visual arts.

The Marlowe and Gulbenkian Theatres in Canterbury and the Theatre Royal in Margate are host to major dance, drama and opera companies. Many small professional and amateur companies perform in the smaller venues and present a wide variety of drama and dance during the 2 weeks of the festival. These have included local companies as well as small foreign companies such as the Brazilian company Teatro Sao Paulo Fabrica, and Hungarian children's theatre Kolibri Theatre.

Other drama companies that have appeared at the festival include the Royal Shakespeare Company, the National Theatre company, Actors Touring Company, Trestle Theatre, Compass Theatre, Shared Experience and Yellow Earth Theatre.

Chichester Festivities

Box Office, 45 East Street, Chichester, West Sussex PO19 1HX
tel (01243) 780192
email info@chifest.org.uk
website www.chifest.org.uk

The Box Office is open for making reservations a month in advance of the festival. At other times consult the website or make contact by email.

Chichester Festivities are programmed over 2 weeks in July and have included performances of classical, jazz and world music, talks, contemporary sculpture in the Cathedral Cloisters, fireworks at Glorious Goodwood Racecourse and outdoor theatre productions. Founded in 1975, the event has attracted performers such as Dame Judi Dench, Jools Holland, Fay Weldon and Nigel Kennedy. The 2003 programme featured productions of *Bartholomew Fair* (Intact Theatre Company), *The Gondoliers* (Chichester Festival Theatre), *Six Characters in Search of an Author* (New Theatre Productions) and *The Water Babies* (Chichester Festival Theatre).

Dumfries and Galloway Arts Festival Ltd.

Gracefield Arts Centre, 28 Edinburgh Road, Dumfries DG1 1JQ
tel (01387) 260447
fax (01387) 260447
email info@dgartsfestival.org.uk
website www.dgartsfestival.org.uk

An annual 10-day festival at the end of May, established in 1979. Founded with the aim of bringing high-quality international events to community audiences that would not otherwise have the opportunity to experience such talent, the festival now also presents local talent of international standing.

The festival programmes a wide range of events covering music –including classical, jazz and folk –dance, theatre, literary, children's and the visual arts. Events take place in a range of venues throughout the region, both large and small, urban and rural.

Edinburgh Festival Fringe

The Fringe Office, 180 High Street, Edinburgh EH1 1QS
tel 0131-226 0026 *fax* 0131-226 0016
email admin@edfringe.com
website www.edfringe.com

The Fringe was started in 1947 to complement the first Edinburgh International Festival. It now breaks its own record every year as the largest arts festival on the planet, bringing thousands of performances of hundreds of shows in more than 200 venues across Edinburgh each August.

The Fringe Society was formed in 1959 to co-ordinate publicity and ticket sales and offer a comprehensive information service to both performers and audiences. It compiles information about venues, press and suppliers and produces a series of publications designed to answer frequently asked questions. The office is open all year round and the staff are available to help by phone, email or personal appointment.

Edinburgh International Festival

The Hub, Castlehill, Edinburgh EH1 2NE
tel 0131-473 2000 *fax* 0131-473 2003
email eif@eif.co.uk
website www.eif.co.uk

Founded in 1947, the Edinburgh International Festival is an annual event held over 3 weeks in August, using all the major concert and theatre venues in the city. In 2003 it presented 168 performances of 80 different productions and concerts, including 3 world premieres and featuring artists from around the world. With music, opera, theatre, film, dance, and the Military Tattoo at the Castle, the festival is now recognised as one of the world's most important celebrations of the arts.

Also offers a programme of year-round activities, with courses and workshops on diverse subjects from playwrighting to the use of digital video, and one-off projects for school children, students and adults collaborating with actors, directors, choreographers and musicians involved in the festival. Performance at the Edinburgh International Festival is by invitation only, issued by the Festival Director.

Fierce!

Birmingham
tel 0121-244 8080 *fax* 0121-244 8081
email fierce@fierceearth.com
website www.fierce.info

Annual festival of performances and events in theatres, bars, clubs, galleries and public spaces across the West Midlands; now in its 7th year. In 2003 the festival took place from 16 May to 28 June and included *Visions of Excess* curated by Ron Athey with UK and international artists, La Ribot's *Take Off*, and Gob Squad's *Room Service*.

Greenwich and Docklands Festivals (GDF)

6 College Approach, London SE10 9HY
tel 020-8305 1818 *fax* 020-8305 1188
email info@festival.org
website www.festival.org

Taking place over the 4 weekends of July, the Greenwich and Docklands Festival programmes multi-disciplinary arts events around East London each summer.

Highlights of GDF 2003 included a theatrical banquet marking the 400th anniversary of the reign of Elizabeth I, a nocturnal gathering of giant giraffes, contemporary dance on skateboards and a military tattoo with an army of petrol-driven insects. As well as programming large-scale, visually impressive work, the festival places emphasis on educational projects and participatory arts.

The International Festival of Musical Theatre in Cardiff

St David's House, Wood Street, Cardiff CF10 1ES
tel 029-2090 1111 *fax* 029-2040 4216
email enquiries@cardiffmusicals.com
website www.cardiffmusicals.com

Following the success of its inaugural festival in October 2002, plans are underway for the next scheduled festival in April 2005. The programme will include a range of music theatre performances and events at venues across Cardiff, including the first major musical theatre production at the new Wales Millennium Centre.

International Playwriting Festival

Warehouse Theatre, Dingwall Road, Croydon CR0 2NF
website www.warehousetheatre.co.uk
Festival Administrator Rose Marie Vernon

The International Playwriting Festival has been in operation since 1986 and has consolidated the Warehouse Theatre Company's role in discovering and developing new writing talent. Launching the career of many successful playwrights, the festival has seen many of its plays transferred to the West End, the Royal Court, Hampstead Theatre and Stratford-upon-Avon.

The 2003 festival was held on 22 and 23 November and received applications from writers in the USA, Hong Kong, Croatia, Holland, Australia, Estonia, Sierra Leone, Italy and New Zealand as well as in the UK.

Lichfield International Arts Festival

The Lichfield Festival Association, 7 The Close, Lichfield, StaffordshireWS13 7LD
tel (01543) 306270
email lichfield.fest@lichfield-arts.org.uk
website www.lichfieldfestival.org

Annual 20-day event held in July and featuring music, poetry, exhibitions, lectures, readings and theatre events. The 2003 festival included open-air performances of *Taming of the Shrew* (MDCC Theatre Company), *The Tale of Beatrix Potter* and Alan Bennett's *Talking Heads* (Intimate Theatre).

London Comedy Festival

20 Chancellors Street, Hammersmith, London W6 9RN
tel 0870-119 611
email info@londoncomedyfestival.com
website www.londoncomedyfestival.com

The London Comedy Festival is a celebration of London's established comedy scene, with many of the capital's top clubs hosting stand-up events, a programme of humour literature events across London's libraries and bookshops including workshops, readings, competitions and debates, and major events at some of London's landmarks, along with other comedy activities.

Highlights in previous years have included the first ever open-air cinema event in Trafalgar Square, the creation of the world's largest cartoon strip, 'Wit Lit' – London's largest ever humour literature event, and the GOSH Gala –a star-studded fundraiser hosted by Graham Norton and Suggs.

Anyone can put on a show as part of the London Comedy Festival. Over the past 3 years the event has encompassed not just comedy clubs but pubs, theatres, galleries and libraries. Registration begins in January with a deadline for inclusion in the Festival Guide of mid-March.

London International Festival of Theatre (LIFT)

19/20 Great Sutton Street,
London EC1V ODR
email info@liftfest.org
website www.liftfest.org
Directors Rose Fenton, Lucy Neal

Started in 1981, LIFT is a biennial summer festival introducing some of the world's most exciting artists and theatre-makers to London. LIFT events have been staged in more than 30 London venues as well as a number of site-specific venues such as streets, disused buildings, the river, parks and open spaces.

Also runs developmental and educational programmes exploring the nature of exchange and creativity for a range of audiences including school children and industry leaders.

London International Mime Festival

35 Little Russell Street,
London WC1A 2HH
tel 020-7637 5661 *fax* 020-7323 1151
email mimefest@easynet.co.uk
website www.mimefest.co.uk
Directors Joseph Seelig, Helen Lannaghan

Founded in 1977, the London International Mime Festival presents innovative visual theatre. Events are non-text-based and can include animation theatre, circus skills, mask, mime, clown and visual theatre. Most of the work programmed will not have been performed in London before.

The 2005 festival will take place from 15-30 January with the deadline for submissions in mid-July 2004. Participation is by invitation only. To be considered, send a VHS video to Helen Lannaghan and Joseph Seelig at the address above with an sae enclosed for the return of material.

Ludlow Festival

email info@ludlowfestival.co.uk
website www.ludlowfestival.co.uk

After 44 years, the Ludlow Festival expanded to 3 weeks in 2003 with a range of music, theatre and exhibitions on offer from 20 June to 30 July. Each year it features open-air Shakespeare productions which are staged in the grounds of Ludlow Castle. Directed by Michael Bogdanov, the 2003 performances were *The Winter's Tale* and *The Merchant of Venice. Twelfth Night* and *Cymbeline* are scheduled for July 2004.

Other highlights in 2003 included appearances by Tasmin Little with the European Union Chamber Orchestra, Courtney Pine and his Band, Barry Norman, Lord Heseltine, the Literary Weekend and Jenny Eclair.

The Mayor's Thames Festival

website www.thamesfestival.org

The Mayor's Thames Festival is a free annual event that takes place on and around the River Thames between Westminster and Southwark Bridges, using the river as a powerful unifying symbol for the whole of London. One of the festival's main aims is to enable more collaborations between artists and community groups. In 2003 it was successful in involving more than 9000 people from 300 London schools and community groups in its work. The 7th Thames Festival attracted an estimated 238,000 people over the weekend of Saturday 13 and Sunday 14 September 2003, with a programme of events that included a night carnival, a fireworks spectacular, mass choirs, music stages, a range of participatory activities, and both artist-led and river-orientated events.

Merseyside International Street Festival

tel 0151-709 3334 *fax* 0151-709 4994
email info@brouhaha.uk.com
website www.brouhaha.uk.com

Now in its 10th year, the Merseyside International Street Festival brings a mix of dance, drama, acrobatics, music, comedy, puppetry and street theatre to around 30,000 spectators in Liverpool each July/August.

Minack Theatre Summer Festival

Porthcurno, Penzance, Cornwall TR19 6JU
tel (01736) 810694 *fax* (01736) 810779
email minack@dial.pipex.com
website www.minack.com

Founded in 1932. An annual, 17-week summer season of plays, musicals and opera held at Minack's unique open-air theatre carved into the Cornish cliffside. Created in 1929 by Rowena Cade and her gardener Billy Rawlings, the Minack lends itself to large-cast plays. Most companies involved are amateur, although approximately 3 each year are professional.

National Student Drama Festival (NSDF)

D14, The Foxhole Centre, Dartington, Totnes, Devon TQ9 6EB
tel (01803) 864836 *fax* (01803) 840693
email admin@nsdf.org.uk
website www.nsdf.org.uk
General Manager (For tickets, administration and sponsorship) Rachel Williams
Director (For general artistic enquiries) Andrew Loretto
Assistant to Director (To enter a production and request an information pack) Ian Abbott

The National Student Drama Festival is a week-long event bringing together students and leading theatre and media professionals. It showcases and nurtures innovative theatre by young people and offers masterclasses, workshops and forums for debate and discussion. A panel of 3 eminent judges awards the prestigious NSDF Prizes, Awards and Bursaries at the end of the festival (31 March –7 April 2004).

NSDF is open to colleges, youth theatres, community organisations and universities, and takes place each spring in Scarborough. Professionals attending in 2003 included Mike Leigh, David Glass, Willy Russell, Howard Goodall, Mark Ravenhill, Sir Alan Ayckbourn, Michael Billington and Frantic Assembly.

The NSDF Ensemble is a company of talented young theatre practitioners from all over the UK. Supported by professional artists, Ensemble members take part in a one-off training/residency. On the recommendation of the NSDF selection team, members are invited to audition each year from the wide range of shows entered for the festival.

National Theatre's Watch This Space Festival

Royal National Theatre, South Bank, London SE1 9PX

tel 020-7452 3400
email info@nationaltheatre.org.uk
website www.nt-online.org

Each summer, Watch This Space programmes a season of international outdoor theatre, music and entertainment outside the National Theatre. Events are free, unticketed and run 6 days a week from June through to August.

The 2003 festival featured performances from Men in Coats, Flying Dudes, Mimbre and the Natural Theatre Company, amongst many others. The season also included a series of Ramayana Workshops for children, exploring the fight between good and evil in the ancient Indian epic.

Push

Almeida Theatre, Almeida Street,
London N1 1TA
tel 020-7288 4938
website www.pushherenow.com

As part of a new artistic collaboration, Push has been based at the Almeida since January 2003 and is currently developing 6 new productions which will be presented as part of Push 2004. A new play, opera, ballet, musical, cross-artform collaboration and television comedy will be produced as part of the Islington-based arts festival in September 2004, with the aim of creating high-quality artistic partnerships between black artists and mainstream arts organisations.

Royal Court Young Writers Festival

Young Writers Festival, The Site, Royal Court Theatre, Sloane Square,
London SW1W 8AS
website www.royalcourttheatre.com/ywp

A biennial festival, the Royal Court Young Writers Programme presents full professional productions of work by the most promising young playwrights aged 13-25. It is the world's largest festival of new playwriting by young people, attracting critical acclaim and the support of leading theatre practitioners including Kathy Burke, Max Stafford-Clark, Hanif Kureishi, Meera Syal and Richard Wilson. The festival has launched the careers of playwrights such as Leo Butler, Nick Grosso, Christopher Shinn, Simon Stephens and Michael Wynne.

Selected scripts for the 2004 festival will be acted and directed by professionals from 1 October to 30 November 2004. For information or application details for the next festival, consult the website or send an sae to the address above. For casting procedures see entry for the Royal Court under *Producing Theatres*.

Salisbury Festival

Festival Office, 75 New Street, Salisbury, Wiltshire SP1 2PH
tel (01722) 332977 *fax* (01722) 410552
email info@salisburyfestival.co.uk
website www.salisburyfestival.co.uk

Established in 1973, for 20 years the festival consisted mostly of classical music events. It is now multi-disciplinary and combines prestigious Cathedral concerts with family street entertainment, circus, theatre and other arts events. There are normally between 30-50 different programmes and projects and a total of some 100 different events which take place at the end of May and beginning of June. The theatre events scheduled for 2004 include the West End hit *Stones in his Pockets* and the French company Au Cul du Loup's environmental show *Monsoon*.

Shrewsbury Summer Season

tel (01743) 281281
website www.shrewsburysummer.co.uk

The first Shrewsbury Summer Season takes place in June, July and August 2004 with a programme of visual arts, music, drama, dance, spoken word and comedy events. Highlights of the current schedule include Shropshire writer Mary Webb's *Precious Bane*, which has been adapted by Bryony Lavery and will be presented for 16 nights by Pentabus Theatre Company. The programme will also include open-air productions of *Macbeth* and *The Comedy of Errors* at Shrewsbury Castle and concerts by the English String Orchestra, the London Welsh Male Voice Choir and the Medieval Babes.

Soho Writers' Festival

Soho Theatre and Writers' Centre, 21 Dean Street, London W1D 3NE
tel 020-7287 5060 *fax* 020-7287 5061
email mail@sohotheatre.com
website www.sohotheatre.com

Soho Theatre's 4th Writers Festival took place from 27 October to 15 November 2003 with a programme of masterclasses, workshops, seminars, talks, rehearsed readings and performances led by some of the UK's leading writers, directors and industry professionals. Festival highlights included talks from *The Guardian* Editor Alan Rusbridger, Howard Jacobsen, Jude Kelly, Allison Pearson, Daniel Kitson, and DV8's Lloyd Newson, plus workshops from Frantic Assembly, Theatre and Beyond, Yellow Earth and Amused Moose Comedy. Panel discussions covered a range of topics from the latest revolutions happening in the theatre world to TV sitcom writing with a line-up of Perrier Award-winning comedy to end each day.

The Stratford-upon-Avon Poetry Festival

Shakespeare Birthplace Trust, Shakespeare Centre, Henley Street, Stratford-upon-Avon, Warwickshire CV37 6QW
tel (01789) 204016 *fax* (01789) 296083
email reception@shakespeare.org.uk (general enquiries only)
website www.shakespeare.org

Established in 1954 by the Shakespeare Birthplace Trust, the festival presents recitals of poetry held over 9 successive Sundays in the summer. Nearly every major British poet from Beowulf onwards has featured somewhere in the festival, along with other poetry written or translated into English.

Over the last 50 years, many leading actors have been involved in the readings, including Judi Dench, Ralph Fiennes, John Gielgud, Ian Holm, Anthony Hopkins, Jeremy Irons, Derek Jacobi, Ben Kingsley, Ian McKellen, Helen Mirren, Vanessa Redgrave, Ian Richardson, Diana Rigg and Robert Stephens. In addition to the 9 traditional recitals the festival now also includes a Local Poets evening.

Role-Play Companies

Actors have long used their craft in promotional areas like selling products and services over the phone and in department stores; work opportunities in these fields are advertised in *The Stage*. More recently, the idea of using theatre skills deeper inside the world of business (and the service professions, like medicine) has grown considerably. Essentially, the high level of co-operation ('interactivity') and the excitement, creativity and inspirational power of good theatre is being grasped by hierarchies 'outside the proscenium arch'. Role-play practitioners today are using techniques evolved by the Theatre in Education movement in the 1960s and '70s – but with far, far better-paying 'customers'.

The established companies – mostly created by actors – have built up a great deal of expertise in this new world and do not take on new 'role players' lightly. It is therefore especially important to research each individual company's 'modus operandi' before spending time and money in contacting them. However, this is a world well worth exploring as an exciting and lucrative alternative area of work.

Barking Productions Ltd.

PO Box 597, Bristol BS99 2BB
tel 0117-939 3171 *fax* 0117-939 3625
email info@barkingproductions.co.uk
website www.barkingproductions.co.uk
Key personnel Christopher Grimes, Neil Bett, Stephanie Weston

Company's work
Creative development and corporate entertainment company run by professional actors and specialising in drama-based training. The company's comedy show, *Instant Wit*, is regularly performed at corporate events. Provides incoming actors with some training in the form of familiarisation with company style and approach. Clients include: Marks & Spencer, Microsoft, Aardman Animations and Orange.

Recruitment procedures
Periodically extends its actor-base. Welcomes letters (with CVs and photographs) and always consults them when recruiting actors. Requires actors to be highly experienced with a businesslike manner (particularly for corporate work) and living in Bristol or London. Advises actors to visit their website and get a good idea of "who we are and what we do" before approaching the company.

Cragrats

The Cragrats Mill, Dunford Road, Huddersfield HD9 2AR
tel (01484) 686451 *fax* (01484) 686212
email jill@cragrats.com
website www.cragrats.com
Creative Director Mark Greenop
Business Director David Bradley

Company's work
A theatrical communications company founded in 1989, specialising in corporate training, TIE and issue-based theatre nationwide. Employs 500 actors per year. Project managers and facilitators are

trained in-house. Clients include: ASDA, NHS, Learning & Skills Councils, and the Royal Bank of Scotland.

Recruitment procedures
Extends its actor-base each month. Recruits actors through its website and through agents, Equity Job Information Service and advertisements in *The Stage*. Welcomes submissions (with CVs and photographs) by post or email from actors with at least 3 years training at an approved drama school. 'We regularly recruit actors aged 21-60. Please contact us. All rehearsals are Yorkshire-based, though work can be anywhere in the UK.'

Interact
Bowden House, 14 Bowden Street, London SE11 4DS
tel 020-7793 7744 *fax* 020-7793 7755
email info@interact.eu.com
website www.interact.eu.com
Directors Derek Hollis, Ian Jessup
Company Administrator Jamie Wright

Company's work
Founded in 1996, the company aims to bring theatre skills to business using the abilities of professional actors, writers, directors and facilitators. Role-play constitutes just 30% of output. Provides incoming actors with some training in the form of a briefing for basic role-play, rehearsal and guidance for complex work. Offers facilitators specific training in project management. Clients include: ACAS, the Foreign & Commonwealth Office, the BBC, and Royal and Sun Alliance.

Recruitment procedures
Periodically extends its actor-base. Recruits actors through its website and through agents, Equity Job Information Service, *PCR* and direct contact. Fluency, confidence and strong acting and improvisation skills are required. Business and forum theatre experience can also be an advantage. Welcomes letters (with CVs and photographs) but not email submissions. Invitations to view individual actors' websites are also accepted. Advises actors that: 'Those with previous experience are most likely to be interviewed. We are unable to reply to submissions. If you are of interest to us, you will be contacted.'

Maynard Leigh Associates (MLA)
Marvic House, Bishops Road, London SW6 7AD
email michaelm@maynardleigh.co.uk
website www.maynardleigh.co.uk

Company's work
MLA is essentially a community of about 25 people who share common values, are committed to their own and other people's personal growth, and are passionate about their work affecting an increasing number of individuals and organisations. They are required to be expert workshop leaders with an interest in the psychological aspects of human potential development. Clients include: Hewlett Packard, Halifax plc, Ernst & Young, BBC TV, Vodafone, Barclay, Virgin and FT.com.

Recruitment procedures
All new consultants and leaders go through a rigorous and lengthy training process regardless of their professional experience. It can take up to 18 months of participation in MLA activities before an actor is allowed to represent the consultancy with clients. There are regular personal development sessions in which people explore how they are doing in MLA and how they need to develop and grow further. As MLA invests heavily in its existing Associates, its pace of growth is limited and it is unable to extend its actor-base regularly. Professional actors with a good

working knowledge of business and corporate life should submit their details by email.

Steps Drama Learning Development
Unit 13.2.2 The Leathermarket, Weston Street, London SE1 3ER
tel 020-7403 9000 *fax* 020-7403 0909
email mail@stepsdrama.com
website www.stepsdrama.com
Account Directors Robbie Swales, Richard Wilkes, Janet Rawson, Simon Thomson, Mark Shillabeer, Angela McHale

Company's work
Founded in 1990, the company supplies training to a wide variety of corporate companies through the use of drama. The work includes role-play, forum workshops and drama facilitation. Incoming actors receive training in the areas of feedback skills, forum workshops, coordinator workshops, facilitation skills and 'train the trainer'. Clients include: J P Morgan, NHS, Weight Watchers, Disney, and the BBC.

Recruitment procedures
Extends its actor-base once or twice a year, selecting 2-3 people from approximately 12-14 applications. Welcomes letters (with CVs and photographs) but not email submissions; consults submitted CVs when recruiting. Actors should have excellent improvisation skills and be able to present themselves realistically as part of the business world in both their dress and language. Requires actors to behave in a professional manner both in their

dealings with Steps and with their clients. Must be organised, reliable and good team players.

Turning Point Theatre Company
20 Couper Meadows, Exeter EX2 7TF
tel (01392) 446818 *fax* (01392) 446279
email turningpoint@eclipse.co.uk
website www.turningpointtheatre.co.uk
Director Lyn Ferrand
Administrator Anne Williams

Company's work
Founded in 1990, the company aims to raise awareness of specific health and social issues using theatre and theatre-related techniques. Gained Pavilion Award for innovations in training (2000). Works in partnership with the corporate, voluntary and statutory sectors. Creates training courses and videos for health and social service professionals. Other activities include national and regional tours, residencies, workshops and conferences. Provides incoming actors with some training in forum theatre techniques if required. Clients include: Devon County Council, the Princess Royal Trust for Carers, Rethink (NSF).

Recruitment procedures
Periodically extends its actor-base in accordance with the demands of specific projects. Actors are recruited via agents and *PCR*. Welcomes submissions (with CVs and photographs) sent by post or email. Showreels and invitations to view individual actors' websites are also accepted.

Other Media

Introduction

The last decade has seen incredibly rapid advancements in recording technology, computers, digital media and the Internet. There has also been an enormous growth in the principal broadcasting companies contracting-out much of their output; this in turn has led to an increase in the number of independent companies employing actors. (There are also companies whose output does not include drama, and other opportunities for actors –these have not been included in the listings.)

Most film and television companies use casting directors, and it's usually a waste of time and money writing to anyone else unless you have a personal contact. It is worth remembering that many companies do work for businesses –training and promotional films, for instance.

Student films may be a somewhat poor relation to Hollywood blockbusters, in terms of pay (if any) and of exposure, but they can provide useful experiences, be a good addition to your CV, and have the potential to lead onto something that is properly paid and much more prestigious. Extracts from such a film could also be useful for your showreel.

Casting for radio is much more akin to that for theatre, although often without the use of a casting director.

Television Companies

These almost always use casting directors who, in turn, will circulate casting breakdowns to agents they trust. However, a carefully timed (and crafted) submission from an individual can occasionally excite interest.

BBC Network Television

For more information, visit the BBC website: www.bbc.co.uk

The new structure

Major restructuring, introduced on 3 April 2000, resulted in the creation of four programming divisions:

- Drama, Entertainment and Children;
- Factual and Learning;
- Sport;
- News.

BBC Broadcast and BBC Production have been abolished. In the areas of sport, children's and education, commissioning and programme-making are now integrated. A New Media division is now developing the BBC's interactive television online activities.

Television genre commissioners in drama, entertainment and features now work with the television channel controllers to strengthen the BBC's output in these areas.

The disbanding of the Independent Commissioning Group has not diminished the value the BBC now places on the contribution of independents. However, in future they will take the same commissioning routes as in-house producers.

The restructuring also gives output guarantees for in-house departments, including Nations and English Regions, and longer-term commissions to enable better planning and a greater focus on creativity.

Casting information

The BBC no longer has a central casting department. Casting advisers are appointed to each specific programme as required. Output includes: *Casualty, Holby City, Doctors, EastEnders, Born and Bred, The Inspector Lynley Mysteries, Waking the Dead, Judge John Deed, Dalziel and Pascoe, Silent Witness* and *Spooks*. The various programmes' casting departments will accept letters from actors previously unknown to them (with CVs, photographs and performance notices). However, actors are advised that while casting personnel are on the lookout for new talent and do attend shows, they are extremely busy and tend to use agents when casting.

The recently launched BBC Talent initiative is designed to offer "raw talent" (actors without formal qualifications or experience) the opportunity to act their way onto a major drama. In 2003 several of the actors cast for the BBC1 drama, *The Canterbury Tales,* were winners of BBC Talent auditions. For the latest information on BBC Talent's projects see the website: www.bbc.co.uk/talent

Drama

BBC Television Centre, Centre House,
Wood Lane, London W12 7SB
tel 020-8743 8000

Drama Development in the North
BBC New Broadcasting House, Oxford
Road, Manchester M60 1SJ
tel 0161-200 2020

BBC Broadcasting Centre
Pebble Mill Road, Birmingham B5 7QQ
tel 0121-432 8888

Drama has departments in London,
Birmingham and Manchester and
produces a broad range of plays, serials,
series and readings for TV, film, BBC
Radio 3, BBC Radio 4 and BBC World
service.

Controller, Continuing Drama Series
Mal Young
Head of Films & Single Drama
David Thompson
Controller, Drama Commissioning
Jane Tranter
Head of Independents Drama Gareth Neame
Head of Drama Serials Laura Mackie
Controller, Innovation & Factual Drama
Susan Spindler
Head of Development Films Tracey Scoffield
Casting Executive, Drama Series
Jane Deitch

*Executive Producer TV Drama Series,
Birmingham* Richard Langridge
*Development Coordinator TV Drama,
Birmingham* Terry Barker
*Executive Producer Radio Drama & Editor,
The Archers, Birmingham* Vanessa
Whitburn
*Executive Producer Radio Drama,
Manchester* Sue Roberts
Head of Drama, BBC World Service
Gordon House
New Writing Initiative Coordinator Lucy
Hannah

The New Writing Initiative
Room 6058, BBC Broadcasting House,
London W1A 1AA
tel 020-7580 4468

Entertainment

BBC Television Centre, Wood Lane,
London W12 7RJ
tel 020-8743 8000
website www.bbc.co.uk/entertainment
Head of Comedy Sophie Clark-Jervoise
Head of Comedy Entertainment Jon
Plowman

Entertainment welcomes new half-hour
TV situation comedy scripts and material
is reviewed by its Comedy Script Unit.
Radio is also a good entry point for new
comedy writers, performers and ground-
breaking innovative series such as sketch
shows and panel games.

Children's

BBC Television Centre, Wood Lane,
London W12 7RJ
tel 020-8743 8000
Head of Drama Elaine Sperber
Head of Entertainment Anne Gildost

There are opportunities for new writers in
this highly competitive area. Unsolicited
material is read by the department, preferably in the form of synopses of ideas. The
preferred genres are contemporary comedy
and drama.

Entertainment and Features, Manchester

BBC New Broadcasting House, PO Box 27,
Oxford Road, Manchester M60 1SJ
tel 0161-200 2020

A bi-media department which makes
programmes for both radio and TV. It is
responsible for a wide range of factual,
entertainment and music programming,
and specialises in spotting new comedy
talent; aims to see all new stand-up
performers/writers in the North West.
Write with details of events to Comedy
Entertainment, Room 4033.

Network Production, Birmingham

BBC Birmingham, Pebble Mill Road,
Birmingham B5 7QQ
tel 0121-432 8888
Editor, Radio Drama The Archers Vanessa
Whitburn

A vast range of radio and TV programming which encompasses Asian, consumer
affairs, leisure, lifestyle, motoring, music
and rural affairs.

World Service

Bush House, Strand, London WC2B 4PH
tel 020-7240 3456
website www.bbc.co.uk/worldservice

BBC World Service provides radio services
in English and 42 other languages, via
short wave and in an increasing number
of cities around the world, on MW and
FM. The English service is also available
24 hours a day in real audio on the
Internet. Classic contemporary drama,
novels, short stories, soap operas and
poetry are all a feature of its English
service, plus a wide range of arts, documentaries, education, features, music, religious affairs, science, sports and youth
programmes. In addition, BBC World
Service provides on-the-spot coverage of
world news, giving a global perspective of
international events.

BBC Northern Ireland

BBC Broadcasting House, Ormeau Avenue,
Belfast BT2 8HQ
tel 028-9033 8000
website www.bbc.co.uk/ni
Entertainment and Events Mike Edgar
Head of Drama Robert Cooper

BBC Northern Ireland produces a broad
spectrum of radio and TV programmes,
both for the BBC's networks and for its
home audience. Output includes news and
current affairs, documentaries, education,
entertainment, sport, music, Irish language
and religious programmes. It also has a
thriving drama department which reads
unsolicited scripts across all genres,
i.e. single, serials, series, feature films and
the short film scheme Northern lights,
which is aimed at new talent from within
Northern Ireland.

In addition to making network radio programmes, broadcasting on BBC Radio 1, 2, 3, 4, and 5 Live and BBC World Service, BBC Northern Ireland also makes programmes for its local radio listeners.

BBC Scotland

BBC Broadcasting House, Queen Margaret Drive, Glasgow G12 8DG
tel 0141-339 8844
website www.bbc.co.uk/scotland
Head of Drama Barbara McKissack

BBC Scotland is the BBC's most varied production centre outside London, providing BBC TV and radio networks and BBC World Service with pivotal drama, comedy, entertainment, children's, leisure, documentaries, religion, education, arts, music, special events news, current affairs and political coverage. Internet development is also a key element of production activity.

Its drama department, along with Scottish Screen, is responsible for the highly successful initiative, *Tartan Shorts*, which promotes film-making in the nation and provides a platform for emerging Scottish creative talent, including actors, writers, directors and producers.

In addition to making network output, more than 850 hours of TV programming per year is transmitted on BBC1 Scotland and BBC2 Scotland. BBC Radio Scotland is the country's only national radio station, and is on air 18 hours a day, 7 days a week. Local programmes are also broadcast on Radio Scotland's FM frequency in the Northern Isles, and there are daily local bulletins for listeners in the Highlands,

Grampian, Borders, and the southwest. BBC Radio Nan Gaidheal provides a Gaelic service on a separate FM frequency for around 40 hours a week.

BBC Wales

BBC Broadcasting House, Llandaff, Cardiff CF5 2YQ
tel 029-2032 2000
website www.bbc.co.uk/wales
Head of Drama Matthew Robinson

BBC Wales provides a wide range of services in Welsh and in English, on radio, TV and online. This including more than 20 hours a week of programmes on BBC1 Wales and BBC2 Wales including the new BBC Wales digital services. Regular output includes the flagship news programme *Wales Today*, the current affairs strand *Week In Week Out*, and the rugby magazine *Scrum V*. A further 10 hours are shown on the Welsh-language channel S4C including the news programme *Newyddion*, the nightly drama serial *Pobol y Cwm* plus a range of programmes for schools. Its 2 radio stations, BBC Radio Wales, broadcasting in English, and BBC Radio Cymru, broadcasting in Welsh, each provide 18 hours a day of news, entertainment, music and sports output. Political coverage on all services has expanded as a result of the creation of the National Assembly for Wales.

BBC Wales also makes popular drama, documentaries, education and music programmes for audiences throughout the UK, including the biennial Cardiff Singer of the World competition, accompanied by the BBC National Orchestra of Wales.

Independent Television

The ITV network

ITV is the biggest commercial television network in the UK. It is made up of a network of 15 different regional licences, each with its own set of obligations and conditions designed to reflect the particular character of their region and the interests of their viewers. ITV plc owns 12 of the ITV licences; the remainder are owned by SMG, Ulster, and Channel.

ITV1 is the most popular commercial television channel in Britain. Watched on average by 45 million people every week, it has the largest programme budget of any commercial channel in Europe. Network programmes are commissioned by the ITV network controllers purely on merit. At least 25% of programmes shown on ITV1 each year come from independent producers. Regional programmes are commissioned by each regional company.

Anglia Television Ltd.
Anglia House, Norwich NR1 3JG
tel (01603) 615151 *fax* (01603) 631032
email angliatv@angliatv.com
website www.angliatv.com

Provides programmes for the East of England, daytime discussion programmes, documentaries and factual programmes for UK and international broadcasters. Does not produce any in-house drama.

Border Television plc
The Television Centre, Carlisle CA1 3NT
website www.border-tv.com

Provides programmes for Cumbria, the Borders and the Isle of Man during the whole week.

Channel Television
The Television Centre, St Helier,
Jersey JE1 3ZD
tel (01534) 816816 *fax* (01534) 816817
email broadcast@channeltv.co.uk

Provides programmes for the Channel Islands during the whole week relating mainly to Channel Islands new, events and current affairs. Does not produce any in-house drama.

Grampian Television plc
Queens Cross, Aberdeen AB15 4XJ
tel (01224) 846846 *fax* (01224) 846800
email gtv@grampiantv.co.uk
Harbour Chambers, Dock Street,
Dundee DD1 3HW
tel (01382) 591000 *fax* (01382) 591010
23-25 Huntly Street, Inverness IV3 5PR
tel (01463) 242624

Provides programmes for North Scotland during the whole week.

Granada Television Ltd.
Granada Television Centre,
Manchester M60 9EA
tel 0161-832 7211
email casting@itv.com
Head of Casting Judi Hayfield

Casting Director, Coronation Street
Gennie Radcliffe
Casting Director June West

Upper Ground, London SE1 9LT
tel 020-7620 1620
Casting Director Janie Frazer
Assistant Casting Director Stephanie Dawes

The ITV franchise holder for the North West of England. Produces programmes across a broad range for both its region and the ITV Network.

Welcomes submissions (with CVs and photographs) from actors previously unknown to the company sent by post or email. As the Casting Department is extremely busy it cannot guarantee to respond to all submissions. Advises actors to call to find out what projects are being cast, and to send in their details as and when appropriate.

HTV Ltd.

HTV Wales, The Televison Centre, Culverhouse Cross, Cardiff CF5 6XJ
tel 029-2059 0590
email public.relations@htv-wales.co.uk
website www.htvwales.com

HTV West, The Television Centre, Bristol BS4 3HG
tel 0117-972 2722
email presspr@htv-west.co.uk
website www.htvwest.com

Provides programmes for Wales and the West of England during the whole week. Produces programmes for home and international sales.

ITV Central

Carlton Broadcasting, Gas Street, Birmingham B1 2JT
tel 0121-643 9898 *fax* 0121-643 4897

Carlton Broadcasting, Lenton Lane, Nottingham NG7 2NA
tel 0115-986 3322 *fax* 0115-964 5552

Central News South, Unit 9, Windrush Court, Abingdon Business Park, Abingdon, Oxon OX1 1SA
tel (01235) 554123 *fax* (01235) 524024

Provides ITV programmes for the East, West and South Midlands every day.

ITV London

101 St Martin's Lane, London WC2N 4AZ
tel 020-7240 4000 *fax* 020-7240 4171
website www.itv.com

Provides ITV programmes for London and the South East from Monday to Friday.

ITV West Country

Langage Science Park, Plymouth PL7 5BQ
tel (01752) 333333
fax (01752) 333444
email westcountryregion@carltontv.co.uk
website www.itv.com

Provides programmes for South West England throughout the week. In-house production is mainly news, regional current affairs and topical features; other regional features are commissioned from independent producers.

LWT

The London Television Centre, London SE1 9LT
tel 020-7620 1620
website www.lwt.co.uk

Broadcasts to Greater London and much of the Home Counties area from 5.15 p.m. Friday to 6.00 a.m. Monday.

Meridian Broadcasting

Televison Centre, Southampton,
Hants SO14 0PZ
tel 023-8022 2555 *fax* 023-8033 5050
website www.meridiantv.com

The ITV franchise holder for the South
and South East. Does not produce any in-
house drama.

SMG TV Productions

200 Renfield Street, Glasgow G2 3PR
tel 0141-300 3000
website www.smgproductions.tv
Drama Coordinator Angela Morton

Network television production arm of
SMG plc, incorporating London-based
Ginger Television. Its client list includes all
UK terrestrial networks and major satellite
and cable channels. Output includes
drama, factual/factual entertainment,
entertainment and children's
programming.

The Drama Department has more than
20 years' experience of producing
network drama for ITV1. Its current
Head is Eric Coulter, who is supported by
Roz Kidd, Head of Development.
Credits include: *Taggart* (now in its 20th
year), *Dr Finlay*, *Rebus* and *Goodbye
Mr Chips*. The Drama team is based at
the SMG TV Productions offices in
Glasgow. Casting procedures differ from
project to project; generally uses
independent casting directors, but also
accepts letters from actors 'on spec'
(with CVs and photographs). Where
appropriate these will be passed on to a
relevant programme or project. The
Drama Coordinator, Angela Morton, is
happy to act as a point of contact for
actors' enquiries. John Hubbard was
responsible for casting the latest *Taggart*
series.

Tyne Tees Television Ltd.

The Television Centre, City Road,
Newcastle upon Type NE1 2AL
tel 0191-261 0181 *fax* 0191-261 2302
email tyne.tees@granadamedia.com
website www.itv.com

Serving the North of England 7 days a
week, 24 hours a day.

UTV

Havelock House, Ormeau Road, Belfast,
Northern Ireland BT7 1EB
tel 028-9032 8122 *fax* 028-9024 6695
email info@utvplc.com
website www.utv.co.uk

Provides programmes for Northern Ireland.
All drama is produced by the ITV network.

Yorkshire Television Ltd. (YTV)

The Television Centre, Leeds LS3 1JS
tel 0113-243 8283 *fax* 0113-244 5107
website www.itv.com
Casting Director Sue Jackson
Assistant Casting Director Faye Styring

Established in 1968, YTV is one of the
biggest ITV companies. Following the new
Communications Act and the merger of
Granada and Carlton, it is part of the new
single ITV plc which began life on
2 February 2004.

YTV continues to produce a range of drama
and light entertainment productions
including *A Touch of Frost*, *Emmerdale*
(shown on the network every weekday
night), and *Heartbeat* –ITV1's most popular long-running drama series. In 2003 a
new sister programme, *The Royal*, attracted
11.3 million viewers and a 41.3% share of
the television audience. In addition to its
drama series, YTV has made a number of
one-off dramas for the ITV network

including *Booze Cruise* and *Brides in the Bath*. With an audience of 9.7 million viewers and a 44% audience share, *Booze Cruise* ranked as the best performing Single Drama from any channel for the whole of 2003.

The Casting Department generally works through agents but will accept submissions (with CVs and photographs) from actors previously unknown to the company if sent by post. As the Department is very busy it cannot guarantee to acknowledge all submissions, but advises actors to enclose an sae for a quicker response. Prefers not to be contacted by telephone or email.

Independent Film, Video & TV Production Companies

Companies in this field start up and close down all the time, and it is very important to have a proper contract if offered work with an independent. If in doubt, check with Equity.

Absolutely Productions
Alhambra House, 27-31 Charing Cross Road, London WC2H 0AU
tel 020-7930 3113 *fax* 020-7930 4114
email info@absolutely-uk.com
website www.absolutely-uk.com
Managing Director Miles Bullough

Founded in 1988. Produces drama and comedy for cinema and TV, and TV entertainment programmes. Recent credits include: *Dead Air* (C4) and *Skin and Blister* (short film).

Apt Films
225A Brecknock Road, London N19 5AA
tel 020-7284 1695 *fax* 020-7482 1587
email admin@aptfilms.com
website www.aptfilms.com
Managing Director Jonny Persey
Director Paul Morrison
Producer Stewart Le Marechal

Young enterprise dedicated to development and production of feature films for national and international audiences. Also produces short films. Recent credits include: *Wondrous Oblivion* and *Solomon and Gaenor.*

Arlington Productions Ltd.
TV D Co, Cippenham Court, Cippenham Lane, Cippenham, Nr Slough, Berkshire SL1 5AU
tel (01753) 516767 *fax* (01753) 691785

Founded in 1994. Television producer specialising in popular drama, with occasional forays into other areas. Only welcomes contact from recognised agents.

Blue Wand Productions Ltd.
2nd Floor, 12 Weltje Road,
London W6 9TG
tel 020-8741 2038 *fax* 020-8741 2038
mob (07885) 528743
email lino@bluewand.co.uk
website www.bluewand.co.uk
Managing Director Lino Omoboni
Executive Producer Martin Cahill
Company Secretary Hazel Arthur

Recently established production company. Aims to produce thrillers, comedy, action and adventure films. Recent credits include: *Camelot* and *The Blue Wand.*

Carlton Television Productions
35-38 Portman Square, London W1H 0NU
tel 020-7486 6688 *fax* 020-7486 1132
Director of Programmes Steve Hewlett

Comprises Carlton Television Productions, Planet 24 and Action Time. Makes drama programmes for all UK major broadcasters (ITV, BBC, Channel 4, Channel 5 and Sky) and regional programmes for Carlton Central, Carlton London and Carlton Westcountry.

Carnival (Films & Theatre) Ltd.

12 Raddington Road, Ladbroke Grove,
London W10 5TG
tel 020 8968 0177 *fax* 020 8968 0968
email info@carnival-films.co.uk
website www.carnival-films.co.uk
Chairman Brian Eastman
Secretary Jude Liknaitzsky

Founded in 1978. Works mainly in TV production, creating drama with a popular and
international feel. Employs actors for
drama. Commissioned by major UK
broadcasters including BBC, Channel 4 and
ITV. Has received various prestigious
awards/nominations, including Oscars and
BAFTAs. Recent credits include: *Poirot*,
BUGS and *Traffic*. Uses freelance casting
directors; does not deal directly with actors.

Chatsworth Television Ltd.

97-99 Dean Street, London W1D 3TE
tel 020-7734 4302 *fax* 020-7437 3301
email television@chatsworth-tv.co.uk
website www.chatsworth-tv.co.uk
Managing Director Malcolm Heyworth

Founded in 1980 the company produces
entertainment, factual programmes and
drama. Has sister companies in TV
distribution and licensing.

Children's Film and Television Foundation Ltd.

Elstree Film and Television Studios,
Borehamwood, Herts WD6 1JG
tel 020-8953 0844 *fax* 020-8207 0860

Involved in the development and co-production of films for children and the family,
both for the theatrical market and for TV.

Collingwood O'Hare Entertainment and Convergence Productions

10-14 Crown Street, London W3 8SB
tel 020-8993 3666 *fax* 020-8993 9595
email info@crownstreet.co.uk
Head of Development Helen Stroud

Founded in 1988. Animation series for
children (COE), documentary series, and
drama films and series (Convergence).
Does not deal directly with actors; prefers
to deal with agents.

Company Pictures

Suffolk House, Whitfield Place,
London W1T 5JU
tel 020-7380 3900 *fax* 020-7380 1166
email enquiries@companypictures.co.uk
website www.companypictures.co.uk
Managing Directors George Faber, Charlie
Pattinson

Founded in 1998. Works mainly in film
and TV production and employs actors for
dramas. Recent credits include: *P.O.W.*,
White Teeth and *Morvern Callar*. Uses freelance casting directors and does not deal
directly with actors.

Cowboy Films

11-29 Smiths Court, Off Great Windmill
Street, London W1D 7DP
tel 020-7287 3808 *fax* 020-7287 3785
email info@cowboyfilms.co.uk
website www.cowboyfilms.co.uk
*Producers and Executive/Managing
Directors* Lisa Bryer, Robert Bray
Production Manager Carly Stone
Head of Features Development
Natasha Marsh

Founded in 1991, originally a commercials
production company. Represents a wide
range of directors including Mike Leigh
(*Topsy Turvey, Secrets and Lies*) and Roger
Michell (*Notting Hill*). Recent film credits
include: *The Hole, Goodbye Charlie Bright*
and *The Soul Keeper*.

Don Productions Ltd.

26 Shacklewell Lane, London E8 2EZ
tel 020-7690 0108 *fax* 020-7690 4333
email info@donproductions.com
website www.donproductions.com

Japanese/English bilingual TV and media production company based in London. Produces TV drama, documentaries, news and sports programmes. Clients include: Japan Broadcasting Corporation, Nippon Television and Channel 4. Provides a casting service.

The Drama House

Coach Road Cottages, Little Saxham, Bury St Edmunds, Suffolk IP29 5LE
tel (01284) 810521 *fax* (01284) 811425
email jack@dramahouse.co.uk
website www.dramahouse.co.uk
Chairman/Chief Executive Jack Emery

Produces drama and drama-documentaries for film and TV. Recent credits include: *Breaking the Code*, *Witness Against Hitler*, *Little White Lies* and *Suffer the Little Children*. Commissioned by major broadcasters including BBC and Channel 4. Hopes that high-profile work will encourage writers and other professionals to come to the Drama House.

Ecosse Films Ltd.

Brigade House, 8 Parsons Green, London SW6 4TN
tel 020-7371 0290 *fax* 020-7736 3436
email info@ecossefilms.com
website www.ecossefilms.com
Director Douglas Rae
Head of Drama Robert Bernstein

Founded in 1988. Works mainly in TV and feature film production and employs actors in dramas and comedies. Recent credits include: *Mrs Brown*, *Charlotte Gray*,

Monarch of the Glen and *Amnesia*. Uses freelance casting directors and does not deal directly with actors.

Elstree Film and Television Studios

Borehamwood, Hertfordshire WD6 1JG
tel 020-8953 0844 *fax* 020-8207 0860
email annahome@cftf.onyxnet.co.uk

Involved in the development and co-production of films for children and the family, both for the theatrical market and for TV.

Eye Film and Television

9/11A Dove Street, Norwich, Norfolk NR2 1DE
tel (01603) 762551 *fax* (01603) 762420
email production@eyefilmandtv.co.uk
website www.eyefilmandtv.co.uk

Independent producers of film and TV drama and documentaries. Also produces corporate, commercial, education and training material. Clients include: BBC, Channel 4, Five, and First Take Films. Eye Film and Television's sister company, Red Eye Pictures, focuses on the development of drama productions, features, shorts and TV output. Recent credits include: *The Secret of Eel Island*.

Feelgood Fiction Ltd.

49 Goldhawk Road, London W12 8QP
tel 020-8746 2535 *fax* 020-8740 6177
email feelgood@feelgoodfiction.co.uk
Managing Director Philip Clarke
Drama Producer Laurence Bowen

Producers of film and TV drama.

Flashback Television Ltd.

9-11 Bowling Green Lane,
London EC1R 0BG

tel 020-7490 8996 *fax* 020-7490 5610
email mailbox@flashbacktv.co.uk
website www.flashbacktv.com
Managing Director and Executive Producer
Taylor Downing
*Company Director and Executive/Series
Editor/Producer* David Edgar
Director of Production Tim Ball

Founded in 1982. Produces factual
entertainment programmes. These
include historical documentaries and
drama-documentaries and a range of
lifestyle programmes. Provides original
and re-versioned programming to British
and American broadcasters including
BBC and Channel 4. Recent credits
include: *The Badness of King George,
D-Day: The Lost Evidence* and *Russia:
Land of the Tsars.*

Focus Films Ltd.

The Rotunda Studios, rear of 116-118
Finchley Road, London NW3 5HT
tel 020-7435 9004 *fax* 020-7431 3562
email focus@pupix.demon.co.uk
Contact Lucinda Van Rie or Lisa Disler

Feature film production company.

Mark Forstater Productions Ltd.

27 Lonsdale Road, London NW6 6RA
tel 020-7624 1123 *fax* 020-7624 1124

Works in film and TV production. Does
not deal directly with actors.

Granada Film

4th Floor, 48 Leicester Square,
London WC2H 7FB
tel 020-7389 8555 *fax* 020-7930 8499
email granada.film@granadamedia.com
Head of Film Pippa Cross

Founded in 1989, the company produces
major commercial feature films and
smaller UK-based films. Does not welcome
unsolicited submissions from actors
unknown to the company; prefers to deal
with casting directors and agents.

Green Umbrella

4 The Links, Old Woking Road,
Old Woking, Surrey GU22 8BF
tel (01483) 726969 *fax* (01483) 721188
email jules@greenumbrella.co.uk
website www.greenumbrella.co.uk
Producers/Directors Steve Gammond,
Mont Tomblesson, Bruce Vigar
Managing Director Jules Gammond

Founded in 1990. Works mainly in video
and DVD production and employs actors
to do voice-overs for sports and special
interest programmes. Recent credits
include: *The Story of Football, Britain in the
50s* and *Fight the Fat.* Does not use
freelance casting directors. Welcomes
voice demos.

Greenwich Village Productions

Greenwich Village Productions, 14
Greenwich Church St, London SE10 9BJ
tel 020-8853 5100 *fax* 020-8293 3001
email info@greenwichvillage.tv
website www.fictionfactory.co.uk/gvtv
Producer/Director John Taylor

An established producer of documentaries
for the BBC World Service and BBC Radio
4, Greenwich Village Productions has
recently undertaken a number of film
projects for broadcast, for sale to the
public and for educational purposes. It
specialises in 'intelligent entertainment'.
Recent credits include: *An Arundel Tomb*
(first in a short film series, *Poems In the
Picture*), and *Pluckley – England's Haunted
Village* (documentary/dramatic
reconstruction of ghost narratives).

Hartswood Films

Twickenham Studios, The Barons,
St Margaret's, Twickenham,
Middlesex TW1 2AW
tel 020-8607 8736 *fax* 020-8607 8744
Producers Beryl Vertue, Sue Vertue,
Elaine Cameron

Founded in 1981. Produces film and TV
comedy and drama. Recent credits include:
Coupling, Men Behaving Badly and *Is it
Legal?.*

Hat Trick Productions Ltd.

10 Livonia Street, London W1F 8AF
tel 020-7434 2451 *fax* 020-7287 9791
website www.hattrick.com
Contact Denise O'Donoghue

Founded in 1986. Situation and drama
comedy series and light entertainment
shows. Recent credits include: *Father
Ted, Drop the Dead Donkey* and *The
Kumars at No. 12.* Aims to nurture new
talent 'both in front of and behind the
camera'.

Hurricane Films Ltd.

19 Hope Street, Liverpool L1 9BQ
tel 0151-707 9700 *fax* 0151-707 9149
email sol@hurricanefilms.co.uk
website www.hurricanefilms.net
Managing Director Solon Papadopoulos
Head of Development Julie Currie

Founded in 2000. Development and
production of creative content. Produces
single films and documentary series
from original ideas. Recent credits
include: *Warship* (in association with
Granada TV), *Comm-Raid on the
Potemkin* (FilmFour) and *Wrecked*
(BBC2).

Kelpie Films

227 St Andrews Road, Glasgow G41 1PD
tel 0141-429 3565 *fax* 0141-429 8438
email info@kelpiefilms.com
website www.kelpiefilms.com

Independent production company. Main
area of work is corporate. Has a number of
commissioned projects, ranging from
short films for cinema distribution to
drama and documentary for television
release. Recent short film/feature credits
include: *Out to Lunch* and *Don't Ask.* Email
fiction.films@kelpiefilms.com for
information on films in production.

LWT and United Productions

London TV Centre, Upper Ground,
London SE1 9LT
tel 020-7620 1620
Controller of Drama Michele Buck

Founded in 1996. Producers of TV and film.

Manic Television and Film

101 Skyline Plaza, 80 Commercial Road,
London E1 1NY
tel 020-7709 0637 *fax* 020-7709 7867
email info@themanicgroup.com
website www.themanicgroup.com
Directors Andrew Bains, David Donigue,
Ian Whittingham
Casting Director Ian Whittingham

Founded in 2002. Works mainly in TV
production and employs actors for dramas
and comedies. Recent credits include: *Rules
of the Game.* Uses freelance casting directors. Accepts submissions (with CVs and
photographs) from actors previously
unknown to the company only if sent by
post. Will also accept showreels. 'We welcome actors to become researchers here
while they're resting.'

Maya Vision International Ltd.
43 New Oxford Street,
London WC1A 1BH
tel 020-7836 1113 *fax* 020-7836 5169
email info@mayavisionint.com
website www.mayavisionint.com
Producer/Director Rebecca Dobbs
Producer Sally Thomas
Director David Wallis

Founded in 1982. Film and TV
production company. Produces features,
TV dramas and documentaries, and arts
programmes. Recent credits include: *In
Search of Shakespeare* and *Conquistadors*
(BBC), *Johnny Panic* (BFI), *Caught Looking*
(Channel 4), and *The World Turned Upside
Down* (BBC2/Arts Council).

Penumbra Productions Ltd.
80 Brondesbury Road, London NW6 6RX
tel 020-7328 4550 *fax* 020-7328 3844
email nazpenumbra@aol.com
Contact HO Nazareth

Founded in 1981. Independent film
and TV producer. Makes contemporary
social-issue drama and documentaries.
Also produces non-broadcast videos when
commissioned.

Picture Palace Films Ltd.
13 Egbert Street, London, NW1 8LJ
tel 020-7586 8763 *fax* 020-7586 9048
email info@picturepalace.com
website www.picturepalace.com
Producer and Chief Executive
Malcom Craddock
Head of Development Katherine Hedderly

Founded in 1970. Works mainly in feature
films and TV drama production. Recent
credits include: *Rebel Heart* (BBC),
Extremely Dangerous (ITV), *A Life for a Life*
(*The True Story of Stefan Kizko*), and the
Sharpe series. Uses freelance casting directors
and does not deal directly with actors.

September Films
22 Glenthorne Road, London W6 ONG
tel 020-8563 9393 *fax* 020-8741 7214
email september@septemberfilms.com
website www.septemberfilms.com
Chairman David Green
CEO Marcus Plantain
Director of Production Elaine Day

Founded in 1992. Has offices in London and
Hollywood and works mainly in TV production. Specialises in factual entertainment,
reality programmes and entertainment formats. Also produces feature films and TV
movies. Commissioned by all major UK
broadcasters including BBC, Channel 4 and
ITV. Employs actors for documentaries.
Recent credits include: *Hollywood Women*
(ITV), *The Investigator* (Channel 4), and
Ozzy Osbourne Uncut (Channel 5). Uses
freelance casting directors and does not deal
directly with actors.

Spellbound Productions Ltd.
90 Cowdenbeath Path, Islington,
London N1 OLG
tel 020-7713 8066 *fax* 020-7713 8066
email phspellbound@hotmail.com
Producer Paul Harris

Small independent production company
specialising in feature films and drama for
television. Current projects include: *Twist
of Fate*, a romantic comedy in
development with Columbia Pictures
(LA), and *Chicane*, a NY crime thriller in
development. Uses freelance casting
directors; *Twist of Fate* was cast by
Hubbard Casting. Accepts letters (with
CVs and photographs) from actors
previously unknown to the company sent

by post and email. Will also accept showreels and invitations to view individual actors' websites. However, advises actors to establish and maintain contact with casting directors.

TalkBack Productions

20-21 Newman Street, London W1T 1PG
tel 020-7861 8000 *fax* 020-7861 8001
website www.talkback.co.uk

Founded in 1981. Produces TV situation comedies and comedy dramas, features, and straight drama. Recent credits include: *Smack the Pony*, *The 11 O' Clock Show* and *Da Ali G Show*.

Tiger Aspect Productions

Drama address: 5 Soho Square, London W1V 5DE
tel 020-7434 0672 *fax* 020-7544 1665
Comedy address: 7 Soho Street, London W1D 3DQ
tel 020-7434 0700 *fax* 020-7434 1798
email general@tigeraspect.co.uk
website www.tigeraspect.co.uk
Head of Drama Greg Brenman

Founded in 1993. Produces TV drama, comedy and sitcoms. 'Investing in and working with the leading writers, performers and programme-makers to produce original, creative and successful programming.'Strives to produce entertaining, challenging and varied drama. Recent credits include: *Teachers* (C4), *My Fragile Heart* (ITV) and *Playing the Field* (BBC1).

Twenty Twenty Television

20 Kentish Town Road, London NW1 9NX
tel 020-7284 2020 *fax* 020-7284 1810
email mail@twentytwentytv.co.uk
website www.twenty-twenty.tv

Executive Producer Claudia Milne
Head of Development Simon Rockell

Founded in 1982. Current affairs, documentaries, science and educational programmes, and reality TV. Began producing TV drama in 2000 and has been commissioned by the BBC and ITV networks. Recent credits include: *Lad's Army* and *Second Sight*.

Walsh Bros Ltd.

24 Redding House, Harlinger Street, King Henry's Wharf, London SE18 5SR
tel 020-8854 5557 *fax* 020-8854 5557
email walshbros@mail.com
Director John Walsh
Casting Director Maura Walsh
Producer David Walsh

Founded in 1993. Award-winning film and TV production company. Employs actors for dramas and documentaries. Recent credits include: *Headhunting the Homeless* – a BBC2 documentary, *Monarch* (FF), *Thex* and *boyz and girlz*. Occasionally holds general auditions. Accepts letters (with CVs and photographs) from actors previously unknown to the company only if sent by post. Will also accept showreels.

Working Title Films

76 Oxford Street, London W1N 9FD
tel 020-7307 3000 *fax* 020-7307 3003
email dan.shepherd@unistudios.com
website www.workingtitlefilms.com
Chairmen Tim Bevan, Eric Fellner
Head of Development (films) Debra Hayward

A film production company founded in 1982. Has produced more than 70 films and won BAFTAs, Academy Awards, and prizes at the Cannes and Berlin Film Festivals. Recent credits include: the popular romantic comedies *Four Weddings and a Funeral, Notting Hill, Bridget Jones's Diary* and *Love Actually,* and novel adaptations *Captain Corelli's Mandolin* and *High Fidelity.*

World Productions Ltd.

Eagle House, 50 Marshall Street, London W1F 9BQ
tel 020-7734 3536 *fax* 020-7758 7000
email firstname@world-productions.com
website www.world-productions.com
Executive Producer Tony Garnett
Executive Producer/Head of Development Simon Heath
PA and Office Manager Helen Saunders

Produces TV drama features, series and serials. Recent credits include: *Between the Lines, Ballykissangel* and *Love Again,* a film about Philip Larkin (BBC). Currently developing more 'unique" drama projects.

Zenith Productions Ltd.

43-45 Dorset Street, London W1U 7NA
tel 020-7224 2440 *fax* 020-7224 3194
email general@zenith-entertainment.co.uk
website www.zenith.tv.co.uk
Managing Director Ivan Rendall
Casting Director Matt Western
Head of Drama Adrian Bate

Founded in 1984. Part of the Zenith Group, which comprises Zenith North and Zenith Productions. Works mainly in producing a wide range of programmes for terrestrial, satellite and cable television, and feature films for worldwide theatrical distribution. Employs actors for dramas, comedies, documentaries and make-over shows. Recent credits include: *Byker Grove, Two Thousand Acres of Sky, Murder Most Foul, Inspector Morse* and *Garden Rivals.* Uses freelance casting directors and does not deal directly with actors.

Film Schools

Although minimally paid (if at all), these are well worth contacting for casting consideration. Although you'll often find yourself in the hands of a director with no idea about actors and acting, the potential of gaining something from the experience is possibly greater than that of participating in a Fringe theatre production – and the end result could contain material worthy of use in a showreel. Some schools keep files of actors' CVs and photographs for students to refer to when casting.

Castings for many low- or non-paid films are advertised in *Shooting People* <www.shootingpeople.org>.

The Arts Institute at Bournemouth
Wallisdown, Poole, Dorset BG12 5HH
tel 01292 533011
Key contact/Lecturer Mike Fisher

Students do not only consider local actors for their short films. Actors are generally offered their expenses and a VHS copy. Welcomes enquiries (containing CV, photograph and covering letter) from new actors. Actors' details are kept on file.

ARTTS International (Advanced Residential Theatre and Television Skillcentre)
Highfield Grange, Bubwith,
North Yorkshire YO8 7DP
tel (01757) 288088 *fax* (01757) 288253
email admin@artts.co.uk
website www.artts.co.uk
Key contact Joy Hebersax

Offers 100% practical training in TV, theatre, film and radio. 1-year courses commence in October and April each year. Also offers hands-on media training, and diplomas in production/operations, directing and acting. There is no formal arrangement with Equity. Students do not only consider local actors. Actors' details are not kept on file.

Brighton Film School
Administration, 13 Tudor Close,
Dean Court Road, Rottingdean BN2 7DF
tel (01273) 302166 *fax* (01273) 302163
email info@brightonfilmschool.org.uk
website www.brightonfilmschool.org.uk
Key contact Franz Von Habsburg

Film-industry recognised. Provides training in all aspects of motion pictures production: screenwriting, directing, cinematography, editing and production management. More than 30 student short films are made each year. Students generally recruit actors through *Shooting People* (www.shootingpeople.org). There is no formal agreement with Equity. Students do not only consider local actors. Actors are generally offered their expenses and a VHS copy. Welcomes enquiries (containing photograph and one-page CV) from new actors if sent by post.

International Film School Wales
University of Wales College,
Caerleon Campus, PO Box 179,
Newport NP18 3YG
tel (01633) 432677 *fax* (01633) 432680
email post.ifsw@newport.ac.uk
website www.ifsw.newport.ac.uk
Head of School Humphry Trevelyan

A recognised Welsh national institution for the production and development of the audiovisual culture of Wales, through training, education and postgraduate research. On average 60-80 student short films are made each year. Students generally recruit actors through agents, casting directors, Equity Job Information Service and public notices at the Royal Welsh College of Music & Drama. There is no formal agreement with Equity. Actors' details are held on file. Welcomes enquiries (with CV, photograph and covering letter) from new actors. Students at BA and MA level increasingly work in production groupings and cast professionally. 'As the main centre for film education and training in Wales we seek, encourage and support the casting of professional actors wherever possible. In addition we will be starting a BA Hons in Performance in September 2004 which will require actors to teach part-time."

National Film and Television School

Beaconsfield Studios, Station Road, Beaconsfield HP9 1LG
tel (01494) 671234
fax (01494) 674042

email admin@nftsfilm-tv.ac.uk
website www.nftsfilm.ac.uk
Key personnel Lindsey Moore

Offers 2-year MA courses including fiction direction, cinematography, production design, editing, sound, animation, and documentary. Students generally recruit actors through casting directors, *Spotlight*, *Shooting People* (www.shootingpeople.org), and from actors' files kept by Lindsey Moore. Has a formal agreement with Equity. Students do not only consider local actors. Actors are generally offered their expenses. Welcomes enquiries (with CV and photograph) from new actors which should be marked for the attention of Lindsey Moore. Actors' details are held on file. Actors are also required throughout the year for workshops, and files are kept for this purpose. Graduation projects are cast by external casting directors.

Radio Companies and Other 'Voice-Work' Opportunities

Unlike in the visual media, many radio directors have their roots in theatre and will go to stage productions to inform their future casting. And, unlike their visual media counterparts, they have a far greater understanding of actors and acting and are far more open to casting against obvious physical type.

The BBC has by far and away the biggest radio drama output, and it also uses actors to read poetry, narrations and stories. Some of this 'output' is made in-house; a good proportion is contracted-out to independent companies. This is one area of work that doesn't very often use casting directors. It is a good idea to listen to radio drama to become aware of its ways – you won't hear much swearing, for instance. Also see 'Voice-Over Agents' (page 76) and 'Showreel & Voice-Demo Companies' (page 258) – some of the latter have excellent advice on making a voice demo on their websites.

BBC Radio Drama
Bush House, The Strand,
London WC2B 4PH
tel 020-7557 1013
website www.bbc.co.uk/drama/radio
Head of Radio Drama Gordon House
Coordinator, Drama Company
Cynthia Fagan
Production Executive, Radio Drama
Rebecca Wilmshurst

BBC Radio Drama Department is the biggest producer of drama on radio in the world. It provides more than 700 hours of drama a year for Radio 3, Radio 4, BBC World Service, BBC7, and the BBC Asian Network. Plays are broadcast every day of the week and can be heard at any time, either on air or on the website. An audience of about half a million people are listening every time a play is aired. Output includes: *Westway* (drama set in a London health centre), *The Archers* (countryside soap opera), the Friday and Saturday plays (thrillers, mysteries and love stories),

afternoon plays, classic serials, Woman's Hour Drama (weekday drama serial), play of the week (from around the world), book of the week (non-fiction) and book at bedtime (fiction including modern classics).

The Radio Drama Company was founded in 1940 as the BBC Repertory Company and is still frequently referred to as The Rep. The company's focus allows new acting talent to work alongside established actors in a variety of radio productions. Actors joing the RDC in August 2003 have already worked with many eminent artists such as Julia Mackenzie, Derek Jacobi, Richard Griffiths, Cheryl Campbell, Anna Massey and Daniel Day-Lewis. Forthcoming productions include a 12-part serialisation of *The Pallisers* by Anthony Trollope for Radio 4 and Ben Jonson's *Volpone* on Radio 3.

Past members of the company have included Stephen Tompkinson, Alex Jennings, Adjoa Andoh, Norman Bird, Emma Fielding, Anthony Daniels,

Ben Onwukwe, Joanna Monro, Ann Beach, Janet Maw, Suzanna Hamilton and Carolyn Pickles.

The RDC does not use freelance casting directors and casting breakdowns are not publicly available. Sometimes holds general auditions and actors can write at any time requesting inclusion. Welcomes postal submissions from individual actors previously unknown to the company but does not accept email enquiries. Voice demos and invitations to view individual actors' websites are also accepted.

The Norman Beaton Fellowship is part of BBC Radio Drama's commitment to place integrated casting at the heart of its output. NBF 2004 aims to provide access to BBC Radio Drama for talented actors from non-traditional training backgrounds, and particularly those from minority ethnic backgrounds who are currently underrepresented in radio drama.

NBF workshops are being held in Cardiff and Edinburgh in 2004 with priority being given to applications from actors resident in, or with strong links to, Scotland and Wales. The winners will be awarded a fellowship, which is a 6-month contract as a member of the Radio Drama Company based at Bush House in London. Up to 4 runners-up will be engaged to take part in a production with BBC Radio Drama.

The Radio Drama Company will also be forging links with theatre companies all over Britain to help develop and nurture new talent for both radio and the stage and to find new NBF bursary winners. Consult the website for information about the next Norman Beaton Fellowship and for details of eligibility requirements.

The Carleton Hobbs Bursary is aimed at students graduating from accredited drama courses across the country. Looks

for distinctive, versatile radio voices to form the next season's Radio Drama Company.

Aims to recruit 4-6 winners from the 2004 event. Students will be seen through an audition process, from which an equal mix of men and women will be selected. Winners receive a 6-month binding contract as members of the Radio Drama Company. Up to 4 runners-up will be engaged as freelance actors in one of the Winter 2004 productions.

Independent radio companies

Bona Broadcasting Ltd.
19 Dalgleish House, Scrimgeour Place, Dundee DO3 6TU
tel (01382) 225403 *fax* (01382) 229300
email enquiries@bonabroadcasting.com
website www.bonabroadcasting.com
Key personnel Turan Ali

Founded in 1994. Staffed by former BBC producers and directors, the company has been a registered supplier to the BBC since 1994. Areas of work include drama, documentaries and light entertainment. Recent drama credits include: *The Confessions of Nostradamus, The Flood* and *Existence.* Casting is through agents only: 'Get a good agent.'

The Comedy Unit Ltd.
Glasgow TV and Film Studio, Craigmont Street, Glasgow G20 9BT
tel 0141-305 6666 *fax* 0141-305 6600
email general@comedy unit.co.uk
website www.comedyunit.co.uk
Producers/Directors Colin Gilbert, Niall Clark, Rab Christie

Founded in 1996. Works in TV and radio productions. Has produced approximately

30 hours of TV and 25 hours of radio. Areas of work include drama, sitcoms, comedy and other light entertainment. Recent drama credits include: *Ronan the Amphibian* and *Coming Home*.

Sometimes holds general auditions. Actors can write at any time requesting inclusion. Submissions from actors previously unknown to the company are accepted if sent by post or email. Voice demos and invitations to view individual actors' websites are also accepted.

CSA Word

6a Archway Mews,
241a Putney Bridge Road,
London SW15 2PE
tel 020-8871 0220 *fax* 020-8877 0712
email info@csaword.co.uk
website www.csaword.co.uk
Key personnel Victoria Williams,
Rosemary Hill, Clive Stanhope

Founded in 1991. Producer of audiobooks, drama, readings, feature programmes and documentaries for BBC Radios 4, 2 and BBC World Service. Areas of work include drama, audiobooks, educational and CD-Roms. Does not hold general auditions as the company tends to use agents for casting. Invitations to view individual actors' websites are accepted.

Culture Wise

1 Chiswick Staithe, London W4 3TP
Key personnel Mukti Jain Campion,
Chris Eldon Lee

Founded in 1988. Areas of work include TV and radio documentaries. Does not hold general auditions. Actors can write at any time requesting inclusion. Invitations to view individual actors' websites are accepted. The company rarely employs

actors, as the primary focus is on factual output: actors are generally used for short readings only within a feature programme.

The Fiction Factory

14 Greenwich Church Street,
London SE10 9BJ
tel 020-8853 5100 *fax* 020-8293 3001
email info@fictionfactory.co.uk
website www.fictionfactory.co.uk
Key personnel John Taylor, Celia de Wolff,
Joanna Green, Roland Jaquarello

Founded in 1993. Makes radio drama and features for the BBC and has recently expanded into video production. Areas of work include drama, documentaries, light entertainment and voice-overs.

Recent drama credits include: *Wild Ride to Dublin*, *A Nursery in the Nineties* and *What Maisie Knew* (Radio 4). Does not hold general auditions. Submissions from actors previously unknown to the company are accepted if sent by post. Voice demos are also accepted. Does not welcome email submissions or invitations to view individual actors' websites. 'It is helpful if showreels contain material appropriate to the kind of work sought; for example, corporate voice-overs or radio advertisements don't necessarily show off acting skills.'

Devlin Morris Productions Ltd.

97b West Bow, Edinburgh EH1 2JP
Key personnel Morris Paton

Producers of theatre, radio and cultural tourism projects. Areas of work include drama and light entertainment. Recent drama credits include: features for BBC Scotland, Radios 4 and 3, and the World Service. Does not hold general auditions. Actors can write at any time requesting inclusion. Submissions from actors previously unknown to the company are accepted if sent by post. Voice demos and invitations to view individual actors' websites are also accepted. Does not accept email enquiries.

Pennine Productions

2 Grimeford Lane, Anderton,
Chorley PR6 9HL
tel (01257) 482559 *fax* 0870-131 8291
email mike@pennine-biz
website www.penine.biz
Producers Janet Graves, Mike Hally,
Clare Jenkins, Mark Whitaker

Founded in 2000. Has been making documentaries and features for BBC Radio 4 since 2001, and will be making programmes for BBC Radio 3 from 2004. Will also be producing book readings for Radio 4 from 2005 onwards. Broadcasts northern, national and international stories. Main areas of work include documentaries and readings.

Recent credits include: *Israel in East Africa, When Jesus Rode into Bristol* and *Land of the Oval Ball* (all Radio 4, 2003). 'We only welcome unsolicited approaches from actors with significant broadcast experience, particularly of book readings –or other audiobook productions. We are too small to be useful to actors trying to break into the network radio or TV.'

Pier Productions

Lower Ground Floor, 1 Marlborough Place, Brighton BN1 1TU
tel (01273) 691401 *fax* (01273) 693658
Managing Director Peter Hoare

Founded in 1993. Independent supplier to BBC Radio 4. Winner of silver and bronze in the Drama category in the 2002 Sony

Radio Awards and gold prize for non-fiction in the Spoken Word Publishers Association Awards. Employs actors for drama programmes.

Recent drama credits include: *The Shepherd Who Couldn't See the Wood for the Trees* and *Perfect Timing* (both Afternoon Plays for Radio 4). Does not hold general auditions. Submissions from actors previously unknown to the company are accepted if sent by post or email. Voice demos are also accepted. Does not welcome invitations to view individual actors' websites. 'We are only a small independent company and it can be hard to reply to everyone.'

Lou Stein Associates Ltd.

14a Tavistock Place, London WC1H 9RD
email loustein@yahoo.com
Producer/Director Lou Stein
Co-Director Deirdrie Gribbin

Lou Stein founded the Gate Theatre, Notting Hill, and was Artistic Director of the Palace Theatre, Watford. Lou Stein Associates was formed to continue Lou's interest in new work, adaptations, music theatre and media. Employs actors for drama programmes.

Recent drama credits include: *Fear and Loathing in Las Vegas* (adapted and directed by Lou Stein, starring Harry Dean Stanton), *My Month With Carmen* (starring Miriam Colon and Julian Glover), and *Grace Notes* by Lou Stein (based on the Bernard MacLaverty novel, starring Amanda Burton). Sometimes holds general auditions; actors can write requesting inclusion at any time. Voice demos and invitations to view individual actors' websites are accepted, but actors are requested to email in the first instance.

Tintinna Productions

Summerfield, Bristol Road,
Bristol BS40 8UB
tel (01275) 333128 *fax* (01275) 332316
email tintinna@aol.com
Producers Ian Bell
Research & Production Sandy Bell

Founded in 1998. Specialises in factual documentaries including history, lifestyle and human interest. Main area of work is documentaries. Does not hold general auditions. Submissions from actors previously unknown to the company are accepted if sent by post. Voice demos are also accepted. Does not welcome email submissions or invitations to view individual actors' websites.

Unique the Production Company

Unit 1B, 50 Lisson Street, London NW1 5DF
Producer Frank Stirling
Editor, Speech Programmes Laura Parfitt

Produces drama, documentaries, comedy and light entertainment for radio. Recent drama credits include: *Dramascape* (BBC World Service), and *Something Understood* (poetry and prose readings for BBC Radio 4).

Submissions from actors previously unknown to the company are accepted if sent by post or email. Voice demos are also accepted. Does not welcome invitations to view individual actors' websites. Advises actors to 'include radio work on demo'.

Whistledown Productions

66 Southwark Bridge Road, London SE1 0AS
tel 020-7922 1120
email davidprest@whistledown.net
website www.whistledown.net
Producers/Directors David Prest, Sarah Cuddon

Founded in 1993. One of the largest independent suppliers to BBC Radio, with a background in features and documentaries. Main area of work is documentaries. Recent credits include: *The Child Migrants* and *Headstrong and Proud*. Does not hold general auditions. Accepts submissions from actors previously unknown to the company. Voice demos are also accepted.

Audiobooks

Barefoot Audio Books Ltd.

123 Walcot Street, Bath BA1 5BG
Director Tessa Strickland
Editor (UK) Natasha Carr

Recent titles include: *Mrs Moon, Animal Boogie* and *Tales of Wisdom and Wonder*. Does not use freelance casting directors. Accepts submissions from actors previously unknown to the company if sent by post, but does not welcome email enquiries. Voice demos and invitations to view individual actors' websites are also accepted. Singing ability is required from actors, and Caribbean and African voices are needed in particular.

Harper Collins Audio Books

77-85 Fulham Palace Road, London W6 8JB
tel 020-8307 4630 *fax* 020-8307 4517
email rosalie.george@harpercollins.co.uk
website www.harpercollins.co.uk
Director Rosalie George
Editorial/Production Manager Nicola Townsend

Has produced more than 1000 titles for both children and adults over the last 15 years. Work spans all genres including crime, comedy, literary fiction, mass market fiction, non-fiction, poetry and classics.

Recent titles include: *Brick Lane* by Monica Ali, *Sharpe's Havoc* by Bernard Cornwell, and *Lovers and Liars* by Josephine Cox.

Foreign languages and regional dialect skills are required from actors. Does not use freelance casting directors. Advises actors to make contact by email or telephone, or preferably through an agent. Also accepts invitations to view individual actors' websites.

Isis Audio Books

7 Centremead, Osmey Mead,
Oxford OX2 OES
tel (01865) 250333 *fax* (01865) 790358
email sales@isis-publishing.co.uk
website www.isis-publishing.co.uk
Audio Production Manager Jeremy Ancock

Founded in 1975. Publishes unabridged audiobooks. Recent titles include: *High Society* by Ben Elton, *Two Women* by Martina Cole, and *The Photograph* by Penelope Lively.

Foreign languages and regional dialect skills are required from actors. Does not use freelance casting directors. Accepts submissions from actors previously unknown to the company if sent by post, but does not welcome email enquiries. Voice demos are also accepted. Actors should have a range of voices and good sight-reading ability.

Macmillan Audio Books

20 New Wharf Road, London N1 9RR
Audio Publisher Alison Muirden
Audio Editorial Coordinator Zoe Howes

Has recently published titles by Agatha Christie, Wilbur Smith and Colin Dexter. Does not use freelance casting directors. Accepts submissions from

actors previously unknown to the company if sent by post, but does not welcome email enquiries. Voice demos are also accepted.

Naxos Audio Books

18 High Street, Welwyn, Herts AL6 9EQ
tel (01438) 717808 *fax* (01438) 717809
email naxos_audiobooks@compuserve.com
Producer/Director Nicholas Soames

Founded in 1984. Produces classic fiction, modern fiction, drama, poetry, children's classics on CD and tape. Recent titles include: *The Canterbury Tales, Heidi* and *King Lear.* Regional dialect skills are required from actors. Accepts voice demos.

Random House Audio Books

20 Vauxhall Bridge Road,
London SW1V 2SA
tel 020-7840 8400 *fax* 020-7834 2509
email gmarnham@randomhouse.co.uk
website www.randomhouse.co.uk
Editor Georgia Marnham
Audio Books Assistant Louisa Gibbs

Created in 1991, the Audiobooks division of Random House acquired the Reed List in 1997. Has recently published titles by Kathy Reich, Chris Ryan, Ruth Rendell and John Grisham.

Regional dialects are required from actors and should be stated in any covering letter. Does not use freelance casting directors. Accepts submissions from actors previously unknown to the company sent by post or email. Voice demos (not advertisements) and invitations to view individual actors' websites are also accepted.

Media Festivals

These are geared towards showcasing directors, rather than actors. However, they can be useful places to network, learn and (if your film is shortlisted) gain extra exposure.

Belfast Film Festival

Unit 18, North Street Arcade,
Belfast BT1 1PB
tel 028-9032 5913 *fax* 028-9032 5911
email info@belfastfilmfestival.org
website www.belfastfilmfestival.org
Director Michele Devlin

Normally held in March/April each year, the Belfast Film Festival brings the best of independent, world, local and classic cinema to screens across Belfast. In addition there are panel discussions, workshops, music events and a series of related club events in venues across the city.

Candidates may submit features, shorts, animation and documentaries for inclusion in the festival. While all categories will be considered for screening, the only competitive category is the Irish short film. To be eligible for the £1000 Kodak Short Film Prize films must have been shot in Ireland during the previous year and last no longer than 20 minutes.

BFM International Film Festival

Suite 9, 5 Blackhorse Lane,
London E17 6DS
tel 020-8527 9582 *fax* 0870-132 2249
email bfm@telerregion.co.uk
website www.blackfilmmakermag.com
Director Charles Thompson

Presenting the UK's premier black film event each September across venues in London, the BFM promotes the range and diversity of black cinema and television around the world. Showcasing an array of award-winning features, documentaries, animation and short films by established international talent alongside black British film-makers, the BFM also screens a substantial amount of high-quality work from up-and-coming film-makers. In addition there are exclusive preview screenings, seminars, workshops and masterclasses on offer. Awards are presented to winners in the following categories: best actor, best actress, best editing, best international feature film, best UK short, best cinematography, and best screenplay.

The 5th BFM International Film Festival took place from 5-18 September 2003, screening more than 70 films by black film-makers from around the world including the USA, Australia, Sweden, France, Canada, Nigeria and the Caribbean.

Birmingham Screen Festival

9 Margaret Street, Birmingham B3 3BS
tel 0121-212 0777 *fax* 0121-212 0666
email info@film-tv-festival.org.uk
website www.film-tv-festival.org.uk
Director Barbara Chapman

A 6-day event in March celebrating the best of film, television and interactive software at venues across Birmingham. The programme features UK premieres, previews, retrospective work, experimental work, shorts, documentaries, animation, international cinema, masterclasses and community events.

Applications are by invitation only; contact the festival for further details.

Bradford Film Festival

National Museum of Photography, Film & Television, Bradford BD1 1NQ
tel (01274) 203308 *fax* (01274) 770217
email a.pugh@nmsi.ac.uk
website www.bradfordfilmfestival.org.uk
Director Bill Lawrence
Contact Adam Pugh

Celebrating its 10th anniversary in March 2004, the Bradford Film Festival presents a number of special guests, tributes, screentalk interviews, masterclasses, spotlights, the Shine short film season, European Cinema, and –in conjunction with Oxfam's Shattered Lives campaign – screenings and seminars on international gun control for 2004.

Features, shorts, documentaries and experimental work submitted for competition must have been completed during the previous 2 years.

Brief Encounters Festival

Watershed Media Centre, 1 Canon's Road, Harbourside, Bristol BS1 5TX
tel 0117-915 0186 *fax* 0117-930 9967
email info@brief-encounters.org.uk
website www.brief-encounters.org.uk

Brief Encounters is an international short film festival which runs for 1 week in November. With more than 20 screenings of diverse new shorts from around the world, special guests and events, parties, awards, seminars, masterclasses, surgeries and focus sessions, the festival offers insights and advice from industry professionals about every aspect of film.

Cambridge Film Festival

Arts Picture House, 38-39 St Andrew's Street, Cambridge CB2 3AR
tel (01223) 500082 *fax* (01223) 462555
email cff@picturehouses.co.uk
website www.cambridgefilmfestival.org.uk

Established in 1977, the festival was relaunched in 2001 after a 5-year hiatus and now runs for 10 days in July. Aiming to screen the best of current international cinema and to rediscover neglected films of the past, it now runs a programme for children supported by events and workshops.

Directors such as Peter Greenaway, Patrice Chereau, Philip Kaufman and Francesco Rosi have presented work at the festival, and many acclaimed films –including *Reservoir Dogs, Intimacy, Barton Fink* and *La Haine* –received their UK premiere in Cambridge.

Chichester Film Festival

Chichester Cinema at New Park, New Park Road, Chichester PO19 1XN
tel (01243) 533081 *fax* (01243) 533081
email info@chichestercinema.org
website www.chichestercinema.org
Director Roger Gibson

An 18-day festival in August/September presenting more than 70 feature films, Q&As with visiting directors, and related talks. More than half the films shown are previews and premieres; the remainder form retrospectives on important contributors to the film world. Also includes an international shorts competition.

The Commonwealth Film Festival

Unit 9, Greenheys Business Centre, Manchester Science Park, 10 Pencroft Way, Manchester M15 6JJ
tel 0161-342 0044 *fax* 0161-342 0055

email info@commonwealthfilm.com
website www.commonwealthfilm.com
Director Mathieu Ravier

Subjects being explored and celebrated in the 2004 programme include 10 years of free, uncensored film-making in South Africa, the growth in gay and lesbian cinema across the Commonwealth, and the recent explosion in low-budget film-making in Nigeria. The festival also presents documentaries, short films, seminars, workshops, industry networking events and parties during its 10-day run across April/May, and is the largest festival showcase for Indian, Canadian and South African cinema in Europe.

Submissions must be made in or co-produced with 1 of the 72 nations of the Commonwealth.

Disability Film Festival

London Disability Arts Forum, 34 Osnaburgh Street, London NW1 3ND
tel 020-7691 4203 *fax* 020-7916 5396
email caglar@ldaf.net
website www.disabilityfilmfestival.net
Festival Coordinator Caglar Kimyoncu

Showcasing the talent of disabled filmmakers, the 6th Disability Film Festival will take place from 1-5 December 2004. The festival offers film-makers, film-goers and industry professionals the opportunity to meet, exchange feedback, network and socialise. It has also become a forum for debate, challenging the exclusion of disabled people either on screen or as filmmakers. Submission forms and guidelines are available to download from the website.

Edinburgh International Film Festival

Filmhouse, 88 Lothian Road, Edinburgh EH3 9BZ

tel 0131-228 4051 *fax* 0131-229 5501
email info@edfilmfest.org.uk
website www.edfilmfest.org.uk
Artistic Director Shane Danielsen
Managing Director Ginnie Atkinson

Celebrating cinema for nearly 60 years, the festival aims to entertain, challenge and inspire audiences for 10 days each August. The programme covers a range of different areas such as British Cinema, red carpet gala events, live interviews with cinema greats, retrospectives, debuts and second films from new film-making talent, short films and special events. Previous events have included the National 48 Hour Film Challenge, Script Factory masterclasses and performed readings, a BAFTA-sponsored interview with Terence Davies, and a Skillset event on Careers in Film.

Submissions should be received by April; all the forms, rules and regulations can be downloaded from the website. Films submitted from outside the UK must have been produced during the 2 years previous to the festival, and British films during the year beforehand.

Foyle Film Festival

The Nerve Centre, 7-8 Magazine Street, Derry, BT48 6HU Northern Ireland
tel 028-7126 7432 *fax* 028-7137 1738
email competition@nerve-centre.org.uk
website www.foylefilmfestival.com
Director Shauna Kelpie
Programmer Brónagh Corr

Established in 1987, the Foyle Film Festival runs for 10 days each November, screening more than 200 films and featuring a number of special guests, events, presentations, workshops and seminars.

Awards are available for the Best Irish Short, Best International Short, Best

Animation, Best Feature and Best Documentary. The application forms and rules and regulations for the competition can be downloaded from the Foyle Film Festival website. Send an email or call the office to request a hard copy.

Hull International Short Film Festival

Hull Film, Danish Buildings,
44-46 High Street, Hull HU1 1PS
tel (01482) 381512 *fax* (01482) 381517
email office@hullfilm.co.uk
website www.hullfilm.co.uk
Director Catherine Litchfield

The festival promotes new work, active audience participation and critical discussion. With the aim of supporting local artists and film-makers, it provides access to industry networks and commissions and has plans to develop film training and production initiatives in the East Yorkshire region. The 3rd Hull International Short Film Festival was held in October 2003 and featured presenters, panelists and delegates from major film and media organisations offering a variety of perspectives and playing a critical role in the training programmes, funding initiatives and distribution circuits of short film.

International Film Festival of Wales

Market House, Market Road,
Cardiff CF5 1QE
tel 029-2040 6220 *fax* 029-2023 3751
email enq@iffw.co.uk
website www.iffw.co.uk
Director Berwyn Rowlands

Celebrating film, TV and new media from Wales and further afield, the festival offers a wide selection of screenings, special guest appearances, debates and programmed industry events each November.

The DM Davies award is open to any short-film director who is of Welsh origin or has been a native of Wales for 2 or more years. It is the largest short-film prize in Europe and previous winners have included Justin Kerrigan (*Human Traffic*) and Sara Sugarman (*Very Annie Mary*). Entries are screened towards the end of the festival with many of the directors in attendance.

Leeds International Film Festival

Town Hall, The Headrow, Leeds LS1 3AD
tel 0113-247 8398 *fax* 0113-247 8494
email filmfestival@leeds.gov.uk
website www.leedsfilm.com
Director Chris Fell

Leeds International Film Festival has been presenting extensive programmes of new and unseen cinema from around the world for the last 18 years, supported by a number of events and workshops for those wanting to get into film and TV. The Yorkshire Short Film Competition highlights emerging new film-making talents in the Yorkshire region, while the Louis Le Prince International Short Film Competition promotes some of the best fiction completed in the last year around the world.

The festival is complemented by the Leeds Children's and Young People's Film Festival held in April each year, with an award for National Young Film-maker of the Year.

London Film Festival

National Film Theatre, South Bank,
London SE1 8XT
tel 020-7815 1322 / 7815 1323
fax 020-7633 0786
email sarah.lutton@bfi.org.uk
website www.lff.org.uk
Artistic Director Sandra Hebron
Programme & Guest Coordinator Sarah Lutton

The Times bfi 47th London Film Festival was held from 22 October to 6 November 2003, attracting 115,000 people who attended 350 screenings. Leading figures in the film industry were there to present their work and the festival featured a number of interviews, profiles, Gala films and special screenings promoting the best in cinema across the world.

Manchester International Short Film Festival

Kinofilm, 42 Edge Street,
Manchester M4 1HN
tel 0161-288 2494 *fax* 0161-281 1374
email kino.info@good.co.uk
website www.kinofilm.org.uk
Director John Wojowski

British New Wave and an International Panorama of film provide the main focus to the festival, with a regional showcase, 'Made up North', aimed at promoting films from local and regional film-makers. Education and Professional Development events are also hosted by the festival and are presented by external curators and organisations.

The festival is open for film submissions each year from January to June, with shortlisted entries being screened at the festival itself in October. Short films on any theme, subject or category and made on any format are eligible so long as they run no longer than 20 minutes and have been made within the 18 months prior to the festival. The Kinofilm Awards acknowledge outstanding achievements in short film, with awards in 8 categories: Best British and International shorts, Best Student and Low Budget shorts, Best Animation, Best Documentary, Best Digital Short, Best Bluefire Short and the Festival Innovation Award. Rules,

regulations and application forms are available on the website.

Raindance Film Festival Ltd.

81 Berwick Street, London W1V 3PF
tel 020-7287 3833 *fax* 020-7388 4938
email info@raindance.co.uk
website www.raindance.co.uk
Director Elliot Grove

Running for 2 weeks in October/November, Raindance is one of the UK's largest independent film festivals and is committed to screening the boldest, most innovative and challenging films from the UK and around the world. Weighted heavily towards new talent, the festival offers more than 100 features (many of which are directorial debuts), 20 shorts programmes and a wide range of events, workshops, parties and awards. The Jury Panel in 2003 included Samantha Morton, Sadie Frost, Trudi Styler and Ian Rankin.

Rushes Soho Shorts Festival

PO Box 2868, London W1A 5QL
tel 020-7851 6207 *fax* 020-7851 6369
website www.sohoshorts.com
Director Joce Capper

Celebrating its 6th year in 2004, shortlisted films will be screened free of charge throughout Soho's cafés, bars and cinemas during the 1st week of August. The festival culminates in an awards ceremony with winners being announced in the following categories: short film, newcomer, animation, music video, title sequence and idents. Patrons of the festival include BAFTA, Directors Guild of GB and New Producers Alliance.

Films for submission should be no longer than 12 minutes and produced in the 12 months prior to the deadline.

Resources

Introduction

This section covers those practical items (and sources of more detailed help and advice) that are, to the professional actor, what tools and a first-aid kit are to a carpenter. Some may be irrelevant to you – for instance, you may feel as though you could never have the organisational skills to set up your own company. Others are essential to all actors: good photographs, for instance. Whatever your needs, time taken clearly to formulate your requirements before approaching any of the contacts listed below will be time well spent.

Equity
Louise Grainger

Equity is the only Trade Union to represent performers and people working creatively across the entire spectrum of arts and entertainment, both live and recorded. The main function of Equity is to negotiate minimum terms and conditions of employment throughout the entire world of entertainment, and to endeavour to ensure that these take account of social and economic changes. We look to the future as well, negotiating agreements to embrace the new and emerging technologies which affect performers – so satellite, digital television, new media and so on are all covered, as are the more traditional areas. We also work at national level by lobbying government and other bodies on issues of paramount importance to the membership. In addition we operate at an international level through the Federation of International Artists which Equity helped to establish, the International Committee for Artistic Freedom, and through agreements with sister unions overseas.

In addition to these core activities, Equity strives to provide a wide range of services for members so that they are eligible for a whole host of benefits which are continually being revised and developed. These include helplines, job information, insurance cover, member's pension scheme, charities and others.

Louise Grainger is a Marketing & Membership Services Officer for Equity.

For more information, visit the Equity website: www.equity.org.uk. For details of Equity's Job Information Service, see entry under *Casting Directories and Information Services*.

London Office
Guild House, Upper St Martins Lane,
London WC2H 9EG
tel 020-7379 6000 *fax* 020-7379 7001

Midlands Office
PO Box 1221, Warwick CV34 5EF
tel (01926) 408638
fax (01926) 408638

North East Office
The Workstation, 15 Paternoster Row,
Sheffield S1 2BX
tel (01142) 759746 *fax* (01142) 759746

North West Office
Conavon Court, 12 Blackfriars Street,
Salford M3 5BQ
tel 0161-832 3183 *fax* 0161-839 3133

Scotland, N. Ireland and Isle of Man Office
114 Union Street, Glasgow G1 3QQ
tel 0141-248 2472 *fax* 0141-248 2473

South East Office
Guild House, Upper St Martins Lane,

London WC2H 9EG
tel 020-7670 0229 *fax* 020-7379 7001

Wales and South West Office
Transport House, 1 Cathedral Road,
Cardiff CF11 9SD
tel 029-2039 7971 *fax* 029-2023 0754

Photographers and Repro Companies

Good photographs (and reproductions of same) are an essential part of an actor's professional armoury and there is absolutely no point in trying to scrimp on them. ('A picture is worth a thousand words.')

Your photograph is a silent, static, two-dimensional representation of vocal, mobile, three-dimensional you. It should be of your head down to your shoulders, reasonably stylish and well produced without necessarily being too glamorous. It should look natural and have life, energy and personality – especially in the eyes, the most important part of your face. Your photo should say, 'Here I am; I know who I am; I'm OK with who I am.' Also, it is very important that your photograph really looks like you when you arrive for interview.

Crucial to the final result is finding a good photographer (a) who understands the world that the end result is intended for and (b) with whom you can work well. In the listings that follow, you'll find a wide range of prices and deals. It is important to research as many of these as possible, without making cost your prime consideration. Ask friends, teachers and your agent (if you have one) for recommendations, and check through *Spotlight* and websites to see samples of work. Read the details under each listing to get a 'feel' for who might produce the 'goods' for you. Once you have a shortlist of possibilities, phone each with appropriate questions (what to wear, studio or natural light, and so forth) in order to get a sense of how well you might be able to work with him/her. Only *after* you've done all this research should cost be a consideration. Even then, a cheap deal could mean that the photographer will spend much less time, and take fewer photographs, than a more expensive one. You might be lucky with the former, but you'll enhance your chances of getting really good results with the latter.

Note Allow plenty of time for this research. Also, bear in mind that as the deadline for *Spotlight* gets nearer, photographers become increasingly busy and it becomes more difficult to book a session.

Digital photography

With digital photography you can see the initial pictures sooner, but not all photographers like this new technology – arguing that the quality is still not as good as film. Provided that you are happy with the quality of an individual's work, the technology they choose is irrelevant to you. Also, it is important to realise that the processing (getting the contrast right, for instance) of the final prints takes just as long on a computer as it does in a conventional darkroom.

Copyright

Under the Copyright, Designs & Patents Act 1988 the photographer owns the copyright on any new photograph, even though you've already paid for the original. That means that you have to obtain his/her permission to have new photographs reproduced in *Spotlight* or anywhere else. Your photographer may be happy to approve such reproduction, but may not be so happy about any cropping or other alterations: you must get permission if you intend to do this. The other important new legal requirement is that your photographer must be credited on any reproduction of the original. Some of the repro companies are now doing this as a matter of course.

Repros

You could get subsequent, high-quality reproductions done by your photographer or by someone else nominated by him/her. However, these will be expensive. The specialist repro companies can do this significantly more cheaply with minimal loss of quality. Once again, check with others about the quality (and service and reliability) of individual companies before taking costs into consideration. It is also useful to overestimate the number of copies you might need over the lifetime (generally, about two years) of your chosen photograph – because (a) you'll almost always find that you underestimate that number in the first place, and (b) you can take advantage of cheaper unit costs.

Note It is often better to send a 10×8in (25×20cm) photograph for submissions; however, high-quality 'jpegs' (at least 300dpi) inserted onto your CV are becoming increasingly acceptable.

Abacus Photography

156 Kingshill Road, Swindon SN1 4LN
tel (01793) 537257 *mob* (07966) 551909
fax (01793) 344208
email nickabacus@fsdial.co.uk
website www.abacus-photography.co.uk

Services & rates
Charges £50 for a photo shoot which includes photographer's fee and studio and equipment costs. This does not include the cost of any 10×8in (25×20cm) prints which are priced at £5 each. A variety of packages is also available. Offers discounts for group bookings. Digital photography is also available at a charge of £50 for 24 images. Always advises clients to bring a change of clothing and discuss their requirements before the shoot.

Work portfolio
Established in 1992. Photographs can be viewed on the website. Has taken publicity shots for around 20-30 actors.

The Actor's One-Stop Shop
54 Belsize Avenue, Palmers Green,
London N13 4TJ
tel 020-8888 7006 *fax* 020-8888 9666
email info@actorsone-stopshop.com
website www.actorsone-stopshop.com

Services & rates
Charges £195 for a photo shoot which
includes photographer's fee, studio and
equipment costs, processing of 1 b/w
36exp, contact sheet and 4 10×8in
(25×20cm) prints. Offers 10% discount for
group (2 or more) bookings. Offers both
pre-shoot and post-shoot consultancy,
advising clients on clothing, image projec-
tion, selection of photos and as well as
general advice on how best to promote
themselves within the acting industry.

Work portfolio
Established in 1997. Photographs can be
viewed on the website or in person by visiting the studio. Has taken publicity shots
for around 250 actors. Recent clients
include: Tagforce (an actor register), Omar
Khan, Samuel L Jackson, Anna Friel and
Rachel Watkins.

Ric Bacon
30 Fortis Green Road, Muswell Hill,
London N10 3HN
mob (07970) 970799
website www.ricbacon.co.uk

Services & rates
Charges £230 for a photo shoot which
includes photographer's fee, studio and
equipment costs, processing of 2 b/w
36exps, contact sheets, 6×4in print of
every shot and all negatives. Offers
reduced rates to students. Shoots in
natural light and offers advice on all
aspects including clothing and make-up.
Happy to look at old photographs of the
client that they particularly like or dislike.

Work portfolio
Established in 1999. Photographs can be
viewed on the website and at The Spotlight
offices. Has taken publicity shots for
around 200 actors.

A Beautiful Image Photography & Design (Debal Bagachi)
31 Church Walk, Brentford,
Middlesex TW8 8DB
tel 020-8568 2122 *mob* (07956) 861698
email debal@abeautifulimage.com
website www.abeautifulimage.com

Services & rates
Charges £150 for a photo shoot which
includes photographer's fee, studio and
equipment costs, processing of 2 b/w
36exps, contact sheets and 2 10×8in
(25×20cm) prints (either hand- or digitally
printed). Occasionally offers 10% discount
for clients sharing a shoot. Digital photography is also available at the same rate;
images can be supplied on CD-Rom. Also
able to provide website and print publicity.
Advises actors to keep make-up simple for
b/w photography and wear unfussy, unpat-
terned tops with simple necklines.

Work portfolio
Established in 1994. Photographs can be
viewed on the website and at The Spotlight
offices. Has taken publicity shots for
around 50 actors. Recent clients include:
Elizabeth Alexander, Patrick Regis, Fiona
Marchant and Diane Cracknell.

Robert Carpenter Turner Photography
The Studio, 62 Hemstal Road,
London NW6 2AD
tel 020-7624 2225 *fax* 020-7624 7731
email Robert@carpenterturner.co.uk
website www.carpenterturner.co.uk

Services & rates

Charges £160 for a photo shoot which includes photographer's fee, studio and equipment costs, processing of 2 b/w 36exps, contact sheets and 4 10×8in (25×20cm) prints. Offers 10% discount to actors who pay in advance. Digital photography is also available at the same rate but there is a charge to supply photos on CD-Rom.

Work portfolio

Established in 1960. Photographs can be viewed on the website. Has taken publicity shots for around 2000 actors. Recent clients include: George Melly, Sir Charles Mackerras, Malcome Billings and Rosie Ashe.

Andrew Chapman

198 Western Road, Sheffield S10 1LF
tel 0114-266 3579 *mob* (07779) 861921
email aschapman@tiscali.co.uk

Services & rates

Charges £65 for a photo shoot which includes photographer's fee, studio and equipment costs, processing of 1 b/w 36exps, contact sheet and 1 10×8in (25×20cm) print. Each extra film is priced at £20 (including contacts) and each extra 10×8in print is £12. Digital photography is also available. Black and bright colours work well in b/w and higher necklines are usually better than low. Always advises people on an individual basis what to bring. Ideally need to allow 1-2 hours for the session and a further hour if digital, as normally review images after the session so that final choices can be written to CD immediately.

Work portfolio

Has taken publicity shots for around 1500 actors. Photographs clients from many agencies including Phillipa Howell

Personal Management, Sharron Ashcroft Management Ltd. and Jane Hollowood Associates Ltd.

John Clark Photo Digital

tel 020-8854 4069
email clarkdigital@btopenworld.com
website www.johnclarkphotography.com

Services & rates

Charges £145 per hour for digital photography.

Work portfolio

Established in 1982. Photographs and advice can be found on the website. Has taken publicity shots for around 500-600 actors. Recent clients include: actors represented by Roger Carey & Associates, Collis Management, Crawfords, Rossmore and Langford Associates.

Angus Deuchar

PO Box 25799, London SW19 1WQ
tel 020-8286 3303 *mob* (07973) 600728
email angus@actorsphotos.co.uk
website www.actorsphotos.co.uk

Services & rates

Charges £225 for a photo shoot taken in natural light. Price includes approximately 120 shots to choose from, a website or contact sheets to view the proofs, 4 finished b/w 10×8in prints and a CD for best-quality repros. Student deals available. Telephone or email for further information.

Work portfolio

Photographs and "advice to actors seeking photographs" can be viewed on the website. Has more than 15 years' experience of taking actors' portraits and used to be an actor himself. Recent clients include: Neil and Adrian Rayment (*The Matrix*

Reloaded), Anne Reid, James Bolam, John Alderton, Richard Lumsden.

Anne Eyre Photography

239 Shakespeare Tower,
Barbican, London EC2Y 8DR
tel 020-7638 1289
email anne@cityphotography.freeserve.co.uk
website www.eyrephoto.co.uk

Services & rates
Charges £250 for a photo shoot which includes photographer's fee, studio and equipment costs, processing of 4 b/w 36exps, contact sheets and 4 10×8in (25×20cm) prints. Extra 10×8in prints are priced at £10 each. Photographs can be shot in the studio, in natural daylight or in a combination of both. Most shoots last around 3 hours to include a full consultation regarding clothing, make-up and hair and 4 rolls at a relaxed pace. Enlargements are printed and retouched by hand. Will also advise on cropping of pictures.

Work portfolio
Established in 1995. Photographs can be viewed on the website and at The Spotlight offices. Has taken publicity shots for thousands of actors. Recent clients include: Julia Sawalha, Sara Crowe, Joe Fraser and Nick Raggett.

Elliott Franks Photography Services

PO Box 29801, London SW19 1WW
tel 020-8544 0156 *mob* (07802) 537220
email frankse@aol.com
website www.elliottfranks.com

Services & rates
Charges £85 (reduced from £160 for *The Actors' Yearbook* readers) for a 2-hour photo shoot in Wimbledon studio with 5 changes of tops, 3 rolls of medium-format film (high quality) with 12 shots per roll and 3 contact sheets. Usually shoots a 4th

roll for fun which is supplied on CD-Rom. One-off 10×8in (25×20cm) prints are priced at £11.31 each; repros of 12 10×8in prints are priced at £1.85 each.

Work portfolio
Established in 1997. Photographs can be viewed on the website and at The Spotlight offices. Has taken publicity shots for more than 300 actors. Recent clients include: actors represented by ICM and Wendy Lee Management Ltd.

James Gill

6 Hanover Gardens, London SE11 5TL
tel 020-7735 5632

Services & rates
Charges £85 for a photo shoot which includes photographer's fee, studio and equipment costs, processing of 1 b/w 36exps, contact sheet and 2 10×8in (25×20cm) prints. Increases to £130 for 2 rolls and 4 10×8in prints. Extra 10×8in prints are priced at £12.50 each. Advises actors to keep it simple. Will take photos of actors as they wish to be presented and will take all the time necessary.

Work portfolio
Established in 1992. Photographs can be viewed at The Spotlight offices. Has taken publicity shots for around 500 actors and in addition has more than 40 years' experience of working in theatres, both in casting and as company manager.

Claire Grogan

12 Calverley Grove, London N19 3LG
tel 020-7272 1845
email claire@clairegrogan.co.uk
website www.clairegrogan.co.uk

Services & rates
Charges £180 for a photo shoot which includes photographer's fee, studio and

equipment costs, processing of 2 b/w 36exps, contact sheets and 4 10x8in (25x20cm) prints. Special packages offered to actors are: 1 36exp plus 2 10x8in prints for £90; and 2 36exps plus 4 10x8in prints for £140. Offers full advice on clothing and make-up when a booking is made. Sessions last 90 minutes in relaxed atmosphere. Aims to take photographs reflecting the actor's personality.

Work portfolio
Established in 1991. Photographs can be viewed on the website and at The Spotlight offices. Takes around 300 publicity shots for actors each year. Recent clients include: Zehra Naqvi, Steve McFadden, Stephen Tompkinson, Jonathan Kydd and Heather Pearce.

Neil Kendall Photography
19 Oakfield Court, Haslemere Road, London N8 9RA
tel 020-8340 4214 *mob* (07776) 198332
email mondo.nez@virgin.net
website www.neilkendallphotography.com

Services & rates
Charges £135 for a photo shoot which includes photographer's fee, studio and equipment costs, processing of 3 b/w 36exps, contact sheets and 2 10x8in (25x20cm) prints. Uses both studio and natural light.

Work portfolio
Photographs can be viewed on the website. Has taken publicity shots for around 30-35 actors. Recent clients include: Vanessa Earl, Peter Ackyroyd, Graham Norton and Liberty X.

L B Photography
36 Nutley Lane, Reigate, Surrey RH2 9HS
tel (01737) 224578
email labowerman@hotmail.com

Services & rates
Charges £90 for a photo shoot which includes photographer's fee, studio and equipment costs, processing of 1 b/w 36exps and contact sheet. Price increases to £135 for 2 sheets. All photos are taken in natural light. 10x8in (25x20cm) prints are priced at £7 each. A discounted rate of £85 for 1 roll is available to students. Advises simple make-up (none for men) and plain tops. Happy to provide guidance on the phone.

Work portfolio
Photographs may be viewed at The Spotlight offices or in *Contacts*. Has taken publicity shots for around 3000 actors. More than 50 agencies send clients on a regular basis, including Narrow Road, Evans & Reiss, Brown and Simcocks and CAM.

MAD Photography
200 Gladbeck Way, Enfield EN2 7HS
tel 020-8363 4182
email madphoto@ukonline.co.uk
website www.mad-photography.co.uk

Services & rates
Charges £110 for a photo shoot which includes photographer's fee, studio and equipment costs, processing of 2 b/w 36exps, contact sheets and 2 10x8in (25x20cm) prints. Offers discounted rate of £55 to students (no prints, 36 contact sheet only). Extra 10x8in prints are priced at £11.75 each. "Hair and make-up should be natural. Bring four tops in any colours: one V-neck, one collar, one t-shirt and one jacket. No white!"

Work portfolio
Established in 1998. Photographs can be viewed on the website and on page 22 of *Contacts 2004*. Has taken publicity shots for 3000-4000 actors. Recent clients

include: Shane Richie, Michael Knowles and Jessica Wallace.

Michael Pollard Photographer
Manchester-based
tel 0161-456 7470
email info@michaelpollard.co.uk
website www.michaelpollard.co.uk

Services & rates
Charges £65 for 15 frames or £95 for 30 frames indoor or outdoor. Shoots medium format, not 35mm. 10×8in (25×20cm) prints are priced at £7.50 each; student rates are available. A 10×8in print is included in the sitting price for 2 or more actors booking and arriving together. Digital photography is also available. Encourages actors to bring 2-3 tops ranging from lighter to darker tones. "Tops should be simple and comfortable with either a round or V-neck. Hair needs to be tidy but do not go to the hairdresser the day before to have it cut. Make-up should be simple and sparing –men can use a simple foundation or cover stick if needed. Women should not use lip liner or lipstick that is too dark or too red. The main thing is to be positive and be prepared. Think how you want to look and how you don't want to look. Enjoy it and be yourself!"

Work portfolio
Established in 1982 (1993 for actors). Photographs can be viewed on the website and at the Northern Actors Centre, Manchester. Has taken publicity shots for around 2500 actors. Recent clients include: Rachel Lindsay (*Brookside*), Adam Rickitt (*Coronation Street*), Tony Audenshaw (*Emmerdale*) and Sophie McDonnell (*CBBC*).

Howard Sayer Photography
Kingston-on-Thames
mob (07860) 559891

email howardsayer@btconnect.com
website www.howardsayer.co.uk

Services & rates
Charges £125 for a photo shoot which includes photographer's fee, studio and equipment costs, processing of 2 b/w 36exps and contact sheets. 10×8in (25×20cm) prints are priced at £6 each. Also offers digital photography at the same rates. Actors can preview images during the photo shoot. Includes a CD containing 10 best images as part of a student package. Images can be reproduced in either colour or b/w.

Work portfolio
Established in 1987. Photographs can be viewed on the website. Has taken publicity shots for around 1000 actors. Recent clients include: actors working for the BBC, Teddington Studios and Benedict Productions.

Catherine Shakespeare Lane
The Monsell Stores, 43 Monsell Road, London N4 2EF
tel 020-7226 7694
email csl@bankval@madasafish.com

Services & rates
Charges £350 for a photo shoot which includes photographer's fee, studio and equipment costs, processing of 2 b/w 36exps, contact sheets and 4 10×8in prints. Offers a student package for £220 (1 roll of 36 and 2 10×8in prints). In special circumstances this package is also available to non-students for £250. Uses natural light and favours a natural look. "My aim is to show my clients at their most interesting."

Work portfolio
Established in 1975. Photographs can be viewed at The Spotlight offices and in

Contacts 2004. Has taken publicity shots for more than 2000 actors.

Peter Simpkin

17 Grove Avenue, London N10 2AS
tel 020-8883 2727
email petersimpkin@aol.com
website www.petersimpkin.co.uk

Services & rates

Charges £305.50 (inclusive of VAT) for a photo shoot which includes photographer's fee, studio and equipment costs, processing of 3 b/w 36exps, contact sheets and 6 10×8in (25×20cm) prints. Student price is £246.75 inclusive of VAT.

Work portfolio

Established in 1973. Photographs can be viewed on the website. Has taken publicity shots for thousands of actors. Recent clients include: actors represented by ARG, Curtis Brown, Christina Shepherd Associates; students from Webber Douglas, LAMDA, Mountview and Bristol Old Vic.

Robert Workman

32 West Kensington Mansions, Beaumont Crescent, London W14 9PF
Studio address: Studio 103B, The Business Village, Broomhill Road, London SW18 4JQ
tel 020-7385 5442
email bob@robertworkman.demon.co.uk
website www.robertworkman.demon.co.uk

Services & rates

Charges £250 plus VAT for a photo shoot which includes photographer's fee, studio and equipment costs, processing of 2 b/w 36exps, contact sheets, 5 10×8in (25×20cm) prints and a CD for duplications. Special student portrait session costs £150 plus VAT. Digital photography is available.

Work portfolio

Photographs can be viewed on the website. Has been taking around 200 publicity shots for actors every year for 20 years. Recent clients include: Caroline Quentin, Jude Law and Philip Middlemiss.

Repro companies

Denbry Repros Ltd.

27 John Adam Street, London WC2N 6HX
tel 020-7930 1372 *fax* 020-7925 0183
email denbrys@vfree.com

Charges £7.20 plus VAT for the initial copy of a b/w negative. Can also reproduce from a digital image.

Repros of a b/w 10×8in (25×20cm) are priced as follows:
£26 for 25, £47.05 for 50, £89.05 for 100, £178.10 for 200, £200.40 for 250 and £393.75 for 500.

Repros of a b/w postcard print are priced as follows:
£19.50 for 25, £36.30 for 50, £66.05 for 100, £132.10 for 200, £133.75 for 250 and £234.95 for 500.

All prices exclude VAT. Colour repros are also available at an increased price.

Other services include a studio for casting photography, downloading images from the Internet and supplying images on CD in colour or b/w.

Denman Repros

Burgess House, Main Street, Farnsfield, Nottinghamshire NG22 8EFF
tel (01623) 882272 *fax* (01623) 882272

Initial scan of a 10×8in (25×20cm) print is free. Can also work with CDs, negatives and transparencies.

Repros of a b/w 10×8in are priced
as follows:
£28 for 25, £39 for 50, £48 for 100, £64
for 250 and £88 for 500.

Repros of a b/w postcard print are priced
as follows:
£24 for 25, £31 for 50, £34 for 100, £39
for 250 and £64 for 500.

Offers additional 20% free to actors
including students. Also runs Denman
Casting Agency, see entry under
*Casting Directories and Information
Services* for further details.

Profile Prints

Courtwood Film Service Ltd., FREEPOST
TO55, Penzance, Cornwall TR18 2BF *tel*
(01736) 365222 *fax* (01736) 350203 *email*
people@courtwood.co.uk
website www.courtwood.co.uk

Charges £2.75 for initial scan of a 10×8in
(25×20cm) print. Can also work with
negatives in colour or b/w, slides or
digital images.

Repros of a b/w 10×8in are priced as
follows:
£29.25 for 25, £47.25 for 50, £87.25 for
100 and £187.25 for 250.

Repros of a b/w postcard print are priced
as follows:
£19 for 50, £33 for 100 and £73.25 for 250.

Specialises in smaller self-adhesive photos
suitable for CVs.

Visualeyes Ltd.

11 West Street, Covent Garden, London
WC2H 9NE
tel 020-7836 3004 *fax* 020-7836 8780
website www.visphoto.co.uk

Charges £5 plus VAT for the initial scan of
a b/w 10×8in (25×20cm) print.

Repros of a b/w 10×8in (25×20cm) are
priced as follows:
£22 for 25, £39 for 50, £70 for 100, £140
for 200, £165 for 250 and £300 for 500.

Repros of a b/w postcard print are priced
as follows:
£15 for 25, £27 for 50, £50 for 100, £100
for 200, £120 for 250 and £225 for 500.

All prices exclude VAT. A 10% discount is
available to members of Equity and/or The
Spotlight, and to students.

Other services include free transmission of
the image to The Spotlight and free blemish clean-up.

The Spotlight, Casting Directories and Information Services

Spotlight is a fundamental part of the fabric of the acting profession, and it is essential to have an entry. (It is a false economy not to have one.) The growth of the Internet has seen a rise in companies offering similar services – usually, for a lower subscription. Once again it is important thoroughly to research the value to you of investing in one of these. As well as trying to assess whether such an investment will really enhance your visibility to employers, an essential part of that research is to read the 'small print' properly.

With some exceptions (major musicals, for instance), most employers do not openly advertise the properly paid acting work they have to offer. It's simpler to contact agents whom they know and trust for casting suggestions. This limits the number of submissions, largely prevents (time-wasting) unsuitable applicants, and goes some way towards ensuring that those suggested for consideration are really suitable for the parts available. Consequently, the time required to consider all the CVs and photographs submitted is contained within reasonable limits. It can take a day's work to go through a thousand submissions to select whom to interview; it can take another day's work to interview just 30 of these.

Casting information services – often allied to Internet casting directories – glean their information from all kinds of sources. The important thing to remember is that much of the information about 'properly paid acting work' is of a second-hand nature – that is, it was not sent directly to them in the first instance. Consequently, it is important to research reputations for accuracy (and 'up-to-dateness') before committing your funds to such companies. However, many Fringe production and student film opportunities are directly advertised in such publications and such opportunities might lead on to 'properly paid acting work'. The most accurate source of reliable casting information is Equity's Job Information Service which was launched in 1999 and is freely accessible to paid-up members on their website and via the phone (0870 9010 900). All the work included is at least reasonably paid (though not necessarily at full Equity-agreed rates), thoroughly checked for accuracy, and the job-providers checked for their record of fair treatment of employees. All this means that there are far fewer jobs advertised than in other information services; however, this is more than compensated for by the accuracy and legitimacy of the information it contains. Since its launch it has gained a great deal of credibility with employers, although that could be jeopardised if too many 'unsuitable applicants' apply.

The Spotlight

Head Office, 7 Leicester Place,
London WC2H 7RJ
tel 020-7437 7631 *fax* 020-7437 5881
email info@spotlightcd.com
website www.spotlightcd.com

Founded in 1927, The Spotlight publishes one of the most famous casting directories in the world. More than 30,000 artists appear in the various formats of *Spotlight*, including actors and actresses, presenters, graduates, children & young performers, and stunt artists.

The Spotlight promotes and supports artists in a number of ways. These include the annual directories containing artists' photographs and contact details, Spotlight Interactive, The Spotlight Link, Artists' Records and an Actors' Advice Service. It also publishes *Contacts* each October listing contact details for every aspect of the Performing Arts.

Spotlight Interactive is an online version of the directories allowing casting professionals to search for actors' details according to specific criteria. Actors' online CVs can now include photography portfolios, voice-clips and a showreel. All artists featured are issued a pin number so that they can update their entry throughout the year. The Spotlight Link allows casting professionals to email casting breakdowns to leading agents, who can then reply with instant suggestions from their Spotlight client lists.

The charge for a half-page entry in the Actors' Directory 2004/5 with the same photo was £116 including VAT. An additional £5 charge is incurred for use of a new photo.

For further details of services offered by The Spotlight, consult the website.

Actors Inc.

FREEPOST NATW1128,
Bracknell RG12 9BR
tel (01344) 449314
email info@actors-inc.co.uk
website www.actors-inc.co.uk

Casting breakdowns are delivered instantly via email, in addition to a weekly jobs newsletter which is sent every Friday afternoon. Members can search the website for information, advice and details of workshops and events as well as the Jobs Notice Board which is updated daily. Actors' details are included in a fully searchable Actors' database which is accessible to

casting professionals. Voice samples can also be incorporated. Actors Inc. also posts job advertisements for casual temporary work geared towards resting actors.

The monthly membership fee is £5 with an option of a 5-week free trial period. Recent auditions posted on the website have included Phoenix Dance Theatre Company, a UK tour of *Starlight Express* and a singer for a funk group.

Castcall

106 Wilsden Avenue, Luton LU1 5HR
tel (01582) 456213 *fax* (01582) 480736

email info@castcall.co.uk
website www.castcall.co.uk
Year established 1986

Details of casting information services
Information service is available in print or online, with emails circulated to sub-scribers at least 3 times each week. Actors should be professionally trained or experi-enced to be included. Charges £34 for 12 weeks. Allows actors to put subscriptions on hold if required and to resume when appropriate. Also offers general advice and free image scanning.

Sources of casting breakdowns have included: Crocodile Casting, Casting Unlimited, Panto People, Layton & Norcliffe, Pippa Ailion, Jayne Collins, Vital Productions, the BBC, Greenwich Films, Nina Gold and many repertory theatres.

Casting People Ltd.

PO Box 26736, London SW17 7FW
fax 020-8672 9738
email info@castingpeople.com
website www.castingpeople.com
Year established 2000

Details of casting information services
Information service is only available online, with emails circulated to sub-scribers on a daily basis. Charges £7.50 per week, £35 for 6 months and £55 for a year. Also produces a free CV for members.

Sources of casting breakdowns have included: film schools, TIE and profit-share companies.

CastNet Ltd.

20 Sparrows Herne, Bushey,
Hertfordshire WD23 1FU
tel 020-8420 4209 *fax* 020-8421 9666
email admin@castingnetwork.co.uk

website www.castingnetwork.co.uk
Year established 1997
Key contact Alyson Sharron

Details of casting information services
The information service is only available online, with information circulated to members by email every day. Casting infor-mation is tailored to the exact requirements of the actor; if an actor is not interested in working in certain areas such as student films or TIE, they will not be sent details of those projects. Information is also filtered according to the skills and physical charac-teristics of actors. When suitable casting opportunities do arise, CastNet will send actors free text messages and emails. Actors may make a submission for any project via the website or by telephone, CastNet will then send their CV, headshot and a covering letter to the casting director.

All reproductions of photos and postage costs are included in the subscription charge. Sends a weekly summary report by email detailing every production for which they have been submitted. CastNet receives casting breakdowns from a range of clients including Fringe theatre, mainstream films and TV.

Details of actors' Internet directories
All actors must meet the following criteria to be included: have graduated from an NCDT-accredited course; have a minimum of 3 professional theatre, film or acting credits (does not include extra or drama school work); be able to use 1 UK-based accent to a 'native' standard; have full membership of Equity (or be eligible); have a professionally taken b/w publicity photograph; must be at least 18 years old at time of application.

Admits new members every week. The CastNet Directory is distributed to more than 1500 casting directors and production companies. Actors' CVs are included on the website, with instant messaging facility for casting directors to contact them by email or text message. Will also include up to 4 photos, showreel and voice demo at no extra charge. Registers personal domain name for each actor and points it directly to their online CV. Anyone can access online directory, but printed directory is only available to industry professionals. Members' online details are updated daily and the book is updated on a quarterly basis. For details of current clients (both actors and casting professionals) consult the website.

The weekly subscription rate is £6.50 and includes all services listed above.

Castweb

7 St Luke's Avenue, London SW4 7LG
tel 020-7720 9002 *fax* 020-7720 2879
email castweb@netcomuk.co.uk
website www.castweb.co.uk
Year established 1999
Key contact Rodney Watney

Details of casting information services
Information service is available online only, with emails being circulated to subscribers every day. The monthly subscription rate is £14.50. Has received casting breakdowns from approximately 150 casting directors and more than 600 production companies. The service is designed for The Spotlight members only; new applicants are entitled to a 7-day free trial with no further obligation.

DannyRose.com Ltd.

106 Graham Road, London SW19 3SS
tel 020-8540 2029 *fax* 020-8715 3470
email enquiries@dannyrose.com
website www.dannyrose.com
Year established 2000
Key contact Charlie Weston

Details of actors' Internet directories
Only accepts actors who have graduated from an NCDT-accredited course or who have a minimum of 3 professional engagements. Admits new members at any time. Offers 2 different subscription rates: standard is available for £20 per year, and professional (includes showreels, voice samples, etc.) for £49. Members' details are available to casting professionals only, although each member receives a web address (www.dannyrose.com/actors'-name) which they can distribute to anyone. Members can log in and update their details as and when appropriate.

Much of the casting work is of a corporate nature with PR companies and large corporates housing their own events or productions. Clients have included: Yahoo, NHS, Sky TV and Merk.

Denman Casting Agency

Burgess House, Main Street,
Farnsfield NG22 8EF
tel (01623) 882272 *fax* (01623) 882272
Proprietor Jack Denman
Casting Director Alison Hope

Established in 1958. Represents hundreds of actors who are also used by other agents. Areas of work include theatre, musicals, television, film, commercials, corporate and voice-overs. *Commission:* 10-12.5% plus VAT

Also offers a repro service; see entry under *Photographers and Repro Companies* for further details.

Equity Job Information Service (JIS)

Guild House, Upper St Martin's Lane,
London WC2H 9EG
tel 0870-901 0900
website www.equity.org.uk

Launched in 1999, this service is now available 24 hours a day via the Equity website in addition to the low-cost telephone service. It is available free of charge to all members. The service provides details of job opportunities in the wide range of fields in which Equity members work. Users of the service can search for jobs in acting, singing, dance, variety, light entertainment and circus, and non-performance work such as stage management.

The effectiveness of this service relies on members only submitting themselves for suitable roles. Too many unwanted applications will make employers reluctant to advertise on JIS in the future and reduce the number of opportunities for actors.

Mandy.com
website www.mandy.com
Posts casting calls for actors for film. See entry under *Publications, Organisations, Associations and Societies.*

Performers Directory
PO Box 29942, London SW6 1FL
tel 020-7610 6699 *fax* 020-7736 6088
email admin@performersdirectory.co.uk
website www.performersdirectory.co.uk
Year established 1995
Directors Antonia Stratton, Clive Stevens

Details of casting information services
Information is available online only with emails being circulated to subscribers every day.

Details of actors' Internet directories
Includes actors' CVs, photos and voice samples in online directory which is accessible only to casting professionals. Members' details are updated as and when requested. Clients have included: Disney, the BBC, Bollywood producers, Universal,

the National Theatre and Royal Shakespeare Company. Has also suggested actors for *The Bill, Jonathan Creek, Jerry Springer the Opera* (West End), Walkers Crisps commercials, Selfridges' Fashion Show and various club events.

Annual subscription rate is £37 and includes all services listed above.

Production Casting Report (PCR)
PO Box 100, Broadstairs, Kent CT10 1UJ
tel (01843) 860885 *fax* (01843) 860899
website www.pcrnewsletter.com
Year established 1968

Details of casting information services
Information service is available in print only and is circulated to members every week. Charges £27.50 for 5 weeks but can also arrange for subscription of varying lengths such as £250 for a full year. Also offers a telephone information line. Sources of casting breakdowns have included: Hubbard Casting, Jeremy Zimmerman Casting, Birmingham Stage, Hull Truck Theatre Company and David Lan.

Other publications available include:

Filmlog, lists feature films in production and forthcoming features with details of studios, locations, key people and addresses (£11 for 3 months, £38 for 12 months);

Theatre Report, covers the whole regional repertory theatre scene and other selected venues with listings of specific companies, regular and special casting and a 'Fringe Focus' (priced as above);

Who's Where, an A-Z of all contacts, updated weekly in PCR (£8 to subscribers with free issue to new subscribers of *PCR* and *Filmlog*);

Who's Where of Casting Directors, a quick reference to UK casting directors (£2);

Who's Where USA, A-Z listing of casting directors in the USA (£7);

Castingdex, A-Z names and addresses of advertising agencies, voiceover specialists, freelance casting directors and production houses (£18).

Shooting People

27 Hedingham Close, London N1 8UA
email contact@shootingpeople.org
website www.shootingpeople.org

Shooting People allows thousands of people working in independent film to exchange information via a range of daily email bulletins, including a daily UK Casting Bulletin. This allows actors to discuss their craft and receive casting calls from directors, producers and casting directors. Currently the bulletin has more than 14,000 members.

Part-membership allows subscribers to receive email bulletins only and is free. Full membership costs £20 per year and entitles user to a range of other services. See entry under *Publications, Organisations, Associations and Societies* for further details.

The Stage

47 Bermondsey Street, London SE1 3XT
tel 020-7403 1818
subscriptions (01858) 438895
email newsdesk@thestage.co.uk
website www.thestage.co.uk
Managing Director Catherine Comerford
Editor Brian Attwood

Established in 1880. A weekly newspaper for professionals in the entertainment industry, with some job advertisements for actors.

Showreel & Voice-Demo Companies

The rapid growth in recording technology has seen an explosion of such companies over the last decade. There has also been a significant increase in the amount of (sometimes contradictory) advice offered on content, length, and so on. Much of this 'advice' is available on individual companies' websites, where you can sometimes also find samples of their work.

Voice demos have been around for several decades and a good one could attract the attention of a voice-agent. However, the world of voice-overs is hard to break into and so a quality-produced demo is very important. Showreels are a more recent innovation and are not yet the 'norm' – some agents and casting directors won't watch them. However, a good one might just tip the balance in your favour.

If you intend to travel down these routes, check the details (including pricing) of each possible company and the quality of their work. You should also assess whether the financial investment(s) involved could produce sufficient return. These additional 'calling cards' need to be of broadcast quality and professionally packaged to have any impact. As with photographers, it is very important to research as thoroughly as possible before committing your meagre funds. Is there a real possibility that one (or both) will enhance your chances of acting work?

Note It is very important that you have permission from the copyright-holders of any material that you intend to use. Some companies will help with this.

The Actor's One-stop Shop

54 Belsize Avenue, Palmers Green, London N13 4TJ
tel 020-8888 7006 *fax* 020-8888 9666
email info@actorsone-stopshop.com
website www.actorsone-stopshop.com
Year established 1997

Showreel services
Offers various 'broadcast quality' packages from £150. Scenes are crafted like film/TV excerpts rather than delivered to camera. Charges £50 per hour to produce a showreel from existing material only. Typical edit lasts 2-3 hours which includes full archiving of material for ease of future updating. Clients can sit in on the edit and will receive finished product on the same day.

Can supply showreel on VHS, CD-Rom or DVD and free 'streamed' copies for agency and Spotlight websites. Also offers free career advice session.

Recommended by The Spotlight, CastNet and E-media plc. Samples are available to view on the website.

Crying Out Loud

Covent Garden, London
tel 020-7379 0177 *mob* (07796) 266265
email simon@cryingoutloud.co.uk
website www.cryingoutloud.co.uk
Year established 1999
Key contact Simon Cryer

Voice-demo services
Supplies scripts for actors to use if desired.
Charges £210 to produce a voice demo
from scratch. This includes the company
fee, studio and equipment costs, recording
and editing of new material and 1 CD copy.
Normally produces voice demos lasting 12
minutes. Charges £40 per hour to produce
a voice demo from existing material only.
Additional CDs are priced at £3.50 each.

A special package is available to students at
a cost of £150. This covers the pre-selection
of material, 1.5 hours of recording time
and up to 2 hours of editing and 1 master
CD with full colour artwork and case.

Each client meets with the director Marina
Caldarone for an hour-long consultation
to select the best material for their voice.
Clients should aim to leave 7 days between
their consultation and their recording so
that they have sufficient time to prepare.

Recent clients have included: Simon Day
(PFD), Beth Cordingly (PFD), Elizabeth
Norman (voice of BT 1571), Evan Roberts
(CAM), Andrew Castle, Annabel Croft,
Jonathan Edwards CBE and Sally Gunnell
OBE.

DannyRose.com

106 Graham Road, London SW19 3SS
tel 020-8540 2029 *fax* 020-8715 3470
email enquiries@dannyrose.com
website www.dannyrose.com
Year established 2000
Key contact Charlie Weston

Showreel services
Supplies scripts for actors to use if desired.
Charges approximately £100 to produce a
showreel from scratch plus £49 registration
fee on DannyRose.com. This includes the
company fee, studio and equipment costs,
recording and editing of new material and
CD-Rom. Additional CDs are priced
between £1.50 and £5.00 depending on
quantities ordered. Normally produces
showreels lasting 90 seconds.

Offer includes professional direction,
rehearsal, access to a script library and
consultation on material chosen,
contrasting background scenarios and host
media on website. Actors wishing to
perform dialogue scenes will need to
supply co-performer. Does not organise
for copyright clearance of material used.

Registration fee entitles member to entry on
casting databases, web address and other
services as described in entry under *Casting
Directories and Information Services*.

Samples of work are available online at
www.dannyrose.com/paulroffman,
www.dannyrose.com/LaurettaLewis and
www.dannyrose.com/DavidDanson

Voice-demo services
Can edit an existing voice CD or audio
tape into a special format which can be
played over the Internet. Takes 2 minutes
of clips and places them on a single file.
The voice-overs are hosted on the actor's
web page and also provided on CD-Rom.
This is included in the showreel offer.

Bernard Shaw

Horton Manor, Canterbury CT4 7LG
tel/fax (01227) 730843
email bernard@bernardshaw.co.uk
website www.bernardshaw.co.uk
Year established 1980

Voice-demo services

Supplies scripts for actors to use if desired. Charges £350 to produce a voice demo from scratch. This includes the company fee, studio and equipment costs, recording and editing of new material and 1 CD copy. Normally produces voice demos lasting 6-15 minutes but this varies according to the wishes and ability of the client. Charges £60 per hour to produce a voice demo from existing material only. Advises actors to reproduce CDs with a specialist duplicator for a cheaper price.

Material is selected in consultation with the client either from their resources or from an extensive in-house library. Does not organise for the copyright clearance of material chosen. Recent clients include: actors from major agencies and broadcasting organisations such as BBC Radio Drama. Has also provided services for actors at the Royal Shakespeare Company, the Royal National Theatre and various drama schools. Work can be heard on the Spotlight online casting directory or on www.excellentvoice.co.uk (select Casting Couch and select Lyndham Gregory or Dian Perry).

Bernard Shaw is a voice-over tutor at the Actors Centres in London, Birmingham, Manchester and Newcastle (see entries under *Short-term and Part-time Courses*) and is the author of *Voice-Overs, a Practical Guide* published by A & C Black Publishers Ltd. He specialises in directing and producing tapes for BBC Radio acting.

Advises actors to attend classes at the Actors Centres (see entries under *Short-term and Part-time Courses*), research voice-over websites, talk to people working in the field and study *Voice-Overs*. Also recommends the publication detailed on www.voiceovercontacts.co.uk

Showreelz

1 Thornhill Court, Crescent Road, London N8 8AY
mob (07885) 253477
email brad@showreelz.com
website www.showreelz.com
Year established 1998

Showreel services

Supplies scripts for actors to use if desired. Charges approximately £250 to produce a showreel from scratch. This includes the company fee, studio and equipment costs, recording and editing of new material and 2 VHS copies. Rates are set at £50 per hour of filming and £30 per hour of editing. Normally produces showreels lasting 5 minutes. Charges £30 per hour to produce a showreel from existing material only. Sends clients to Stanley Productions for duplicate VHS copies. Will offer 10% discount to actors quoting *The Actors' Yearbook*.

Offers free consultation to actors ascertaining the roles they are most likely to be cast in and selecting pieces accordingly. Does not organise for copyright clearance of material used.

Recent clients include: Marjie Campie (*Brookside*), Rosemary Ashe (*Les Miserables, Phantom of the Opera*), Alex Ferns (*Eastenders*) and Chris Gascoyne (*Coronation Street*).

Advises clients to do the edit on paper before arriving –i.e. rewind tapes, reset the video counter and make a note of minutes and seconds as each clip starts. This saves the client a lot of time and money. Clients with a good range of clips can opt for a montage sequence at the beginning consisting of 10 2-second clips of extreme close-ups, big gestures, etc. These would be put together, sound stripped and a music soundtrack overlaid. This is often an effective strategy as, even if a viewer does not watch the tape through, they have at least a glimpse of the range on offer.

Voice-demo services
Supplies scripts for actors to use if desired. Charges approximately £150 to produce a voice demo from scratch. This includes the company fee, studio and equipment costs, recording and editing of new material and 2 CD copies. Rates are set at £30 per hour. Normally produces voice demos lasting 3 minutes. Will offer 10% discount to actors quoting *The Actors' Yearbook*.

Offers free consultation suggesting different scripts and looking at any pieces brought by the client. Advises on the suitability of all pieces chosen. Recent clients include: Helen Bang and Siobhan McGill.

Silver-Tongued Productions
Sidcup, Kent
tel 0870-240 7408 *fax* 020-8309 0659
email contact-us@silver-tongued.co.uk
website www.silver-tongued.co.uk
Year established 1996

Voice-demo services
Supplies scripts for actors to use if desired. Charges £25 per hour plus £50 mix down. Additional CDs are priced at £5 each, £9 for 2, £24 for 6, £38.50 for 11. This

includes postage and packing by recorded delivery and complete labelling of the CDs and cases. Publicity photos can be included on the front cover for an extra charge of 50p per CD. Average duration of voice demo is 6-8 minutes.

Material is selected in consultation with the actor. Advises a range of styles for commercials such as straight read, comedy, hard sell and soft sell. Actors can choose readings from plays, books, poetry or prose if they wish. Does not organise for copyright clearance of pieces chosen. Advises actors to show off talent with accents or characters but keep within capabilities. "Try to show variety in the subject matter so that the finished CD is entertaining to listen to. Preparation is everything!"

Recent clients include: Jeremy Edwards, Aidan McArdle, Pip Torrens and Guy Masterton. Agency recommendations include: Ken McReddie Ltd., Hobson's Voices, Foreign Voices.

Funding Bodies

The competition for funding is so fierce that it is important to allow sufficient time for research, planning and proper presentation of your proposed project. It is well worth checking to see what information is available on the websites listed in this section. Many funding bodies are happy to advise on form-filling, what kind of projects stand a chance and what could constitute a realistic amount to ask for. It is also well worth going on one (or more) of the Independent Theatre Council's (ITC; see page 126) courses for assistance in the complex world of funding applications. Bodies that offer individual funding should be approached with similar care and attention.

National Arts Councils

Arts Council England
14 Great Peter Street, London SW1P 3NQ
tel 0845-300 6200 *fax* 020-7973 6590
textphone 020-7973 6564
email enquiries@artscouncil.org.uk
website www.artscouncil.org.uk

Arts Council England is the national development agency for the arts in England, promoting excellence, innovation and diversity within the arts. It awards grants to individuals, arts organisations and national touring projects using public money from Government and the National Lottery.

Grants for individuals are generally between £200 and £30,000, while those for organisations range from £200 up to a maximum of £100,000. Most grants, however, will be under £30,000. National touring grants are available for individuals and organisations touring to 2 or more Arts Council England regions and normally vary between £5000 and £200,000. Grants for individuals, organisations and national touring can cover activities lasting up to 3 years.

All applicants should apply to the region in which they are based. Application forms, guidance notes and information sheets can be downloaded from the website. A wide range of resources, publications, links and information about other funding sources is also accessible on the website.

Arts Council of Northern Ireland
MacNeice House, 77 Malone Road,
Belfast BT9 6AQ
tel 028-9038 5200
email publicaffairs@artscouncil-ni.org
website www.artscouncil-ni.org

The prime distributor of public support for the arts, the Arts Council of Northern Ireland is committed to increasing opportunities for artists to develop challenging and innovative work. In addition to funding schemes for organisations and community groups, the council has developed a special programme of schemes to extend support for the individual artist. This programme includes the General Arts Award which provides funding for specific projects, specialised research and personal artistic development and the Major Individual Award which supports established artists in the development of ambitious work.

Arts Council of Wales

9 Museum Place, Cardiff CF10 3NX
tel 029-2037 6500
email info@artswales.org.uk
website www.artswales.org.uk

Responsible for funding and developing the arts in Wales using money from Welsh Assembly Government and the National Lottery. Provides arts organisations and individuals in Wales with the opportunity to apply for funding towards clearly defined arts-related projects. Scheme Guidelines for the funding programmes in 2004/5 will be available on the website. Anyone applying for more than £5000 should speak to an Arts Development Officer in the South Wales Office to discuss how well the project aligns with national and regional priorities.

Scottish Arts Council

12 Manor Place,
Edinburgh EH3 7DD
tel 0131-226 6051
email help.desk@scottisharts.org.uk
website www.scottisharts.org.uk

The Scottish Arts Council is the principal channel of public funding for the arts in Scotland, distributing money from the Scottish Executive and the National Lottery to those working at a professional level in the arts. Funding is available to individuals and organisations for arts projects, productions and presentation of work, research and development including short-term or one-off training courses, conference fees, master classes, mentoring, travel to see work, establishing contacts and partnerships and exploring opportunities for future projects. In support of the UK initiative European Year of Disabled People 2003, additional funds are available to support skills development for disabled artists and performers.

Those wishing to have their work evaluated by the Scottish Arts Council before applying for funding for a future drama project should contact Carole Ross (carole.ross@scottisharts.org.uk) with full details of performance times and venues at least 8 weeks in advance. If possible an evaluation will be arranged and a report will be completed 6 weeks after the work has been seen.

Regional Arts Council Offices

Arts Council England, East

Eden House, 48-49 Bateman Street,
Cambridge CB2 1LR
tel 0845-300 6200 *fax* 0870-242 1271
textphone (01223) 306893

Area covered: Bedfordshire, Cambridgeshire, Essex, Hertfordshire, Norfolk, Suffolk; and unitary authorities of Luton, Peterborough, Southend-on-Sea, Thurrock.

Arts Council England, East Midlands

St Nicholas Court, 25-27 Castle Gate,
Nottingham NG1 7AR
tel 0845-300 6200 *fax* 0115-950 2467

Area covered: Derbyshire, Leicester shire, Lincolnshire (excluding North and North East Lincolnshire), Northamptonshire, Nottinghamshire; and unitary authorities of Derby, Leicester, Nottingham, Rutland.

Arts Council England, London

2 Pear Tree Court, London EC1R 0DS
tel 020-7608 6100 *fax* 020-7608 4100
textphone 020-7608 4101

Area covered: Greater London.

Arts Council England, North East

Central Square, Forth Street, Newcastle
upon Tyne NE1 3PJ
tel 0845-300 6200 *fax* 0191-230 1020
textphone 0191-255 8585

Area covered: Durham, Northumberland;
metropolitan authorities of Gateshead,
Newcastle upon Tyne, North Tyneside,
South Tyneside, Sunderland; and unitary
authorities of Darlington, Hartlepool,
Middlesbrough, Redcar and Cleveland,
Stockton-on-Tees.

Arts Council England, North West

Manchester House, 22 Bridge Street,
Manchester M3 3AB
tel 0845-300 6200 *fax* 0161-834 6969
textphone 0161-834 9131

Area covered: Cheshire, Cumbria,
Lancashire; metropolitan authorities of
Bolton, Bury, Knowsley, Liverpool,
Manchester, Oldham, Rochdale, St Helens,
Salford, Sefton, Stockport, Tameside,
Trafford, Wigan, Wirral; and unitary
authorities of Blackburn with Darwen,
Blackpool, Halton, Warrington.

Arts Council England, South East

Sovereign House, Church Street,
Brighton BN1 1RA
tel 0845-300 6200 *fax* 0870-242 1257
textphone (01273) 710659

Area covered: Buckinghamshire, East
Sussex, Hampshire, Isle of Wight, Kent,
Oxfordshire, Surrey, West Sussex; and uni-
tary authorities of Bracknell Forest,
Brighton & Hove, Medway Towns, Milton
Keynes, Portsmouth, Reading, Slough,
Southampton, West Berkshire, Windsor
and Maidenhead, Wokingham.

Arts Council England, South West

Bradninch Place, Gandy Street,
Exeter EX4 3LS
tel 0845-300 6200 *fax* (01392) 229229
textphone (01392) 433503

Area covered: Cornwall, Devon, Dorset,
Gloucestershire, Somerset, Wiltshire;
unitary authorities of Bath and North
East Somerset, Bournemouth, Bristol,
North Somerset, Plymouth, Poole, South
Gloucestershire, Swindon, Torbay.

Arts Council England, West Midlands

82 Granville Street, Birmingham B1 2LH
tel 0121-631 3121 *fax* 0121-643 7239
textphone 0121-643 2815

Area covered: Shropshire, Staffordshire,
Warwickshire, Worcestershire; metropoli-
tan authorities of Birmingham, Coventry,
Dudley, Sandwell, Solihull, Walsall,
Wolverhampton; and unitary authorities of
Herefordshire, Stoke-on-Trent, Telford and
Wrekin.

Arts Council England, Yorkshire

21 Bond Street, Dewsbury, West Yorkshire
WF13 1AX
tel 0845-300 6200 *fax* (01924) 466522
textphone (01924) 438585

Area covered: North Yorkshire;
metropolitan authorities of Barnsley,
Bradford, Calderdale, Doncaster, Kirklees,
Leeds, Rotherham, Sheffield, Wakefield;
and unitary authorities of East Riding of

Yorkshire, Kingston upon Hull, North Lincolnshire, North East Lincolnshire, York.

National and Regional Film Agencies

UK Film Council
10 Little Portland Street,
London W1W 7JG
tel 020-7861 7861
email info@filmcouncil.org.uk
website www.filmcouncil.org.uk

Established by the Government in 2000, the UK Film Council supports the development of the British film industry and film culture. Offers a variety of funding schemes to nurture new film-making talent and provides money to regional film agencies for distribution to local projects.

For general enquiries about any of the UK Film Council's short film schemes, and to be kept informed of future opportunities, *email:* shorts@ukfilmcouncil.org.uk

The Northern Ireland Film Commission
21 Ormeau Avenue, Belfast BT2 8HD
tel 028-9023 2444
website www.nifc.co.uk

Scottish Screen
249 West George Street, Glasgow G2 2ND
tel 0141-302 1761
email info@scottishscreen.com
website www.scottishscreen.com

Sgrin Media Agency for Wales
The Bank, 10 Mount Stuart Square,
Cardiff CF10 5EE
tel 029-2033 3300
website www.sgrin.co.uk

East Midlands Media
35-37 St Mary's Gate, Nottingham
NG1 1PU
tel 0115-934 9090
email info@em-media.org.uk
website www.em-media.org.uk

London Film & Video Development Agency
114 Whitfield Street, London W1T 5EF
tel 020-7383 7755
email lfvda@lfvda.demon.co.uk
website www.lfvda.demon.co.uk

North West Vision
c/o FTC North West, 109 Mount Pleasant,
Liverpool L3 5TF
tel 0151-708 9858
email info@northwestvision.co.uk
website www.northwestvision.co.uk

Northern Film & Media
Central Square, Forth Street,
Newcastle-upon-Tyne NE1 3PJ
tel 0191-269 9200
email info@northernmedia.org
website www.northernmedia.org

Screen East
c/o Anglia Television, Anglia House,
Norwich NR1 3JG
tel 0845-601 5670
email info@screeneast.co.uk
website www.screeneast.co.uk

Screen South
Folkestone Enterprise Centre,
Shearway Road, Folkestone,
Kent CT19 4RH
tel (01303) 298222
email info@screensouth.org
website www.screensouth.org

Screen West Midlands

31-41 Bromley Street, Birmingham B9 4AN
tel 0121-766 1470
email info@screenwm.co.uk
website www.screenwm.co.uk

Screen Yorkshire

40 Hanover Square, Leeds LS3 1BQ
tel 0113-294 4410
email info@screenyorkshire.co.uk
website www.screenyorkshire.co.uk

South West Screen

St Bartholomews Court, Lewins Mead,
Bristol BS1 5BT
tel 0117-952 9977
email info@swscreen.co.uk
website www.swscreen.co.uk

Other sources of funding

Actors' Benevolent Fund

6 Adam Street, London WC2N 6AD
tel 020-7836 6378 *fax* 020-7836 8978
email office@abf.org.uk
website www.actorsbenevolentfund.co.uk

For more than 120 years the Actors'
Benevolent Fund has provided financial
assistance to actors unable to work due to
poor health, an accident or old age.

Calouste Gulbenkian Foundation

98 Portland Place, London W1N 1ET
tel 020-7636 5313 *fax* 020-7908 7950
email info@gulbenkian.org.uk
website www.gulbenkian.org.uk

Awards grants to professional organisations or professional artists developing
new art in any artform.

Department for Education and Skills

tel 0845-60 222 60
website www.dfes.gov.uk/dancedrama

The Dance and Drama Awards (DaDAs)
were introduced to provide national scholarships for the most talented dance and
drama students. The awards are offered to
students by their provider on the basis of
talent demonstrated at audition. 525 new
awards are available each year for students
joining courses at the 22 participating
private providers.

Those wishing to apply for a DaDA should
inform their course provider when
requesting an audition/interview.
Information about the course and application details will be sent in due course. As
demand for this type of training is very
high, early applications are strongly
recommended.

Although providers will select the
most talented applicants in accordance
with DfES Code of Practice when
awarding DaDAs, they will also take into
account financial circumstances when
choosing between applicants of equal
talent.

Details of participating course providers
are available to download from the
website or by calling the DfES Publications
line, choosing option 3 and quoting
reference D4.

Equity Trust Fund

222 Africa House, 64 Kingsway, London
WC2B 6BD
tel 020-7404 6041 *fax* 020-7831 4953

The trust seeks to further education
through support and development of the
performing arts and to provide for the
welfare and health of professional

performers, former performers, their relatives and dependants.

The Esmée Fairbairn Charitable Trust

11 Park Place, London SW1A 1LP
tel 020-7297 4700
website www.esmeefairbairn.org.uk

Offers Arts & Heritage grants with the aim of increasing provision of original and high-quality arts in areas of the UK less well served than others. Activities must take place outside London.

First Light

Progress Works, Heath Mill Lane, Birmingham B9 4AL
tel 0121-693 2091 *fax* 0121-693 2096
website www.firstlightmovies.com

Supports short films which are made by or in collaboration with young people.

The Jerwood Charitable Foundation

22 Fitzroy Square, London W1T 6EN
tel 020-7388 6287
email info@jerwood.org
website www.jerwood.org.uk

Awards grants to young people, mainly aged 20-35, who have demonstrated achievement, commitment and excellence, particularly in the performing arts. Financial support has been offered to young actors, dancers, choreographers, playwrights, film-makers, singers, musicians and others in the performing and visual arts, as well as to young engineers, chemists and doctors. The foundation seeks to make grants which will produce tangible and visible results and whose beneficial effects will extend beyond the immediate recipient of the grant.

NESTA (National Endowment for Science, Technology and the Arts)

Fishmongers' Chambers,
110 Upper Thames Street,
London EC4R 3TW
tel 020-7645 9500
email nesta@nesta.org.uk
website www.nesta.org.uk

Offers a variety of funding schemes to promote innovation within the fields of science, technology and art.

The Oxford Samuel Beckett Theatre Trust Award

PO Box 2637, Ascot, Berks SL5 8ZN
email info@osbttrust.com
website www.osbttrust.com
Director Romilly Walton Masters

Aims to support experimental theatre by encouraging new generations of creative artists, whether dramatists, dancers, musicians, painters, sculptors or poets. Through this award, it is looking to help an artist, or a group, of high calibre to realise a fully resourced professional production. Innovation and quality weighs more heavily than potential commercial success or public appeal.

A grant of up to £30,000 and a 3-week run at the Riverside Studios (Studio 3) in November was offered in 2004. Further support was offered in the form of a mentor, administrative and artistic guidance from the team at Riverside Studios, a week of technical rehearsals in Studio 3 and help in finding a subsidised rehearsal space.

The Royal Theatrical Fund

11 Garrick Street, London WC2E 9AR
tel 020-7836 3322 *fax* 020-7379 8273
email admin@trtf.com
website www.trtf.com

Founded in 1839, the Royal Theatrical Fund makes grants which will alleviate the suffering, assist the recovery, or reduce the need, hardship or distress of theatrical artists or their families/dependants. To be eligible to receive a grant, a person must have professionally practised or contributed to the theatrical arts (on stage, radio, film or television) for a minimum of 7 years.

Sophie's Silver Lining Fund

17 Silver Street, Chacombe,
Banbury, Oxon OX17 2JR
tel (01295) 711155
email TheLarges@aol.com
website www.silverlining.org.uk

Provides assistance to needy acting and singing students with the cost of their training.

The Wellcome Trust

UK Exhibitions and Science and Art Initiatives (SCIART),
210 Euston Road, London NW1 2BE
email k.arnold@wellcome.ac.uk
website www.wellcome.ac.uk/en/1/
pinpubscisocart.html
Contact (SCIART initiatives) Dr Ken Arnold

SCIART supports collaborations between art and science, providing 3 different kinds of award for projects in which visual art, music, digital media, film, creative writing or the performing arts interact with scientific research in an exciting way. Projects should aim to explore new modes of enquiry and stimulate fresh thinking and debate in both disciplines, whilct being accessible to diverse audiences.

Experiment Awards (up to £5000) assist artists and scientists in the fledgling stages of an arts project informed by science. This might take the form of a feasibility study, workshops or an in-depth research into a scientific area. Research Development Awards (between £5000 and £15,000) aim to support the further development of an idea in its formative stages. Production Awards (between £15,000 and £100,000) will be awarded to substantial projects likely to make a significant impact on the public's engagement with science. They can be used to fund major activities such as exhibitions, art projects, programmes for TV and radio, theatre, time-based media, public performance or events programmes.

Publications, Organisations, Associations and Societies

This section contains details of all kinds of ways of getting involved, sourcing useful information, learning, finding interesting lectures, networking, and simply keeping in touch with what's going on. It is important for the 'jobbing' actor to keep up-to-date with developments within the industry, and getting involved in related activities can pay dividends in the future.

Actorclub Ltd.
17 Inkerman Road, London NW5 3BT
tel 020-7267 2759
email johncunningham@actorclub.fsnet.co.uk
website www.actorclub.co.uk

A club which allows actors to workshop selected plays. Scenes are chosen to suit the actors attending and are then explored in a variety of ways. Most workshops cost £20 and may be attended by a maximum of 10 actors. Also runs career focus workshops (£30) and Meisner Technique evenings (£10).

Actors' Benevolent Fund
See entry under *Funding Bodies.*

Actors' Centre (London)
See entry under *Short-term and Part-time Courses.*

Actors' Centre North-East
See entry under *Short-term and Part-time Courses.*

The Agents' Association (GB)
54 Keyes House, Dolphin Square,
London SW1V 3NA
tel 020-7834 0515 *fax* 020-7821 0261
email association@agents-uk.com
website www.agents-uk.com

Established in 1927 to represent and enhance the interests of entertainment agents in the United Kingdom and to standardise practice. Boasts a membership of more than 430 agencies, covering all fields of the entertainment industry.

Arts & Business
Nutmeg House, 60 Gainsford Street,
Butlers Wharf, London SE1 2NY
tel 020-7378 8143 *fax* 020-7407 7527
email info@aandb.org.uk
website www.aandb.org.uk

With support from the Department for Culture, Media Sport and Arts Council England, Arts & Business delivers a range of services to arts organisations of all sizes across the UK promoting the effectiveness and creativity of business and arts partnerships.

Services include sponsoring seminar workshops, training courses, a resource centre, development forums, one-to-one advice sessions and a wide range of publications. Contact details for regional offices are available on the website.

Arts Councils (National and Regional)
See entries under *Funding Bodies.*

Arts Venues
website www.arts-venues.co.uk

Commissioned by the Arts Council
England, this online guide brings together
detailed information from venues,
promoters and festivals across England.

The guide provides extensive information
on each organisation, including contact
details, artistic policy, programmes of
work, artforms covered, spaces and stages
available, facilities for companies, facilities
for patrons, and details of public services
available. Also provides each organisation's
email address and website, plus a detailed
location map. All material for the entries is
supplied directly by the venues, promoters
and festivals themselves.

Artsline
54 Chalton Street, London NW1 1HS
tel 020-7388 2227 *fax* 020-7383 2653
minicom 020-7388 2227
email access@artsline.org.uk
website www.artsline.org.uk

Founded in 1981 with the aim of increasing disabled people's participation in the
arts, and to provide them with accurate
information about access to arts and cultural events in London. In collaboration
with the London Disability Arts Forum, it
began producing *Disability Arts in London*
(*DAIL*) magazine in 1986 and now provides a newly launched access database
with details for arts and entertainment
venues across London, including:
theatres, cinemas, museums, art centres,
tourist attractions, comedy, music venues
and selected restaurants. For details of

other publications, projects and services
available, consult the website.

**Association of Professional Theatre for
Children & Young People (APT) / ASSITEJ
UK (International Association for
Children & Young People)**
Warwick Arts Centre,
University of Warwick, Coventry CV4 7AL
tel 024-7652 4252 *fax* 024-7652 3883
website www.apt.org.uk / www.assitej.org
Contact Brian Bishop

Supporting the provision of professional
theatre for young people, APT encourages
and enables the exchange of ideas,
experience and advice between theatre
companies in the UK and abroad.
Information about member companies
and their work is available on the website.

Barbican Library
Barbican Centre, London EC2Y 8DS
tel 020-7638 0569
website www.cityoflondon.gov.uk/
leisure_heritage/libraries_archives_
museums_galleries/city_london_libraries/
barbican_lib.htm

Situated on the Library floor of the
Barbican Centre, this is the largest
lending library in the City of London. In
addition to the general library, the strong
arts and music sections reflect the
Barbican Centre's emphasis on the arts.
The library is fully accessible by wheelchair
and has a number of other access facilities
including hearing induction loops and a
reading magnifier machine. Open
9.30 a.m.-5.30 p.m. (Monday, Wednesday),
9.30 a.m.-7.30 p.m. (Tuesday, Thursday),
9.30 a.m.-2.00 p.m. (Friday) and
9.30 a.m.-4.00 p.m. (Saturday).

British Academy of Dramatic Combat

3 Castle View, Helmsley,
North Yorkshire YO62 5AU
email enquiries@badc.co.uk
website www.badc.co.uk

See entry under *Short-term and Part-time Courses* for further details.

The British Academy of Film and Television Arts (BAFTA)

195 Piccadilly, London W1J 9LN
tel 020-7734 0022 *fax* 020-7734 1792
email membership@bafta.org
website www.bafta.org

Founded in 1947, BAFTA provides facilities for screening and discussions, runs a popular and varied events programme coverings all aspects of film, television and interactive entertainment, encourages research and experimentation, and presents the annual Orange BAFTA Awards.

Approximately 4 events are available to members each month. These range from major industry debates to pre-release screenings of film or television productions, followed by a question-and-answer session with the producer, director, writer and/or cast. A series of Networking Evenings was launched in 2001 to facilitate informal meetings and the exhange of ideas between industry professionals. One of the key events in the programme is the annual David Lean Lecture which was given by Ken Loach in 2003.

Applicants must have a minimum of 3 years' professional experience in the film, television or interactive entertainment industries (or any combination of these) and must be able to demonstrate a significant professional contribution to the industry.

British Arts Festivals Association (BAFA)

3rd Floor, The Library, 77 Whitechapel High Street, London E1 7QX
tel 020-7247 4667 *fax* 020-7247 5010
email info@artsfestivals.co.uk
website www.artsfestivals.co.uk

Provides information and a professional network for the festivals movement in the UK, working to promote the profile and status of arts festivals. As well as the arts festivals website, which catalogues festivals in the UK and provides links to festivals in Europe, BAFA also publishes a free Calendar and Directory of the 105 festival members in print, and produces an advance festivals press pack each January.

Members have the opportunity to attend BAFA conferences, training courses and focus meetings. Membership is open to all arts festivals in the UK and associate membership to other arts organisations. Does not promote individual artists, companies or tours.

British Council

Arts Group, 10 Spring Gardens,
London SW1A 2BN
tel 020-7389 3194 *fax* 020-7389 3199
email artweb@britishcouncil.org
website www.britishcouncil.org/arts

Norwich Union House, 7 Fountain Street,
Belfast BT1 5EG
tel 028-9024 8220 *fax* 028-9023 7592
email collette.norwood@britishcouncil.org

The Tun, 3rd Floor, 4 Jackson's Entry,
Holyrood Road, Edinburgh EH8 8PJ
tel 0131-524 5714 *fax* 0131-524 5714
email kate.burwell@britishcouncil.org

28 Park Place, Cardiff CF10 3QE
tel 029-2039 7346 *fax* 029-2023 7494
email mary.tapley@britishcouncil.org

The British Council is the UK's public diplomacy and cultural organisation and works in 100 countries, in arts, education, governance and science. The Arts Group supports around 2000 arts events every year encouraging international collaborations, performances and exchanges with some of the top UK artists. In addition they support arts-based workshops, seminars and online events.

The form of support which is offered varies according to the project. In most cases the Council acts as an advisory body and brokers partnerships with overseas contacts such as artistic programmers and producers, venues, choreographers and festival directors. Although most work is geared towards young people aged 16-35, this isn't an exclusive emphasis and classic or traditional work is supported, especially if it has a modern slant.

Resources available on the website include an annual directory of UK drama, dance, live art and street art companies that have work suitable for overseas touring; specialist information about drama/performing arts education in the UK; and *Britfilms* –a portal site for the UK film industry with information about international film festivals, UK film directors and films, making a film in the UK, training and careers advice.

Not open to the public except by appointment. Write, phone or email to establish contact or get in touch with an artform specialist.

British Film Commission
See UK Film Council International.

British Film Institute (BFI)
bfi National Library,
21 Stephen Street, London W1T 1LN
tel 020-7255 1444

email library@bfi.org.uk
website www.bfi.org.uk
National Film Theatre, Belvedere Road, South Bank, Waterloo, London SE1 8XT
tel 020-7928 3535
email nft@bfi.org.uk

Established in 1933, the *bfi* strives to increase the level of understanding, appreciation and access to film and television culture. In addition to the *bfi* National Library which holds the largest film archive in the world, the organisation runs the National Film Theatre and London Film Festival (see entry under 'Media Festivals'), and the *bfi* IMAX Cinema. It also publishes books, releases films in cinemas, on video and DVD, runs educational programmes and has one of the largest collections of film stills and film posters in the world.

British Music Hall Society
82 Fernlea Road, London SW12 9RW
tel 020-8673 2175
website www.music-hall-society.com
Secretary Daphne Masterton

Founded in 1963 and with offices across England, the society aims to preserve the history of music hall and variety, to recall the artistes who created it and to support entertainers working today. Members receive copies of the society's quarterly magazine *The Call-Boy* containing news, views and information about the sector; they also have the opportunity to attend evening and weekend study group meetings. Arranges live theatre shows and it is possible for members to take part in such performances on these occasions.

Casting Directors Guild
PO Box 34403, London W6 OYG
tel 020-8741 1951
website www.castingdirectorsguild.co.uk

A professional organisation which represents casting directors working in film, television, theatre and commercials. The Casting Directors Guild aims to standardise professional working practice and to enable the exchange of information and ideas between members.

Election to the Guild is at the discretion of the Committee. Full members must have worked in 1 or more areas of the industry for at least 5 years and are entitled to use the initials CDG after their name. Probationary members must have worked as an assistant to a casting director for 3 years.

Members are listed on the website with information about their areas of work and recent credits.

Conference of Drama Schools (CDS)

PO Box 34252, London NW5 1XJ
email enquiries@cds.drama.ac.uk
website www.drama.ac.uk

Founded in 1969 to strengthen the voice of member drama schools and encourage the highest standards of training, the CDS also helps students understand the range of courses on offer and how to apply for them. The CDS played a key role in the negotiations which led to the formation of the National Council for Drama Training (see entry below).

The 21 member schools offer courses in Acting, Musical Theatre, Directing and Technical Theatre training. CDS members offer courses that are professional, intensive and vocational. They are often mentally and physically demanding and, unlike most degree courses at universities and colleges, do not generally contain a high proportion of academic work.

Produces an annual official guide to UK drama schools for careers officers, teachers and applicants, providing a description of each member school, its policy and the courses it offers together with information about funding. It also provides details of summer schools. The printed version is available free of charge by writing to the address above and enclosing an sae. Alternatively it can be downloaded from the website.

Contacts

See separate section on The Spotlight.

Co-operative Personal Managers' Association

The Secretary, c/o 1 Mellor Road, Leicester LE3 6HN
tel 0116-233 8432 *fax* 0116-223 5537
email cpmauk@yahoo.co.uk

Council for Dance Education and Training (CDET)

Toynbee Hall, 28 Commercial Street, London E1 6LS
tel 020-7247 4030 *fax* 020-7247 3404
email info@cdet.org.uk
website www.cdet.org.uk

Founded in 1979, the Council for Dance Education and Training (CDET) promotes excellence in dance education and training. It accredits courses at vocational dance schools, advocates on behalf of the private dance training and teaching communities, and provides a comprehensive information service about dance education and training. CDET offers advice and support to students, parents, teachers and artists. It also informs the work of government and other agencies working in dance.

Dance UK

Battersea Arts Centre, Lavender Hill, London SW11 5TN

tel 020-7728 4990 *fax* 020-7223 0074
email info@danceuk.org
website www.danceuk.org

Dance UK began in 1982 and works with and on behalf of dance, providing information, publications, networks, forums for debate and conferences and a unified voice for all its members. It has about 130 corporate members, including most of the major dance companies, venues, agencies, funders and educational institutions. Individual members include individual dance artists, choreographers, administrators, managers, technicians, teachers, students, writers and members of dance audiences.

The organisation is active in 3 main areas: Communication, Professional Development and Healthier Dance. As well as the website, Dance UK manages email groups for choreographers, dance managers and independent dance artists, and produces *Dance UK News* which is mailed quarterly to members. Has set up a number of practical initiatives to promote longer-lasting careers and professional development in dance including insurance schemes for teachers, the UK Choreographers Directory, and books and information sheets on floors, pensions, insurance and copyright.

Promoting the health and well-being of dancers it also generates research, educational talks and events, posters, information sheets and books. The Practitioners Register is a telephone help-line providing contact information for local medical and complementary therapists with experience of working with dancers. For information about other dance organisations and performing companies visit the links page on their website.

Department of Culture, Media and Sport (DCMS)

Information Centre, 2-4 Cockspur Street, London SW1Y 5DH
tel 020-7211 6200
email enquiries@culture.gov.uk
website www.culture.gov.uk

The DCMS is responsible for Government policy on the arts, sport, the National Lottery, tourism, libraries, museums and galleries, broadcasting, film, the music industry, press freedom and regulation, licensing, gambling and the historic environment.

Arts policies are carried out in partnership with Arts Council England and its Regional Arts Councils, other government departments such as the Department for Education Skills, and with regional bodies such as local authorities.

The Information Centre contains an archive of DCMS publications and press, and Parliamentary material (Culture, Media & Sport Committee papers). Open from 9.00 a.m. to 5.30 p.m. visits are by appointment only.

Directors Guild of Great Britain

Acorn House, 314-320 Gray's Inn Road, London WC1X 8DP
tel 020-7278 4343 *fax* 020-7278 4742
email guild@dggb.org
website www.dggb.org

Founded in 1982, the Directors Guild of Great Britain represents directors in all media including film, television, theatre, radio, opera, commercials, corporate, multimedia and new technology. It is a trade union, offering help with contracts, a campaigning voice, policy to influence the future of the industry, and advice for members to meet and share their skills. It also organises many events with a focus on training such as masterclasses (topics have included working with actors, theatre for young people), panel events, career advice sessions and short courses.

Actors can obtain information about the Guild's members and their career profile using the online searchable database. For information on directors who are not members of the Guild, the DGGB has a number of suggestions on their website. Actors may wish to consult the following websites for information on international directors:

www.dga.org (Directors Guild of America) www.dgc.ca (Directors Guild of Canada) www.asdafilm.org.au (Australian Screen Directors Association)

Drama Association of Wales
The Old Library, Singleton Road, Splott, Cardiff CF24 2ET
tel 029-2045 2200 *fax* 029-2045 2277

Founded in 1934 and a registered charity since 1973, the Drama Association of Wales aims to increase opportunities for people in the community to be creatively involved in high-quality drama.

Its main activities are an extensive mail-order library service with more than 200,000 volumes of plays, biographies, critical works and technical theatre books, and training courses in all aspects of theatre, including a 7-day residential summer school and a winter school in the Mediterranean.

Also runs several new writing schemes offering a script reading service, a play-writing competition, workshops and support for first productions, and organises the Welsh National Drama Festival from January to June, culminating in the Wales One Act Festival. Assists in founding and

sustaining youth theatre companies and encourages cooperation between professional and amateur theatre.

UK membership costs just under £12 per year for individuals and £29 a year for Amateur Societies.

Dramaturgs' Network
139b Tooting Bec Road, London SW17 8BW
tel 020-8767 6004
email info@dramaturgy.co.uk
website www.dramaturgy.co.uk

The Dramaturgs' Network is a professional organisation which promotes the role of the dramaturg in the UK. Providing members with a network of support the organisation brings dramaturgs, literary managers and script editors together to create opportunities for debate and sharing of information and experiences. In collaboration with other professional bodies such as the Directors Guild of Great Britain and Equity, the organisation seeks to standardise the definition and working practice of dramaturgs in the UK.

CVs of members and details of training opportunities are available online.

Equity
See separate section on Equity.

Fringe Theatre Network (FTN)
Unit 5a, Imex Business Centre, Ingate Place, London SW8 3NS
tel 020-7627 4920 *fax* 020-7978 2631
email Frank.Fisher@fringetheatre.org.uk
website www.fringetheatre.org.uk
Coordinator Frank Fisher

The FTN provides services, support and a network of contacts for venues, producing companies and individuals working on the London Fringe with the aim of increasing the level of professionalism in Fringe theatre. Acting as an umbrella organisation, the FTN puts forward the interests of Fringe theatre in its dealings with statutory authorities, funding bodies, policy-makers and other arts organisations.

Independent Theatre Council (ITC)
12 The Leathermarket, Weston Street, London SE1 3ER
tel 020-7403 1727 *fax* 020-7403 1745
email admin@itc-arts.org
website www.itc-arts.org

Founded in 1974, the Independent Theatre Council negotiates contracts and has established standard agreements with Equity and other unions, on behalf of all professionals working in theatre. With more than 500 members, the ITC provides management and legal advice, contractual negotiation and conciliation services, networking, advocacy, information exchange, and training and personal development services for perform ing arts organisations, individuals and venues.

Working across a variety of artforms including drama, dance, opera, music theatre, puppetry, mixed media, mime, physical theatre and circus, ITC members usually operate on the middle and small scale and are dedicated to producing innovative work, often in unconventional performance spaces.

The ITC has commissioned a wide range of publications which offer guidance on potentially difficult aspects of working in the performing arts, advice on good practice and further sources of information. Courses and seminars run by the ITC cover a similar range of topics and issues.

Also offers in-house training and other services. For details of how to join and other benefits available to members, consult the website.

International Federation of Actors
Guild House, Upper St Martin's Lane, London WC2H 9EG
tel 020-7379 0900 *fax* 020-7379 8260
email office@fia-actors.com
website www.fia-actors.com

Works internationally to represent and coordinate the interest of performing artists and their professional organisations.

The Knowledge
CMP Data & Information Services, CMP Information Ltd., Riverbank House, Angel Lane, Tonbridge, Kent TN9 1SE
tel (01732) 377041
email knowledge@cmpinformation.com
website www.theknowledgeonline.com

Covering all aspects of production, the Knowledge Online contains contacts and services for the UK film, television, video and commercial production industry. Its *Know-How* section contains studio and post-production charts, production guidelines, articles and maps, and in 2003 it introduced an overview of international co-production by the British Film Commission.

Limited access can be gained by registering online, but for full access to all 17,500 entries and access to the *Know-How* users must pay a £50 annual subscription.

Mandy.com
website www.mandy.com

An online service providing a directory of 33,000 technicians, facilities and producers and a vacancy list for jobs in production, crew, art departments and post production. Also posts casting calls for actors, classified ads and information about films for sale and distribution on its website.

National Association of Youth Theatres (NAYT)

Arts Centre, Vane Terrace,
Darlington DL3 7AX
tel (01325) 363330 *fax* (01325) 363313
email naytuk@aol.com
website www.nayt.org.uk

Founded in 1982, the National Association of Youth Theatres is the leading membership organisation for youth theatre practice in England and Wales. On behalf of members it works with the Department for Education & Skills (DfES), Arts Council England, Regional Arts Councils and local authorities to achieve greater recognition and improved funding for the sector.

Membership is open to any group or individual using theatre techniques in their work with young people, outside of formal education.

The NAYT provides a range of resources, information and support for its members including training programmes; advice on a wide range of policy and strategy issues such as fundraising, constitutions, insurance, health safety, child protection, scripts, practitioners, access and equal opportunities; an archive with project reports, surveys and case studies; and a monthly *Bulletin* containing the latest news on funding, training, performances and vacancies. With online information and contact details for more than 700 members, the organisation also enables young people to contact youth theatres directly.

National Council for Drama Training (NCDT)

1-7 Woburn Walk, London WC1H 0JJ
tel 020-7387 3650 *fax* 020-7387 3860
email info@ncdt.co.uk
website www.ncdt.co.uk

The National Council for Drama Training is a partnership of employers in the theatre, broadcast and media industry, employee representatives and training providers who work together to increase support for professional drama training and education.

It seeks to maintain the highest standards and provides a credible process of quality assurance through accreditation for vocational drama, reassuring students that the courses they choose are recognised and respected by the drama profession.

Following a process of re-evaluation and reform of both the NCDT and its system of accreditation, a new structure will be announced in 2004 and a new system of accrediting vocational acting, musical theatre and technical courses will be ready for piloting in the 2004/5 academic year.

National Operatic and Dramatic Association (NODA)

58-60 Lincoln Road,
Peterborough PE1 2RZ
tel 0870-770 2480 *fax* 0870-770 2490
email everyone@noda.org.uk
website www.noda.org.uk
Patron Lord Lloyd-Webber

Founded in 1899, NODA is the main representative body for amateur theatre in the UK. It has a membership of around 2300 amateur/community theatre groups and 3000 individual enthusiasts throughout the UK, staging musicals, operas, plays, concerts and pantomimes in a variety of performing venues, ranging from professional theatres to village halls.

Produces a quarterly national magazine, *NODA National News*, containing advice and information for the amateur theatre sector, listings of performances in the National Theatre Diary and classified ads. Also holds area and national conferences, workshops and summer schools.

Northern Actors Centre
See entry under *Short-term and Part-time Courses.*

Personal Managers' Association
Rivercroft, 1 Summer Road, East Molesey, Surrey KT8 9LX
tel 020-8398 9796 *fax* 020-8398 9796
email info@thepma.com

Founded in 1950, the PMA is an association of artists' and dramatists' agents which provides members with a forum to exchange ideas and information. The association maintains a code of conduct and acts as a lobby when necessary.

Professional Casting Report (PCR)
See entry under *Casting Information Services.*

Rogues and Vagabonds
13 Elm Road, London SW14 7JL
tel 020-8876 1175
email admin@roguesandvagabonds.co.uk
website www.roguesandvagabonds.co.uk

A subscription website for theatre-lovers and industry professionals providing news, amusement, information, interviews, reviews, quotes and profiles covering all aspects of theatre. With specific resources for actors including free casting information, links to useful websites and information about a wide range of services offered to actors, the site also provides details of awards, plays, musicals, producers, theatres and directors.

While some areas are available to non-subscribers, the majority are only accessible to those who pay the annual subscription charge of £10.

Royal National Theatre Platforms
South Bank, London SE1 9PX
tel 020-7453 3000
email angus@nationaltheatre.org.uk
Platforms Producer Angus MacKechnie

A programme of pre-performance events exploring all aspects of the arts. These offer the chance to learn about the National's work and discover more about theatre in general. Platforms usually start at 6.00 p.m. lasting for 45 minutes. There are also occasional afternoon events, usually starting at 2.30 p.m. Tickets: £3.50 (£2.50 concessions).

Alan Ayckbourn, Michael Gambon, Peter Hall, Michael Pennington and Stephen Unwin were just some of the names participating in the programme for spring 2004.

Royal Television Society (RTS)
Holborn Hall, 100 Gray's Inn Road, London WC1X 8AL
tel 020-7430 1000 *fax* 020-7430 0924
email info@rts.org.uk
website www.rts.org.uk

Provides the leading forum for discussion and debate on all aspects of the television industry, with opportunities for networking and professional development for people at all levels and across every sector. The RTS has 14 national and regional centres in the UK which draw up an annual programme to suit the needs of their members.

Events organised by the RTS include dinners, lectures, conventions, conferences and awards ceremonies. In addition it produces a monthly magazine *Television* outlining key industry debates and developments.

The Royal Theatrical Fund

See entry under *Funding Bodies*.

The Screenwriters' Workshop

Suffolk House, 1-8 Whitfield Place, London W1T 5JV
tel 020-7387 5511
email screenoffice@tiscali.co.uk
website www.lsw.org.uk

Runs a series of informal seminars with writers, agents, producers, directors and script editors. Also offers a programme of screenwriting courses and workshops covering all aspects of writing for the film and television industry. All courses are run by professional writers and qualified teachers. Membership costs £40 per year.

Shooting People

27 Hedingham Close, London N1 8UA
email contact@shootingpeople.org
website www.shootingpeople.org

Shooting People allows thousands of people working in independent film to exchange information via a range of daily email bulletins. These include:

- Daily UK Film-makers Bulletin –for directors, producers and crew to share information on the latest technologies, get advice, find crew, locations, production deals, events & screenings, training and more. Currently more than 22,000 members
- Daily UK Screenwriters Bulletin –writers all over the UK use this email network to discuss writing, share ideas and

hear about competitions, opportunities and training. Currently more than 13,000 members

- Daily UK Casting Bulletin –for actors to discuss their craft and receive casting calls from directors, producers and casting directors. Currently more than 14,000 members
- Weekly UK Script Pitch Bulletin –a weekly collection of script pitches offered to producers and directors by the writers on the Screenwriters Network. Currently more than 11,000 members

Both part and full membership are available. Part membership allows subscribers to receive email bulletins only, and is free. Full membership costs £20 per year and entitles user to a range of other services. Full members can create an actors' personal profile with a photograph and be listed in the online directory, post to any bulletin and download guides on various confusing aspects of film-making such as actor contracts, health & safety and distribution. They are also entitled to create member cards and browse other member cards to find potential local collaborators.

Shooting People also organises a number of parties, screenings, workshops and other events for which full members receive advanced notice.

The Society of Teachers of Speech and Drama (STSD)

73 Berry Hill Road, Mansfield, Nottinghamshire NG18 4RU
email stsd@stsd.org.uk
website www.stsd.org.uk

Protecting the professional interests of qualified, specialist teachers of Speech & Drama, the STSD encourages good standards of teaching and promotes the study and knowledge of speech and dramatic art in every form. Has established close links with drama schools and examination boards and its publications are read world-wide.

Members receive copies of its newsletters, information sheets and the journal *Speech & Drama*. They are entitled to free advice, to be included in a register of members and to attend its summer conference.

Students of Speech & Drama can search for suitable teachers using the online database.

The Spotlight

See separate section on The Spotlight.

The Stage

47 Bermondsey Street, London SE1 3XT
tel 020-7403 1818
subscriptions (01858) 438895
email newsdesk@thestage.co.uk
website www.thestage.co.uk
Managing Director Catherine Comerford
Editor Brian Attwood

Established in 1880. A weekly newspaper for professionals in the entertainment industry, with reviews, comments and job advertisements.

The Theatre Museum

1e Tavistock Street, London WC2E 7PR
tel 020-7943 4700 *fax* 020-7943 4777
email tmenquiries@vam.ac.uk
website www.theatremuseum.org

The Theatre Museum is the National Museum of the Performing Arts and a branch of the Victoria Albert Museum (V&A). With a wide range of documents, artefacts and works of art recording the history of the performing arts in Britain from the 16th century to the present, it holds the world's largest and most important collections relating to the British stage. Using costumes, designs, manuscripts, books, video recordings (including the National Video Archive of Stage Performance) posters and paintings, the museum reconstructs details of past performances and the lives of performers, past and contemporary.

All the live performing arts are represented, including drama, dance, opera, musical theatre, circus, puppetry, music hall and live art, and are made available through exhibitions, educational programmes, events, publications, study facilities and the website.

Theatre Record

305 Whitton Dene, Isleworth,
Middlesex TW7 7NE
tel 020-8737 8489 *fax* 020-8893 9677
email (subscriptions)
ruth@trsubs.demon.co.uk
website www.theatrerecord.com

Established in 1981 as *London Theatre Record*, the magazine was renamed in 1990 to cover work across the UK. *Theatre Record* publishes the complete, unabridged reviews of all new shows covered by national press and leading listing magazines. Fringe shows get extra attention from the critical teams of *Time Out* and *What's On*, while special supplements cover festivals and seasons such as Edinburgh (official and Fringe), LIFT and the London International Mime Festival.

As well as reviews, each show is represented by a full listing of cast, technical credits and, where possible, production photographs. Also lists opening nights for forthcoming productions. Issued fortnightly.

Theatre Royal Haymarket Masterclasses

Theatre Royal Haymarket,
London SW1Y 4HT

tel 020-7389 9660 *fax* 020-7389 9697
email masterclass@trh.co.uk
website www.trh.co.uk/masterclass
Patrons Sir Peter Hall, Sir David Hare,
Maureen Lipman CBE

Masterclass is an arts initiative which
allows young people aged 17-30 to attend
workshops and talks given by leading
actors, directors, designers and writers
working in theatre today. All events take
place at the Theatre Royal Haymarket and
are free of charge to young people aged
17-30. People over the age of 30 may also
take part and contribute to the project by
joining the Masterclass Friends scheme.

In addition to the masterclass events, the
programme includes a longer-term new
writing project and a series that gives career
advice and support. Previous Masters have
included Steven Berkoff, Simon Callow,
Mike Leigh, Alan Rickman, Prunella Scales
and Janet Suzman. For details of forthcoming events, consult the website.

Theatres Trust

22 Charing Cross Road, London
WC2H OQL
tel 020-7836 8591 *fax* 020-7836 3302
email info@theatrestrust.org.uk
website www.theatrestrust.org.uk

Established by an act of parliament in 1976,
the Theatres Trust's remit is to promote the
better protection of theatres across the
whole of the UK. Local authorities are
required by government to consult the
Trust when evaluating any planning applications involving land on which there is a
theatre.

Provides help and advice on theatre planning issues, architecture and design to theatre managements, government agencies,
local groups and grant-making bodies, and
campaigns generally on behalf of theatre
buildings. It also publishes a quarterly
newsletter, a series of Advice Notes, occasional books and other papers. It is unable
to award grants but is sometimes able to
help support studies into the best use, or
adaptation, of theatre buildings and has
worked with local groups to help bring
dark theatres with potential back into current use. Has records of more than 3400
theatres both past and present; these are
being added to their online database.

UK Film Council

See entry under *Funding Bodies*.

UK Film Council International (formerly British Film Commission)

10 Little Portland Street, London
W1W 7JG
tel 020-7861 7860 *fax* 020-7861 7864
email
internationalinfo@ukfilmcouncil.org.uk
website www.britfilmcom.co.uk

A division of the Film Council, the
international arm seeks to encourage and
enable overseas film-makers to locate their
productions in the UK. Publishes annual
newsletters and fact sheets covering
different aspects of film-making and hosts a
number of domestic and international
events. The website offers basic information
and links through to other events associated with the international film industry, and
an online directory with contact information for a range of companies and organisations working in film across the UK.

Westminster Reference Library

35 St Martin's Street, London WC2H 7HP
tel 020-7641 4638
website
www.westminster.gov.uk/libraries/westref/

General reference library with an extensive performing arts section. Open from 10.00 a.m. to 8.00 p.m. Monday to Friday and 10.00 a.m. to 5.00 p.m. on Saturday.

Women in Film and Television (WFTV)

6 Langley Street, London WC2H 9JA
tel 020-7240 4875
email emily@wftv.org.uk
website www.wftv.org.uk
Membership Events Manager Emily Compton

A membership association open to women with a minimum of 1 year's professional experience in the television, film or digital media industries. With more than 800 members including writers, actresses and directors, the WFTV promotes the interests and diversity of women working at all levels in these industries. Offers a network of national and international contacts with an online directory of members, and provides a number of social forums, workshops, seminars and preview screenings.

Bibliography

Books for aspiring, student and young actors

Margo Annett, *Actor's Guide to Auditions and Interviews* (3rd edition, A & C Black, 2004). A useful guide outlining some of the techniques needed for success.

Peter Barkworth, *The Complete About Acting* (Methuen, 1991). Another very good book about acting and getting work.

Simon Dunmore, *An Actor's Guide to Getting Work* (4th edition, A & C Black, 2004). A practical, comprehensive guide covering all aspects of marketing yourself as an actor.

Simon Dunmore, *Alternative Shakespeare Auditions for Women* (A & C Black, 1997). A collection of 50 less well-known speeches for women.

Simon Dunmore, *MORE Alternative Shakespeare Auditions for Women* (A & C Black, 1999). Another collection of 50 less well-known speeches for women.

Simon Dunmore, *Alternative Shakespeare Auditions for Men* (A & C Black, 1997). A collection of 50 less well-known speeches for men.

Simon Dunmore, *MORE Alternative Shakespeare Auditions for Men* (A & C Black, 2002). Another collection of 50 less well-known speeches for men.

Ellis Jones, *Teach Yourself Acting* (Hodder & Stoughton Ltd., 1998). A good overview of acting and the profession.

Anna Scher, *Desperate to Act* (Lions, 1988). Brilliant, basic advice for those so 'desperate', from a lady who should know.

William Shakespeare, *Hamlet, Prince of Denmark*. Especially Hamlet's advice to the players (Act 3, scene 2), which is some of the best advice on acting ever given.

Bernard Graham Shaw, *Voice-Overs, A Practical Guide* (A & C Black, 2000). A useful guide which explains and teaches the skills of voicing radio and television commercials.

Clive Swift, *The Job of Acting* (Harrap, revised 1984). Although some of it is out-of-date, this book is a wonderful read from an experienced and caring professional.

Malcolm Taylor, *The Actor and the Camera* (A & C Black, 1994). Another good 'primer' for the beginner.

Other career advice books for actors
Ed Hooks, *The Audition Book* (3rd edition, Back Stage Books, 2000). Excellent reading if you're thinking of trying your hand in the USA. It's also worth looking at Ed's website for his excellent 'Craft Notes' <www.edhooks.com>.

Peter Messaline and Miriam Newhouse, *The Actor's Survival Kit* (3rd edition, Simon & Pierre, 1999). Well worth reading if you're thinking of trying your hand in Canada.

Books for any actor
Stephen Aaron, *Stage Fright: Its Role in Acting* (University of Chicago Press, 1986). Fascinating book, written by a psychotherapist who is also an experienced director and teacher.

Brian Bates, *The Way of the Actor* (Century Hutchinson, 1986). Very interesting insights into the inner workings of the actor's psyche.

Peter Brook, *The Empty Space* (Penguin, 1990). Written in the 1960s, but still essential reading.

Adrian Cairns, *The Making of the Professional Actor* (Peter Owen Publishers, 1996). A fascinating study of the history, and possible future, of the art of acting.

Simon Callow, *Being an Actor* (Penguin, 1995). Autobiographical books by famous actors are generally useless in terms of practical career advice. However, this one –part autobiography and part advice –has a great deal of down-to-earth common sense. His famous 'manifesto' on directors' theatre is spot on.

Nicholas Craig, *I, an Actor* (Pavilion Books, 1988). A very funny send-up of the starry actor's autobiography. A must.

Uta Hagen, *A Challenge for the Actor* (Macmillan, 1991). The best book on acting ever written.

Richard Hornby, *The End of Acting: a radical view* (Applause Books, 1992). Revelatory insights into the processes of acting.

David Mamet, *True and False* (Faber & Faber, 1998). This book cuts through much of the mythology that surrounds acting.

Kenneth Rea, *A Better Direction* (Calouste Gulbenkian Foundation, 1989). A very thorough inquiry into directors and the need for more training opportunities.

Patsy Rodenburg, *An Actor Speaks* (Methuen, 1997). An entirely practical guide with excellent advice and exercises to help develop the performer's voice.

Michael Sanderson, *From Irving to Olivier – A Social History of the Acting Profession* (Athlone Press, 1984). A very expensive, but nevertheless fascinating, study of the actor's world over the last century.

Michael Shurtleff, *Audition* (Walker & Company, 1984). An American book which should be read. It contains brilliant insights and thoughts to help any actor.

The Spotlight, *Contacts* (The Spotlight, annually in October). Contact details for everything you can think of (and more) that relates to the performing arts in general.

Webography

Training

www.actorscentre.co.uk (Actors Centre London)

www.actorscentrene.co.uk (Actors Centre North East)

www.dfes.gov.uk/dancedrama (Department for Education & Skills)

www.drama.ac.uk (Conference of Drama Schools, with links to member schools' websites)

www.ncdt.co.uk (National Council for Drama Training)

www.northernactorscentre.co.uk (Northern Actors Centre)

www.youthdrama.ie (National Association for Youth Drama in Ireland)

www.nayt.org.uk (National Association of Youth Theatres)

www.nyaw.co.uk/nytw.html (National Youth Arts Wales)

www.nymt.org.uk (National Youth Music Theatre)

www.nyt.org.uk (National Youth Theatre)

www.scottishyouththeatre.org (Scottish Youth Theatre)

art.ntu.ac.uk/scudd/ (Standing Conference of University Drama Departments)

www.ucas.ac.uk/ (UCAS, the central organisation that processes applications for full-time undergraduate courses at UK universities and colleges)

www.youth-music-theatre.org.uk (Youth Music Theatre: UK)

Agents and casting directors

www.agents-uk.com (Agents' Association, Great Britain)

www.castingdirectorsguild.co.uk (Casting Directors Guild)

Theatre

www.arts-venues.co.uk (online guide brings together detailed information from venues, promoters & festivals across England)

www.artsfestivals.co.uk (British Arts Festivals Association, with an online calendar of British arts festivals)

www.festivals.demon.co.uk (British Federation of Festivals for Music, Drama Speech)

www.edfringe.com (Edinburgh Festival Fringe)

www.eif.co.uk (Edinburgh International Festival)

www.euro-festival.net/Efichome (European Festivals Association)

www.fringetheatre.org.uk (Fringe theatre network, with listings of and

links to London Fringe venues)
www.itc-arts.org (Independent Theatre Council homepage with links to member companies' websites)
www.assitej.org (International Association for Children & Young People)
www.apt.org.uk (International Association for Children & Young People UK)
www.nsdf.org.uk (National Student Drama Festival)
www.youtharts.org.uk (Youth Arts Wales, with links to TIE and Young People's Theatre Companies)

Other media

www.bafta.org (British Academy of Film & Television Arts)
www.bbc.co.uk (BBC homepage)
www.bbc.co.uk/drama/radio (BBC Radio Drama)
www.bernardshaw.co.uk (Author of *Voice-Overs, A Practical Guide,* website contains advice, information and details of voice services available to actors)
www.bfi.org.uk (British Film Institute)
www.em-media.org.uk (East Midlands Media)
www.excellentvoice.co.uk (Information and advice for voice-over artists with examples of good voice demos online)
www.imdb.com (Internet Movie Database; catalogues all sorts of information on more than 250,000 films and the 900,000 people who helped to make them)
www.lfvda.demon.co.uk (London Film & Video Development Agency)
www.mandy.com (Provides a directory of 33,000 technicians, facilities and producers and a vacancy list for jobs in production, crew, art departments and post production. Also posts casting calls for actors)
www.nifc.co.uk (Northern Ireland Film Commission)
www.northwestvision.co.uk (North West Vision)
www.northernmedia.org (Northern Film & Media)
www.scottishscreen.com (Scottish Screen)
www.shootingpeople.org (Shooting People, issues daily email bulletins for those working in low-budget films)
www.sgrin.co.uk (Sgrin Media Agency for Wales)
www.screeneast.co.uk (Screen East)
www.screensouth.org (Screen South)
www.screenwm.co.uk (Screen West Midlands)
www.screenyorkshire.co.uk (Screen Yorkshire)

www.sound.co.uk (Information and advice for voice-over artists with links to many other sites)

www.swscreen.co.uk (South West Screen)

www.filmcouncil.org.uk (UK Film Council)

www.voiceovers.co.uk (A forum for voice-over artists to advertise themselves)

www.wftv.org.uk (Women in Film & TV)

Resources

www.artscouncil.org.uk (Arts Council England)

www.artscouncil-ni.org (Arts Council of Northern Ireland)

www.artswales.org.uk (Arts Council of Wales)

www.artsline.org.uk (Arts-Line, provides access information on arts venues)

www.asdafilm.org.au (Australian Screen Directors Association)

www.britishcouncil.org/arts (British Council Arts Page)

www.culture.gov.uk (Department for Culture, Media & Sport)

www.dga.org (Directors Guild of America)

www.dgc.ca (Directors Guild of Canada)

www.dggb.org (Directors Guild of Great Britain)

www.equity.org.uk (Equity)

www.londontheatre.co.uk/online (London Theatre Guide, with news, listings, reviews, seating plans, tickets, maps and venues)

www.nesta.org.uk (NESTA: National Endowment for Science, Technology & the Arts)

www.pcrnewsletter.com (PCR: Professional Casting Report)

www.roguesandvagabonds.co.uk (Rogues and Vagabonds, with news, information, interviews, reviews, quotes and profiles covering all aspects of theatre plus specific resources and links for actors)

www.scottisharts.org.uk (Scottish Arts Council)

www.officiallondontheatre.co.uk (Society of London Theatre website with news, reviews and booking information)

www.spotlightcd.com (The Spotlight, publishes actors' directories and offers a career advisory service)

www.thestage.co.uk (*The Stage*, contains news, information and job advertisements which are updated each Thursday)

www.theatrenet.com (Theatre Net; news, events and special offers and links to agents, producers, theatre companies, venues and more) www.theatrerecord.com (Theatre Record)

www.uktw.co.uk (UK Theatre Web, with information, events and tickets for theatre in the UK)

www.vl-theatre.com (Virtual Library of Theatre & Drama, listing resources in more than 50 countries)

www.whatsonstage.com (A UK theatre listing service with search facilities and a ticket-ordering service)

Index

Q20 Theatre   182
Queen Margaret College, Edinburgh   27
Queen Margaret University College   19
Queen Mary, University of London   27
Queen's Theatre   118
Questors Theatre Ealing, The   39
Quicksilver Theatre   182

Radcliffe, Gennie   103, 209
Raindance Film Festival Ltd.   232
Random House Audio Books   227
Rattlebag Actors Agency Ltd.   88
Ray Cooney Plays   127
RDF Management   70
Red Room, The   151
Regional Arts Council Offices   256
Rejects Revenge Theatre Company   151
REP College, The   19
Replay Productions   183
Repro companies   236, 237, 238, 239, 240, 242
Repros   237, 239, 240, 243, 244, 245
Reynolds, Simone CDG   103
Rho Delta Ltd.   132
Richard Jordan Productions Ltd.   130
Richmond Drama School   20, 39
Richmond Drama School   20, 39
Richmond Productions   151
Riverside Studios   168, 260
Robert Carpenter Turner
  Photography   238
Robert Fox Ltd.   128
Roehampton, University of Surrey   27
Rogues and Vagabonds   271
Ronnie Marshall Agency   64
Rose Bruford College   20, 39
Rosebery Management Ltd.   89
Rosemary Branch Theatre   168
Rosenthal, Suzanna Ltd.   152
Rossmore Personal Management   70
Royal Academy of Dramatic Art
  (RADA)   20
Royal Court Theatre   118
Royal Court Young Writers Festival   198
Royal Exchange Theatre   119

Royal National Theatre   119
Royal National Theatre Platforms   271
Royal Scottish Academy of Music and
  Drama   21
Royal Shakespeare Company (Casting
  Department)   120
Royal Television Society (RTS)   271
Royal Theatrical Fund, The   272
Royal Welsh College of Music and
  Drama   21
Royce Management   71
Rushes Soho Shorts Festival   232

Salisbury Festival   198
Salisbury Playhouse   120
Sandra Griffin Management Ltd.   58
Sandra Singer Associates   103
Saraband Associates   71
SCA Management   71
Scat Theatre Company   183
School of the Science of Acting, The   21
Scott Marshall Partners   64
Scott, Laura CDG   103
Scottish Arts Council   256, 281
Scottish Screen   258, 280
Scottish Youth Theatre   279, 5, 110
Screen East   280, 258
Screen South   280, 258
Screen West Midlands   259, 280
Screen Yorkshire   259, 280
Screenwriter's Workshop, The   272
September Films   217
Sevenoaks Stag Theatre   171
Sgrin Media Agency for Wales   258, 280
Sgript Cymru   152
Shakespeare 4 Kidz   184
Shakespeare Lane, Catherine   46, 242
Shakespeare's Globe   93, 121
Shared Experience   152, 193
Shaw, Bernard   38, 252, 253
Shaw, Philip   103
Sheringham Summer Theatre   152, 153
Sherman Theatre   121
Shining Management Ltd.   76
Shooting People   220, 221, 250, 272, 280